7 Bury Place
Regent's Park
St Pancras Town Hall
arley Court
BLOOMSBURY
Russell Square
FITZROVIA
Conway Hall
MARYLEBONE
7 Bury Place
Oxford Street
10 Soho Street
22 Betterton St.
ble Arch
COVENT GARDEN
SOHO
India House
MAYFAIR
Route of Rathayatra
Piccadilly
de Park
Trafalgar Square
St James's Park
Buckingham Palace
Royal Albert Hall
Westminster Abbey

All summer long, as the sun shone in a clear sky, devotees and guests gathered round him on the Manor lawn. He answered their questions, spoke philosophy, told stories, and laughed with them.

'When the sun shines,' he said, 'England is one of the most beautiful places on earth.'

OTHER BOOKS OF INTEREST FROM THE BHAKTIVEDANTA BOOK TRUST

When the Sun Shines

THE DAWN OF HARE KRISHNA IN BRITAIN

To dear Manorama

RANCHOR PRIME

Hare Krishna

Ranchor

THE BHAKTIVEDANTA BOOK TRUST

Readers interested in the subject matter of this book or who wish to contact a Hare Krishna community anywhere in the world can contact:

ISKCON Reader Services
P. O. Box 730
Watford, WD25 8ZE
United Kingdom

Phone: +44 (0)1923 851000
readerservices@pamho.net
www.iskcon.org.uk

Design by Govinda Cordua
Line drawings and map by Ranchor Prime

Set in Minion

www.krishna.com

ISBN 978-1-84599-070-1

Printed in Germany 2009

CONTENTS

To Yamuna Devi,
who introduced me to Krishna
and told me her story.

INTRODUCTION

Mr Fitzgerald: Could you explain to me the difference between the monistic idea that Krishna is everything, and the idea that this world of illusion is somehow distinct from Krishna?

Prabhupada: This is very easy to understand. You are recording my speeches in the tape recorder. When you play it back it will speak just like I am speaking, but I am not there. Is it not a fact?

Mr Fitzgerald: Yes.

Prabhupada: It will appear that I am speaking from beyond this world.

– Recorded in Prabhupada's room, London, 9th August 1971

Are there people who speak from beyond this world, who know the secrets of life, whose glance penetrates in a way that you can't understand, who see inside your heart, who exist within their own spiritual aura and yet at the same time walk right beside you, sit down next to you, and enter your world – like someone who comes into your dream who is so real that you are jolted awake and left gasping in the darkness wondering, Who was that?

I found such a person – at least I think I did. I still don't know for sure if I found him or he found me. Being with him was like a flash of understanding, a shudder of intense emotion, like falling in love. For a moment, just briefly, I knew what life could really be.

This story is about love. It is about the emotional connection that arose between a handful of young men and women and the one who inspired them to strive for the highest goal. Were these young men and women lost, more than any others in this world are lost? More needy? Less grounded in reality? I don't think so. They were prompted to look for something different and so they found what others did not see.

The events in this book happened when I was a young man. Their memories are etched on my mind. I carry them like treasures that I can take out when I need inspiration. Bringing them into the open I turn them to the light and let them glint and sparkle. Sometimes when I do this I mourn for the one I lost, a true and loving guide – and for the young man he left behind long ago; but mostly I am filled with gratitude for the things he taught me and for the memories of him that strengthen me in this world where time takes everything away.

I wish I had stopped at the time to write these stories down. It is a tragedy that the good things in life cannot last and that even their memory must fade. In the eternal world of the spirit, though, whatever is of value is never truly lost. So in this book I have recovered the stories – my own and those of more than eighty friends who were there with me.

I first met Srila Prabhupada when he arrived at Heathrow Airport in 1971. I remember seeing a small figure whose presence extended far beyond his physical form to make him seem large. He glowed with a warmth that enveloped those around him and bathed the whole scene in a golden light. Others saw this light; one man even said he saw a dazzling halo around Prabhupada like the haloes painted round saints' heads in Italian frescoes. Some would say these visions were fantasy, but I think we were seeing a field of energy that our rational side normally edits out. Our faith made us wide open so we could see it just that once.

Ultimately I am mystified by so much of what happened between Prabhupada and his disciples. Who was he and how did he come to be among us?

PRABHUPADA'S JOURNEY TO THE WEST

Abhay Charan De, who later became Bhaktivedanta Swami Prabhupada, was born in Calcutta on 1st September 1896. His father, a cloth merchant whose family belonged to an aristocratic lineage, brought him up to be devoted to Krishna. At the age of twenty Abhay enrolled at Scottish Churches College[1] in Calcutta to study English, Sanskrit, Philosophy, and Economics. At the end of his four-year course, as a protest against British rule, he refused the BA diploma offered to him. He married and began work as manager at a large pharmaceutical laboratory. Two years later, in 1922, he met his guru, Bhaktisiddhanta Saraswati, in Calcutta.

At their first meeting the teacher made a prophetic request of Abhay: 'Why don't you preach Sri Chaitanya's message throughout the world?' Abhay was sceptical; his priority was to see India become an independent nation. 'I was politically minded at that time,' he later said, but recalled how Bhaktisiddhanta had refuted his arguments and convinced him to accept the task of teaching Chaitanya's message.

The mission that Bhaktisiddhanta urged upon Abhay Charan had been inherited from Bhaktisiddhanta's father, Bhaktivinoda Thakur. To understand this inheritance, and how significant it was, we must know something about Sri Chaitanya and about nineteenth-century Bengal.

SRI CHAITANYA

The fifteenth-century charismatic reformer Sri Chaitanya (1486–1534) transformed the face of Hinduism in East India. Known as Gauranga, 'the golden one', he was born in Bengal at a time when Hindu culture was dominated by Muslim rulers and led by a weakened priestly class. He preached a simple Vaishnava faith based on the worship of Krishna as the sustainer of all life. He taught that the self is *sat-chit-ananda:* eternal and full of knowledge and bliss. Above all, he emphasised the simple truth that salvation depends on the grace of Krishna, as taught in the *Bhagavad-gita.* He rejected caste Hinduism and thus transcended cultural boundaries, leading his followers in publicly chanting Krishna's names, a practice which proved to have both a universal appeal and a powerful effect.

Sri Chaitanya left only a single poem, the eight-verse *Shikshashtaka,* as a record of his teaching. Its third verse went to the heart of his appeal: 'One who feels lower than the grass, who is more tolerant than a tree, who expects no personal honour, but who gives all honour to others, can easily chant the name of the Lord constantly.' This spoke to the innate spiritual capacity in everyone, regardless of birth or status, to cultivate the inner life of the spirit.

The immediate disciples of Chaitanya expanded his teachings to produce a body of literature derived from classic Sanskrit sources, setting out a complete manual for spiritual life in the modern age.[2] These disciples believed Sri Chaitanya to be an incarnation of Krishna, and spread his teachings throughout Bengal and Orissa.

THE BENGAL RENAISSANCE

In 1765, within a few years of the Battle of Plassey, the British East India Company took control of most of eastern India, and introduced its own administration, law courts, colleges, and schools. At first, British scholars took very seriously the culture and religion of the Hindus. These British Orientalists learned Sanskrit, translated Vedic writings into English, and explored Indian history. Using their own empirical methods they portrayed to their colleagues at home an Indian culture of philosophical sophistication and accomplishment. At the same time the Bengali elite learned English, were exposed to the ideas of eighteenth-century Europe, and reassessed their own Hindu culture and history in the light of Western rationalism. These educated Bengalis were known as *bhadraloka,* literally, 'well-mannered people'. The forum for their new ideas was Hindu College, established by them in Calcutta in 1817 to nurture the ideals of free thought, liberty, and truth.[3]

This early period of British-Indian interaction, which brought the heritage of Vedic India for the first time into sustained contact with the European Enlightenment, was marked by mutual interest and regard between Hindus and Christians. However, from 1813, when Christian missionaries began operating in Bengal, and particularly after a government resolution of 1835, which established through British education a systematic method to replace Hindu culture and religion with Western ideas and Christian values, the two sides drew apart. A strong reaction to British and Christian cultural dominance was provoked among the *bhadraloka,* who fought to establish their own Bengali identity. This nineteenth-century period of intense social and intellectual transformation in Bengal was called the Bengal Renaissance. Out of its ferment emerged a form of Vaishnava spirituality rooted in India but capable of speaking to a modern cosmopolitan world. The principal channel of this spiritual evolution was Kedarnath Datta Bhaktivinoda (1838–1914), who drew his inspiration from Sri Chaitanya, whom he called 'our Eastern Saviour'.

BHAKTIVINODA THAKUR

Bhaktivinoda Thakur, the father of Bhaktisiddhanta Saraswati, was brought up in the midst of the Bengal Renaissance. He attended Hindu College, where he learned the ideals of free thinking that were to influence his religious outlook. Bhaktivinoda belonged to a generation of Indians equipped with Western rationalism but inspired by a fierce desire to preserve and reform their Hindu tradition and identity. This identity was defined for him by his faith in Sri Chaitanya. In his youth Bhaktivinoda had been sceptical of his religious heritage, a tradition he saw as full of superstition and prejudice and in need of modernisation and reform. Then in 1868 he learned about the teachings of Sri Chaitanya. His discovery transformed him from an eclectic scholar of religion to a committed teacher and reformer who laid the foundation for the modern movement of Chaitanya Vaishnavism.

Chaitanya's teachings attracted Bhaktivinoda in part because they expressed devotion for one God. This feature of Vaishnavism closely paralleled what Bhaktivinoda and many of his contemporaries most admired in Christianity. The other feature that made Chaitanya so relevant for Bhaktivinoda was his rejection of caste Hinduism and his transcendence of cultural boundaries.

In 1898, R W Frazer, a contemporary English observer, recorded Bhaktivinoda's conviction of the future relevance of Chaitanya's message: '[Chaitanya's] devout and aged follower, Sri Kedar Nath Dutt, Bhakti Vinod, … declares his firm faith that, from a devoted love to Krishna shown by constant repetition of his name, a movement will yet take place to draw to the future church of the world' – and here Frazer cites Bhaktivinoda's own words – ' "all classes of men, without distinction of caste or clan to the highest cultivation of the spirit. This church, it appears, will extend all over the world and take the place of sectarian churches which exclude outsiders from the precincts of the mosque, church or temple." '[4]

THE FIRST LONDON MISSION

When Bhaktivinoda died, his fourth son, Bhaktisiddhanta Saraswati, formed the Gaudiya Mission, which by 1933 had sixty-four branches in India. Following his father's wish to see Chaitanya's teachings taken to the West, he sent three preachers preachers to London, led by his disciple, Swami Bon, giving them a grand send-off from Bombay on 10th April. They sailed aboard the S S *Victoria* on a ten-day voyage to Naples, from where they went by train to London, arriving on 22nd April. Their first temporary residence was in Bloomsbury, foreshadowing the Radha-Krishna temple that would be inaugurated there thirty-six years later.

Despite the numerous letters they carried introducing them to former governors and viceroys, they found it hard to establish themselves. 'It is extremely difficult for an Indian to find a furnished flat in London,' reported Swami Bon. 'The colour-question is rather strong with the average English men and women.'[5]

Eventually they managed to rent a flat in South Kensington at 39 Drayton Gardens, where they opened their monastery. From there they cultivated influential contacts and addressed meetings of learned societies. The principal of the School of Oriental and African Studies held a reception to introduce the monks to polite society. The summit of their progress came that summer when the Marquess of Zetland, former Governor of Bengal, presented them to King George V at a garden party on the lawns of Buckingham Palace.

Following this they launched the Gaudiya Mission Society. In announcing the Society's aims Swami Bon chose almost the same phrase later adopted by Bhaktivedanta Swami: 'Back to God and back to Home is the message of the Mission to mankind.'

Bon wrote of the many kindnesses of his hosts and their apparent willingness to listen to what he had to say, but so far as his records tell he was unable to get more than a token hearing. After two years without tangible success the party returned to India, stopping on the way for a preaching tour in Germany. Their mission was brought to an end by Bhaktisiddhanta Saraswati – in part because they had not been able to raise financial support in London and were being funded entirely by the Gaudiya Mission in India.

BHAKTISIDDHANTA'S PREDICTION

The preachers returned to Calcutta in September 1935, and Abhay Charan was at their reception. He was keen to hear of Swami Bon's experiences for, as was known to Abhay's close friends, his heart was set upon preaching in the West to fulfil the order he had been given when he had first met Bhaktisiddhanta Saraswati. He had been twenty-six in 1922 when he had met Bhaktisiddhanta. For the next ten years he had pursued his business career and raised a family of four children before eventually accepting initiation from Bhaktisiddhanta in 1933 and receiving the name Abhay Charanaravinda. Thereafter his guru had repeated his original request that he take Chaitanya's mission to the West.

When Bhaktisiddhanta Saraswati welcomed his disciples home in 1935 he expressed disappointment at the apparent failure of the London mission, but in his speech that day he made a prediction: 'However long in the future it may be, I predict that one of my disciples will cross the ocean, and that devotee will bring back the whole world.'[6]

A few weeks before he left this world, at the end of 1936, Bhaktisiddhanta wrote his final instruction to Abhay Charanaravinda, repeating his wish: 'I have every hope that you can turn yourself into a very good English preacher if you serve the mission to inculcate the novel impression of Lord Chaitanya's teachings in the people in general, as well as philosophers and religionists.'

PREPARING TO CROSS THE OCEAN

The rest of Abhay's life in India, until 1965, was spent in preparing himself for his momentous mission. The failure of the London expedition in the 1930s strengthened his resolve to aim for America, where he hoped to find a more receptive audience. 'He told me he had made a solemn vow,' remembered his friend Devi Prasad Maskara, who knew him in Calcutta in the 1920s and '30s. 'His guru had told him he should go to the foreign countries and preach about Lord Krishna. He did not have enough money to go to America, and many times he consulted me, asking, "How will I go?" '[7]

Abhay launched his own English-language magazine, *Back to Godhead,* in 1944, and did all the writing and distribution himself. As he became more absorbed in his spiritual work, his interest in material affairs waned. His business – the manufacturing and marketing of Ayurvedic medicines – failed to live up to its early promise. He saw this as the will of Krishna pushing him to dedicate himself fully to carrying out the mission his guru had given him.

In 1953 he started a League of Devotees, supported by the dwindling profits from his business, but when the business faltered and finally collapsed, rather than striving to find a new means of income he devoted his time to *Back to Godhead* and the League of Devotees. In 1954 he separated from his family to devote himself fully to preaching, leaving his wife and grown children in the care of his sister and her five adult sons. He moved to Vrindavan, seat of Krishna devotion in northern India, and in 1959 was ordained as a *sannyasi,* thus renouncing all ties save the service of Krishna.

In Vrindavan he took up residence in two small rooms at the Radha-Damodar temple. 'During those years he was consumed in writing his translations and purports of *Srimad-Bhagavatam,*' recalled his friend

Narayana Maharaj.[8] He eventually published the first three volumes of his translation of the *Bhagavatam*. When these were ready he made his final preparations to leave for America.

During the 1940s and '50s, when he was still living in Calcutta, Abhay would pray at the shrine of Sri Advaita in Shantipur, West Bengal. Advaita was the fifteenth-century associate of Chaitanya dedicated to uplifting the most disadvantaged members of society. The priest at the temple there remembered his regular visits. 'He would sit at the back and chant *hari-nama* on his *mala* very quietly and deeply. I noticed that he came on the weekends, every month or two. His presence was profound. Sometimes his eyes would be full of tears and his voice would be choked up.'

He didn't visit Shantipur for several years after his move to Vrindavan, but one day in August 1965, dressed in the saffron robes of a *sannyasi,* he went to West Bengal and reappeared at the little temple.

> Again he sat for a long time chanting Hare Krishna in concentrated devotion. He was weeping unabashedly even more than he used to while he took the holy name. I asked him, 'Who are you?' He replied, 'My name is Abhay Charanaravinda Bhaktivedanta Swami. I am an unworthy disciple of Srila Bhaktisiddhanta Saraswati Thakur, my divine master. I have been coming here for such a long time because my *gurudeva* has given me an impossible mission. His desire was for me to go across the ocean to the Western countries and spread the sublime teachings of Sri Chaitanya Mahaprabhu … I have not known how this mission of his will be successful, so I have been coming here to this special house where Advaita, Nityananda, and Sri Chaitanya would gather to plan the sankirtan movement. It was here that they launched the inundation of love of God that swept India…. I have been praying earnestly that they will give me their mercy and guide me…. Tomorrow I am leaving for Calcutta to go upon a ship across the ocean to America. I do not know what will befall me there.'[9]

So it was that A C Bhaktivedanta Swami Prabhupada, having been given free passage onboard a cargo steamer of the Scindia Line, the S S *Jaladuta,* sailed from Calcutta, bound for New York, on the 13th of August 1965.

Four years later, in September 1969, Prabhupada arrived in London, and that was when I had my first experience of him. This was just around the time when Hare Krishna was becoming known in England. Five days after his arrival I saw him interviewed on television. Here's how I remember it:

His face is strong and kind. His eyes hold unspoken truths. Opposite the youthful presenter he is old, his memory large. He carries treasures from another world. I know at once I must hear what he has to say.

'My mission is to teach how to love God. People have forgotten God, and I have come to remind them.'

Hearing these words I am reminded that all my life people have taught me about God. But what have I learned? Precious little. Has this messenger, appearing so unexpectedly on a tiny black and white screen, something to tell me of God? I strain forward as the interviewer asks a question.

'Is this the same God we worship in the West, the Christian God? Or is this some other God?' The question excites me. It is just what I myself want to ask. During my school days I was taught about the Christian God, but I was curious to know about other ways of seeing God. My teachers dismissed my questions. What they taught was enough, they said. The rest was a distraction. Now I am with the interviewer – he has asked my question for me. What will the answer be?

'Yes, I am speaking of the same God. There is one God whom we all worship, Christians and Hindus alike, and he has many names. One of his names is Krishna.'

I had always thought my teachers were mistaken when they refused to speak of other ways of knowing God. Now here is proof. This man knows about God; even separated from him by radio waves and a hundred miles, I can see it written on his face: he knows what he is saying.

'I have come to teach anyone how to see God. It is possible to talk with God. Just as we are talking to each other now, you can talk with God.'

Now I feel he is speaking directly to me. He has my full attention. The flickering screen is all that stands between us. For this moment it is my whole world.

I have long wanted to evoke that world for another generation, to let people hear what Prabhupada taught and to experience how he guided us – and how we responded to him. In this book I have not followed the usual conventions of nonfiction: I have told the story as it happened, without commentary or analysis. Others will investigate the development of the Krishna consciousness movement, its sociology and psychology. That is not my purpose here. I just want to tell the authentic story from the point of view of those who were there – as they experienced it. I have included around seventy characters, all of whom are real people. I have used their words and their memories. These seventy are drawn from the three hundred men and women whom Prabhupada initiated in England.[10] I would like to have included all three hundred, but that would have made my book too long.

To keep to a reasonable length I have abbreviated their stories, but kept their words so that through their eyes a picture of Prabhupada will emerge. Using recordings and transcripts of his lectures and conversations I have tried to transmit faithfully his voice and presence as it felt to those who were with him. I have abbreviated his discourses and explanations but preserved the actual words he used. In real life Prabhupada interspersed his dialogue with Sanskrit terms and scriptural quotations, which I have omitted here to make his words more widely accessible. Wherever I have used an archived source I have added a reference at the back of the book so that those who want to study the original will know where to look.

ACKNOWLEDGEMENTS

My gratitude goes to the seventy disciples of Srila Prabhupada who gave me their stories in interviews or written form. Here are their names:

Abhirama, Adikarta, Advaita Acharya, Akhandadhi, Amita, Ashtasakhi, Bala Gopala, Bhajahari, Birasingha, Chitraketu, Dayananda, Devamaya, Dhananjaya, Gokularani, Govardhan, Gunarnava, Harernamananda, Haripriya, Ishvara, Jagat Bandhu, Jagannatheshvari, Janakaraja, Janaki, Janananda, Jaya Lakshmana, Jayatirthacharan, Jijñasi, Jñanadas, Julia Burroughs, Kishor, Kripamoya, Krishnadas Swami, Krishnavesha, Kulashekara, Lilashakti, Mahavishnu Swami, Manjuali, Mohan, Mondakini, Nabasvati, Narahari, Nikunjavasini, Padmalochana, Partha, Prabhavishnu, Prabhupada (Dr Vishnu Sharma), Prithu, Radhapriya, Bhakti Chaitanya Swami, Ramadevi, Riddha, Rohininandan, Shailendriya, Sakshi Gopala, Samba, Sanatana, Sarvamangala, Sharadiya, Shilpakarini, Srikama, Subhaga, Shuchi, Sudurjaya, Svayambhur, Tribhangananda, Trivikrama, Vichitravirya, Vrajendra Kumar, Yaduvendu, Yamuna, Yashashvini.

I was privileged to personally interview fifty-four of the above persons. I am specially thankful to Yamuna, who gave me three days of her time and shared much of her store of memories, which she is recording in her own memoir.

Another important source was the collected audiotapes and video recordings of storytelling sessions held at Bhaktivedanta Manor between 1993–2003, which featured Dhananjaya, Gurudas, Jyotirmayi, Lilashakti, Malati, Mondakini, Mukunda Goswami, Rebatinandan, Shyamsundar, and Tribhuvanatha. I made frequent reference to books written by godbrothers and godsisters: George Harrison's *I Me Mine;* Gurudas's memoir, *By His Example;* Hari Sauri's *Transcendental Diary;* Hayagriva's *Hare Krishna Explosion;* Kshirodakshayi Vishnu's *Sweet Memories of Srila Prabhupada;* Mulaprakrti's *A Friend To All;* Siddhanta's *Memories* volumes 1 and 2; Satsvarupa Das Goswami's two-volume biography *Srila Prabhupada-lilamrita;* Shrutakirti's *What Is the Difficulty;* Tamal Krishna Goswami's *TKG's Diary;* and Vedavyasa's *Srila Prabhupada in Germany.* I also referred to Yadubara's DVD series *Following Srila Prabhupada.* I am grateful to all these authors and filmmakers. My companion throughout was the five-volume edition of *Srila Prabhupada's Letters* published by the Bhaktivedanta Archives.

Arya gave me access to her sound archive with permission from the Oxford Centre for Hindu Studies, Janananda das Goswami recorded interviews in Australia, Riddha recorded an interview in South Africa.

Several friends kindly gave time to read drafts at various stages and help me with their comments. They were Bhajahari, Ian Roberts, Jayadvaita Swami, Julia Evans, Mukunda Goswami, Sakshi Gopala, Shyamsundar, Vegavan, Yaduvendu, and Yamuna. My daughter Anasuya read the manuscript twice during its production and gave me invaluable feedback.

The origin of this book owes much to Gauri, former president of Bhaktivedanta Manor, who encouraged me in 2002 when I proposed the idea; he became my advocate to the Bhaktivedanta Book Trust, which commissioned me to write the book in 2005, and to the management council of ISKCON UK which subsequently added an investment of its own.

Crucial additional support came at a time when I was running out of resources during the extended period of research and writing from Kalapi Jani and family of Nairobi, Dr Harshad and Monika Desai of Stourbridge, Pundarika and Harekrishnadasi of Nottingham, and Ian and Andrea Roberts. As well as helping me financially, Ian and Andrea gave me shelter and retreat at their house in Rydall for extended periods of writing. At the outset, when I needed a quiet place to find my way into the book, Sitarama lent me his garden cabin in Aldenham, and my friend Nicky and her husband David Briffa lent me their guest wing in East Sussex. On the final stretch, when I was emotionally worn out, my friend Keshava Bharati das Goswami gave me shelter and support in his ashram beside Govardhan Hill, where I finished the first draft.

Many thanks to Bhargava, Gurudas, Shyamsundar, Visakha, and all the other BBT photographers for taking so many pictures of Srila Prabhupada, and to the BBT Archives for preserving them. I'm also grateful to Clive Arrowsmith and Michael Brennan for letting me use their photos.

Thanks, too, to the production staff at the Bhaktivedanta Book Trust, who worked countless hours to turn my manuscript into this beautiful and lavish book, and to Grahila for indexing it.

Finally my biggest thanks goes to my companion of thirty years, Lilashakti, for her endless patience in the presence of an anguished writer.

NOTE TO THE READER

In describing events of more than thirty years ago it is unavoidable that inaccuracies will occur. I have done my best to check the facts in this book and provide references where possible. If mistakes are found I ask my readers' understanding and invite them to send me any corrections for incorporation into future editions.

I have tried to give a balanced account of those days. However, my own voice and the voices of my sources are intrinsic to the story. Prabhupada taught that spiritual life is personal and full of varieties, and he was personal with his disciples. It is natural, therefore, that my telling of this story is personal and is simply one among many that could be written about Prabhupada in Britain.

I am grateful to my editors and reviewers for their help in making my text as accurate and impartial as possible. Any deficiencies that remain are entirely my own.

PROLOGUE

LONDON, 7TH SEPTEMBER 1977

We scrambled into the temple van and drove out to Bhaktivedanta Manor, knowing this might be the last time we would see Prabhupada in England. Each of us sat silently, scarcely noticing the journey from Bloomsbury through the morning rush hour to the countryside north of the city.

At the Manor the hallways and corridors were filled with anxious faces waiting for Prabhupada's appearance. We were told he would be carried down from his rooms to spend an hour with his disciples in the temple room while we sang to him, as had happened each morning since his arrival.

When I saw him I didn't cry, as some did, or feel sad to see how emaciated he was. Instead I was mesmerised by his beauty. I had seen him so many times – heard him lecture, sat and laughed with him, followed his footsteps as he walked through parks and fields – but I had never seen him so transfigured. His features were intensely golden. His head appeared larger, perhaps because the rest of his body was smaller, sitting wasted in a chair carried by sturdy bearers. His ears seemed to have lengthened, their lobes extending downwards. There was something familiar. What was it? Yes, I realised, he reminded me of images I had seen of the Buddha. Aloof from the world, saturated with wisdom, transcendent. Yet his eyes glistened with tears, and his soft hands were joined in prayer.

He was too weak to talk, so his secretary, Tamal Krishna Goswami, stood on the dais beside him and made a speech recounting the prominent events of his life. While Tamal spoke, my mind travelled back to the first time I had seen Prabhupada. It seemed a lifetime ago, but it had only been six years. His disciple Shyamsundar had befriended me the day I had walked into the London temple – he a carpenter and sculptor, me an architect and artist; he with his easy West Coast drawl, me with my modest English diction. A few weeks later, after I had moved into the temple, Shyamsundar went to India with his friends. A year elapsed before he returned, this time with Prabhupada. Then he brought me into His Divine Grace's room, sat me down before him, and generously introduced me.

'This is Ranchor, Prabhupada. He will be working on the plans for your Mayapur temple.'

Prabhupada had wanted to know about me. I did my best to answer his questions, but in his majestic company I felt clumsy. Over the ensuing weeks Shyamsundar, with his relaxed and friendly ways, helped me to feel more at ease and accepted in Prabhupada's presence.

I listened to Tamal's confident voice rise and fall as he continued to narrate Prabhupada's story, speaking about his first days in San Francisco – how he had lived with his disciples in Haight-Ashbury and made friends with the hippies, how he had danced by the Pacific Ocean and captured their hearts – although they had no idea where he would lead them.

As I listened, the gilded walls of the temple, its luxuriant curtains and chandeliers, the crowd of attentive devotees, the weight of my own responsibilities – all these receded and my attention rested on Prabhupada's golden figure. I remembered how the story began, as Shyamsundar had told it to me.

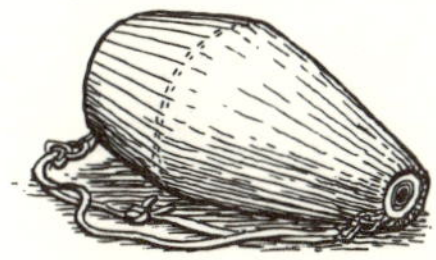

BOOK ONE

From the Mystic West
1967–68

CHAPTER 1

Children of the Fifties

Sam Speerstra inherited the American dream in abundance. He grew up in Salem, Oregon, in the 1950s when the hardships of the war years were giving way to an era of plenty. He was fair-haired and athletic, and his relaxed demeanour and penetrating intellect won him popularity.

At Reed College in Portland, where he studied philosophy, his best friend was Michael Grant, a music student and jazz pianist. Michael's sensitive and thoughtful nature, dark good looks, and easy charm gave him an air of mystery and distinction.

Both were college rebels, seeking a deeper understanding of life. Sam was outgoing and Michael more reserved; they complemented each other. They spent their summers in San Francisco exploring the Californian counterculture. Their eyes were drawn to the western horizon.

For thousands of years this horizon had been no more than a

dream in the minds of their European ancestors. In Europe the western horizon, where the sun sank behind the waves, had been the end of the world, the mystic path to the afterlife. A few bold explorers had ventured over it, in search of the fabled land of India. Making landfall, pushing inland and traversing a continent, some had reached this Pacific shore and settled round the Bay, renaming it after their patron saint, San Francisco. It seemed a land that promised all.

Sam and Michael grew up in that promised land, but like their ancestors they were still explorers, and they still looked west. There, beyond the Pacific Ocean, lay the promise of India. It was their mystic West.

Joan Osland had been a friend of Sam's since high school. Her long hair was swept back to reveal her fine forehead and raised cheekbones. Her face showed strength and emotional depth, and her voice was rich and soulful. In the early sixties she moved from Oregon to California, where she and a friend opened a gallery in North Beach, San Francisco. There she lived as a potter and calligrapher and wrote poetry.

Joan's younger sister Jan had the same high cheekbones and thick dark hair, with a soft beauty and laughing eyes full of warmth and good nature. She met Michael at Joan's house in 1965. Jan and Michael fell in love, and in 1966 they moved to New York, where he found success playing jazz clubs with Thelonious Monk and making his own music. In his spare time he explored mysticism.

In 1965 Sam won a Fulbright scholarship and went to spend a year in Switzerland studying the German philosophers and furthering his search for truth. On his return he moved to San Francisco where he met Melanie, who matched his quick wit with her own irrepressible energy and enterprise. Melanie's good humour, self-assurance, and wild beauty attracted attention wherever she went, and soon the couple established themselves at the heart of the psychedelic rock community in Haight-Ashbury.

Sam and Melanie loved the California counterculture, but they were disillusioned by its drug scene. They escaped for the summer to the mountains of central Oregon, where Sam found a job as a fire lookout for the National Park Service. They were hoping the time away would allow them to make a fresh start. On their lonely watchtower they immersed themselves in reading about yoga and Tibet, and began to think of looking for a spiritual teacher.

In 1966 in New York a spiritual teacher had arrived, and Michael and Jan were to play a key part in the unfolding of his extraordinary story. Bhaktivedanta Swami came from India with the mission to teach Westerners how to love Krishna. His guru, in line from the fifteenth-century saint Sri Chaitanya, had asked him to give Krishna consciousness to the English-speaking world. When Bhaktivedanta Swami had first received this order in 1922, India was still ruled by Britain; his generation looked upon her as the world's foremost power. But war and the struggle for Indian independence had undermined Britain's influence. The United States now led the world. So when he was at last ready to travel west, Bhaktivedanta Swami decided to begin his mission in America. After a month at sea on board a small cargo steamer, he sailed into Boston Harbour on 17th September 1965, where he stood on the deck, facing the grey warehouses of an unknown continent, and prayed to Krishna: 'You have brought me here to speak about You. Now, my Lord, it is up to You to make me a success or failure, as You like.'

Six months later, after enduring many struggles,[1] Bhaktivedanta Swami moved into his first private accommodation – a narrow, unfurnished room in a Manhattan block overlooking the Hudson River. Although the room was cramped and bare, he began lecturing to the few seekers who found their way to his door. Drawn by the force of his personality and message a small group of regulars formed, and when he needed help to relocate, they found him a loft amid the artists and down-and-outs of the Bowery. Bhaktivedanta Swami had to share the space, but it was large. At the foot of its four flights of stairs it had its own front door. His listeners grew in number.

It was here during the summer of 1966 that Michael first came to listen to the swami from India. He saw in the elderly teacher a simplicity and dignity he had not encountered before, and felt touched by an ancient wisdom. A few days after that first meeting Michael returned to the swami's loft and found the teacher sitting on the floor at his portable typewriter, his trunk serving as his writing desk.

'Come in,' Bhaktivedanta Swami said, pleased to see Michael again and beckoning him into his curtained-off section of the loft. There, with his washing hung behind him, he was working among piles of manuscripts. Michael sat down beside him. Evidently the swami slept there on the floor amid his few possessions. Although he was hard at work, he was ready to talk with Michael for hours, and they quickly became friends. He showed Michael a set of three large volumes and explained that he had written and published them in India in preparation for his mission to the West. They were the first of a projected sixty-volume compendium of spiritual life. Even now he was working on future instalments.

'I am here always working on something, reading or writing, twenty-four hours a day,' said the swami. 'When I feel hungry I take some food, and when I feel sleepy I go to bed. Otherwise I don't feel fatigued.'

He concluded by inviting Michael to attend his lectures every Monday, Wednesday, and Friday evening. Michael promised to return, then made his way down the long flight of stairs, bearing the treasured volumes he had agreed to buy. After that he went regularly, bringing Jan with him. The loft would fill up with an eclectic crowd, and the swami would lead them in chanting the Hare Krishna mantra. Some joined in while others simply sat and listened. Most of them had little idea of what the swami was teaching, but they liked the atmosphere, and above all the chanting.

One day Michael and Jan met the swami in the street. The swami's eyes lit up.

'Are you chanting?' he asked Jan.

'Sometimes,' she replied, not wishing to disappoint him. Something about him made her want to please him and to do what he asked, even if it was hard.

A few weeks later Michael received an unexpected appeal for help. The swami had been made homeless and was staying with Carl and his wife, who were among his new students. He urgently needed a secure place of his own. Here was Michael's opportunity to ensure that this extraordinary teacher received the hearing he deserved among the young and open-minded of New York's Lower East Side. The next day he found an ideal location: a small gift shop on Second Avenue with a courtyard and flat behind. He took the swami there to meet the landlord, who was won over by his prospective tenant. When Bhaktivedanta Swami presented him with his three books, the landlord agreed on the spot to become a trustee of the swami's yet-to-be-formed society and even to pay a subscription. Michael arranged for phone and electricity and for the first month's rent. Within a week, Swami, as his students had started to call him, was installed there and able to resume his regular lectures. Above the storefront a prophetic sign, left over from the store's days as a gift shop, read 'Matchless Gifts'. This was to be the first ashram and temple of the Hare Krishna movement.

Joan, still in San Francisco, received some unexpected news from her sister. 'Michael and I are getting married. Please come to the wedding,' wrote Jan. Swami had told her and Michael that if they were living together they should be married. He had also offered to perform the wedding.

Joan was ready for a change and flew straight to New York. As soon as she arrived she was taken for lunch at the swami's apartment. There she met an elderly gentleman with laughing eyes and a ready smile. A dozen young men sat on the floor around him eating, while he served them. After the introductions, she joined them.

The food had been cooked by the swami. The chillies made her eyes water, and the strong flavours were far removed from the macrobiotic simplicity she was used to. After lunch the swami reached into a large jar and pulled out a sticky sweet. It was a *gulabjamun,* a spongy brown ball soaked in sugar syrup, much favoured by him. He held it out to her.

'No, thank you. I enjoyed lunch, but I can't eat another bite.' Everyone smiled.

'No, you take,' he insisted. 'Now!'

Reluctantly she held out her hand, then bit into the sticky sweet, contradicting every dietary rule she lived by. The syrup exploded in her mouth, while everyone cheered and the swami smiled broadly. Joan thought him fascinating, but she didn't expect to eat there again.

However, the next day she was back for lunch, and again the day after. The swami asked if she could help cook her sister's wedding feast and she found herself agreeing readily. She laboured in his kitchen for six hours while he prepared a twenty-course feast for forty guests. He taught her to make a pastry stuffed with potato he called *kachori,* and that day he won her over. Each remaining day of her short visit she returned for his company.

Jan and Michael accepted initiation from Swami on 9th September 1966 to become his first Western disciples, receiving the names Janaki and Mukunda. Their wedding was held a few days later. Swami was a *sannyasi,* a celibate monk who had renounced the world, but for the sake of his young disciples he broke with tradition to perform a full Vedic marriage ceremony. As the flames of the sacred fire burned their offerings of grains and fruits, the couple felt their worldly ties fall away. Their immediate thought was to go on pilgrimage to India, and with this in mind they planned to return to the West Coast along with Joan.

Bhaktivedanta Swami had thought of visiting California as soon as he had arrived in the United States,[2] so hearing that Mukunda and Janaki were heading west he asked for their help. Before going to India, could they find a place in San Francisco and help start a second branch of Krishna consciousness on the West Coast? If they found a place, the swami promised, he would come. So Mukunda and Janaki agreed to postpone their India plans. Joan, inspired by her encounter with Swami, decided to help as well. They would look for a small store similar to the one on Second Avenue where they could introduce their friends to the swami.

On their way back to the West Coast the three of them made a detour to visit Sam and Melanie, driving straight to their lonely lookout tower high among the Oregon old-growth firs. Sam noticed right away that something was different about Michael and Jan – they seemed to be smiling a lot, and they refused meat and intoxicants. The friends talked about their spiritual searches. Michael spoke about his new guru, and together they chanted Hare Krishna late into the night.

The following morning came the first snowfall of winter and a call on the radio telling Sam and Melanie that they were free to leave. By then they were curious about the swami, so when they heard of Mukunda's intention to bring him to San Francisco, they decided that they would come along and help search for a place.

In San Francisco, they soon found a store that seemed just right. It was at 518 Frederick Street, beside Golden Gate Park, in the heart of Haight-Ashbury. Next door, Mukunda rented two apartments on the second floor, one for Swami and one for Janaki and himself. Joan, Melanie, and Sam shared a house in the Mission District. Over the following weeks Sam observed his old friend Michael, now Mukunda, and saw the change in him wrought by his contact with Bhaktivedanta Swami. Mukunda and Janaki seemed to have found a new happiness and fulfilment. If the swami could influence his friends so deeply, thought Sam, he must be a special teacher.

One day in Haight-Ashbury, Joan met and made friends with Roger Siegel. Roger was a photographer who had spent years working with Martin Luther King and Stokely Carmichael in the civil rights movement. He was interested in Eastern philosophy and mysticism, and had a great sense of humour. His open features and confident manner appealed to Joan, and before long the two of them moved into an apartment together. So Sam and Melanie, Joan and Roger, and Janaki and Mukunda were brought together, ready to play their parts. Mukunda wrote to the swami with the news: they had a temple. Swami replied that he would come.

Haight-Ashbury was at the centre of the sixties' shift in American consciousness. This was the time and the place for spiritual revolution. Young people, disillusioned with the Vietnam War, were coming there seeking freedom and adventure. In this fertile ground, amid a flowering of music, literature, art, and self-expression, a haven was being prepared where the swami's clear teachings and inspired chanting would find a ready audience. Here the six friends would learn all about Krishna consciousness. Eighteen months later they would bring it to London.

CHAPTER 2

The Teacher Lives Among Them

That December of 1966 the friends transformed the Haight-Ashbury shop into a temple, not unlike the one in New York. They painted the walls and built a raised seat for Swami, above which they hung a decorated Indian cloth. Over the double doors they put a sign that said 'Radha Krishna Temple'.

During this same time and only two blocks away in Golden Gate Park, a great 'gathering of tribes' had been called. It was the eve of San Francisco's Summer of Love, and the promise of psychedelic mind expansion had taken firm hold among America's young. Word had gone out that Timothy Leary, Allen Ginsberg, and musicians such as the Grateful Dead would lead the way to mass enlightenment at a Human Be-In. On the appointed day, 14th January 1967, close to a hundred thousand young people turned up. 'Turn on, tune in, and drop out,' declared Timothy Leary, and Allen Ginsberg led the crowds in chanting Hare Krishna. LSD was given away free at the park gates. But despite the chanting and the LSD – and the optimism of so many young seekers – mass enlightenment did not arrive, and in the aftermath disillusioned souls wandered the streets of Haight-Ashbury.

Meanwhile, to help fund the temple and spread the word, Sam and Mukunda were busy organising their own event, a Mantra-Rock Dance – their opportunity to introduce Swami to San Francisco. The owner of the Avalon Ballroom, a popular rock venue, was a friend of Sam's. He agreed to lend the Ballroom for the night of 29th January. Sam used his genius for personal contacts to persuade the top rock bands in the Bay Area to appear in support of the new temple. Allen Ginsberg agreed to be there. The night was billed as 'Krishna Consciousness Comes West', and the guest of honour was to be Bhaktivedanta Swami.

When all was ready Mukunda sent Swami a ticket and, on 16th January, just two days after the great Human Be-In, he flew into San Francisco – the first time he had ever been in an aeroplane.

Fifty young people dressed in rainbow colours, with beads, bells, incense, and flowers, waited at the airport. Melanie and Sam came with their pet dog; Joan was there with Roger, his camera at the ready; and Janaki and Mukunda were there to personally welcome Swami. The plane taxied to a halt on the runway, and a small figure emerged, effulgent in saffron robes. He descended to the tarmac, followed by a young New York disciple carrying his coat, and crossed toward them. They burst into song, playing their musical instruments and filling the airport with the sound of Krishna's names.

As Swami entered the arrivals hall he smiled broadly and sat down among them. Allen Ginsberg came forward with a bouquet and touched his feet. The crowd fell silent and watched intently as Swami took out his *karatals*, brass hand cymbals, and wrapped the ribbons round his fingers. He closed his eyes and began to chant. The crowd was spellbound. When the time came for them to join in he looked around and smiled his encouragement. He seemed majestic, golden, unassailable, yet with his strength was a sweetness and humility.

Reporters were there to interview him. Would hippies be welcome at his temple?

'We welcome everyone in any condition of life,' he promised. 'Come to our temple and hear the message of Krishna. Whatever you are – what you call, acidhead, hippie? – whatever. Everyone is invited to come and chant Hare Krishna.'[1]

After a brief exchange, Swami left for the waiting car and the crowd followed, chanting around him, unable to take their eyes off him as he distributed the flowers they had given him, one for each person who had come to welcome him to California.

Swami stayed in San Francisco for four months and made good his promise. The temple doors on Frederick Street were open from seven in the morning until nine every night, and it became a haven for the spiritual seekers, and sometimes the spiritual casualties, of Haight-Ashbury.

He sat in his apartment above the temple, just as he had in New York, his typewriter on his trunk, his books at his side. He spent his time teaching, counselling, and befriending the young men and women who came to see him. Whenever he had time he returned to his writing. He was finalising his translation and commentary on the *Bhagavad-gita,* which he would title *Bhagavad-gita As It Is,* because he had added no interpretation of his own but simply followed the authorised teaching of his tradition. Hayagriva, a disciple who had followed him from New York, assisted with the book's editing.[2] Swami established a pattern during these days that would remain part of his life from then on: dictating in the early hours into a Dictaphone and sending the completed tapes to his disciples for transcription. After completing the *Gita* he immediately started on a new book, *Teachings of Lord Chaitanya.*[3]

One of his first visitors was the poet Allen Ginsberg, who arrived early one morning after being up all night. The swami greeted him as he greeted all his visitors: with a *gulabjamun*. The two sat and talked while Roger recorded them on a reel-to-reel tape recorder. Soon their conversation turned to the hippies.

‘They will all fall by here at one time or another,’ remarked Ginsberg, comparing them to the young LSD-takers of New York’s Lower East Side.

‘You have not had LSD, Allen?’

‘I have.’

‘It is dependence, Allen.’

‘It resolves certain inner things.’

‘Krishna consciousness resolves everything. Nothing else is needed.’

They discussed the Mantra-Rock Dance that was scheduled for that evening, six days after the swami’s arrival in San Francisco. Ginsberg said he would get the audience to join him in chanting Hare Krishna.

‘I am not ready to be a full-on devotee, but I chant Hare Krishna every day,’ he assured Swami. ‘And I will continue to chant until I leave this earth.’

‘And if you are chanting Hare Krishna mantra daily, then everything in your life will be perfect.’

Swami smiled, and Allen touched his feet before leaving with a supply of *gulabjamuns*.[4]

The Avalon Ballroom was frequented by Janis Joplin and bands such as Jefferson Airplane, the Grateful Dead, Moby Grape, and Big Brother and the Holding Company. Theirs was the kind of music normally appreciated under the influence of LSD. Posters and publicity for the event ensured a good audience, but this event would not revolve around the rock stars or LSD: its undisguised focus for the evening was to be Bhaktivedanta Swami and his chanting.

On the night of 29th January, heroes of the psychedelic revolution – Timothy Leary, Owsley Stanley, who had synthesised LSD, and others – all showed up. On stage was Allen Ginsberg, leader of them all. By 9.30 the Ballroom was filled to capacity. Strobe lights flashed, music thumped, and incense mingled with clouds of marijuana smoke.

Into this heady mix entered Swami, distinctive in his plain saffron robes. As he reached the stage, Janis Joplin and her band fell quiet. Someone projected slides of Krishna overhead, and to a huge ovation

Swami took his seat. Ginsberg draped a garland round his neck and introduced him, praising his work and recommending the temple, particularly the early-morning chanting sessions for those recovering from LSD trips. Then Swami spoke.

'Anyone can chant the *maha-mantra*. There are only three words: Hare, Krishna, and Rama. Hare is the energy of the Lord.'

He explained the mantra briefly before handing the microphone back to Ginsberg, who led the chanting on his harmonium. The mantra quickly took hold, and for half an hour it filled the hall as the audience joined hands and danced with abandon, their singing backed by the rock musicians. It ended with Swami's voice vibrating Sanskrit prayers over the sound system. '*Om vishnupada paramahamsa...*' he chanted, and finished with, 'All glories to the assembled devotees!' Then he made his way down from the stage, passing through the crowd like a messenger from another realm.

The following day Mukunda introduced Sam as the one who had organised the event. Swami congratulated him and asked how much money it had raised. When Sam told him they had made around two thousand dollars Swami was impressed.

'Those who make the money should know how to spend it,' he said. On the spot he made Sam the temple treasurer and invited him to come every day to learn how to keep books.

During these daily sessions, Sam found that nothing he had experienced could match the tranquillity and exhilaration he felt when he was with Swami. He wanted to stay close to him for the rest of his life. Swami, he concluded, was destined to be his personal teacher. Soon he and Melanie asked if they could be initiated, and Swami agreed at once, asking that they also get married. The next day he performed their initiation, and a few days later their marriage. He gave Melanie the name Malati, after the perfumed night blossom beloved of Krishna, and Sam he named Shyamsundar, after Krishna, whose beauty is like a dark rain cloud.

Every morning Swami came down to the temple at seven, and his presence lit up the small room. He kept to the same routine he had started in New York. At first the numbers were few – Janaki, Mukunda, and one or two others – but each day more came. Swami showed them everything by his personal example: how to bow in front of the picture of Krishna, how to sing, how to dance in time with the singing, and how to chant on beads. The mornings began and ended with chanting. He led the kirtans, always playing his *karatals* and singing Hare Krishna, Hare Krishna, Krishna Krishna, Hare Hare/ Hare Rama, Hare Rama, Rama Rama, Hare Hare. As he chanted he closed his eyes in deep concentration, occasionally opening them to glance round the room. Then he lectured from the *Bhagavad-gita, Srimad-Bhagavatam,* or on the life of Sri Chaitanya.

At seven in the evening he would again enter the temple, serious and purposeful. The evening meetings, when the dancing and chanting were at their most energetic, attracted larger numbers. Gradually, as regular visitors began to recognise one another, a community started to form. With a brief smile Swami would take his seat and chant the Sanskrit prayers in honour of his predecessor teachers. Then he led them in singing Hare Krishna for at least an hour. Soon the congregation would be on their feet, swaying, clapping, playing instruments, absorbed in chanting or in watching Swami chant Krishna's name. As the ecstasy mounted Joan's strong voice would call out *'hari hari bol!'* and the dancing would increase. Swami would build the tempo to a climax and suddenly bring the kirtan to a halt. As everyone sank to the floor he intoned more prayers. Then he spoke, patiently explaining the philosophy of Krishna consciousness.

His advice was always the same.

> Mantra is a combination of two words: *man* means 'mind' and *tra* means 'to deliver'. The Vedic mantras, or hymns, are meant for delivering us from mental concoctions. Our present difficulties are experienced on the mental and psychological planes. The psychedelic movement is on this platform. They are speaking of expanding the mind, but you should know that beyond the mind is intelligence, and beyond intelligence is the soul. The mantra delivers us from this mental psychological plane and establishes us on the spiritual.[5]

Or,

> When you chant Krishna's name he is with you in your heart. He and his name are connected, for it is a transcendental sound vibration. When we chant 'water, water', that is a material sound and our thirst is not quenched, but when we chant the Hare Krishna mantra the sound *krishna* and Krishna himself are the same. This process is so easy even a child can do it. So please chant and be happy.[6]

One evening as Swami was about to start his lecture, they were disturbed by a loud thumping coming through the wall from the ice cream parlour next door – a meeting place for the local Hells Angels, bikers with a reputation for being violent and reckless. Swami called Roger over and asked him to go and see what the problem was. Nervously, Roger went round and explained that Swami wanted to give his lecture now. Would they mind being quieter so his audience could hear? He added that they were welcome to come and listen too. There was an awkward pause.

'It was your singing that made us dance, but the wall got in the way,' their leader said with a grin. 'Hey, if the swami wants to speak, that's okay with us. Your guru's heavy, man.' The speaker was Sonny Barger, notorious leader of the Angels' Oakland chapter, based just across the bay. From then on a friendship developed between the two groups, with Sonny Barger and the bikers regarding themselves as guardians of the devotees.

Through their regular contact with him, Swami's students began to love him more and more and to want to do whatever they could to please him. They began to call him Swamiji, a more affectionate form of 'swami'. In his lectures Swamiji often spoke about the life of the founder of the Hare Krishna movement, Sri Chaitanya. In one lecture he told his audience how Sri Chaitanya used to lead his followers in procession through the streets of sixteenth-century Bengal, chanting the names of Krishna.

One day some of Swamiji's followers decided to go outside and chant. It was their spontaneous decision, without prompting, to do as Sri Chaitanya had done. A group with drums and cymbals went on a procession round several city blocks, ending up beneath Swamiji's apartment. He came to the window, happy to see them, and called them up. They crowded into his room and sat round him on the floor. His smile showed that he was immensely pleased with what they had done.

'Lord Chaitanya has given you the intelligence to chant in the street so more people can hear the holy names. Do this every day,' he said as he handed out his sticky brown sweets.

Day by day the chanting party grew, gathering banners and musical instruments and venturing further into the city. Through these regular excursions, the sight of joyful Hare Krishna chanters became an accepted part of San Francisco life.

In the beginning they often made their way to Golden Gate Park, collecting people as they went. Once in the park music-makers flocked to them: flute players, drummers, and flower-decked young men and women with guitars and tambourines. Together they sang and danced for hours beside a grassy hill, among exotic trees and shrubs, and afterwards some followed them back to the temple.

On Sundays Swamiji came out to join them. He chanted, sitting on the grass with his eyes closed, and began to chant, weaving a mystical energy field that drew a widening circle of flower children, who joined hands and danced round and round.

'That is how Krishna danced with the cowherd girls,' he said after one such occasion. 'Each *gopi* wanted to dance with Krishna, so he multiplied himself and danced in a circle beside each one of them. Every *gopi* thought Krishna was hers.'

In the temple, Swamiji was the focus of worship. His seat, from where he lectured and sang, was itself their altar. He was their direct link with Krishna. By watching him and hearing his voice they felt themselves in Krishna's presence.

One day Krishna came to them in another way. Malati found a small painted wooden figure in an import store, with a 'made in India' sticker on its base. She took it home and put it on her mantelpiece.

Shyamsundar brought it to show Swamiji, and Swamiji's response took everyone by surprise. As soon as he saw the little figure on his desk he bowed his head to the floor and recited prayers.

'This is Jagannath, Lord of the Universe,' he said, and told them the story of how Jagannath had come to be installed in one of India's grandest and oldest temples at Jagannath Puri, Orissa, and how Sri Chaitanya used to see him every day.

'Jagannath is Krishna himself, and he is worshipped along with his sister Subhadra and his brother Balaram. There should be three figures. Where are the other two?'

Malati went back and found two more that matched.

'Jagannath has come to us. It is Krishna's will that we worship him.'

Swamiji asked Shyamsundar if he could carve three-foot-high versions of the figures. When the figures were complete, he said, the devotees would take them in procession to the beach. He described the great Rathayatra festivals that took place in Puri every year, when the three deities were borne on huge chariots through the street.

Shyamsundar and Malati visited a dockyard where barges were dismantled and chose some large pieces of timber. Shyamsundar then set up a workshop on the veranda of their apartment, overlooking Buena Vista Park. He immersed himself in his assignment. First he used a saw to rough out the wooden shapes, then whittled them down with rasps and chisels until the forms of Jagannath, Subhadra, and Balaram began to emerge. One day he was hard at work and didn't notice Swamiji enter his apartment.

Thwack!

Shyamsundar's pack of cigarettes flew across the floor. He turned in surprise to see Swamiji, his cane raised, with a look of satisfaction on his face. He had been out walking and had stopped by to see Shyamsundar's work when he had spied the cigarettes on the floor at Subhadra's feet. He had done the natural thing. He laughed, but then spoke with concern.

'Why let a small stick of tobacco stand between you and Krishna?' As he said this he indicated with his fingers something very small. 'Yes, it's difficult to stop. Just take one less every day, and in that way you'll soon be finished.' This friendly and practical hint was all Shyamsundar needed, and he stopped smoking that day.

Each morning Janaki and her sister spent time with Swamiji learning to cook. Janaki loved being with Swamiji – cooking for him, ironing his clothes, sharing jokes, asking questions – anything to feel close to him. Once she asked him if he had any children.

'You are not my child?' he immediately responded. 'Aren't all these boys and girls my children?' And she knew he meant it.

Once she dreamed they were on another planet with Swamiji, all clapping and chanting Hare Krishna, and the whole world was coming to join them. She described the dream to him.

'Oh, such a lovely dream,' he smiled.

A drum arrived from Calcutta – a twin-headed clay *mridanga*. It was a traditional drum of Bengal, designed to be played while sitting, standing, or dancing, and had accompanied Sri Chaitanya's original chanting parties. Swamiji had been waiting for this drum since he had arrived in New York, when he had sent money to India and ordered it to be freighted over. The morning it arrived he raced Mukunda down two flights of stairs. As soon as Mukunda unpacked the drum Swamiji stepped forward. He tore a piece of cloth from his robe and wrapped it round the sacred instrument.

'This cloth must never be removed,' he instructed.

That day in kirtan he brought the drum to life. It sounded like a new voice joined to their chanting with its high-pitched ring and deep resonant bass. Everyone was excited by the new arrival and especially astonished at Swamiji's mastery of it. Mukunda was keen to learn how to play, and Swamiji started giving him lessons the next day. Mukunda loved those times that they spent together, filled with Swamiji's patient attention. So their friendship continued to grow.

Malati took charge of the kitchen. Many hungry mouths needed feeding, and through a combination of collecting donations and careful shopping, she managed each day to feed up to a hundred people.

Swamiji taught her to cook dal, rice, chapatis, and many other delicious recipes. The food was offered to Krishna and sanctifed as prasadam, 'God's mercy', and it gained a reputation throughout Haight-Ashbury as food for body and soul. More than that, it was a bond that united the growing community with each other and with Swamiji.

Roger had felt from the moment he had first seen Swamiji at the airport that Swamiji was his guru. As the weeks went by another feeling gained strength: Swamiji was also his friend. He looked for ways to get into Swamiji's room so he could talk with him, and Swamiji always welcomed him. Roger found that each step he took toward his teacher was rewarded by his teacher taking many steps toward him. One day Mukunda called Roger.

'Swamiji wants to speak to you.'

Roger hurried into Swamiji's room.

'Is Pentax a good camera?' Swamiji's down-to-earth question took Roger by surprise. He had expected something more mystical.

'A friend in India wants me to get him one,' he explained.

Roger showed him his own camera, a Nikon, and Swamiji, curious, played with it for a long while, trying the different controls. Handing it back he asked if Roger could research prices for both Nikon and Pentax cameras. This was the first time Swamiji had asked Roger to do something for him, and Roger felt good to be able to offer this service. Conscientiously he reported back with the information, and from then on photography became his service for his teacher.

One day Swamiji asked Roger to take his photograph: the devotees in New York had requested a portrait for use in his publications. Aware of how special this opportunity was, Roger planned carefully. He scheduled the session for the afternoon, when Swamiji was not so busy and when he could take advantage of the warm late afternoon sunshine that streamed into Swamiji's back room. He covered a mattress with a printed Indian cloth to create a seat, and Swamiji offered his own grey *chadar* to hang as a backdrop. Patiently he sat chanting on his beads.

'Bring the *Bhagavatams,*' he said, indicating his three volumes with their brightly illustrated covers. He had them placed beside him on the mattress. Roger was overwhelmed with the intimacy of the occasion, just him and Swamiji, and he had to concentrate as he took first a few colour shots and then a reel of black-and-white.

When he developed the film he was astonished by the results. Swamiji's eyes gazed from the prints with a compassion that seemed to reach out, while a stillness hung in the air around him. Most surprising of all, behind him, the grey *chadar* glowed with unexpected hues, showing a faint aura round Swamiji's head.

Joan was seeing Swamiji at least twice a day, taking every opportunity to observe him. She was utterly captivated by him – his voice, his grave countenance, his personal grace and beauty, his laughter, his penetrating gaze, and his fatherly presence. She started a journal to record his sayings and found herself transformed into a devoted disciple. She took a special interest in cooking for him, and always wanted to learn more about what he liked to eat. Cooking provided a good way for her to serve him and to remain in his company. When Swamiji directed her personally Joan felt a special thrill. He taught her new recipes every few days, and these periods in the kitchen with Swamiji were her favourite times.

Shyamsundar's work of carving the Jagannath deities neared completion. He painted their three-foot forms with bright primary colours in careful imitation of the miniature originals. Swamiji had set the date for installing the deities as 26th March 1967, which was the anniversary of Sri Chaitanya's birth that year. Under his direction the altar was rebuilt with a redwood shelf strong enough to hold the three deities above the painting of Sri Chaitanya dancing with his associates. Shyamsundar built a new platform and lectern for Swamiji and placed it on one side of the room so that Swamiji could sit in the midst of his guests and look to his right to see Jagannath.

When the day came for the installation they fasted, and sat together to read about the life of Sri Chaitanya[7] and to chant. By evening they were light-headed from the fasting and absorbed in chanting Krishna's names. The temple filled with guests, and the deities were installed on their shelf.

Swamiji spoke about the practice of devotional service, explaining how worship of Jagannath would now be part of that process:

> Here is Krishna. Krishna's form, Krishna's colour, Krishna's advice, Krishna's instruction, Krishna's sound – everything Krishna. There is no difficulty. Whatever you are hearing, you should repeat to others. You are hearing about Krishna, and you have to think, then you have to speak – otherwise it will not work. And you should worship. Therefore you require this deity for worshiping. We have to think of, we have to speak, we have to hear, we have to worship. And should we do this occasionally? No. Regularly. This is the process.[8]

Swamiji then led his audience in the ancient rite of offering a flame to the deities, using a simple candle on a plate. Each devotee and guest took a turn offering the flame in a circle in front of Jagannath while everyone else sang Hare Krishna. When all had made their offering, he demonstrated how to feel the heat from the sanctified flame by passing his hand over the candle and touching his forehead. Then he had the candle carried round the room.

'Show everyone. Whatever they can contribute…' The flame was taken round the room, and following his hint, guests dropped coins in the plate. As this was going on he made a request.

'When you come to the temple, you bring one fruit and one flower and offer it to the deity.'

When all was done and the rising full moon signified the moment of Sri Chaitanya's birth, they all sat on the floor in rows to eat a wonderful feast.[9]

From that day on visitors brought offerings of fruit, flowers, and all kinds of other items; garlands were made daily for Jagannath; more paintings went up on the walls; each night the simple ceremony was re-enacted, with more and more worshippers offering the flame to Jagannath. The temple flourished.

Joan and Roger asked Swamiji if he would conduct their marriage just as he had for their friends. Swamiji agreed, but first he wanted them to become initiated disciples.

'Why not do it tomorrow?' he asked, and they agreed.

The next day they sat with him in a circle round the sacred fire, which had been lit in front of Jagannath. Chanting devotees surrounded them. Smoke filled the small temple while Swamiji chanted mantras and added fuel, and the initiates offered grains and fruit into the flames. He made it all seem so natural, yet the initiates were making a serious commitment. No meat-eating, no illicit sex, no intoxication, and no gambling – these were the vows Swamiji required of all his initiated disciples. They promised to chant the Hare Krishna mantra sixteen times round their string of 108 japa beads, an obligation that would take them about two hours a day. They were able to make such promises because his living example inspired them and gave them faith in the spiritual path – and because they loved him.

He gave Joan the name Yamuna, after the river in which Krishna played, and Roger he named Gurudas, 'personal servant of the guru.' The date was 7th April 1967. In those first three months there were others who took initiation: fourteen young men and women, some of whom also got married.

One afternoon the devotees went with Swamiji down to the seashore. Being with their spiritual guardian beside the vast Pacific Ocean was an unforgettable experience.

'Because the ocean is great, it is tranquil,' he said, looking out to sea. 'Something so great will naturally be calm because it has nothing to fear.'

As the sun sank beneath the waves they lit a driftwood fire. While potatoes roasted in the embers, they danced round the flames with Swamiji, singing Hare Krishna. When the chanting ended he recited prayers, then raised his arms and faced the sea.

'All glories to the Pacific Ocean!' he repeated three times.

'Hare Krishna!' they responded.

As the stars came out Swamiji sat on a weathered tree trunk washed ashore by the tide. His disciples sat round him, and together they ate baked potatoes covered in butter.

Two weeks later Swamiji returned to New York, where his other disciples awaited him. Before leaving he entrusted Mukunda to guide the temple in his absence and promised to return for their Rathayatra festival in July, when they would again go to the beach, bringing Jagannath with them.

The original six friends had expanded into a community of brothers and sisters tied to one another and to Swamiji by deep bonds. He was their friend, teacher, master, and loving father. They had become family.

CHAPTER 3

The Idea of London

Shyamsundar was the first to talk about going to London in early 1968, when swinging London, home of the Beatles, was becoming a focus of youth culture. He proposed the idea to Swamiji, not knowing that opening a temple in London had been on Swamiji's mind all along.

Swamiji had always intended to start a worldwide movement. This had been clear in 1966 when he had incorporated his new society and named it the International Society for Krishna Consciousness. He now had centres in New York and San Francisco. In March of 1967 he approved a third temple in Montreal, in neighbouring Canada. This fulfilled the word 'International', but it was only the beginning.

'After Montreal, if I can establish one branch in London it will be a great success of our mission,' he wrote in a letter to the New York devotees in late March,[1] and a week later he added, 'I wish that at least four centres may be established in the Western countries, including one in London.' He wrote this last comment to Kirtanananda, one of his leading New York disciples, and it was to him that he first turned later in the year to fulfil his ambition.

All plans for expansion, however, were interrupted when on Sunday 28th May Swamiji suffered a heart attack and was rushed to Beth Israel Hospital in New York. That night both in New York and San Francisco devotees stayed up chanting and pleading with Krishna to let Swamiji live. For a few days his life hung in the balance, but gradually he pulled through. He made no secret of his dislike of being in the hospital and his lack of faith in the doctors: he preferred to depend on Krishna and on his disciples' care. He gave them a prayer to recite: 'My spiritual master has not yet finished his work, so please let him finish.'

For ten days the devotees ministered to him from his bedside, taking turns massaging him. Almost immediately he resumed his letter-writing, dictating slowly and painfully from his bed.

'Please inform all the boys and girls, especially Janaki, that I am progressing well,' he wrote to Mukunda. 'As soon as I get a little strength I shall come to San Francisco. In the meantime I shall be glad to know what arrangements you are going to make for the Rathayatra festival.'[2] After ten days in hospital he discharged himself and was taken by his disciples to a beach house in New Jersey, where a week later he wrote to his anxious followers in New York, 'Due to your sincere and ardent prayer, Krishna has saved my life. I was to die certainly but because you prayed sincerely I am saved. I am improving gradually and coming to my original condition.'[3]

The heart attack forced Swamiji to change his plans. He would return to India for Ayurvedic treatment and to convalesce in Krishna's spiritual homeland, Vrindavan. Although he thought it likely he might die before he could return to America – it was all in Krishna's hands – his purpose remained fixed and he counted on his disciples to make sure everything continued in his absence. 'Even in my broken health I shall try to propagate my mission through my disciples like you and others,' he again wrote to Mukunda. 'I don't mind whether I die here or in Vrindavan. Wherever there is Krishna, that is Vrindavan.'[4]

At the beginning of July Swamiji returned to California, hoping to attend the first Rathayatra festival in the Western world, but he was too weak, so the devotees rented him a bungalow on the oceanfront at Stinson Beach just north of San Francisco. There he rested while they celebrated Jagannath's chariot festival without him. Afterwards, they drove Jagannath across Golden Gate Bridge and over the headland to his bungalow.

For ten days they visited him in ones and twos. Then he left them for India. He wanted a hot climate and to be in Vrindavan again. He took only Kirtanananda with him as an assistant. His departure on 9th April was an emotional occasion because no one knew when – or if – they would ever see him again.

The flight to India was long and interrupted. He changed planes in New York and again in London. Swamiji set foot for the first time on English soil on 24th July 1967 when his flight was delayed and he was put up for the night at the Excelsior Hotel (which to him appeared like a 'dream palace') near Heathrow. Then, via Moscow, he flew to Delhi, where he disembarked and eventually reached Vrindavan. The change of climate worked.

'Dear children at New York,' he wrote, 'it was about midnight when we stepped out of the plane, and I KNEW IT WAS INDIA! It was like walking into a solid wall of HEAT. But that's what I've been wanting, and it felt good to me.'[5]

Once Swamiji entered Vrindavan his health improved. Soon he began to plan an American Centre there where he could bring his disciples to be trained. At the same time he sent a constant flow of letters to encourage them. His brush with death had made him more determined than ever to push forward his mission. By late September he was ready to return to America, but he had to wait for a new entry visa.

In his absence his Society continued to expand. Centres were developing in Boston and Montreal and new ones opened in Santa Fe and

Los Angeles. But despite the expansion in the United States, London still occupied his thoughts.

In Vrindavan he initiated Kirtanananda as a *sannyasi*. Swamiji considered Kirtanananda a capable man, one who could pioneer the London centre that his own guru, Bhaktisiddhanta, had wanted to see.

'I always said that if I could get the American boys and girls to take to this movement, the rest of the world would join,' he had once written.[6] Now he wanted to put his theory to the test by asking Kirtanananda Swami to stop in London for a couple of weeks on his way back to the United States and to look into the possibilities of starting a centre there. He gave him a letter of introduction to his godsister Miss Bowtell, who had been initiated as Vinoda Vani following the Gaudiya Math mission to London in 1933–35.

However, Kirtanananda passed through London without stopping. When Swamiji heard this he was deeply disappointed. He asked another New York disciple, Rayarama, to go instead. But then he withdrew the request. Getting his *Bhagavad-gita* published was more urgent, and Rayarama was now editing it.[7]

Mukunda worked hard to get Swamiji a new U.S. visa, and in November he succeeded. This was what Swamiji was waiting for. He had promised Janaki he would come to San Francisco first upon his return, and to fulfil this promise he flew by the Pacific route into San Francisco on 14th December 1967.

When he stepped off the plane Swamiji appeared strong and his bearing was erect. For the first time, his disciples saw him carrying a *tridanda,* the staff made of three bamboo poles wrapped in saffron cloth that signified his status as a renounced monk.

This time they arranged for him to stay in a spacious flat on Willard Street, a block from the temple. It belonged to Yamuna and Gurudas, but the couple moved out to make way for him. Newly renovated with its white walls and hardwood floors, the place was spacious and bright, with enough room for his servant and a secretary to stay there with him.

That afternoon Swamiji sat on a cushion in a bare room, his *tridanda* leaning on a nearby wall. He seemed to illuminate the room more than the late-afternoon sunshine. The joy of meeting him again filled his disciples' hearts. He opened his suitcase and took out a pile of fine cotton saris from Bengal. With a look of great care he handed one to each of the women.

Someone asked about the small cloth bag tied to the top of his *danda*. He opened it and revealed three garlands of crushed silk.

'These are for Lord Jagannath,' he said with a big smile. At this time Jagannath had no clothes. Sometimes the devotees gave him flowers, but he wore no other decoration. This was their introduction to the idea of making ornaments and clothes for the deity.

Three weeks later Swamiji travelled to Los Angeles, where Mukunda and Janaki, helped by others, had opened another storefront temple along with a nearby apartment for him. It soon became apparent that he had not completely recovered his health.

'I am at the present moment physically unfit,' he wrote to Yamuna. 'I am having always a buzzing sound in my brain. I cannot sleep soundly at night, but still I am working because I try to be in my position of spiritual platform.'

On receiving this news Yamuna travelled down from San Francisco to help her sister cook for Swamiji. They wanted to put him on a healthy eating programme. They tried to remove sweets from his diet, but he protested, and would have none of it.

He simply rose above the physical, and a great sense of urgency imbued his work. His time in India had allowed him to take stock of the previous two years. Whereas his first trip to America had for him been a journey into the unknown, now he had seen young Americans embrace Krishna consciousness, and their lives transformed as a result. He was convinced that Krishna was calling him to something extraordinary.

'I expect that all of you will combine together to open at least 108 centres before I leave this world,' he had written from India.[8] Now he was back, determined to fulfil his plan. He communicated a sense of boundless possibility to his disciples, and pushed them to help make his dreams come true.

Central to Swamiji's vision was what he called a World Sankirtan Party. It would be made up of at least twelve devotees who would travel with him from country to country. On a morning walk round Stowe Lake in San Francisco Yamuna asked him what it meant.

'Sankirtan is Lord Chaitanya's mission. It means a devotee goes to a place, chants Hare Krishna, and attracts others to chant Hare Krishna. Then, when their faith is a little strong, they become devotees and you go to another place. We will go to many places and do this.'[9]

It was not long after this that they began to discuss among themselves the idea of going to London. Shyamsundar saw that the focus of youth culture was shifting from San Francisco to London, where the Beatles were.

'Wouldn't it be great to meet the Beatles and get them to chant Hare Krishna?' he kept saying to Mukunda and Gurudas.

George Harrison in particular seemed open to hearing about Krishna. He had met Ravi Shankar in 1966 and had stayed with him in India, visiting Kashmir and Varanasi. He had also been composing songs such as 'Within You Without You', which clearly showed he was on a spiritual search.[10]

George had briefly visited Haight-Ashbury the previous summer, hoping to witness for himself the spiritual awakening he had heard about. While there he had met some of the local Hells Angels on the street and reportedly invited them to visit him in London. But he was dismayed by the decadence of the San Francisco youth culture. His disappointment had been reported in a local underground paper, together with his advice that the truth could be found by chanting mantras, not by taking drugs. 'Through the musical you reach the spiritual,' he had told a reporter. Mukunda had read the reports and written George a letter.

'It's the mantra itself that's important, not the music,' Mukunda wrote, 'because the mantra is the name of God.' He recommended the Hare Krishna mantra and addressed the letter care of the newspaper, hardly expecting it to reach its destination.[11]

Just after Swamiji had returned from India, the Beatles made their celebrated pilgrimage to Maharishi's ashram in Rishikesh to learn meditation. George and his wife Pattie loved it there and stayed, along with John and Cynthia Lennon, for two months of daily meditation and yoga.

Because of all this, Shyamsundar was convinced that if he went to London he could get the Beatles to listen to him. Young people considered the Beatles their spokesmen. If the Beatles would chant Hare Krishna the world would listen and people everywhere would follow their example.

Shyamsundar told Swamiji of his plan, assuring him that the Beatles would be personally ready to meet the guru of the Hare Krishna movement. Swamiji liked his bold approach and responded with enthusiasm.

'I am very much eager to open a centre in London,' he wrote to Mukunda, who was in Los Angeles. 'If Shyamsundar and Malati go there, then I may also go for some time to deal with the Beatles, who are so much anxious to understand about spiritual knowledge.'[12]

This was in May 1968. Malati was pregnant, so Swamiji decided the group should wait until after her baby was born. In early June Swamiji went to Montreal while his U.S. visa was being renewed. He accepted the delay in getting the visa as an indication that this was a good time to begin his mission in Europe. This would be the start of his World Sankirtan Party.

The obstacle was lack of money. How could they afford the travel and accommodation? Just then an unexpected cheque arrived in the mail for Shyamsundar: the return of almost two thousand dollars owed to him from two years earlier. Between them it was agreed that with this money the three couples – Mukunda and Janaki, Yamuna and Gurudas, and Malati and Shyamsundar – would go to London. They put their proposal before Swamiji. Shyamsundar's original plan had been just to meet the Beatles, but now it had grown into something much more: they would start a Hare Krishna temple in London, as Swamiji had so long wanted.

Malati and Shyamsundar's daughter was born on 17th June 1968. They called Swamiji with the news, and over the phone he named her Saraswati, goddess of wisdom. He suggested that mother and child rest for a month, and then the whole party could travel to England. After a second Rathayatra was staged in San Francisco, Shyamsundar bought a consignment of redwood timbers, sufficient to adorn a small temple, and shipped them to London. Then the six of them, with baby Saraswati, set off for Montreal to spend a last few days with Swamiji.

The party arrived to find the Montreal temple located in a former bowling alley. The devotees had hung blankets to partition the large open space, its floor still marked out into bowling lanes. Living like this for their two-week visit would be austere, but their family spirit and the excitement of their assignment made it manageable.

The first thing they wanted to do was find Swamiji, who was living in a house nearby. Janaki and Malati, carrying baby Saraswati, went searching for his house and found it – it was the one with saffron cloth hanging out to dry. They went straight in to see him.

'Oh!' he looked up. 'This very morning I dreamt of this child.'

Swamiji wanted to give them musical training before they went to England. He hoped they would perform beautiful kirtan wherever they went and so attract people to Krishna. He had explained this to Shyamsundar a few weeks before.

> If we can organise a nice Kirtan party, which Mukunda can do because he is music master, and if we travel in the European countries supported by our books and literature, I am sure it will be a great successful missionary work.[13]

So each morning they met him in the temple room and sang the temple prayers while he corrected their rhythm and pronunciation. He taught them an afternoon melody to add to the morning one they already knew, and instructed them to keep their singing simple and pure, using just these two basic tunes.

He decided to award them second initiation. He gave them the *gayatri-mantra* 'as a matter of recognition to those who are chanting sixteen rounds regularly and following the four principles of restrictions.'[14]

Over the two days before they left they celebrated Krishna's birthday, Janmashtami, and Swamiji's birthday, Vyasa Puja, the day of homage to the guru.

Recently, disciples had begun to call Swamiji by a new name. They had heard that 'Prabhupada' was an address of love and respect traditionally given to great spiritual masters in the line of Sri Chaitanya. The name had two meanings: 'one who stays at the feet of Krishna, the supreme master', and 'one who has got many *prabhus,* or masters, to abide by his order'.[15] The same name had been offered to Rupa Goswami, the sixteenth-century disciple of Sri Chaitanya, as well as to Swamiji's own spiritual master, Bhaktsiddhanta Saraswati. The devotees had asked Swamiji if they could call him Prabhupada and he had accepted. Gradually it became, for them, simply his name.

On his birthday Prabhupada cooked a sumptuous feast. When it was ready he called the six devotees going to London and gave them the words of the *gayatri-mantra* on pieces of paper to learn by heart. Then he placed threads round the shoulders of the men, handed threads to the women, and told them they must chant the mantra three times daily.

They sat together in the temple room to eat the feast, he on his raised seat and they around him on the floor, enjoying his heavenly cooking. While they ate he gave half of one of his *gulabjamuns* to Malati so her baby could suck the juice.

In the evening they went over to Swamiji's house. He was in a jolly mood and played with baby Saraswati. Picking her up he held her out in front of him with one hand. Then he pulled her close again, wrapped his garland round both of them, and had their photo taken.

'If my godbrothers in India saw this they would say, "What kind of *sannyasi* is he?"' he joked. Then he spoke more seriously. 'This means so much to me – sending my disciples to London.' He recalled the big send-off his own guru had given his disciples when they had left for London in 1933. Those devotees had been mature swamis, but now he was sending six young householders to achieve what those swamis had not. He was counting on them, and he spoke long to them, filling them with inspiration, determination, and hope.

That evening Gurudas was admiring a painting of Narasimha, the fourth incarnation of Vishnu, that appeared on the cover of the new *Back to Godhead* magazine lying on Prabhupada's desk. To an untutored eye it seemed a fearful image, showing a supernatural being with a man's body and the head of a lion.

'Swamiji, when we go chanting on the streets in London, can we wear Lord Narasimha masks?' he joked.

'Why not?' Prabhupada responded calmly, using the playful suggestion to make a serious point. 'What great men do, others will follow.' He told them about a Charlie Chaplin film he had seen in his youth. Chaplin had played a man at a dance whose coattails were torn so that they swung out behind him as he danced. When he realised what had happened and that people were laughing at him, he deliberately tore them all the way up to his collar and then began to dance with abandon. Other men rushed to imitate him and a fashion was born. Prabhupada laughed heartily and his disciples laughed with him. Only later did they realise the significance of what he had told them: be bold and the world will follow you.

Their plan for London was certainly bold. They would get the Beatles to chant Hare Krishna and spread it all over the world. But whatever they may or may not achieve, Prabhupada wanted a temple in London, and if they tried their best to fulfil his desire he would shower them with his blessings.

Prabhupada told them that London was the hub of the world, the most important city on the planet. He told them how Bhaktisiddhanta had conceived of sending devotees there from India. He lent them a thousand dollars from his personal fund, and gave them the addresses of Miss Bowtell and a Hindu family, the Kohlis, in London. He called their adventure the London *yatra,* explaining that *yatra* means journey. This journey, he said, would be the start of a pilgrimage to bring Krishna consciousness to the world.

'Chant, feast, dance, study our philosophy, and share it with others.

This is our peace formula,' he said. 'It will do good to you and good to others as well.'

When the time came to say goodbye, Malati had one last request. She had seen Hindus touching Prabhupada's feet. She knew he didn't much care for it, but she had heard that the dust of the feet of a great soul could dissipate ten thousand years of sinful life. So she asked if he would allow them this benediction.

Gravely he stretched out his lotus feet. They each touched their head to his soles, and as they did so he rubbed the backs of their heads. When Yamuna's turn came she kissed Prabhupada's feet. They were soft and pink, like pictures of the Vrindavan sky, she thought. She had never experienced a touch so profound. Any doubt about the outcome of their mission was removed. Failure was not part of their mentality. They were ready.

Those nine days they spent with Prabhupada in Montreal were a turning point in their spiritual lives. He had initiated them into the *gayatri-mantra*, he had trained them in kirtan, and he had given them unlimited blessings.

They said goodbye on 19th August 1968. Within twenty-four hours they were at the New York temple. From there, by Icelandic Airways on one-way tickets costing sixty-five dollars each, they flew to Amsterdam, then by ferry they crossed the English Channel.

BOOK TWO

Finding Krishna in London 1968–70

CHAPTER 4

Searching for George

HERNE HILL, SOUTH LONDON, 4TH SEPTEMBER 1968

From their attic window Malati and Shyamsundar looked out over a rolling urban landscape. In front of them rose the slender spire of St Paul's, parish church of Herne Hill, a genteel South London suburb whose sheltered tree-lined streets, with their nineteenth-century terraced houses, afforded views eastward to the wooded parks of Forest Hill and Sydenham, and westward to Clapham and the distant chimneys of Battersea Power Station.

They had crossed from Calais by hovercraft with their six-week-old baby, reaching Dover on 4th September, then caught the train to London and come straight to the Kohlis, who owned a semi-detached house divided into bedsits at 80 Herne Hill. Here they had been given refuge.

The house was on the southern slope of a low ridge that reached northward from Dulwich toward the centre of the city. A red London bus regularly passed by their doorstep, travelling in the direction of the distant dome of St Paul's Cathedral. In half an hour it could carry them – through Camberwell with its art college and hospital, along the length of Walworth High Street, home of Charlie Chaplin and bustling street markets, past workshops and warehouses on Southwark's riverside, across the soaring arch of Waterloo Bridge – to the banks, insurance offices, and trading halls of the City of London.

Within a week the others had made the crossing[1] into England, and Shyamsundar, who had lost no time in buying an old pickup van, a red Ford Popular that cost him £65, had met them at Victoria Station and brought them down to Herne Hill, where each couple now occupied their own bedsit at the same address.

As soon as they were assembled they strolled down to Brockwell Park and climbed a gentle hill to the pedimented porch of Brockwell Mansion, a once grand house that now served as a teashop for the people of Herne Hill. From here they could see the metropolis stretching away north, beyond the city, to the distant hills of Highgate and Hampstead.

If they wanted to be noticed they knew they had to be in the city, not at this safe distance from it, so their first task was to find a place for a temple amid the busy streets of Central London, where they could live together and invite guests. This would be difficult here, where apart from the Kohlis they knew no one, but Prabhupada had instilled in them the faith that if they attempted something for Krishna, Krishna would help them. So to this immediate task they bent their efforts.

Seven days after Shyamsundar and Malati had arrived they all drove into town in their van and, after parking in Covent Garden, ventured onto the streets to chant Krishna's names. With Mukunda carrying his drum, they set off through the crowded side lanes until they came to Charing Cross Road, where they turned downhill toward Trafalgar Square. Here at the base of Nelson's Column, they decided, would be the right place to inaugurate their London *yatra*. Mukunda started on the drum and led them in chanting, first the prayers to the guru, then to Sri Chaitanya, and then the Hare Krishna mantra. The sound of their voices and the chiming of the brass *karatals,* together with the boom of the *mridanga,* echoed from the grand frontages of the National Gallery and the High Commissions of Canada and South Africa. People crowded round to watch the exuberant dancing of these charismatic young men and women and wondered who they could be. The devotees concentrated on their chanting. Behind them stretched Whitehall and the Houses of Parliament, with Admiralty Arch leading down the Mall to Buckingham Palace; this was the crossroads of the old empire. As onlookers gathered, the chanters felt protected by the sound of Krishna's names and by the knowledge that they were fulfilling Prabhupada's sacred mission.

Afterwards, a friend of Dr Kohli took them to the Hindu Centre in Grafton Terrace, on the north side of town in a row of houses at the foot of Hampstead Hill. The centre had been opened two years earlier by leading members of London's small Hindu community, composed mainly of professionals in the diplomatic service, medicine, and law, and wealthy Indian families with a London home. There the devotees led worshippers in chanting Hare Krishna and made a lasting impression among their hosts, who had never dreamt of meeting Western devotees of Krishna.

The next morning Malati wrote to Prabhupada with a report of their first public outing, and a week later came his reply, dated 18th September:

> My dear Malati,
>
> It was my Guru Maharaj's desire that there should be a centre established in England, and by his mercy you have successfully begun this mission. Please keep me informed how you are progressing there. I am very anxious to hear in every letter.

From that moment they lived to hear the sound of the postman. Prabhupada would write to one or another of them almost daily, and they would share his letters so that they always had new words of encouragement. Prabhupada sent a special handwritten letter to Janaki, whose sensitive nature made the London assignment especially challenging.

My dear Janaki,

Your letter dated 13/9/68 is so nicely written that I have read the matter twice, I am writing herewith in my hand, Hare Krishna: Please try to open the London temple as quickly as possible, and I am ready to start for London at any moment on receipt of the news.[2]

Although their bedsit was small, Yamuna and Gurudas hosted the others and started inviting guests to chant with them and share their meals. The Kohli family lent their front room for larger meetings and introduced them to their friends. For the young devotees, lack of money was an obstacle: they had no savings and no support, nor did their visas allow them regular employment. The only solution was to look for casual work. Shyamsundar did carpentry for his landlord, Mukunda offered piano lessons and transcribed music, and Gurudas looked for ways to sell his photos to newspapers.

Since they had no place of their own in which to hold public meetings, they went out to meet the public. During the day they called on estate agents, followed up contacts, and in the evenings, almost nightly, visited Hindu homes.

They were soon bound to get themselves noticed, especially when the men decided to shave their heads for the first time. It was a big step, but it left them feeling refreshed and free. They bought a bolt of cotton cloth and dyed it saffron, so that the men could wear saffron robes and the women saffron saris. Now when they went out in public they drew instant attention. It was their chanting, however, that caused the real sensation.

DRURY LANE, OCTOBER 1968

One of the first places to welcome their chanting was the Arts Lab. Along with the *International Times* newspaper and the Roundhouse, the Arts Lab was a focal point of the alternative London scene. It was housed in two adjoining small warehouses at 182 Drury Lane, near Covent Garden Market. Under the leadership of Jim Haynes, an American army veteran and now a much-respected creative entrepreneur among

London's arts community, the Arts Lab had established itself as an exciting venue for theatre, poetry, film, and happenings of all kinds. Its basement cinema, its floor covered with old mattresses, was renowned as a place to see all-night film shows, meet artists, poets, and music-makers, and generally hang out. Even John Lennon and Yoko Ono were sometimes seen there, their white Rolls Royce parked outside.

Upstairs the devotees were given a regular spot on Wednesday and Friday evenings. They sat in a darkened room with candles and incense burning and chanted for hours with whoever came. The sessions attracted much attention. Here they met John Peel, who hosted a radio programme for the BBC called Night Ride. Peel showcased new music, and a few words from him could make or break an artist. He invited the devotees onto his show and gave airtime to a version of the Hare Krishna mantra from his own collection of world music, even before the devotees had made their own recording. Later he wrote about the experience in his column in the *International Times:*

> The followers of the Hare Krishna movement have visited the jaundiced Peel. Each of them radiates more love and joy than a hundred busloads of archbishops.

Peel went on to defend the paper's right to print nude photos, to which the archbishops objected, and implied that the Hare Krishna devotees, being so full of love, were obviously more enlightened and liberal-minded in their views.

They quickly made friends among the hippies, who were a growing presence in London. The members of the English underground, through music, art, and radical politics, had extensive links with their hippie cousins in San Francisco, and between the two cities a kindred community had begun to emerge, pioneering hippie culture on opposite sides of the Western world. The organisers of the London hippies were often Americans, so it was not surprising that six young American mystics with a new spiritual lifestyle to teach would be perceived as part of this flow of inspiration and welcomed as an exciting addition to the London scene.

One night the devotees went to the Arts Lab and told Jim Haynes about their need for a place in the centre of town. Haynes said he might be able to help. He was co-founder of the *International Times,* which was vacating a building just round the corner.

The newspaper had been forced to abbreviate its name to IT after being sued by *The Times* newspaper. IT was outspoken in exposing corruption and injustice, but it had also been accused of printing obscenity and promoting drugs – charges it vigorously denied. All this made the IT popular with the young, and secured its credentials as the journal of the English underground. Jim sent them round to IT, whose staff welcomed them as fellow conspirators and spiritual brothers and sisters. The paper was about to move to a larger building and it seemed that their present offices might be available, at least temporarily, to the devotees. The editor, Graham Keen, explained that the building was owned by a wealthy young businessman, Nigel Samuel, proprietor of a chain of high street jewellers.

'You should go and see Nigel,' said Graham. 'Ask if he'll let you stay here. I think he might help you out.' And Graham made a phone call to arrange an appointment for them.

'You do the talking, Gurudas,' urged Shyamsundar and Mukunda. 'You always find the right words on these occasions.'

The three of them called on Mr Samuel in his penthouse overlooking Portland Square and found him a ready listener. He recognised his visitors as possessing a spiritual depth that appealed to him, and their calm and friendly presence put him at ease. They talked of books, which were his special interest – Gurudas mentioned the *Bhagavad-gita* – and about the new freedom and spirit of adventure that connected San Francisco and London.

'So how can I help?' he asked courteously.

'We need a place to live in Central London, and we were hoping we could stay in your building on Betterton Street,' ventured Gurudas. Samuel took a moment to think. His principal tenants had just moved out and he had no new ones lined up. His second-hand book service,

Bibliophile, had books in storage there and an office on the upper floor, so he was in no hurry to let the building.

'Yes, why not? You can use the lower floors for a while. I've an office on the top floor, where I sometimes come, and there's another tenant up there with me – but we won't bother you.'

The three could hardly believe their good fortune, but there was more. 'I won't charge you rent,' added Samuel generously, and they shook hands on it.

Now the devotees were together in one place, with an address and a phone number in the heart of London. They had only to step outside their door and in one minute they could be at the Arts Lab, or, if they turned the other way, they could be in Piccadilly Circus in just five minutes.

The house at 22 Betterton Street was a four-storey building. Large windows gave light to the upper front rooms, while at pavement level a grim steel shutter secured the warehouse space. On either side were ageing apartment buildings with brickwork stained by London soot. Opposite sat a grim council block, Betterton House, and a launderette. Residential buildings extended down either side of the narrow thoroughfare, which was used as a shortcut by taxis crossing from Covent Garden toward Holborn. The ornate Covent Garden Market buildings, open for business at two each morning to supply London's fruits, flowers, and vegetables, were a few streets south. Drury Lane, with its famous theatres and the Royal Opera House, was at the end of the street. Betterton Street itself was narrow, admitting little daylight. Only when the sun climbed high in the sky did it reach the devotees' windows, and never during the winter.

Here all streets rang with the tramp of ceaseless footsteps, the roll of cart wheels, the echo of tradesmen and -women down the centuries, side by side with the twentieth-century publishing and entertainment industries. From the tranquillity of Herne Hill the devotees found themselves thrown into this workhouse of the past, and workshop of the future.

The ground floor of their building was mostly taken up with stacks of old IT issues, but Shyamsundar cleared a space between them so he could start carving a set of Jagannath deities. Again he used reclaimed timber, this time taken from the boat-breaking yards of East London's docks. At the rear of the building he fitted out a small kitchen, where Malati took charge. Beside it he partitioned off a small room where she could look after baby Saraswati and watch her while she cooked. Out the back was a rough lean-to bathroom where they made a simple shower arrangement. They had no money for a hot water heater, so as December approached they bathed in cold water, accepting the hardship as part of their adventure.

On the second floor were private rooms for the other two couples, and on the first floor, in the only large space, they created their temple. Shyamsundar built a simple tiered altar. On the middle shelf stood small Jagannath deities, the originals from San Francisco that had inspired the carving of the larger ones. Beneath these was a framed photo of Prabhupada chanting in Golden Gate Park surrounded by young men and women. The top shelf was reserved for the large new Jagannath Shyamsundar was carving, and before long he took his place, smiling down beneficently.

The new temple lifted their spirits. It meant they could start and end each day in one another's company. Each morning they could sit together to chant on their beads. Prabhupada had always emphasised that if they did this all other difficulties would be resolved.

> My dear Malati,
>
> Try to take care of Lord Jagannath as far as possible after doing your household duties, but you should be strict only in completing the sixteen rounds of chanting. That will save you from all discrepancies. As a householder, even there are some flaws in following the rules and regulations, it doesn't matter. You should try your best and Krishna will help you.[3]

They read to one another from the *Srimad-Bhagavatam,* discussing Prabhupada's commentary and increasing their faith in his words. The women now had a kitchen, even though it was small and poorly equipped, where they could practice the culinary skills Prabhupada had so carefully taught them. Now that they had somewhere to invite guests, they advertised Sunday Love Feasts. People came in increasing numbers.

The devotees could not relax, though, for they knew that as soon as Mr Samuel needed the space they would have to vacate the building. He had promised them at least a couple of months; they could become homeless at any time. So while they made the most of what Krishna had given them, they kept up their search for a permanent temple.

THE ROUNDHOUSE, NOVEMBER 1968

At the Arts Lab they had been gathering a regular audience who would come and sit in a large circle and chant. Now they held these same chanting sessions regularly in their new temple. One day Jim Haynes arranged for them to perform at the Roundhouse in Camden. It had been built a hundred years earlier as an engine shed accommodating a giant turntable for steam engines, but now it was London's newest performance space and a venue for early Pink Floyd concerts. The devotees sat in a circle, as they had been doing at the Arts Lab, but this time they were joined by hundreds of chanters. They built a sacred fire in the centre of the performance area, and soon the flames flickered in the cavernous space, sending light dancing into the shadows.

Yamuna, sitting with the harmonium, saw faces fading into the distance all around her. An expectant hush fell.

'When we start to chant, please join in,' she asked, her voice resonating calm. 'And if you feel inspired, you can shout *haribol!*' She demonstrated the joyful cry, then started the chant, closing her eyes as she always did when she sang so she could focus without distraction upon the sound of the holy name, as she had learned from Prabhupada.

They chanted for a long time. Incense filled the air, and bells, drums, and guitars sounded from all sides in accompaniment to their chanting. Most of those present had never chanted a mantra. This was their initiation into a new realm of mystical experience.

As the sound rippled through the assembly an eighteen-year-old boy gave himself over to the mantra and felt its energy sweep through him. His name was Colin Jury, and he was an apprentice printer from the East End. He had seen the devotees at the Arts Lab, but until this day he had not experienced the power of their chanting.

'*Haribol!*' he called repeatedly into the darkness, overcome with emotion. He felt transformed by the mantra. His friends, who belonged to an anarchist group called the Tribe, couldn't understand what Colin was experiencing. In the last year his involvement with them had led him on a downward spiral and turned his life upside down. He realised he needed to get away. When the chanting was over he told his friends he wanted to be on his own and left the Roundhouse to digest his spiritual experience. A few mornings later, having become homeless and after staying up all the previous night, he met Mukunda at the Indica bookshop in Southampton Row.

'Come round to our temple and have breakfast with us,' offered Mukunda, and Colin gladly accepted. After an amazing breakfast of hot *halava* cooked by Yamuna – it was unlike anything he had ever tasted – Colin stayed and helped her for the rest of the day. He had never felt so at home. The next day the devotees allowed him to move in with them.

Colin's close friend Dick Withy came to see him and he also moved in, followed by another friend, Tim, both of them from South London. These three young men, Colin, Dick, and Tim, became the first English Krishna devotees.

On Christmas Eve the devotees placed a phone call to Prabhupada in Los Angeles, using Mr Samuel's office phone. Such phone calls were rare – they even wrote to Prabhupada first to ask if they could call him. They needed to hear his voice and to share with him some of their successes. They put Colin on the line.

'So you have learned how to make chapatis?'

'Yes, Prabhupada.' He hadn't – but now he would.

The expanding group of devotees heard that Ravi Shankar was going to be at the Indian High Commission and thought his visit would provide them a good opportunity to meet some leading people, as Prabhupada had always said they should try to do. They arrived in their Ford

Popular and talked their way past the policemen at the gate. A man in livery was announcing the guests, and he introduced them as well.

'International Society for Krishna Consciousness.' Everyone looked up. The High Commissioner, S S Dewan, was a Communist, and his guests were surprised when he called the devotees upstairs to talk with them in private. Afterwards he invited them back for dinner and they chanted with him and showed him slides of Prabhupada and Krishna. They became friends that night, and later, after they had introduced him to Prabhupada, the High Commissioner became a valuable supporter of Krishna consciousness.

COVENT GARDEN, NOVEMBER-DECEMBER 1968

The regular chanting sessions at the Arts Lab encouraged them to practice their musical skills. With Mukunda as their musical director they began to incorporate more Indian instruments into their repertoire. Shyamsundar learned to bow the *esaraj* – something like an Indian violin – and Colin took to the *mridanga* like a born drummer, Mukunda mastered the tambura, and Yamuna played the harmonium, leaving Malati and Gurudas on *karatals*. Mukunda composed a version of the *Brahma-samhita,* the prayers of creation, based on a tune he had heard Prabhupada sing, and together they rehearsed it at the Arts Lab, eventually borrowing the makeshift recording studio there to produce a demo tape. They were now an authentic band of musicians, and they posed with their instruments for a group portrait in front of Jagannath's altar.

Their friendship with the people at IT gave them a natural way to communicate with London's youth through the underground paper. Yamuna designed a cover for IT that included the Hare Krishna mantra written out in her calligraphic hand, and Mukunda wrote an article explaining the art of chanting. They contributed the story of Prahlada, the child saint who led his friends in chanting Krishna's names, illustrated with paintings by Govinda Dasi of San Francisco. The story, written by Gurudas, covered six pages and was serialised in two issues. The spirituality of their features amid IT's radical articles and provocative images announced their presence in London's alternative culture.

A new musical called *Hair* was attracting record audiences in London. It had originated in New York off Broadway as a protest against the Vietnam War. It told the story of a hippie tribe's search for happiness and peace, ending with one of them being forced into the army and killed in Vietnam. Such stories were a reality for peace-loving young Americans, including a good number who aspired to be Hare Krishna devotees. A high point in the musical was a choreographed version of the Hare Krishna mantra performed by the whole cast. *Hair* was a sensation on both sides of the Atlantic and was popularising the mantra. It was all make-believe – the hippies on stage were professional actors – but it expressed a real yearning that existed among young people for spiritual revolution and for the dawn of a new age – the Age of Aquarius.

The devotees chanted nightly to the crowds on the pavement outside the Shaftesbury Theatre, where *Hair* was showing. They were not actors; they were the real thing – dedicated to their search for truth and peace. One night the members of the cast invited them in to chant on stage.

The cast of *Hair* performed the Hare Krishna chant each night, but they did so while naked. A cultural revolution was in progress, of which *Hair,* with its naked dancers, was one manifestation. Its intention was to change people's consciousness. John Lennon had just written its anthem, his song 'Revolution', in which he sang that, while people say they want to change the constitution, 'You'd better free your mind instead.'

The generation that grew up after the Second World War was determined to find its own truths, and in this time of self-discovery and spiritual adventure the Beatles were leaders of the revolution. If they became Krishna conscious, others would surely follow.

SAVILE ROW, DECEMBER 1968

The Beatles were looking for new talent. They had been exploited by the corporate music world, so now, following the untimely death of their manager Brian Epstein, they had started their own company, Apple Corps, to support independent artistic expression. 'Send us your ideas,' they announced.

Taking them at their word the devotees launched a campaign to get the Beatles' attention. They sent them a gift each day for a week – a photo of the New York devotees, arms upraised and with smiling faces, and the invitation, 'Come sing with us!'; the Prahlada story and Yamuna's IT cover; then a walking clockwork apple with the Hare Krishna mantra painted on it and a home-baked apple pie. The gifts got through with the help of an American girl working as George Harrison's secretary. Finally, hoping they had excited some curiosity, they delivered their demo tape of the *Brahma-samhita* prayers and a photograph of themselves.

They had no way of knowing if their campaign had been fruitful, but the opportunity to find out came in early December when Shyamsundar received an unexpected phone call.

'Hi, I'm at the airport with some friends. Can you come and get us?' It was Rock Scully from San Francisco. Years before, he and Shyamsundar had shared a room as Fulbright scholars in Switzerland. Later in California, when Rock was managing the Grateful Dead, he had helped Shyamsundar put on the Mantra-Rock Dance. Now he was asking a favour.

'There's a few of us – Ken Kesey with a Buddhist friend, and Sonny and Frenchy with their old ladies from the Oakland Hells Angels. We're tired and hungry with nowhere to stay.'

Shyamsundar drove to the airport, and three hours later the ageing Ford Popular rounded the corner into Betterton Street crammed with passengers and laden with two Harley-Davidson machines. The whole party trooped upstairs, and after removing their heavy leather boots, settled down to the hearty meal that Malati, Yamuna, and Janaki had prepared for them, their grimy bikers' outfits and tattoos incongruous among the incense and images of Krishna. The two Hells Angels – their friend from San Francisco, Sonny Barger, and his mate Frenchy – had come to pay a visit to George Harrison in response to the invitation they claimed he had given them the previous year in Haight-Ashbury.

Rock Scully had organised the expedition and Ken Kesey had come along for the ride.

Gurudas had been friends with Kesey previous to meeting the devotees. As author of the cult novel *One Flew Over the Cuckoo's Nest* Kesey was a folk hero of sixties America. The two of them spent the evening discussing philosophy, while the other guests, having feasted on prasadam, fell into a deep sleep on the floor. When they awoke it was evening and they wanted to explore the city. Kicking their Harley-Davidsons into life, they roared off into the night. A few days later Rock called Shyamsundar again.

'We've got an appointment to meet George Harrison tomorrow. You can come too.'

Bringing another apple pie, Shyamsundar walked to Savile Row, home of Apple Records. By the time he arrived the rest of Rock's party was inside causing the peaceable Apple staff a good deal of apprehension. Before going in Ken Kesey had posed outside for a photo, dressed in his leather gear and a cowboy hat. But Shyamsundar, whose name was not on the list, was having trouble persuading the doormen to let him in. Just then Yoko Ono arrived and recognised him from the Arts Lab.

'You must be a friend of George's,' she said kindly. 'Come in with me.'

Once in the crowded foyer he delivered his pie to the receptionist, who promised to pass it on to George, then found somewhere to sit. The room was filled with the noisy visitors from California, so Shyamsundar decided to stay quietly in a corner and chant on his beads. Word came that all four Beatles were in a meeting. Time passed, and people came and went. One by one, John, Paul, and Ringo emerged and hastened to the exit without acknowledging the visitors. The party became restless and some left. Finally, when the foyer was half empty, George appeared. He looked round the room, spotted Shyamsundar, and came straight over to him.

'Where have you been?' he exclaimed.

George sat down beside Shyamsundar and his words came tumbling out. He had so much to say. It was as if he and Shyamsundar were old friends who hadn't met for a long time.

'I've been waiting ages to meet you. I've seen Krishna people in America, but I couldn't just go up and talk to them. Then a friend gave me Bhaktivedanta Swami's record. I can't stop listening to his voice. I started chanting Hare Krishna along with him. I've listened so many times I've worn the record out.'

Shyamsundar listened in amazement as George told him how he had not only learned the chant but had listened carefully to Prabhupada's recorded explanation of Krishna consciousness. The words had sunk deep. He had even taught the mantra to John Lennon, and together they had chanted Hare Krishna on a yacht in the Greek islands.

'We carried on until our jaws ached. As soon as we stopped chanting, it was like the lights went out. It was amazing.'

Shyamsundar asked if George had received any of their gifts.

'Oh, yeah, we got everything. The apple pies didn't last long – they were delicious. And more than a year ago I got a letter from one of you guys in San Francisco. I'm sorry I didn't reply – there's been too much happening. I've just been waiting for the chance to meet you.'

'Well, Krishna seems to have arranged that now,' laughed Shyamsundar. George would never know how much he had prayed for this day.

'So where is Bhaktivedanta Swami now?'

'He's in Los Angeles, but he'll come to London soon.'

'I feel like I already know him – I've heard his voice so much. I really want to meet him face to face. And I want to talk more with you, too, but we can't talk properly here. Can you make it out to my place this Sunday afternoon? Then we can spend as much time as we like and we can chant together.' George drew a map to show the route to his house, and after thanking Shyamsundar for coming, saw him to the door.

ESHER, SURREY, SUNDAY 8TH DECEMBER 1968

Dressed in his best robes, his head clean-shaven and his forehead freshly marked with clay *tilaka,*[4] Shyamsundar rang George's doorbell.

He carried a parcel of savouries and sweets specially prepared by Yamuna. George opened the door and invited him in. While George's wife Pattie took the delicacies to the kitchen to prepare afternoon tea, George led his guest into a spacious room decorated with paintings of Hindu deities: Shiva performing his cosmic dance encircled by flames, the benign elephant-headed Ganesh, and Saraswati, goddess of the arts, holding her stringed vina. On the mantelpiece sat framed photos of George's yoga masters, Yogananda and Yukteswar, with incense burning before them, and a picture of Prabhupada.

George was no stranger to the yoga path or to chanting mantras. Three years earlier he had met Ravi Shankar and gone to India to study sitar with him. Then he had met Maharishi, and for three months in early 1968 he had stayed at Maharishi's ashram in Rishikesh to learn mantra meditation. George had lots of questions, and Shyamsundar did his best, in his relaxed way, to answer them. George especially wanted to know more about Bhaktivedanta Swami.

'Prabhupada represents an unbroken line of teachers that stretches back thousands of years,' explained Shyamsundar. 'Although he is deeply learned and has written several books, he thinks of himself as everyone's servant. He always says that his qualification to be a guru is that he is teaching us exactly what he has heard from his own guru. He hasn't added anything or taken anything away. That's why we trust him.' George listened.

'The essence of Krishna consciousness is to love Krishna. We do that by serving Krishna in everything we do and by chanting Krishna's names. Prabhupada says the name of God and God himself are non-different. When you chant Krishna's name Krishna dances on your tongue.'

'But how do you avoid being distracted by *maya*?' George knew about *maya,* the illusion of material life, and how hard it could be to follow the yoga path when you are surrounded by people intent on other goals.

'That's the power of chanting,' Shyamsundar replied, and he described how as long as you chanted Krishna's name you were with Krishna. Consequently *maya* had no power over you. Prabhupada had written all about this in his edition of the *Bhagavad-gita*,' he said. 'It has just been published in New York, and soon we'll have copies here in London. I'll give you one.'

'Yes, I'd like that very much,' said George. 'But why do you only chant to Krishna? What about Shiva or Saraswati?'

'Our spiritual master says that Krishna is the origin of all other forms of God. He is the original candle from whom all other candles have been lit: each candle has equal brightness, but the first candle is the source of all the others. So Krishna includes all other deities – there is no need for us to chant to them separately. We depend on Krishna for everything.'

They talked for a long time, comparing their experiences. Then they sat and chanted together, George playing his Indian harmonium, Shyamsundar keeping time with the *karatals*. Pattie joined in. When the afternoon ended, George knew he had found someone he could talk to frankly and openly about his spiritual path. He became thoughtful.

'I would like to do something for you people,' he said.

But Shyamsundar didn't ask for anything. He knew that the Beatles must be constantly targeted by people asking favours. He was glad just to be there talking to George. All the austerities of the past few months had been worth it now that he was on such intimate terms with the one person he had most wanted to meet in London – in the world.

George wanted to meet and chant with the rest of the devotees, and he had developed a taste for their cooking. So it was agreed that in a week or two, as soon as he could get free, he would visit their temple in Covent Garden.

'See you soon, then,' said Shyamsundar as he climbed into his car. 'Hare Krishna!'

'Hare Krishna!' answered George, waving goodbye. They each felt they had found a friend.

ROYAL ALBERT HALL, 18TH DECEMBER 1968

The Arts Lab people organised an event at the Albert Hall. They called it the Alchemical Wedding. It was intended as a fund-raiser for the street theatre group the Human Family, and was the idea of Jack Moore, an American activist who worked with Jim Haynes. The high point of the event, Moore said, would be a shared silence. Haynes booked the Hall and came round to see the devotees.

'Can you cook some of your delicious food for the performers, and then sit with us for the group silence?' he asked.

'We can be there and we can cook,' they agreed. Gurudas added, 'But in Krishna consciousness we don't practice silence. For us, silence means chanting.' Haynes agreed to let them chant.

Posters were designed at the Arts Lab and full-page ads printed in IT. Word spread that John and Yoko would be there, and maybe even the recluse poet-singer Leonard Cohen. As the evening approached no one knew exactly what to expect. The Albert Hall was a vast round space that could hold over 5,000 people. Would they be able to fill it?

On the night of 18th December people streamed into the hall. The devotees decided they would station themselves at the head of each of the six aisles that radiated upward from the empty central space in front of the stage. At a signal, they would advance down the aisles, chanting their way to the middle.

Soon the hall was full of London's beautiful people, all buzzing with excitement. John and Yoko sat near the stage with many other luminaries of the alternative scene. The lights went down, leaving a single spotlight on the empty space. An expectant hush fell when the diminutive figure of Jack Moore stood momentarily in the centre under the spotlight and lifted a finger to his lips. Silence spread around the empty space. It grew long and deep, engulfing the vast multitude. Minutes ticked by. Then it was broken by a single word.

'OM,' chanted a voice.

Janaki had stayed alone near the edge of the arena. Suddenly she stepped forward into the spotlight, her arms upraised, crying *'Haribol!'*

At this sign the devotees stepped from the wings, moving forward slowly, swaying to Mukunda's beating *mridanga* and chanting the *maha-mantra.* As they moved through the crowd the chant was taken up until the whole assembly was with them. From all sides their singing rose, backed by waiting musicians. The place erupted. People were swept off their feet and the space in front of the stage filled with dancing figures. They held hands in ever-increasing circles, chanting Hare Krishna with abandon. It seemed to be the culmination of years of spiritual searching, a communal act of transcendence. Momentarily all differences were forgotten as musicians played and bodies swayed and swirled.

'The Hare and the Krishnas came forth playing their bells,' wrote David Mairowitz in the IT the following week. 'Bald and robed vegetarian loveliness. They were joined by any number of dancers and children and musicians, and suddenly the valley was alive with enthusiasm and the silence was filled. It was a promise of things to come, like a kiss across the lagoon from a naked mermaid.'

The harmony could not be sustained for long, and the dancing became more and more wild. A girl stripped off her clothes, and when officials moved to apprehend her, a scuffle broke out. Police emerged from the shadows to impose order, and confusion spread. Someone turned off the sound system, the house lights came up, and officials began herding the audience toward the exits. The devotees quickly left.

The next morning the naked girl was in the *Daily Express* – Gurudas had unintentionally captured her with his camera, a fact that was discovered in the newsroom when he had rushed his film to Fleet Street that night. The headline read 'MAD RAVE-IN AT ALBERT HALL.' Gurudas cut out the picture of the girl and the word 'MAD' in the headline and sent the rest of the page to Prabhupada.

NEW YEAR'S DAY 1969

Mukunda was working hard to register their society, and all the paperwork was now in place. He had been steered through the legal process by Tom Driberg, one of Allen Ginsberg's friends. Driberg had made a name for himself in the 1930s (under his pen name, William Hickey) as an acerbic columnist at Lord Beaverbrook's *Daily Express*. When he tired of writing gossip he got himself selected as a Labour Member of Parliament. Now, himself an object of gossip rather than reporter of it, he used his many contacts to assist the devotees and get them noticed.

To launch their newly registered International Society for Krishna Consciousness the devotees invited friends and supporters to a meeting at their Betterton Street temple on New Year's Day 1969. With Driberg's help they attracted a good crowd. The focus of the meeting was to be a recorded address from Prabhupada sent over from the U.S. for the occasion.

The Betterton Street room was bare save for the colourful altar upon which stood the large form of Jagannath overlooking the space with his broad smile. Above him hung a life-size painting of Prabhupada, based on the photograph Gurudas had made two years earlier in San Francisco. Seventy guests, many in suits and ties, sat awkwardly on the coarse mat that covered the floor.

They had been invited with the promise that they would meet celebrities, though none came unless you counted Barry Miles, who owned the fashionable Indica bookshop, and Tom Driberg. Few of the guests had any idea what to expect. Gurudas turned on the tape recorder and Prabhupada's voice rose from the speaker, intoning Sanskrit prayers.

'Ladies and gentlemen,' Prabhupada began, 'please accept my greetings in the happy New Year of 1969, and blessings of Sri Krishna, the Supreme Personality of Godhead, for your kindly participating in this happy meeting of Krishna consciousness.'

When they heard his voice brimming with confidence and affection, his disciples were reminded that in this city far from home he was the inspiration for all they were trying to achieve.

'Krishna appeared on this earthly planet five thousand years ago and gave us the universal philosophy and religious principles of Krishna consciousness in the shape of the *Bhagavad-gita*.'

The audience listened intently as Prabhupada, in his distinctive Indian diction, described how Sri Chaitanya had revived Krishna consciousness in India five hundred years earlier.

'Lord Chaitanya's special gift to the fallen souls of this age of quarrel was to induce the people to chant the holy name of Krishna. When we chant the Hare Krishna mantra we immediately contact Krishna and become purified from all dirty things in our heart. In such cycle of birth and death, I, you, and every one of us have identified with this material form of life and are subjected to material pangs in the shape of birth, death, old age, and disease. Human society is struggling fruitlessly against these perpetual problems of life.'

Prabhupada's voice, strong and determined, stood against the confusion of that struggle, which raged daily through the city of London, threatening them all. Everyone had his or her difficulties to face, and he was offering a solution.

'Krishna consciousness is the art of changing our heart by purification of the dust of material desires. Anyone who wants to be free from the pangs of material existence should take to the process of chanting Hare Krishna.'

He went on to warn against being misled by those who deny God or put themselves in God's place. Instead, he offered an ancient wisdom.

'Hear the message of Krishna as it is in the *Bhagavad-gita*,' he said, then concluded: 'The consciousness is there in you. Cleanse it of all dirty things. Make it clear Krishna consciousness in pleasant method by chanting the glorified holy name of God – Hare Krishna, Hare Krishna, Krishna Krishna, Hare Hare/ Hare Rama, Hare Rama, Rama Rama, Hare Hare.'[5]

When the recording finished, each of the three male devotees stood and spoke about ISKCON in America and the new society being registered in London, and about the need for a permanent temple. Then the feast was served using cutlery borrowed from the nearby Swedenborg Society. Despite the awkward seating arrangements – everyone had to sit on the floor – the strangeness of the place, and the lack of comforts, the guests went away feeling rewarded. Ten days later, on Sunday 12th January, an article appeared in the *Sunday Times* written by the fabled Atticus, whose column was a staple of middle-class Sunday breakfast tables across the nation. The accompanying photo showed Malati and Yamuna, and between them Gurudas and Shyamsundar, holding baby Saraswati. Their faces, marked with clay lines of *tilaka*, were austere, even mystical. The men's shaven heads and faraway gazes contrasted with the baby sucking on Shyamsundar's large round japa beads. In the background, at the apex of the tightly composed triangle, rose Mukunda's head and shoulders. This was the first sight most readers had ever had of the Hare Krishna devotees. The article, titled 'Atticus Feels the Benefit', was full of appreciation:

> They're very gentle people, a bit unworldly, but not at all ingenuous. What they're aiming to do is found a London temple for the Society for Krishna Consciousness, and they are hoping to rent a warehouse which they can convert. What they're propagating – in simple terms – is spiritual advancement. Believing what you eat, you are, their diet is confined to pure grain foods and dairy products. They have renounced all meat, intoxicants, illicit sex, and speculative gambling – a programme which differs vastly from the Beatles' old Maharishi. Tame, you might think, but they look very well on it. What's likely to earn them a public is their chanting. They want to try their chants on tourists, derelicts, and businessmen. They're quite prepared, they say, to go into action outside the Stock Exchange. It's an intriguing idea, and what it might do for the economy, Krishna only knows.

TWICKENHAM FILM STUDIOS, 16TH JANUARY 1969

'Hi, it's George here. I want to ask you a favour, Shyamsundar. Can you come out and meet the gang? We're filming at Twickenham.'

Shyamsundar listened on the phone to George's Liverpudlian tones and his excitement mounted.

'I've been away visiting my family for a few days,' George continued. 'Now I'm back working with the boys. Things have been a bit tense lately. It'd do us good to have someone like you around to talk to. You could tell the others about Krishna and that. What d'yer think?'

Shyamsundar didn't need to think very hard. 'Sure. When should I come?'

'How about lunchtime today?' George never did like to waste time.

Shyamsundar drove west through the suburbs to Twickenham Film Studios, where the Beatles were filming 'Let It Be'. At the gate, with his shiny bald head, his bright yellow robes, and his blue waistcoat he looked exotic even by Beatles standards. He soon found his way onto the film set. The group were just breaking for lunch, and George invited him to follow them upstairs. They settled into comfortable chairs in the studio's lounge. George sat Shyamsundar in the middle.

'So, what's it all about?' asked John.

Shyamsundar was used to being put on the spot. Prabhupada had trained all his disciples to speak boldly, and the past months had given Shyamsundar plenty of opportunity to do just that. With no clear idea what to say, he thought of Prabhupada and began speaking. As he spoke he forgot how nervous he was and instead felt Krishna giving him the words. Soon his usual confidence asserted itself and he spoke to the Beatles just as he would to any intelligent audience. He could see that John in particular was listening intently.

'Simply put, God is a person. Some call him Allah or Jehovah – we call him Krishna. In the Vedic scriptures we get a lot of information about who God is – what he looks like, how he plays, what he does and doesn't like, and what he says. We also get to know who *we* are – eternal spirits – and what's our relationship with God.'

'But how d'yer know it's all true?' interrupted John.

'We're lucky. You can't understand this heavy stuff so easily, but we have a spiritual master who can explain it to us and show by his own example how it all works.'

Paul wanted to know Shyamsundar's opinion of Maharishi, Ringo was interested in how he got involved with Krishna consciousness, and John asked about the chanting.

'Is your music the language to communicate with God?'

'Yes. Although you can sing or chant or pray to God in any language, the Hare Krishna mantra is called the great mantra because it's the most powerful and the most attractive to chant.'

The conversation went on for an hour, and afterwards John in particular thanked Shyamsundar.

'We must do this again sometime,' he said warmly.

As George saw Shyamsundar to the gate he assured him the meeting had been a success – they had liked him – and he promised he would visit the temple soon.

Colin was cleaning the temple's front entrance out in the cold February air. He had been instructed to keep a lookout for George. A large black Mercedes sped down the narrow street, and with two wheels mounted the pavement immediately opposite 22 Betterton Street. Colin recognised its occupant immediately.

'Shyamsundar, he's here!' he called upstairs, just as George bounded into the building in his big fur coat. He was met by Shyamsundar racing down the steps to greet him. The two went upstairs, followed by Colin, and George was introduced to Mukunda and Gurudas. They all sat together on cushions and chatted. The devotees felt at ease with George and he was at ease with them.

Jim Doody arrived and joined them. Jim lived in a studio round the corner where he ran his lightshow business – the first in London. He had invented his own light machine, which projected moving patterns of coloured light onto walls and ceilings. He called his business Krishna Lights, and took his machine to parties and events, donating part of his profits to the temple.

The three women in the kitchen hurried to finish frying *samosas* and puris, dusted themselves down, and emerged carrying dishes to offer on Jagannath's altar. As Malati lit incense and recited the prayers to bless the food, Yamuna and Janaki came over and Shyamsundar introduced them. Then they too sat down, and Yamuna pulled out the harmonium. Closing her eyes, she began to sing.

As soon as the chanting started George was absorbed. He joined them as a fellow traveller on the path, sinking deep into the now familiar vibrations of the mantra. The chanting did not last long, but they each felt the intensity of the occasion: for the devotees it was an affirmation from Krishna that they should be sharing this with George Harrison, and for George it answered his prayers for spiritual comradeship. Everyone felt Krishna's presence.

Once the chanting was over, prasadam was served. They spread a cloth on the floor as they always did, like a big tablecloth, and arranged plates along it. They sat round the edges either side of George and watched him eat with gusto. When Yamuna came round with seconds, George accepted eagerly.

'I like the way you sing,' he told her. 'Your mood, your voice – I've heard you sing before, you know.'

Yamuna was stunned. 'How is that possible?'

'At the Arts Lab. I was there one night,' he confided. 'We were out on a lark and I crept in wearing a disguise. I sat in the dark and chanted with you for half an hour.'

'But my voice is like a croaking frog,' Yamuna laughed.

'No, your voice is special. It's mesmerising.'

Yamuna lowered her eyes modestly. She thought this must all be Krishna's magic.

Before he left, George invited the devotees to come to his home in Esher for a long kirtan the following Friday evening. He would get a few friends round and they would really push the boat out, he said.

Back downstairs by the door Colin grew bold and asked George how he liked their temple.

'You know where the *real* temple is, don't yer?' George retorted. 'It's in your heart.' Grinning, he poked Colin in the chest with his index finger.

At George's home the women made friends with Pattie as they followed her into the kitchen. Together they cooked another feast, something really special this time, while George showed the men his studio and introduced them to Billy Preston, a brilliant young keyboard player he had brought over from America.

Once back in the living room they moved the furniture and laid a saree down the centre of the space. Then, in their accustomed style, the women sat everyone down and served a luxurious meal. When the plates were finally cleared away, the devotees got out their instruments and settled down with a sense of anticipation for the main event – the kirtan.

Billy Preston played the electric organ, George sat at his white upright harmonium to begin with, then picked up a bass guitar, Mukunda beat the *mridanga,* Colin played George's tablas, Shyamsundar the *esaraj,*

Gurudas the tambura, and Janaki and Malati the *karatals*. Yamuna sang the lead, at times calling *'Haribol!'* at the top of her lungs. They chanted for an hour or so, switched instruments, and chanted again. For three hours the chant went on – long, deep, and languorous. George had learned to love chanting by hearing Prabhupada's album, and now that he had others to share the chanting with he didn't want to stop.

That night, after chanting together for hours, something changed. A deep connection was forged between them, a sense of spiritual community that transcended any differences they might have on the material plane. At the end, as the devotees were preparing to leave, George spoke the words that were on everyone's mind.

'We have to make a record.'

This was what the devotees had longed for. Even back in San Francisco they had sometimes dreamt of what it would be like to record the Hare Krishna mantra with the Beatles. Now, without artifice, the door was opening. It was more of Krishna's magic.

As Colin left George came up to him. 'I saw how much you enjoyed the tablas,' he said. 'They're yours, man. Look after them.' And George handed him the drums.

A week later George came round to the temple. He had just been to Spain. 'I wrote a song about you guys,' he said. 'It's called "Here Comes the Sun." '[6]

After that George became a regular visitor at the temple, and the devotees sometimes went to his home.

HANOVER SQUARE, 10TH FEBRUARY 1969

After their initial expedition to chant on the streets in September, the devotees had been stopped by police whenever they had again tried to sing in public. They were told they needed official permission to chant on the public highway. Mukunda made a formal application to the authorities, and after a three-month delay while they registered their society, permission was granted – on the condition that they didn't obstruct the pavement.

One clear crisp day in February they resumed their public chanting.

The men's heads were freshly shaven and they wore their saffron robes, with jackets over them to keep themselves warm. Round Gurudas's neck hung a double row of large red japa beads. Colin played the *mridanga* with his usual verve. They started off in front of Apple's offices in Savile Row, then made their way through Mayfair, past private galleries and expensive boutiques, to Hanover Square, just south of Oxford Street. There they stationed themselves in the gardens at the centre of the square, and in the bright sunshine sang to the lunchtime crowds of office workers. A policeman approached, but before he could intervene Mukunda stepped forward to show him their permit. Bemused, he warned them not to make an obstruction and continued on his way. As they chanted, a photographer took pictures and a small crowd gathered, smiling good-naturedly in the winter sun. The next edition of the *International Times* carried a photo of them chanting,[7] accompanied by a short piece about the power of the Hare Krishna mantra. They sent the news cutting to Prabhupada. Its headline, arranged around three sides of the photo, read 'Beautiful Blue Smiling Cowherd Boy Steals Their Hearts'.

Prabhupada had stationed himself at the Los Angeles temple for the past four months. He wanted the temple to become a model for his fast-growing international society. By the start of 1969 ISKCON had thirteen centres across North America and two in Europe: Hamburg and London. Every other day Prabhupada wrote half a dozen letters to his disciples and fledgling leaders – not short letters, but long, detailed epistles offering inspiration, personal guidance, rebukes, instructions, solutions, congratulations, and encouragement, always pushing them to increase their efforts.

One area uppermost in his thoughts was book publication and distribution and how to finance it. In America he encouraged his disciples to sell *Back to Godhead* magazines, alongside *samkirtan*, public chanting, and it was going well. The Los Angeles devotees had been particularly successful at producing a steady income from magazine sales while increasing their outreach through chanting. Seeing this, Prabhupada had concluded that the combination of street kirtan and selling literature was the best way to advance the movement. When he heard from Mukunda that the London devotees had resumed their public chanting, he quickly responded.

> My dear Mukunda,
>
> Immediately my request to you is that you try to sell at least 2 to 3 thousand Back to Godhead… I think you have now got licence for kirtan on the street so you can follow the same principle… When I was young and lost my father, I was very sorry, but by Krishna's grace, I have now many American fathers and mothers, so I am appealing to all my American fathers and mothers to help me by this contribution.[8]

Mukunda understood from the tone of this letter that Prabhupada knew he was making big demands of his disciples. Still, it was also clear that he depended on their dedication. Prabhupada made a similar plea to the women.

> My dear little mothers, Yamuna, Malati, Janaki,
>
> I lost my mother when I was only 14 years old, so I didn't get much affection in my childhood. But in my old age Krishna has given me so many young mothers to take care of me…[9]

His appeal to the women as mothers invoked their feelings of affection for him, so although they found it hard to go out on the street and sell magazines, they tried their utmost to do as he asked.

MONTREAL, CANADA, JUNE 1969

One day John Lennon saw Gurudas at the Apple offices.

'Oh, Gurudas! Come on in. I'm going to work for peace.' He told Gurudas about his and Yoko's plans to lead a worldwide campaign to stop the Vietnam War.

A few weeks later John and Yoko crossed the Atlantic. After being denied entry into the U.S. they checked into the Queen Elizabeth Hotel in Montreal, where they stayed in bed for a week dressed in their pyjamas. Their slogan was 'Make love, not war', and their way of promoting it was to receive the press from the double bed in their hotel room. This was their second 'bed-in' to promote world peace – the first had been in Amsterdam. Each day John and Yoko's room filled with friends, reporters, and local celebrities. Between conversations the couple, sitting side by side in bed, openly chanted Hare Krishna in front of their guests. On the last day they invited the Montreal Hare Krishna devotees to chant with them and to join them and their friends in recording a song John had written to promote peace. The song ended with the names of its singers.

> John and Yoko, Timmy Leary, Rosemary, Tommy Smothers, Bobby Dylan, Tommy Cooper, Derek Taylor, Norman Mailer, Allen Ginsberg, Hare Krishna, Hare Krishna. All we are saying is, Give Peace a Chance.

Lennon had always followed his own path regardless of what people thought of him, but despite his determination not to be led, he showed appreciation for the power of Krishna's names. 'We get our energy from Hare Krishna – that's where it comes from,' Yoko told a reporter from the *Montreal Star*. The song was released as 'Give Peace A Chance' under the impromptu name the Plastic Ono Band, and became a worldwide hit.

BURY PLACE, 5TH JUNE 1969

Five minutes' walk north from the lanes of Covent Garden, across the broad east-west thoroughfare of New Oxford Street, were the sheltered residences of Bloomsbury, home to University College and the British Museum. The massive raised plinth and Doric columns of the museum recalled a time when England thought herself the home of learning for the betterment of humanity. Although those dreams had faded, the streets around the museum retained an atmosphere of studious refinement with their college buildings, portered mansions, antiquarian bookstores, and antique coin shops. Just in front of the museum, on a quiet street called Bury Place, stood a vacant five-storey warehouse and office building. It had served as a book depository, and now it needed a new tenant.

One day the estate agent representing this building was standing in line at his bank in Holborn. In front of him, a tall, shaven-headed young man wearing saffron robes attracted his curiosity. The estate agent had once known someone in San Francisco who had joined the Hare Krishna religion. Perhaps this man knew him.

'Excuse me,' he began, and Gurudas turned to see who was speaking. 'I wonder if you know a friend of mine, a Sam Speerstra?'

'I certainly do,' replied Gurudas. 'He lives with me – just nearby.'

The two began to talk, and soon Gurudas had told the estate agent about their London *yatra*. When Gurudas learned that his companion was an estate agent, he explained that the devotees were looking for a permanent home. 'We thought a warehouse would be the ideal sort of place,' he said. 'We could convert it into a temple. But we can't afford to pay much.'

'I think I have just the place for you. I can take you there now if you like – it's only round the corner.'

Gurudas followed the estate agent until they stood in front of 7 Bury Place. It was a narrow building adjoining a block of mansion flats on one side and the Bull and Mouth public house on the other. On the ground floor was a well-proportioned entrance beside a large arched window. Above were four diminishing storeys with stone-dressed windows surrounded by honey-coloured London brick, topped by a circular attic porthole with an ornate pediment and the date 1893. The building had until recently been the London headquarters and depository of the Trinitarian Bible Society, dedicated to 'publishing and distributing the holy scriptures throughout the world in many languages'.

'There's a dispute over the ownership,' the estate agent said. 'It seems the owner has gone away and no one knows how to contact him, so our instructions are to rent it out cheaply until the dispute is sorted out. We can arrange something favourable for you.'

Gurudas hurried back to tell the others, and a full viewing was arranged. Everyone agreed the place was ideal, and its past religious connections seemed a good omen. Shyamsundar's friend set the rent at forty-five pounds a week – a small sum for a five-storey building in one of London's most desirable locations. The agreement was quickly

Gurudas's iconic portrait, photographed in the late afternoon sunlight at Swamiji's apartment in San Francisco.

One of his first visitors was the poet Allen Ginsberg.

The temple flourished, and visitors brought offerings of fruits and flowers.

Swamiji with Gurudas, speaking on television.

With Yamuna outside the ABC studios.

He chanted sitting on the grass among the flower children, with his eyes closed.

In the beginning Swamiji was the focus of worship in the temple.

By Stowe Lake in Golden Gate Park, Swamiji told Yamuna his plans for a World Sankirtan Party. (Left to right: Shyamsundar, Malati, Swamiji, Yamuna, Gaurasundara)

Janaki, with Mukunda at her side, pretends to steal Swamiji's air ticket so he cannot leave San Francisco.

sorted out, underwritten with George's help by Apple Corps, and signed on 5th June 1969.

Shyamsundar surveyed the ground floor and started to plan a masterwork of carpentry to convert it into a temple. It was his ambition to build a beautiful shrine in London, for which he would use the hefty Californian redwood timbers he had shipped over and which were now stored in stashes all over London.

They were all anxious to get the work done as soon as possible so they could invite Prabhupada to London. Prabhupada himself wanted to come and had written many times that he was ready whenever they called for him. In February he had written to Mukunda and Colin,

> Pending your search for a suitable temple-house, immediately rent an apartment for me, and on hearing from you I shall start for London. Please let me know your decision on this matter so that I can prepare my London-Yatra.[10]

Despite such letters the devotees hadn't felt they could receive Prabhupada properly until they had a temple of their own. Prabhupada had accepted their judgement, and in February he had travelled to Hawaii instead of to London, telling them to take their time to find the right place. Now, months later, they were able to write him with the good news. He replied,

> My dear Shyamsundar,
>
> With great joy I understand that at last you have secured one nice house which can accommodate twenty or thirty people. I have immediately asked Trivikrama das Brahmacary of Buffalo to go there. I am also advising Bibhavati and Ishandas to go there. I shall expect your final word as to when you would like me to start for London. Accordingly I shall make my plan.[11]

Trivikrama was a university graduate who, after studying sociology and doing a spell in the Navy, had joined Prabhupada in Buffalo. Ishan and his wife Bibhavati were from Montreal. He was a jazz musician and she was a new mother. Further in his letter Prabhupada revealed for the first time his ambition to establish a London temple of Radha and Krishna:

> Regarding the altar, I wish that underneath the Jagannaths a throne of Radha-Krishna should be there.[12]

Shyamsundar reckoned he would need three months to get the work done. It was decided that Tim, Colin's friend who had followed Colin and moved in with the devotees, would become his assistant carpenter, and the other devotees would take cleaning jobs to help finance the construction. Without waiting for such formalities as planning permissions or building approvals, Shyamsundar got straight to work. He removed an intermediate wall and had the redwood delivered and hoisted in through the ground-floor window. Other walls and bits of floor were soon stripped out, and the rubble transported away.

The neighbours, particularly a Mr French, who was a tradesman in the Covent Garden fruit and vegetable market, were outraged at what they saw as a hippie invasion of their quiet street. Soon inspectors arrived from Camden Council. They said the building was zoned neither as a place of worship nor as a residence and that the building plans were unsafe. All work was halted.

Gurudas and Mukunda set about making friends at the council offices and completing the necessary forms. Their near-celebrity status as friends of the Beatles, and their lease backed by Apple, helped win support for their cause. The two officers dealing with the case, Mr Black and Mr Savage, made allowances and advised Shyamsundar how he could make his structural modifications safely. Two large steel beams were required, they said. Mick Jagger of the Rolling Stones paid for these. The Stones and the Beatles were rivals in the pop charts, but in private they were all good friends, and George had introduced Shyamsundar to Mick Jagger at the Apple studios.

While the devotees waited for planning approval they faced other complications. They had been living rent-free at Betterton Street. Now Nigel Samuel told them they had to make way for paying tenants. The single men – Trivikrama, Colin, Dick, and Tim – set up a *brahmachari* ashram, a place for celibate monks, in the bare upper rooms at Bury Place, although they still had no proper permission to live in the building. The three married couples again found bedsits in the suburbs. Shyamsundar and Malati moved to Balham, Gurudas and Yamuna to Clapham, and Mukunda and Janaki to Hackney. Scattered like this across the capital, the women felt the strain. They were not out and about like the men, and now they had nowhere to come together.

ABBEY ROAD STUDIOS, 7TH JULY 1969

Although their living arrangements were in disarray their relationship with George was progressing wonderfully. They had recorded a three-hour chanting session at his house, and during April and May had worked on perfecting their sound, rehearsing either at the temple or at the Apple studios on Savile Row. Near the end of the work Colin brought the tablas George had given him to the studios and sat with George in a sound room to overdub the recording while Gurudas and Shyamsundar watched from the mixing room. Eventually George was satisfied and took the demo tape to play to the other Beatles. He wanted them to agree that he and the devotees could record a Hare Krishna single on the Apple label.

These were difficult months for George. Relations between the Beatles were strained, and Apple Corps was a headache for all four of them as disputes over song rights raged on. Then George's home was raided by the police and he and Pattie charged with possession of cannabis. Despite these troubles it was a time of heightened creativity during which George produced some of his best songs – 'All Things Must Pass,'[13] 'Something,' and 'Here Comes the Sun' – songs in which he hinted at his spiritual leanings. He sometimes called Shyamsundar on the telephone, and they would meet for dinner at his house or at the temple. Whenever they met, George wanted to chant. He would get so deep into the chanting that all his worries seemed to go far away.

One thing George really liked about Krishna consciousness was the idea of God being a person. Until then he had thought of God as cosmic consciousness – an impersonal oneness that pervaded the universe. Now he began to think of God as an all-beautiful and all-loving person who existed beyond the oneness – a person to whom he could sing and offer his love.

George's proposal was approved, and the Radha Krishna Temple was signed by Apple. Recording time would be found for them at the Abbey Road Studios, where all through July and most of August the Beatles were working together for the last time, on their *Abbey Road* album.

It was important to get the chant down to three-and-a-half minutes – George insisted on it so the recording could be played on the radio – without losing its vitality and spirit. They spent a lot of time rehearsing it.

On 7th July a call came through from George – he had the studio booked for recording 'Here Comes The Sun' and had managed to free up a session for the Radha Krishna Temple. The devotees dropped everything and rushed over, taking prasadam and blankets with them. When they arrived, Paul McCartney and his wife Linda were in the control booth with Derek Taylor and George.

The devotees sat in the cavernous studio ready to record while George issued firm instructions. He knew how to get the best from them. He moved them about the studio while they recorded up to thirty takes, until at last he had the sound balanced to his satisfaction. He wanted Yamuna to sing the lead – hers was the strongest voice – but he wanted her double-tracked with a male voice to give extra depth, so he had Shyamsundar's voice in unison and sometimes in harmony with hers. Away to the side Colin played the *mridanga,* Gurudas and Dick the *karatals,* and in the chorus Malati and Janaki were accompanied by the other new English devotees – Tim, and Pamela, who had recently joined them. Derek Taylor played George's harmonium, which was painted all over with psychedelic flowers. When everything was finally to George's satisfaction they did three last takes.

By now it was evening. On the third take all seemed to go well, but as the chant ended, Malati, thinking there was still another verse to go, struck a large gong that was hanging invitingly beside her in the studio.

It was spontaneous, but it threatened to mar what would otherwise have been the best take of the day – until they heard the playback.

The chant started in the same meditative mood of their kirtans in the temple, with Yamuna's lone voice and the sound of clapping hands keeping time. When the chorus repeated for the second time the shimmer of *karatals* came in, followed on the third round by the drum. In the fourth the tempo picked up and the mood lifted. By the fifth repetition the kirtan was flying, carried forward with the trumpeting conch on an unstoppable wave toward a final moment of stillness, in which the vibrations of Malati's gong echoed with the lingering drone of the harmonium.

'We've got it!' exclaimed George. Everyone agreed that the gong made a perfect ending. Later George added guitar and more harmonium to give it his final touch.

Three weeks later they recorded the 'B' side. Colin arrived early at the Abbey Road studios and watched while the Beatles wrapped up their afternoon recording session. By the time it had ended the rest of the devotees had arrived, and Yamuna and Malati went round applying *tilaka* to everyone's forehead, including George's and the producer George Martin's. When all was set they recorded 'Prayers to the Spiritual Masters'. This was an atmospheric version of the Sanskrit verses they recited every morning to the gurus and previous teachers in their line.

The track began with a deep, soulful drone, over which came first the chiming of the *karatals,* then the voices of the devotees singing in unison the Sanskrit obeisance to their guru. After repeating the prayer several times they sang the praises of Sri Chaitanya, founder of the Hare Krishna movement, followed by the names of his intimate disciples, who had propagated his message in sixteenth-century Bengal.

The public could not know whom the prayers were addressing, but their singing was a powerful expression of devotion which needed no explanation. The record was now complete – the *maha-mantra* on one side, these prayers on the other – ready to go out into the world to awaken and inspire many sleeping hearts.

HYDE PARK, SUNDAY 27TH JULY 1969

Shyamsundar had been busy. A brightly-coloured temple on wheels, nearly forty feet high, stood in the road on the north side of Hyde Park. London had never seen anything like it. Earlier in the week George Harrison had given an interview to Radio One's audacious Kenny Everett.

George: If anyone happens to be walking from Hyde Park down Park Lane along toward Piccadilly and down Trafalgar Square at 1.30 on Sunday they'll be in good company.

Everett: Who'll be there, George?

George: Er, God.

Everett: Oh?

George: He'll be there. Lord Jagannath, and Krishna – and all the gang, Balaram – and they're all gonna be there at that million-dollar bash. Starts 1.30, Marble Arch. Great chanting and, er, fun.

Everett: Fun?

George: Fun.

Everett: Oh, well, if it's fun, then we might go.

Ever since Shyamsundar had carved the first Jagannath deities in San Francisco and built the float to take them to the Pacific shore, he had had a special feeling for Jagannath. Now here in London he had decided to build his biggest ever Jagannath chariot. The other devotees all knew how much Prabhupada liked Rathayatra, so they agreed to organise London's first Jagannath festival, although it would strain their meagre resources to the limit. Gurudas and Mukunda met with the police at Scotland Yard and got permission for a procession route right through the centre of town, and Shyamsundar began work on the chariot.

Shyamsundar could divert his energies from his work on the temple because Camden Council had temporarily halted work at Bury Place. He set up an open-air workshop in the back garden behind their bedsit at 11 Balham Park Road. His landlady looked on as the chariot rose into the trees overhanging her garden. He was aided by Tim and a team of volunteers, with Malati providing them plenty of refreshments. Each day they gathered a few more pieces of wood, funded by donations and the devotees' earnings. Yamuna worked in her flat to sew the chariot's canopy and a large Hare Krishna banner.

Shyamsundar built more for scale than durability. The finished chariot was nearly forty feet high and wide enough to take up two traffic lanes. The morning before the procession Gurudas and Mukunda came over to help drag the chariot to the centre of town. They set off at first light, one of them walking in front to make sure the road before the chariot was clear. Shyamsundar towed the chariot with his red pickup, and the other two pushed it from behind. Even with help from passersby, who seemed to take the procession in their stride, the devotees needed all day to make the journey – up Balham Hill and across Clapham Common, over Albert Bridge and, following the embankment, to Marble Arch. The road was bumpy, and along the way they mounted several curbs. All this loosened the structure and weakened the wheels.

They had covered the town with advertising and George had done his bit on the radio, so about two thousand people showed up at Marble Arch – by the famous Speaker's Corner – to witness the Jagannath deities, dressed by Yamuna, carried up a ladder onto the platform, which was now festooned with bunting, coloured fabric, and flowers. Beside Jagannath sat several devotees, who attended to the deities and led the chanting.

David Naysmith was in the crowd that day. He was an assertive young man with a friendly, inquisitive nature, who had come down from Scotland six months earlier to work as a civil servant. He had met Krishna devotees on the street – one of the women had once tried to sell him a *Back to Godhead* magazine – but he hadn't been interested. Today would be different. When David was nine years old he had received a strong premonition that his twenty-first birthday would be special for him. A voice had told him that he would have a life-changing, religious experience on that day. Today was David's twenty-first birthday. He arrived at Hyde Park not knowing what to expect but compelled to keep his date with destiny.

When David reached Speaker's Corner he saw a crowd made up

mostly of Indians gathered around a tall, brightly-coloured float. When he went closer to investigate, he saw that everyone around him was smiling and singing. At that moment Trivikrama, who had just arrived full of enthusiasm from America, stepped from the crowd.

'Come over here,' he beckoned to David with a big smile. 'You look like you could help us move this thing. Could you push from the back?'

David joined a few others and together they pushed. Slowly the chariot inched forward, groaning under its own weight. After just a hundred yards the wheels began to creak ominously. Then all of a sudden the front right wheel collapsed and the chariot lurched to a lopsided halt. Soon a huge traffic jam built up, and the devotees had no choice other than to dismantle their creation piece by piece and clear the road, as the police looked on.

The day was not entirely lost; the procession continued, without the chariot, to Trafalgar Square, where many people experienced kirtan for the first time.

Still, the devotees were devastated. Gurudas wrote to Prabhupada full of apologies. He believed the failure was his fault because he lacked devotion. He was so distressed that his letter trailed off without a signature. Prabhupada's reply was full of reassurance.

> My dear Gurudas,
>
> I could understand that you are immersed in great confusion on account of the wheels giving way. I think it was a mistake of engineering calculation. The load was heavier than the wheels could carry. So there is no question of being disappointed. As in the material world failure is sometimes considered the pillar of success, similarly in the spiritual order the same principle can be applied. So don't be disappointed. Maybe Krishna's desire is something higher in this connection. In any case, don't be disappointed. Keep your enthusiasm. Be patient, and Krishna will reward your attempts with success.[14]

Two weeks later Prabhupada wrote to Shyamsundar. This time he revealed how much personal emotion was invested in the efforts of his young disciples in London.

My dear Shyamsundar

When I first heard the news of the car collapsed it was so great a shock to me that the whole day I was sick and morose, and now after receiving this letter and your pictures I am very much enlivened. The car was on the road and the photo is taken with a multitude of people. That is your success and as a result of the collapse you have got now the sympathy of the Indian community as well as all the people of London.[15]

At Trafalgar Square that day, Mukunda had asked for volunteers to help the devotees decorate the new temple. David had put up his hand and given his address. The next day Colin had gone to visit David in Crouch End in North London, and brought him back to Bury Place. There he gave him prasadam and played him a recording of Prabhupada singing and speaking. David was impressed, and he decided to move into Bury Place to help Shyamsundar with the construction. Before moving in he distributed his few possessions among his Scottish flatmates and spent the last of his money on one of the handsome, three-volume sets of *Srimad-Bhagavatam,* the only books the temple had for sale. On that first visit to the temple, when David heard Prabhupada's voice, he recognised him as his spiritual master.

At the end of July a letter came from Prabhupada initiating the three English boys. Colin was named Kulashekara, Dick became Digvijaya, and Tim became Tirthapada.

SYDENHAM HILL, 28TH AUGUST 1969

The 'Hare Krishna Mantra' was released by Apple on 29th August. The 45-rpm single came with Clive Arrowsmith's now classic portrait of the Radha Krishna Temple on the cover. Arrowsmith was known for his stylised portraits, and he had arranged the devotees – there were now thirteen of them, including baby Saraswati – sitting on the floor with their life-size painting of Prabhupada stretched out before them. Behind them stood the three Jagannath deities on a raised platform. The devotees looked serene, blissful, and mysterious.

Apple organised a press launch the day before the release, paying for a marquee in a private garden in Sydenham, a mile from where the devotees had lived in Herne Hill when they had first arrived in England less than one year previously. They marvelled at how in that short time their fortunes had so changed.

George was there as the record's producer and to present the devotees to the press. He chanted with them, sitting on the grass while Yamuna led the kirtan and the group posed for photographs. The eighty or so journalists who turned up got a surprise that day: they were served a delicious vegetarian feast. The atmosphere became more like a picnic than a press conference.

Three days later George was at the Isle of Wight pop festival with his friend Bob Dylan. Before Dylan's set, which was to be the grand finale, George had the new Hare Krishna record played again and again to the 100,000 fans waiting for Dylan to appear. Within a few days the recording was in the top twenty. Prabhupada wrote to congratulate Shyamsundar.

> Regarding your recording of Nama Om and Hare Krishna, it is very very good and everyone says it is technically all-perfect. So your endeavour to induce the Beatles to cooperate with us is successful to a greater extent. Now when I shall go to London I shall carry with me various other recordings sung by me, and under my direction we can produce at least one dozen Hare Krishna recordings in various tunes. I am sure people will like them very much when they are presented by Mr George Harrison and his company.[16]

The day before the record launch, George had joined John, Paul, and Ringo at Tittenhurst Park, John and Yoko's new home, into which they had moved on 11th August. There at Tittenhurst the Beatles were photographed together for what was to be the last time, in the ornamental grounds and inside the house. George talked with John about the devotees, telling him how while they were converting their new temple they were living scattered around the city and still had nowhere to bring their spiritual master.

John made a generous offer: they could come and stay at Tittenhurst if they would help him fix the place up. It seemed the perfect arrangement. So after launching their record, the devotees made their way to Tittenhurst, twenty-three miles west of London. There they were accommodated in a row of four gardener's cottages a hundred yards from the main house. One of the cottages was set aside for Prabhupada.

The devotees had succeeded in holding a Rathayatra, their new temple was being prepared, they had just released a record, and now they had been given a fitting place where they could bring their spiritual master. Mukunda wrote to Prabhupada, telling him all was ready and inviting him to come and live with them at Tittenhurst Park.

CHAPTER 5

Underneath the Cedars

HEATHROW AIRPORT, 11TH SEPTEMBER 1969

A light drizzle fell from a grey sky as Prabhupada descended the steps from the plane at Heathrow. He was met by an immigration official and a policeman, whose job it was to take him directly to the VIP lounge. From behind a barrier his disciples waved and called. With his escort Prabhupada broke away from the huddle of disembarking passengers and came straight over to them. As he approached they fell to the wet tarmac, their tears mixing with the rain. Still on their knees they laughed and cried as Prabhupada reached down to rub their heads. Only Gurudas, busy with his camera, remained on his feet.

Once in the VIP lounge they enthroned him before the waiting press, garlanded him, and sat at his feet. He was swathed in saffron and heaped with flowers. To their eyes he looked like an emperor returning to his people. Gurudas did his best to continue taking photographs, but the next day when he developed his pictures he found them out of focus. 'It's hard to photograph with tears in your eyes,' was all he could say.

Prabhupada began to chant, playing his *karatals* and singing with abandon. When he finished, Mukunda stood and invited the reporters' questions.

'I am trying to teach what you have forgotten,' began Prabhupada, addressing the newsmen. These words, delivered with an urgency and conviction the reporters did not expect, opened his mission to the people of England. The press conference, organised with Apple's help, was his first face-to-face encounter on English soil with the people whose culture and ideas had dominated his childhood. He went straight to the heart of what he had to teach.

'Some of you are saying there is no God or that God is dead, and some of you are saying that God is impersonal or void. I want to teach that there *is* God. It is a challenge to the atheistic people. There *is* God.'

The British Empire had dominated India for close to two hundred years, including the first fifty years of Prabhupada's life. During that time the British had imposed their ideas upon India; now he would not compromise in what he had to tell them.

'As we are sitting here face to face, similarly you can see God face to face if you are serious and sincere.'

Around forty journalists had come to meet the Beatles' new guru. George Harrison had given the public something unexpected – a mantra, the 'Hare Krishna Mantra', released on the Apple label by a group calling themselves the Radha Krishna Temple. Their chanting was so magical, so different, that it had captivated London. The reporters wanted to know what it was all about. Prabhupada was there to tell them.

'Unfortunately we are trying to forget God. Therefore we are embracing so many miseries. I am simply teaching that you be Krishna conscious and *be happy*. Don't be swayed away by the waves of illusion.'

Two years earlier the Beatles had met Mahesh Yogi, known as the Maharishi. For a few months, Maharishi's long hair and beard, beatific smile, and armfuls of flowers had represented, in the eyes of the Western media, the archetypal image of an Indian guru. But Prabhupada was a different kind of guru. He was no trendy swami; he was penetrating and intense, and he demanded to be taken seriously. One of the reporters spoke up.

'Sir, is this singing essential to the sustenance of your faith?' This was the sort of question Prabhupada liked. He had hoped for such questions in Britain, and he responded immediately.

'This singing is the process for clearing the dust accumulated on the heart. Our relationship with God is eternal and cannot be broken. Due to contact with *maya* we are trying to forget him, but if we chant this holy name of God, Hare Krishna, then *maya* will not act and we shall very quickly understand our relationship with God.'

He cited several Sanskrit verses that explained the qualifications one needed to become Krishna conscious. But he was not here to convert the British to his religion; he was not concerned with such sectarian ideas. When a reporter asked about the fighting between Christian denominations in Ireland, which by 1969 had reached new levels of violence, Prabhupada did not hesitate. 'We are not Christians or Hindus or Muslims. We are God's servants. Among God's servants there is no disagreement. First-class religion teaches how to love God. It doesn't matter if it is Christian or Muslim or Hindu. If you are Christian and you have developed your sense of loving God, then you are perfect.'

As he spoke, his disciples punctuated his words with ripples of laughter and cries of '*haribol!*' They were unable to contain their emotions, and their unrestrained expressions of love contrasted with their teacher's dignified gravity.

'These are not ordinary boys and girls,' Prabhupada said, indicating his disciples. 'They are very elevated. Their qualities are greater than any mundane scholar's. For anyone who has developed love of Krishna, all good qualities will automatically arise in them. Let anyone come and test these people and you shall see.'

Prabhupada had good reason to be proud of his young followers, for they had succeeded in laying a foundation for Krishna consciousness in Britain where, thirty-five years earlier, his seasoned godbrothers had failed. They had succeeded because they loved to sing Hare Krishna and they loved their teacher and wanted to do whatever they could to please him. They were not driven by ambition; they simply wanted to make their teacher happy. That made *them* happy, and their happiness communicated itself to those around them.

Once the questions were over the devotees led Prabhupada to the waiting Rolls Royce. The driver helped him into the car, and as they looked lovingly at Prabhupada, who appeared so wonderful sitting alone in the back seat, the car glided away. Only then did they realise that no one had accompanied him, not even his servant Purushottama, who had come with him from America.

The car and driver had been sent by John Lennon. For nearly two weeks the devotees had been living at Tittenhurst and preparing for Prabhupada's stay. Their numbers had grown now to fifteen. There were the three English men, David from Scotland, and two new women – Vishakha, who had come from Dundee, and Pamela from London. Then there were the three devotees recently sent by Prabhupada from America to help: Ishan and his wife Bibhavati (and their baby, Braja), and Trivikrama, whose Navy training had equipped him to take charge of *brahmacharis*.

John Lennon had kept the devotees busy as soon as they had arrived at Tittenhurst. Slacking was not allowed. Their first job had been to assist John and Yoko to move in. Kulashekara had helped John carry his personal belongings out of the back of his Rolls. Then they had begun to redecorate the main house. John had wanted it stripped of unnecessary furniture and carpeting and painted white. There was much to be done in the garden under the guidance of the seasoned gardener, who had served the previous owners.

Near the main house was the gallery, originally a music room, with a high ceiling and good acoustics. John let the devotees use this room as their temple for as long as they were at Tittenhurst. Shyamsundar and Tirthapada were busy working on Bury Place, so it was Ishan who converted the gallery into a temple. He built an altar for their small Jagannath deities and created a raised seat for Prabhupada, with steps leading up to it and a lectern for his books. Yoko lent a rug from the main house, which David spread across the tiled floor. In preparation for Prabhupada's arrival they hung the room with greenery and garlands.

The four cottages that served as their quarters were traditional two-up, two-down brick dwellings – a little dilapidated, but otherwise quite serviceable. They chose a central one for Prabhupada, and cleaned and decorated it. The *brahmachari* ashram was next door to Prabhupada's place, and the two cottages on either end were assigned to the women and to married couples.

In those first few days before Prabhupada arrived they had started meeting in the new temple morning and evening for kirtan and class. John and Yoko had attended a few times and sat at the back listening, with John occasionally joining in the chanting. Once, George had come down with Pattie, and he too had chanted with the devotees.

The chauffeur drove on in silence. Prabhupada had just spent two weeks in Germany, where he had been encouraging the members of the new Hamburg centre, led by his American disciples Shivananda and Krishnadas.[1] Now as he sat alone in the spacious back seat of the car, he chanted quietly on his japa beads. From the airport the road crossed the Thames at Staines and, overhung by tall trees, skirted Windsor Great Park and the gardens of Virginia Water. Prabhupada saw a green, undulating landscape, whose sandy soil supported woods of pine and oak, interspersed with fern and gorse, and patches of grass where wild deer grazed. After only a few miles they reached the gates of Tittenhurst Park.

The mansion at Tittenhurst, set in seventy-two acres of landscaped grounds, was built in 1737. During the eighteenth century fashionable people were attracted to the wooded commons and heaths of Berkshire, where for little money they could acquire large landholdings and, dispossessing the poor who had eked out a living there for generations, build for themselves secluded summer homes to escape London's foul air. Living at places like Tittenhurst they could mingle with high society at the Ascot races, be close to the Royal Family at Windsor Castle, and drink the health-giving waters of the chalybeate springs. During the nineteenth century Tittenhurst Park had belonged to the great philanthropist Thomas Holloway who, after amassing a fortune by selling pills and ointments and by lending money to the French government during the Franco-Prussian War, built and endowed Royal Holloway, the first women's college of London University, and Holloway Sanatorium for the mentally ill. For these institutions he constructed two colossal turreted edifices nearby on the heath, close to Virginia Water. On the grounds of Tittenhurst itself he planted a profusion of ornamental trees, mostly New World conifers, including two rare weeping blue atlas cedars. Holloway labelled each tree with a brass nameplate denoting its species and its common name. These nameplates were still in place when John Lennon bought Tittenhurst from the Cadbury family.

Like Holloway, John Lennon wanted to leave his mark on the world – but by promoting peace and bringing about a revolution in consciousness. Yet although he was lavishing money on renovating Tittenhurst, he no longer felt comfortable in England. America was safer from reporters and lawyers. But the American government refused him a visa. So he and Yoko, with her six-year-old daughter, sought sanctuary at Tittenhurst instead. The place suited him for the same reason it suited his predecessors: it was secluded but within easy reach of London, and it was close to Heathrow Airport. It was somewhere he could retreat with his new family, entertain friends, compose and record his own music without corporate interference – and have time to think. A temporary refuge for a troubled genius.

Tittenhurst would also serve as a retreat for Prabhupada; it was a place where he could live quietly for a few weeks with his disciples, work on his new book about Krishna, and write letters to his disciples. The two contrasting figures, John and Prabhupada, were both only passing through Tittenhurst, and though they would share its cedar groves they would hardly meet. John, when he was not away recording the Beatles' last album at Abbey Road or working on his solo music with Yoko, ranged through his mansion's empty rooms, while Prabhupada lived quietly in the cottage or walked among the trees with his disciples in the early mornings.

Still, John was deeply intrigued by Prabhupada. He had met Prabhupada's disciples and engaged them in serious discussions enough times to know that Prabhupada was a man to be taken seriously. He was not going to be like the Maharishi, whom John had found disappointing. John had a serious nature – he liked to ask penetrating questions and then to hear, carefully, what people had to say. After hearing he would make up his own mind about life, and say what he thought without compromise.

Having watched Prabhupada's car leave the airport the devotees scrambled into their Land Rover, borrowed from John, and set off in pursuit. They hoped to arrive ahead of Prabhupada so they could show him to his quarters. But when they reached Tittenhurst they found him standing alone in the driveway with his luggage. The rain had stopped and he waited patiently.

'Where should I go?' he asked in a relaxed mood.

Gurudas led the way down the path to Prabhupada's cottage, through an arched front door, and up bare wooden stairs to a suite of two small rooms. The front room was a bedroom that overlooked the entrance courtyard; in the rear, with its small adjoining bathroom, was a cosy square sitting room with a high ceiling and a view across the garden. Prabhupada would spend most of his time in this room – chanting japa, dictating onto his big reel-to-reel tape recorder, answering correspondence, and receiving guests. Here he would also worship, overseeing the *puja* for his small Radha-Krishna deities whose altar was in the closet in the corner, and singing songs to them with his harmonium. Apart from a set of shelves for his books, a low table for his desk, a cushion for his seat, and a borrowed carpet, the room was empty. This was how he liked to live: simply, as a *sannyasi*.

Downstairs the kitchen at the rear was organised by Yamuna and Malati, who were to cook for Prabhupada and the devotees. Janaki's service would be to clean his quarters. Purushottama, who was given the front room, would be his secretary and personal attendant, while Trivikrama, who lived next door with the *brahmacharis,* would give him his daily massage.

As soon as Prabhupada's luggage was deposited in his rooms he wanted to see the temple room. The devotees went with him and crowded in. He made his obeisances before the small Jagannath deities, then settled on his raised seat, looking down at his disciples.

'Yamuna? Come and lead a kirtan.'

Yamuna sat on the floor in the middle of the room with the harmonium and sang the familiar words to her guru: '*Nama om vishnu padaya…*' and the devotees sang their heartfelt response: 'I offer my humble obeisances unto Bhaktivedanta Swami, who is very dear to Lord Vishnu, having taken shelter at his lotus feet.'

It was a wonderful moment. For a full year Prabhupada's emissaries had laboured to serve him in London. Now, with their new British brothers and sisters gathered round them, they were reunited with their master in kirtan.

The chanting swelled and Prabhupada smiled with pleasure. He gestured to them to dance around Yamuna in a circle, and for half an hour they went on, until he brought the kirtan to a close and began to speak.

David Naysmith sat, trying to be attentive. He had been told that Prabhupada liked his disciples to ask questions, and he found himself distracted from Prabhupada's talk by a strong impulse to ask one question in particular. When at last Prabhupada fell silent, his hand shot up.

'Yes?'

'When can I take initiation?'

Prabhupada paused to observe this eager young man.

'That is another thing. We shall see.'

Prior to encountering Prabhupada, David had not even known he was looking for a spiritual master. Seeing Prabhupada and hearing him speak confirmed beyond doubt that this was his teacher and master.

Now that he had made his desire known he did not mind if he was made to wait; Prabhupada had not rejected him.

Another spiritual seeker was present that day. George Harrison had come down to Tittenhurst, eager to meet the person whose voice had fascinated him for so long. He had arranged with John Lennon that they would see Prabhupada together. While Prabhupada returned to his rooms, John and George joined the devotees for a late lunch – the arrival feast Yamuna and Malati had prepared. John, Yoko, George, and Pattie sat together cross-legged in the temple room while the feast was served from pots and bowls spread around them on the floor. It was a moment of friendship and informality before the serious meeting that would follow.

A sunken path led from the main house, down the slope, overshadowed by dense clusters of laurels and rhododendrons, to Prabhupada's cottage, which lay hidden beneath the trees in a fold of the rolling lawns. After the meal was over, John, Yoko, and George made their way with Shyamsundar down the path to the cottage entrance and up the narrow flight of stairs to Prabhupada's small sitting room.

Fortune had arranged this encounter, in this secluded spot amid the shifting landscapes of the late sixties, bringing two of the most influential young men of their generation together with Krishna's personal envoy.

Yoko sat on the bare floor next to her husband and looked around her. She saw the simple way Prabhupada lived, with no furniture save for his low study table and a few cushions for visitors. In one corner incense burned before Radha and Krishna, and a harmonium stood at the foot of their altar. Beside his desk stood a shelf of books.

Prabhupada smiled benevolently as his guests settled themselves and Shyamsundar garlanded each of them. John and George sat facing Prabhupada, with Yoko taking her place beside her husband. She understood that he was searching for answers, exploring whatever life presented to him, and she was there to support his search. Pattie had not accompanied George. This was his path and she had to let him follow wherever it would lead.

John wanted a role in the world beyond being a musician, to make a difference, with his declarations for Revolution, for Love, Not War, and his challenges to the establishment. That was why he had asked Prabhupada and the devotees to come and stay. He recognised them as comrades from whom he might learn, and he wanted to help them bring their change in their way. All this was apparent to Prabhupada.

'By the grace of Krishna you are leaders,' he began, addressing John and George together. 'Thousands of young men follow you. They like you. If you give them something nice, the face of the world will change.'[2]

Prabhupada's voice was soft and amiable as he spoke of Krishna as the universal father. 'We are all Krishna's children,' he said, quoting the *Bhagavad-gita*. 'If we think of him, we chant Hare Krishna, we will have everything to gain and nothing to lose. Chant Hare Krishna, everyone. Dance in ecstasy. My request is that you try to understand this Krishna consciousness philosophy, and make your own judgement.' They listened with concentration and respect.

'You want peace – I have read your statements,' he spoke directly to John. 'But we must know the process. Krishna says, "I am the enjoyer, I am the owner, I am the friend." ' These were the words Prabhupada always referred to as the 'Peace Formula'.

'Why do we claim "This is mine?" Krishna is the Lord of every place. We come here in the kingdom of God and we claim, "This is my property." Is it not insanity?' He smiled at John, and looked around him and out of the window at the beautiful gardens. John, whose claim to Tittenhurst was the obvious example, remained silent.

'Krishna is the friend of everyone. He is such a nice friend that he is living with me in my heart. Therefore I think people should have one God, Krishna; one scripture, the *Bhagavad-gita;* one mantra, Hare Krishna; and one activity, to serve Krishna. Then there will be peace all over the world.'

Had John read his edition of *Bhagavad-gita,* Prabhupada asked. John murmured that he had dipped into the *Gita* during his three-month stay at Maharishi's ashram in Rishikesh but had not read Prabhupada's commentary. Right now he seemed content just to sit here and go on hearing Prabhupada speak.

'We want people to be happy,' continued Prabhupada. 'Be happy and make all others happy – that is Krishna consciousness. But here in the material world you cannot be happy because everything is temporary.' This was something John could understand. He had achieved immense success, but he was at odds with the world and tortured by drug addiction. Prabhupada's words were self-evident, and John listened closely as he explained that the soul, which is eternal, cannot find happiness in a temporary world. The solution, Prabhupada said, was to go to the eternal world to be with Krishna, to join in Krishna's *rasa* dance.

Understanding that his guests were musicians, Prabhupada wanted them to hear Vedic mantras, so he chanted some verses from the *Srimad-Bhagavatam*. The verses he chose, although he didn't explain them to his guests, had special relevance to this meeting. His voice filled the room with deep and melodious tones.

'*Matir na krishne paratah svato va ...*,' he sang. The verses said that people addicted to material life, to 'chewing the already chewed', were not attracted to Krishna. They were like the blind following the blind, misled and bound by miseries, and their only hope of freedom was to find the shelter of a pure devotee of God.[3]

'You don't have to understand the words,' he assured them. 'Just hear the sound vibration and it will benefit you. All Sanskrit verses – for example, the verses of the *Bhagavad-gita* – are mantras that can be sung like this.' He encouraged them to use such verses to create sacred music.

John would go on searching, Prabhupada knew. Still, he was helping Krishna's devotees and listening with respect, so his spiritual progress was assured. George was different. He heard with rapt attention as Prabhupada went on to describe the power of the Hare Krishna mantra.

All at once John broke his long silence. He and George had both received private mantras from the Maharishi, and he was curious to know why Prabhupada thought the Hare Krishna mantra was special among all other mantras. 'All mantras are just the name of God,' said John, 'so it doesn't matter which one you sing, does it?'

'Oh, but it does matter,' Prabhupada corrected him. 'You must take the medicine prescribed for you. In this age, the Hare Krishna mantra is recommended by the great authorities.' He stressed that the mantra should be received through the right channel.

'If your mantra doesn't come through an authorised channel, it won't work,' he pronounced. Now, after listening in submission for twenty minutes, John was provoked.

'But how do you know who is authorised?' he interjected. This question of authority was crucial for him. 'Maharishi said he was authorised. How are we to tell one from another?'

'It's a matter of personal taste isn't it?' suggested George. 'One person prefers roses, another carnations.'

'That's all right – you may choose any flower,' Prabhupada agreed. 'But still, the rose is considered the best. Similarly, God will present himself to you in whatever form you desire, but if you study the *Bhagavad-gita* carefully you will realise that Krishna is the source of all other forms of God.'

After they had been going for an hour, Prabhupada's audience relaxed and became talkative, as he repeatedly emphasised the need to accept authority, specifically the authority of the *Bhagavad-gita* spoken by Krishna. But whose version of the *Bhagavad-gita*, they wanted to know.

John again voiced his concern. 'How do you distinguish one authority from another?'

'The world is full of authorities,' added George, who had read many books on mysticism.

'I take a little from here and a little from there,' said John.

Prabhupada chuckled. They went on discussing the problem, and all the while he kept bringing them back to Krishna and the *Bhagavad-gita*.

'Anyway, Vivekananda said books are secondary,' put in George. 'You don't have to read books in order to perceive the truth.'

'Then why Vivekananda wrote so many books?' responded Prabhupada, and everybody laughed. Ultimately, he explained, all gurus accept Krishna as the authority because they rely on his words from the *Bhagavad-gita*.

'But we've gotta keep going round, asking advice, sifting through like sand to see who's the best,' sighed John. George felt differently.

'I'm not saying Krishna isn't the supreme. I believe he is,' he said with assurance.

'Then if you want to know who represents Krishna, see who is always chanting Krishna's name, who is addicted to Krishna.'

This was Prabhupada's last word. They had talked for nearly two hours and it was getting late.

'Bring the prasadam.'

Yamuna handed round plates of fruit, fresh from being offered to Radha and Krishna. Finally George was passed the harmonium, and invited to bring the meeting to a close by leading them all in chanting the Hare Krishna mantra.

John and Yoko made their way down the steep stairs. She was impressed by Prabhupada's patient expounding of his topic and his serious mood, and by his friendly nature: he was clearly genuine about his mission. As they left the cottage she turned to John. 'Could you live that simply?'

Gurudas, following behind, heard the admiration in her voice. John made no answer. It was common knowledge that he had no wish to be anyone's disciple, but it was clear that he had formed a genuine regard for Prabhupada.

One beautiful September day soon after his arrival, Prabhupada said he would like to see London. As a boy growing up in Calcutta he had imagined it as a fabulous city. Now he was curious to see for himself the seat of power that had once ruled his world. At the same time he wanted to inspect the new temple that was under construction at Bury Place.

Shyamsundar, Gurudas, and Mukunda accompanied him for the day, and John allowed the group to use his white Rolls Royce. On the way into London Prabhupada spoke about England's former wealth. The Tittenhurst Estate had once provided work for twenty men; now it was overgrown, with only one elderly gardener maintaining it. 'England has been reduced,' he said. 'At one time she ruled the world. The British governed India with just a handful of men. But now because of their karma the British are in decline.'

He had often said that London was the most important city in the world. But what he saw that day disappointed him. They crossed the Thames at Westminster. 'It's just a canal,' he said on seeing the tidal stream.

They drove round Trafalgar Square and down the Mall, but even Buckingham Palace failed to impress. In India the British had used the vast resources of the subcontinent to build on a monumental scale. They had created the Viceroy's Palace in Calcutta and many grand state capitals, culminating in the fabulous imperial capital in New Delhi, completed in 1929. But here in London everything seemed so much smaller than he had expected.

He made fun of the English weather.

'Isn't it a beautiful day?' people greeted him.

'Oh, yes,' he would answer – then, 'They think the weather is beautiful if the sun shines for just one day.'

It was not until Prabhupada entered the shell of Shyamsundar's half-built temple in Bloomsbury that at last he beamed with pleasure. Under Shyamsundar's hands and with the help of Tirthapada, a hidden gem was emerging, transforming the ground floor of the former Bible warehouse into a shrine for Radha and Krishna. Having removed the walls, Shyamsundar was crafting an elaborate vaulted temple in the empty space.

His artistic inspiration came from the caves of Ajanta, whose arched and ribbed vaults had been hewn into a cliff face in the Deccan two thousand years before in a powerful expression of early Buddhist monasticism. Shyamsundar had transposed their design to twentieth-century London, and in a reversal of the usual process, in which early timber structures were later imitated in stone, he was imitating stone forms in wood, using the redwood he had shipped from California. His choice of material expressed the American roots of the London temple, and his design adapted Buddhism to Krishna consciousness in what had once been a Christian building. By combining all these elements his temple demonstrated the ideal Rupa Goswami had taught in the sixteenth century – that everything should be employed in the service of Krishna. Prabhupada loved it.

Planning obstacles had been overcome by the patient persuasion of Gurudas and Mukunda, and now only details remained to be agreed upon, such as where to put the sign. They explained to Prabhupada that the council said a sign could not be displayed outside the property.

'But this is inside,' he protested with a mischievous grin, standing on the front step of the house to indicate that the line of the building was inside the property boundary.

From where he stood he could see the British Museum at the northern end of Bury Place, and this pleased him. It was a prestigious location for a temple. He did have one reservation though: this temple was too small. For now it would have to suffice, but his ambition was for something far grander. He wanted to take over churches, as he had written to his wealthy friend, Sethji, in India:

> It is a great necessity to construct a very big Radha Krishna temple here, so I am trying to find out some redundant churches to turn into temples.[4]

The Church of England had recently declared a list of redundant churches. Prabhupada had several times written in letters that he wanted not one but four or five temples in England, and these churches seemed to offer a good opportunity. So while they were in London the group went to Westminster Abbey where, with help from Lord Sorensen, Mukunda had arranged a meeting with the Dean, Dr Edward Carpenter.

Dr Carpenter received Prabhupada with great cordiality in his private residence, hidden from view among the inner cloisters of the abbey. They sat in his reception room, overlooking the Jerusalem chamber, where in 1611 the first Authorised English translation of the Bible had been compiled.

The Dean was a mild and open-minded man known for his interest in all faiths, and his wife was a vegetarian and friend of the Dalai Lama. When the Dean and Prabhupada met they found a mutual understanding that required few words. Their conversation was relaxed and friendly, and did not directly address Prabhupada's wish to convert churches into temples. While Lord Sorensen looked on, the Dean fetched Prabhupada a glass of water and then sat comfortably by his side, the two men of God content to be with each other mostly in silence.

Early in the mornings, as daylight broke through the mist at Tittenhurst, Prabhupada walked under the dew-dripping trees. He felt at home in nature. Wherever he went he was at home, because everywhere he saw Krishna, but here Krishna's material energy was especially beautiful. Among the soaring redwoods were chestnuts, oaks, beeches, and yews. Grassy passages wound between banks of rhododendron and laurel, opening onto fields of unkempt grass, where layered Cedars of Lebanon stood tall. In a grove all their own the blue atlas weeping cedars spread their fringes to the ground, their canopies forming a sea green tent.

He wrapped himself against the morning chill with a black overcoat and Russian hat, and wore Wellington boots against the damp grass. On his hand was his bead bag. His disciples took turns to walk with him. Sometimes Yamuna would follow him in her black hooded cloak, while her husband scrambled through the bushes with his camera to capture Prabhupada on film. He appeared as if he was keeping company with Krishna, as he walked with his head held high and his gaze aloft, then sometimes, softly chanting Krishna's names, he would lean his head to one side and look down, absorbed in his private thoughts.

One morning Gurudas saw a worm crawl unharmed beneath Prabhupada's foot. Looking behind him he also noticed with surprise that the grass, though trampled by his own and Yamuna's steps, was hardly marked where Prabhupada had been. It was as if he floated on the dew.

'If you tread on some grass and it dies, what happens to the souls?' asked Yamuna.

'They take human birth.'

She bent down and pulled up a tuft of grass from under his feet, and he laughed. He stopped and pointed with his cane. A clump of dried grass contrasted with the lush green that surrounded it.

'Why is this grass yellow?'

'Is it because the soil is not fertile?' guessed Gurudas.

'No. It has become detached at the root. A plant is nourished through its roots. Therefore as soon as the roots are detached there is difficulty. Similarly, when we are detached from Krishna we are in difficulty, but as soon as we are attached to him our lives become successful.'

Another morning they followed the trail left by a tractor through a field of hay. Either side the hay rose almost to head height, bathed in the glow of the rising sun. Kulashekara asked Prabhupada about the song they had recorded the previous day. Each afternoon Prabhupada had a recording session in his room, working through the songs of Narottama and Bhaktivinoda. He sang and played the harmonium, while Kulashekara, under his tuition, accompanied him on the drum and Purushottama played the *karatals.* Prabhupada had just recorded *Shikshastaka,* the eight verses taught by Sri Chaitanya.

'That was a song by Lord Chaitanya.' Prabhupada stopped and turned to face his companions, his cane on one arm. 'This is the time when he would come out – when the sun has just risen but not yet climbed in the sky. This is when Lord Chaitanya would dance with his devotees.' As he spoke he held up his arms and swayed from side to side. 'And this is how he would dance.' His skin shone gold, reflecting the golden light in the sky and the golden field of hay.

Prabhupada made friends with the gardener. Frank was past retiring age, but as an expert gardener he had agreed to John Lennon's request to stay on, and lived with his wife in a cottage on the estate. Although he was struggling to maintain the grounds with little help, he still managed to keep a well-stocked kitchen garden, which he proudly showed Prabhupada.

'Come and see my mushrooms,' he said one day.

'Mushrooms grow in the dark,' replied Prabhupada, 'so I'm not fond of them.'

'Then let me show you my melons,' went on Frank with undiminished enthusiasm. He liked Prabhupada, and it gave him pleasure to share his work with him. Together they went into a large heated greenhouse where an impressive crop of melons was ripening.

'Do you grow lady's finger?' asked Prabhupada, after admiring the melons. This was an exotic vegetable that Frank had never heard of. They went on chatting.

'How old are you?'

'Sixty-five.'

'Do you still have all your teeth?'

'Well, as a matter of fact no. I'm too fond of sweets,' replied Frank with some remorse.

'I'm seventy-three and I'm also very fond of sweets, but I still have all my teeth!' Prabhupada showed Frank his full set of gleaming teeth.

'How have you managed that?' asked Frank with admiration.

'Because I eat the right kind of sweets,' replied Prabhupada. Then he told Frank how to make burfi and other milk sweets. They chatted every day.

One incident that brought John and the devotees together was what became known as the 'ghost affair'. John had hired a builder to construct his new recording studio. The builder was staying in one of the Tittenhurst cottages, an old dwelling dating back hundreds of years to when the estate had formed part of the Great Forest of Windsor. Lately the builder had been looking tired, and his work for John was suffering. One morning he came late to work and confided to Kulashekara and David that he and his wife were having trouble sleeping.

'She's 'earing things in the night.'

'What sort of things?'

'Well, she says moans, chains, bodies dragged across floors – that sort of thing. I'm sure it's just rats in the roof.' He said he was going to go round and seal all the gaps.

Next morning the builder was extremely agitated. He had sealed the gaps and other entrances and got off to sleep as usual. But that night he had awoken to find his wife, still asleep, bouncing up and down on the bed as if shaken by an invisible force. He had woken her and they had both dashed out of the house in terror. None of the seals had been broken. Now he was on the point of handing in his notice.

'Tell John we can get rid of this ghost,' Prabhupada told Mukunda when he relayed the story. But John insisted on getting his own exorcist. The man came, dressed in a long purple coat, but within five minutes of entering the cottage he withdrew. He said there was an old panel above the fireplace with occult signs on it. He dated the house back to Tudor times, and thought the ghost had probably been the original inhabitant. The ghost, he said, refused to leave, and he was powerless to do anything about it.

After John heard this he accepted the devotees' offer of help. During his massage Prabhupada instructed David what to do.

'You should all chant Hare Krishna and blow a conch loudly in each room. The combination will force the ghost to leave. Ghosts cannot tolerate the purity of the holy name or the sound of a conch shell.'

They opened all the doors and windows, sprinkled them with Ganges water, burned incense, and held a resounding kirtan, blowing conches and playing all sorts of musical instruments. As the kirtan reached a crescendo Kulashekara felt a sudden release of pressure and saw a bright light leave the house like a whirlwind.

'I think that noise you made really scared away those rats,' said the builder the next day.

'No, dear,' corrected his wife. 'Their chanting purified the atmosphere and we felt something leave.'

Every morning for the next three weeks Prabhupada passed the cottage on his walk. 'So, how is the ghost?' he would enquire. Finally, when there seemed nothing further to report, he said, 'If they want, they can have him back.'

One night in his room Prabhupada explained that the original resident of the house was probably envious. He said such persons could be forced to remain as ghosts in their old homes. Ghosts lived in subtle bodies, he explained, which did not allow them to eat or drink, so they were always frustrated. 'There are many more ghosts in the stables,' he told them, 'but if we chant Hare Krishna they won't bother us.'

John was grateful to the devotees for the exorcism, but he and Yoko were haunted in other ways. He was doing his best to be a conscientious host, unfailingly polite and taking a genuine interest in his guests. Some days he and Yoko would chant with them and maybe listen to Prabhupada speak. At other times they were cold and distant, withdrawn into their private world. This was because they were weaning themselves painfully off their drug habit.

On one of his better days John invited Prabhupada up to his house to hear a song he had just recorded called 'Cold Turkey'. It described the painful experience of withdrawal from heroin addiction, and in the song John graphically described the agony he had been going through. Playing it to Prabhupada might have been a cry for help or a desire to share with him what he had learned about the dangers of drug addiction and about karma. John wanted to make a fresh start, and Prabhupada was someone who would understand.

That evening after dark Prabhupada sat on a large sofa with his assistant Purushottama in John Lennon's white drawing room, with Yoko sitting nearby. John stood beside some expensive audio equipment, trying to get it to play his tape. Somehow he couldn't make it work. After a few frustrating minutes he gave up the attempt and apologised to Prabhupada, explaining to him what the song had been about.

'Temperature's rising, fever is high,' went the song. 'Can't see no future, can't see no sky.' It described the inner torture John was experiencing, how he wished he were dead and prayed to be set free. It ended with the plea, 'Get me out of this hell – cold turkey has got me on the run.'

Prabhupada listened patiently as John explained that now that he had given up drugs he wanted to tell people how destructive they were.

'Never mind,' Prabhupada said, 'we can listen to another song. I have brought my own recording to play to you.' Only that afternoon he had recorded one of his favourite Bengali songs, '*Hari hari biphale,*' by Narottama Das. He asked Purushottama to play the tape on his own portable tape recorder. It opened with words expressing the lament of a pure-hearted Vaishnava:

> O Hari, my life has been wasted. Although I have been given this rare human birth I have not served Radha and Krishna. Instead I have deliberately drunk poison.
>
> From the spiritual world comes the chanting of Krishna's names – why am I not attracted to them? Day and night my heart burns in the fire of samsara, yet I do not try to find relief.

These words appealed directly to John's situation. For a few minutes they sat together. Prabhupada explained the meaning of the song, urging John to chant Hare Krishna, then looked at his watch. 'You must excuse me,' he said. 'It's getting late and I still have work to do. Thank you for inviting me.'

As he walked back toward the cottage David and Trivikrama heard his footsteps crunching on the gravel and emerged from their hiding place. They had wanted to be there with him but had not been invited. Unknown to anyone, they had concealed themselves in the bushes outside the drawing room window and had peeped through a crack in the shutters.

'Oh, you saw everything?' chuckled Prabhupada. He didn't ask what they were doing or disapprove of their boyish behaviour. For David the experience was a valuable one: he saw that despite his wealth and fame, John Lennon was full of anxiety, whereas he, being accepted as Prabhupada's disciple, felt fortunate and secure.

'Your name is Dhananjaya,' said Prabhupada a few days later, handing David his beads. 'It is a name for Arjuna which means "conqueror of wealth". You will have no difficulty acquiring money: it is flying in all directions. You simply have to catch it.' As he spoke he raised his hands and plucked imaginary notes from the air.

An initiation ceremony was being held in the temple, and there were other initiates too. Pamela, who had been with the devotees since February, was given the name Pritha. A few days later, Denise and Dave, a young English couple with their infant son Dylan, were also initiated. Before meeting the devotees they had kept a stall on Oxford Street, where Dave had sold hippie bells and beads. He and Denise had planned to escape London – their dream was to find a croft in his native Scotland and work the land. But fate had intervened.

Dave had seen the devotees come past his stall, chanting. He had loved it. He would fold up his stall and dance down the street after them. Denise had seen them chanting too. She thought them an odd crowd – particularly Ishan, who dressed in a leopard-print *dhoti* and played a trumpet. Yet all day long at their flat, she listened to the Hare Krishna record. When Prabhupada gave his first public lecture they both attended. Denise was spellbound. She couldn't understand his words, but she drank in the whole vibration of his being. She asked the devotees if she could join them, and they had invited her and her family to come and live with them at Tittenhurst. Within days she and Dave had sold their belongings and found a friend to drive them out there, where they were given a room in the cottage next door to Prabhupada's. As Denise was unpacking, Malati put her head round the door. 'Quick, come with me. Prabhupada's in the temple room.'

Denise ran after her up the path and got there just in time to see Prabhupada blessing Ishan and Bibhavati's baby. While Denise bowed down, Prabhupada prepared to leave.

'These people have just come to join us,' announced Malati, introducing Denise, Dylan, and Dave.

'Hare Krishna,' Prabhupada said, and smiled broadly at Denise as he walked past her.

When he looked down at her Denise felt overwhelmed, as if she had come through many universes and lifetimes to meet her spiritual father. A week later Gurudas told her and Dave that Prabhupada would give them initiation and perform their marriage at the same time.

Now the temple hall was filled with chanting devotees. A small square fire pit had been built with bricks and sand on the floor near the altar. Dave took his place on one side and Prabhupada sat opposite, facing him. Dylan fidgeted on Malati's knee. Denise was led in, dressed in Yamuna's red silk sari.

First Prabhupada initiated them as his disciples. He gave Denise the name Draupadi, after the wife of the Pandava brothers, and Dave he named Devadatta, 'gift of God'. Little Dylan he renamed Dhruvananda after the sage Dhruva, lord of the polestar.

'Generally the child comes after the wedding,' Prabhupada remarked, 'but in this case the child is here to see his parents married. Don't laugh,' he corrected Gurudas, who was giggling as he loaded another roll of film into his camera. Then he turned to Malati.

'Take the child outside so he doesn't see the wedding.'

Soon the couple's vows were made, and under Prabhupada's deft hands the fire flickered into life and grew higher with each ladle of ghee he added.

'Swaha,' he chanted, and all responded. Eyes watered as smoke from the sacred fire filled the room. As soon as it was over everyone streamed out into the sunlight and the fresh air.

A few days later Prabhupada asked the couple to accompany him on his morning walk. They set off at his side, past the main house and down a long slope through the rose garden. Light was just breaking over the horizon, bathing the scene with a soft glow. As mist hovered among the trees, they followed a track leading to the paddock, where John kept a donkey. In the chill morning air Prabhupada stopped at the gate.

'Mankind is like this donkey,' he said gravely. 'He works all day, chasing a carrot on a stick for just a few handfuls of hay.' Then he added, with a twinkle in his eye, 'And at night he enjoys sex at the risk of being kicked by his wife.' He burst into laughter and turned back up the hill toward the cottages. As they walked Devadatta realised that he and his wife had been taken to see the donkey so that they could understand this simple lesson about the power of the senses and the importance of self-control on the spiritual path.

'Thank you very much,' Prabhupada ended, smiling as the newly-wed couple took their leave.

One morning a few days later, while Prabhupada was lecturing in the temple, little Dhruvananda crawled up the steps of his seat and climbed into his lap. Prabhupada continued to speak undisturbed, and after a short time the child curled up and fell asleep.

With Prabhupada in their midst, the community was now complete: a full-fledged ashram where disciples served their guru. Their activities revolved around him, as life's rhythms follow the rising and setting of the sun.

Keeping up with Prabhupada was no easy task. Each night he rose in the small hours, first to quietly chant japa on his beads, then to do his translation work. At this time he was working on a book exclusively about Krishna, recounting the stories preserved in the ancient *Srimad-Bhagavatam*. It was to be called, simply, *KRSNA, The Supreme Personality of Godhead*. By the time Purushottama and Yamuna came to join him in his room for arati it was still only four o'clock, and he had already been up for hours. When his private arati was over he walked with them to the temple, where all the devotees met for the first arati of the day. He would then lecture from *Srimad-Bhagavatam* followed by a kirtan.

At 6.30 every morning, rain or shine, he went for his walk, accompanied by one or two devotees. From her kitchen door Malati watched him leave, wishing she could join him. She cooked for the devotees and did the shopping, helped by the newly-initiated Draupadi, while their two children played together. One day Saraswati was playing as usual when she saw Prabhupada and ran out to catch hold of his hand as he went past.

'You're not properly dressed,' he told her as she clung to him, refusing to let go. Then he patiently waited for Malati to bring out Saraswati's little coat, and took her with him on his walk.

While he was out walking, Yamuna and Janaki prepared his breakfast and cleaned his rooms. The rest of the community chanted their japa in the temple, or while walking in the grounds. On his return he would take his Ayurvedic medicine followed by a light breakfast.

Yamuna's special service, apart from cooking for Prabhupada, was to learn how to worship the deity. He planned to install Radha-Krishna deities in the new London temple and wanted her to be in charge of looking after them. At the cottage he trained her to serve his own small deities, first by demonstrating while she watched, then by letting her do everything. This was her initiation into being a *pujari*. Each morning she would bathe and dress the deities, decorate their altar, and perform their arati ceremony, offering simple items – incense, lamp, water, and a few flowers. On returning from his walk Prabhupada would come to see how she had done and tell her how she could improve.

One day she and Malati collected armfuls of roses and dahlias from the gardens. They brought them triumphantly to Prabhupada's room and pinned them around Radha and Krishna, arranging them as a backdrop. When he came in he opened his eyes wide in pleasure and astonishment.

'Oh, this is very nice,' he said. Then he paused before adding, 'But it could be even better.'

'How?' Yamuna was eager to learn. 'Please show me how.'

He sat on the floor before the deities and took down all the flowers, then quickly and deftly reassembled them. She saw how, by using perspective from large blooms to small, he framed Radha's and Krishna's forms to reveal them to their best advantage. He explained that this principle also applied to dressing: reveal Krishna's form; don't cover it. In worshipping Krishna, he stressed to Yamuna three things above all: 'Be clean. Be punctual. Be fully present in all that you do.' And he concluded, 'The essence of deity worship is to chant Hare Krishna. Do your best to chant without offence.'

One night he called Yamuna to his room. An Indian friend had donated ten-inch brass deities of Radha and Krishna. Prabhupada asked if she could paint them. She protested that she couldn't paint – that she would spoil them – but he said he would teach her how. She got some of the paints Shyamsundar had used to paint Jagannath, and the following evening she sat with Prabhupada late into the night. By the light of his desk lamp and under his watchful gaze, she painted the deities' eyes, outlining them with a black line, gave them solid red lips, and made lotus petal designs on their bases. Prabhupada kept these deities until the time would be right for them to be worshipped.

Janaki was Prabhupada's first female disciple, and her relationship with him was special. She loved to surprise him. Once, she presented him with her valuable diamond ring, and he treasured it. Whenever she especially tried to please him, he called her his little mother. But sometimes, when she was moody and obstinate he called her his naughty daughter.

One morning she decorated his breakfast plate with small paper umbrellas from Chinatown, their bright colours sprouting from the fruit. When Yamuna brought in the plate, Janaki stood outside the door, peeping in to see his reaction.

'Oh, who has made this plate? She must be inspired by the *gopis*.'

'It was me, Swamiji,' she called from the doorway.

'Radharani is expert in many arts. You must be her maidservant!'

A happy smile lit Janaki's face.

While Prabhupada lived in the Garden House surrounded by nature and with few visitors, he was more relaxed than when he stayed in one of his established temples. After breakfast he spent an hour in solitary bhajan in his room. Sitting on the floor at his harmonium, he sang the Bengali prayers of Bhaktivinoda or Narottama, or hymns from the *Brahma-samhita*. When she could, Yamuna listened, sitting out of sight at the foot of the stairs. At her request he included one or two chapters every day from the *Bhagavad-gita*. While hearing her guru's voice wafting down the stairs, full of love for Krishna, she stored up the precious memory of those days.

At ten o'clock he turned his attention to managing his mission. If necessary he would meet with Mukunda or Gurudas, and perhaps dispatch them to London on business – to finalise the registration of ISKCON, visit the bank, meet council officials, or organise preaching engagements. This was also when the sankirtan party would leave for London. Managing them was Trivikrama's responsibility. Each day they went out to chant in the West End and sell magazines. They had mixed results, but Prabhupada always encouraged them.

'So the people are appreciating the *harinam*?' Prabhupada asked Trivikrama when he reported the sales figures. The party brought in a small daily income, which Mukunda and Gurudas gratefully received. Money was tight.

'Our business is not to make money,' Prabhupada reassured him. 'We just want to distribute our literature. By hearing and appreciating the *harinam* party the public will make spiritual progress. Even if they don't join, if in their minds they think these are good people, they will be benefited.'

From his small study underneath the cedars Prabhupada kept in close touch with his disciples all over the world. His preferred method of communication was by letter – he avoided the telephone. During the two months he spent at Tittenhurst he sent over eighty letters. Most of these letters were long and detailed, responding minutely to his disciples' questions and concerns. His aim was always to encourage and inspire them to preach. In a letter to Prahladananda he wrote,

> The transcendental sound vibration of Hare Krishna and preaching of *Bhagavad-gita* philosophy will act on everyone, regardless of whether or not they are understanding at first. When preaching you only repeat what you have heard from the disciplic succession and this will act.[5]

In some letters he pushed forward key priorities for ISKCON. He gave much thought to the long-term survival of his society, which had now grown to more then twenty centres in five countries. He wrote to Tamal Krishna in Los Angeles that he wanted to create a governing council. He was well aware of the dangers of factionalism in a religious society, having seen it at first-hand among his godbrothers in India.

> In the future we can form a central governing body for the whole institution… In my Guru Maharaj's institution different godbrothers took the words of Guru Maharaj in different interpretations and the whole mission was disrupted… I am always afraid of this crack, but I am sure if our aim is to serve Krishna sincerely and the spiritual master simultaneously, that will be our success.[6]

At the forefront of his attention was the need to set up an independent publishing operation for his books. He wrote about this to Gargamuni in New York.

> We shall produce immense literature. If the press goes on nicely, I shall be able to give you material for publishing a book every two months ... Ramakrishna Mission has their own publication organisation; Bible Society has their own arrangement. So why Iskcon should fail to have its own organisation? You seriously consider the whole situation along with Tamal and let me know your definite opinion what to do.[7]

He also wanted a German press so his disciples in Germany could publish translations of his books and a German version of *Back to Godhead*. Kulashekara had been apprenticed to a printer before he joined the temple, and he had also recently married Vishakha. Prabhupada decided to send them both to Germany, to assist the temple in Hamburg and help set up the press.

Every day punctually at noon he set aside whatever problems of management had concerned him that day, wrapped a simple cloth about his waist, and sat on the floor for his massage. Since the crisis in his health in 1967, which led him to convalesce in India, this daily treatment had become an essential part of his health regime. During his stay at Tittenhurst the privilege of giving him his massage was shared between Trivikrama and the newly initiated Dhananjaya, neither of whom had any previous experience.

Prabhupada assured them that they simply had to begin with his head and work down to his feet. No book on the art of massage was necessary, as Trivikrama had expected. 'This is not necessary. Just read the *Bhagavad-gita* and Krishna will tell you how to do.'

Prabhupada liked hard massage – the harder the better. Sometimes the session could last for two hours. Their arms would ache with the effort.

Trivikrama found that by being with him every day, intimately touching his body, he gained inner strength and the determination to remain celibate. At the age of twenty-six he was contemplating marriage. He found Prabhupada kind-hearted and considerate, and through his personal association he got relief from his restless mind.

In a lecture one morning Prabhupada spoke of his own married life, and how in later years his guru appeared in his dreams and called him repeatedly to retire from family life and fully devote himself to preaching. 'How could I do that with five children?' he recalled. 'But by my guru's mercy I took *sannyasa* and now I have gained so many children – and without the botheration of a wife!' he added, to much laughter.

Next day Trivikrama was massaging him.

'Yesterday you said you have so many children without the trouble of a wife...' he began, intending to ask about the question of marriage, but Prabhupada cut him off.

'I said that?' he mused, feigning surprise, and Trivikrama knew what he meant. Prabhupada had often said it didn't matter, married or not – the important thing was to be Krishna conscious. Krishna consciousness itself was the sacrifice – it might call for austerity, but it could also be joyful. The important thing was to be motivated by love, thought Trivikrama, as he continued massaging the one he loved.

Another time during the massage he praised Prabhupada. 'Last night at the lecture you really gave it to them, Prabhupada.' He was referring to Prabhupada's stern response to a heckler at a public meeting. 'Sit down – you are nonsense!' he had commanded. Trivikrama had not seen his spiritual master act like that before, and it was a revelation. He was chattering away as he worked, feeling as if he were preparing Prabhupada for another knockout performance.

But Prabhupada interrupted him. 'No!' Then in a small voice that seemed to come from deep inside he murmured, 'I am just a humble servant.'

Dhananjaya was given the service of massaging Prabhupada when his name was still David – within days of Prabhupada's arrival. Trivikrama, who was suffering from a bad toothache, asked David to stand in for him.

'But I've never massaged anyone in my life!' David protested.

'Don't worry, Prabhupada will tell you what to do.'

David went upstairs, taking with him two bottles, one of sandalwood oil for Prabhupada's head, and one of mustard oil for his body. He rubbed his hands to make them warm, as Trivikrama had instructed him, and nervously presented himself for duty.

Prabhupada sat on the floor ready for his massage and questioned his aspiring young disciple.

'Where are you from?'

'Scotland.'

'How far is Edinburgh from London?'

'About four hundred miles.'

'And how long does it take by train?'

'About six hours.'

'Where did you go to school?'

'In Scotland.'

'Did they teach you British history?'

'Yes.'

'When was the Battle of Trafalgar?'

'1805.' David was confused. He was expected to be asked if he had read the *Bhagavad-gita* or what he knew about Krishna, but he was being tested on history.

'When was the Battle of Waterloo?'

'1815.' Prabhupada seemed satisfied.

'I also studied British history at Scottish Churches College in Calcutta. At my college Lord Zetland, a Scottish lord, gave out diplomas at the end of each academic year. He became the Governor of Bengal and was a very powerful man.'[8]

The massage was a long one, and by the time it was over, almost two hours had passed. David was covered in perspiration. Trivikrama had told him that if Prabhupada started to fall asleep that was the sign the massage was a good one, and a couple of times Prabhupada had seemed to drift off. David felt happy to have been given this one chance of intimate service. The next day Trivikrama felt better and resumed his role.

'How is your toothache?' asked Prabhupada with concern, wanting to know what treatment he was taking. He always took a paternal interest in his disciples' health. After the massage Trivikrama came looking for David.

'You must have done something right,' he said with resignation. 'Prabhupada says from now on he wants us to take turns.'

So it was that David, soon to be initiated as Dhananjaya, to his great delight regularly massaged his spiritual master for the rest of his stay in England.

After his massage Prabhupada bathed, chanted *gayatri-mantra,* then had lunch in his room. Following this he usually chanted japa, then slept for a couple of hours. When he woke he had a little fresh juice and his door was open for anyone to visit. This was the time when devotees could sit with him and talk informally. In the evening at 6.30 he attended the arati ceremony in his room.

Little Saraswati was a frequent visitor and he loved to play with her. In the evenings she was often there when Yamuna offered arati, attended by Prabhupada and whoever wished to join them. Once, just after the flower had been offered, Saraswati decided to get up and leave. Prabhupada, sitting on the carpet, took the flower and tossed it at her, hitting her on the back of the head. Saraswati picked up the flower and ran back to Prabhupada with it. He put out his hand, but to his and everyone's amusement she dropped the flower into his mouth. He laughed and gave it back to her.

'Now you can go,' he said with a smile.

Yamuna came down with fever. She used to wear herself out working for Prabhupada and never had sufficient sleep, so her strength simply left her. As she languished in her room, separated from Prabhupada next door by the brick wall between them, she could hear his occasional movements. She tried to chant, and listened for the comforting sound of his voice through the wall. After two days she began to feel better and ventured out onto her small balcony, which adjoined Prabhupada's. Simultaneously he stepped out onto his own balcony, his hand in his bead bag. She looked across at him.

‘Swamiji, I love you so much,’ she called out with great emotion. He looked up.

‘I know,’ he nodded gravely. Their eyes met, then he turned back to his room where Trivikrama was preparing to administer his massage.

In the evening, if there was a speaking engagement, Prabhupada would be driven there. If not, he would stay in his room and receive visitors. By eleven he would be in bed.

He was eager for every opportunity to go out and speak. This period in the countryside was for him an enforced holiday that he would willingly have foregone. But for his disciples it was a time of family intimacy they would always remember.

CHAPTER 6

Spreading the Word

BBC TV STUDIOS, 16TH SEPTEMBER 1969

It was a coup for Gurudas and Mukunda to get Prabhupada on Late Night Line-Up. TV had been around since before the war, but only now, when almost every household in Britain had one, was it coming into its own. BBC's evening discussion programme aired every weekday evening at ten, and was the recognised forum for arts and intelligent discussion. Each night the presenter covered a different topic and spoke to well-informed or provocative people – perhaps a playwright or a politician – doing his best to put them on the spot. Tonight, on 16th September, in the hot seat was a venerable Indian guru.

Prabhupada sat back, comfortable and relaxed under the bright studio lights, while opposite him perched the presenter, Tony Bilbow, young and quick-witted, wearing thick, horn-rimmed glasses and leaning forward in his penetrating interviewer's style. He introduced Prabhupada as a guru from India who had come to Britain to open a branch of his movement. With unusual deference he asked Prabhupada about his purpose.

'My mission is to teach how to love God,' Prabhupada began, his face appearing strong and kindly. Compared to the youthful presenter he seemed old and wise, but with surprising energy and a ready smile. 'People have forgotten God, and I have come to remind them.'

Bilbow was not entirely at home with this topic on a programme where the 'God' word was rarely mentioned, but he pressed on.

'Is this the same God we worship in the West – the Christian God? Or is this some other God?' he wondered. This was a question many viewers would have shared. They were not used to hearing about religion from non-Christians. This Indian guru, though, evidently spoke of God with deep conviction.

'Yes, I am speaking of the same God,' answered Prabhupada in a matter-of-fact voice. 'There is one God whom we all worship, Christians and Hindus alike, and he has many names. One of his names is Krishna.'

In middle-class sitting rooms across the country people sat up and took interest. Religion, unfashionable in sixties Britain, had recently made a comeback in the guise of yoga and Eastern mysticism, as pioneered by the Beatles.

'I have come to teach anyone how to see God. It is possible to talk with God. Just as we are talking to each other now, face to face, you can talk with God.' Prabhupada smiled, encouraging his interviewer.

'But *how* can we see God?'

'By chanting the names of God, that's all. Just sing God's names. We don't say you must chant only the name "Krishna". You can chant any name and it will act.'

'Would you like to demonstrate your chanting?' invited Bilbow.

'Oh, yes!' Prabhupada gave a broad smile. Together they stood up and crossed the studio to where a group of devotees were already seated in a semicircle on the floor, holding their instruments. Bilbow went round with his microphone to where Shyamsundar sat. Bending down he asked him about himself, and listened as Shyamsundar told how he had met Prabhupada in San Francisco and become a devotee of Krishna. His shaved head, with his forehead bisected by vertical lines of *tilaka,* shone under the bright lights, adding to his striking appearance.

Prabhupada sat in their midst, right there on the studio floor, and the chanting began. First came the *karatals* played softly, then the drone, a combination of harmonium and tambura. Then Yamuna led the singing, weaving a web of mystical sound that stretched from the studio right across the country, entering millions of homes.

As the closing credits of the programme scrolled down the screen, the devotees faded from sight along with their chanting. For some viewers that night, the sound of the mantra seemed proof of Prabhupada's words: by chanting God's names you can see God. It was just as he had once told Shyamsundar: 'This is the simplest, most beautiful system there is. Just chant Hare Krishna. It's proven – time-proven.'

CONWAY HALL, 6TH OCTOBER 1969

Knowing Prabhupada's desire to preach in the city, Mukunda and Gurudas arranged a series of lectures for him. The venue they chose was Conway Hall. Built in the 1920s in Red Lion Square, Holborn, the hall had a reputation for radicalism, being the home of the British Humanist Association. The Society had begun as a group of Christian nonconformists in 1793, united in their rejection of the doctrine of eternal hell and in supporting the abolition of slavery. Eventually they had moved away from formal Christianity and embraced Humanism. Their commitment to free thought meant their doors were open to anyone of any creed. This commitment was expressed in the inscription displayed in large letters above the proscenium arch in their main hall: 'To thine own self be true.'[1]

The main lecture hall seated three hundred people, with room for more on the balcony, and the devotees worked hard to fill it. They publicised Prabhupada's lectures, planned to extend over ten weeks, by handing out invitation cards in the West End and spreading the word around their Hindu friends. The first talk was scheduled for 6th October at seven in the evening, and was entitled 'Teachings of the *Vedas*'. An audience of 150 showed up and the talk went well. Prabhupada was sufficiently pleased with it to send the tape to Boston to be used as the introduction for his translation and commentary of *Sri Ishopanishad*, which was about to go to press.

The second talk was on Wednesday 15th October. That evening Prabhupada set off from Tittenhurst in the car that was hired for him each week. The car came with a driver, whose name was Eddie. Prabhupada sat in the front passenger seat, while in the back were Yamuna, carrying his small Radha-Krishna deities in a box, and Purushottama. The others followed in Shyamsundar's pickup, with Saraswati riding on Malati's lap. Mukunda had gone ahead to arrange things at the hall, where close to a hundred people came to hear, many of them from the Hindu community.

Prabhupada took his seat on the stage on a table covered with an embroidered cloth. To his right, on an altar improvised by Yamuna, stood his small Radha-Krishna deities next to a vase of flowers and incense burning in a bowl. Behind hung a large banner with the words of the Hare Krishna mantra. He started with chanting, joined by the devotees, then gave his lecture.

'Ladies and gentlemen, I thank you very much for coming to this meeting,' he began. Each week Gurudas advertised a different topic, and Prabhupada treated the occasion as a formal lecture, setting out his message to the people of England. This week's topic was sankirtan, chanting the glories of God.[2]

'One who chants the glories of God is a *mahatma*,' he said, quoting from the *Bhagavad-gita*. The Hindus in his audience regarded the *Gita* as their highest authority. They also admired Mahatma Gandhi as the embodiment of a wise man. Prabhupada wanted to point out to them that the term *mahatma*, 'great soul', was used in the *Bhagavad-gita* to describe a person who always chanted God's glories.

'This human form of life is meant for enquiring about *brahma*, spirit. *Aham brahmasmi*,' he cited the *Vedanta-sutra*. 'I am not this body – I am spirit soul. Englishman or German or Indian; American or

Russian or Chinaman; Christian or Hindu – these are all designations.' His teaching was for everyone, regardless of race or creed.

'In your childhood you had a body just like this child's body,' and he gestured toward Saraswati, who sat nearby on her mother's lap. 'Now that you are grown up, where has that body gone? Change of body is going on in every moment, in every second, imperceptibly. And the final change is called death. But actually there is no death: when you leave this life you accept another body.' This was the foundation of his teaching. Everyone's real identity was eternal spirit.

'When I understand that I am spirit, then' – he quoted the Sanskrit word from the *Gita* – '*prasannatma*, all anxiety is finished and at once I become joyful. Finally I will realise that God, or Krishna, is the origin of everything. In quality I am one with God, just as a particle of gold is also gold. As the nature of God is to be blissful, so also my own nature is to be blissful. That is the way to end suffering – by realising my own spiritual nature.'

He spoke as he always had – directly and without compromise. These truths were not to be understood by fools, he asserted, only by people with intelligence, after many lifetimes of searching. Otherwise, for those who were not on the spiritual path, this world was a place of suffering.

'Even if you think this is a good place to be, still nature will kick you out. You do not know when you will have to leave. Therefore an intelligent man asks, What is my position? Why am I suffering? Why am I forced to die?' His task as a teacher was to remind them of uncomfortable facts they might prefer to forget.

'Always remember these four things: birth, death, old age, and disease. Simply being advanced in eating, sleeping, mating, and defending does not make you actually advanced. The advanced soul is broadminded and realises, "I am not English or Indian; I am not old or young. I am eternal spirit," and so surrenders to God.'

He concluded his talk with a verse from one of the Bengali songs of Bhaktivinoda Thakur, his great nineteenth-century predecessor.

'This world is an ocean of forgetfulness, ruled by *maya*. Don't be washed away by the waves of material nature, from one body to another, from one to another.'

The solution he had to offer was a simple one.

'You don't need to study many books. Krishna consciousness is there in everyone – it just has to be invoked. The process of invoking it is to chant Hare Krishna, Hare Krishna, Krishna Krishna, Hare Hare/ Hare Rama, Hare Rama, Rama Rama, Hare Hare. You will clear your heart and very quickly understand that Krishna is God. There is no loss. We are not charging any money. We have our books, *Bhagavad-gita As It Is, Teachings of Lord Chaitanya.* But there is no need of philosophy. Simply chant. Thank you very much.'

When he finished the devotees gave him a rousing cheer.

In the audience was an eighteen-year-old girl from Sweden, Lena Engvall. She had come to London with her twin sister to find the meaning of life. The easiest way for a Swedish girl in the 1960s to get to England was to come as an au pair, so she and her sister had taken positions caring for the small children of well-to-do Jewish families in Finchley. Before leaving Sweden she had heard the 'Hare Krishna Mantra' on the radio. She thought it the most amazing sound – something stirred inside her making her jump up and down – and she felt she must find out more.

On their first day off in London the two sisters escaped to the West End for some sightseeing, when all of a sudden on Oxford Street they heard that same Hare Krishna song, chanted by a group of strange people dressed in orange. They crossed the road and Lena asked one of the men what it was all about.

'It's a kind of Hinduism,' he said vaguely. 'We are trying to purify our hearts.' Then he gave them an invitation to Conway Hall. 'Come and hear our spiritual master, who is giving talks here every week.'

They came early. The devotees still appeared strange to them, with a penetrating look in their eyes unlike other people. When Prabhupada started to speak Lena found she couldn't understand much. He seemed to her to be stern, and she was a little frightened. But at one point during his lecture little Saraswati ran up to him, and although he was in the midst of speaking he gave her his full attention. He even started to play with her. Lena was charmed when she saw this, and decided he must really be a kind and saintly man.

At the end of the talk, when he called for questions, an Indian woman stood up to voice her doubt.

'What are you doing to relieve all the suffering in the world?'

'Join us,' he replied earnestly, and with a smile, looking around at the devotees onstage, he added, 'we are not suffering.' They showed their agreement by laughing with him.

That was a turning point for Lena. She was all too aware of the suffering in the world, but his answer seemed plain enough: the Krishna people had found happiness and perhaps so could she. An ecstatic kirtan began, with Ishan playing his trumpet, and she and her sister both joined in. They were so swept away by the chanting that afterwards they danced their way to the tube station, down the escalator, along the platform, into the carriage, and all the way home. After that Lena began visiting the temple whenever she could.

The following week the audience was again a good one, with many respectable and cultured people. The topic for the night was 'You Are Not This Body'. Prabhupada used an analogy of a car and its driver to illustrate the difference between body and soul, and everyone in the room seemed to understand what he was saying. Afterward the kirtan took off. He got up and started dancing, raising his arms and leaping in the air. Yamuna sat on the floor beside him with the harmonium, leading the kirtan. She was singing Hare Krishna, but Prabhupada was singing a new mantra she had never heard before.

'Narada muni bhajaya vina radhika ramana namine,' he chanted again and again, signalling to her to continue her singing. She closed her eyes and carried on, not knowing what was happening. Then he sang Hare Krishna in unison with her in a voice that rang out across the auditorium.

The kirtan seemed to shift to a new dimension, one they had not experienced before. All of a sudden the audience was on its feet. The devotees jumped off the stage and danced round the hall. As they looked back toward the stage, some of them noticed that Prabhupada's feet were not touching the ground. He seemed to be levitating. At least that was what they thought they saw.

As they got in the car, the driver, Eddie, who had been at the back of the hall, turned to Prabhupada. He used to address him as 'Padre'.

'Well, Padre, you got a bit out of control tonight, didn't you?' And he nudged him with his elbow. 'It's just like you were saying: this car's no good without a driver.'

The following morning Yamuna asked Prabhupada what had happened.

'Narada Muni came to our kirtan. Didn't you see?'

'No, I didn't see him.'

'Well, he came.'

Prabhupada had taught his disciples about Narada Muni, the divine being who travelled throughout space and time continuously chanting Krishna's names. 'Narada Muni, Lord Shiva, Lord Brahma – they all came and danced with us, and I sang to them. That was why the kirtan was so full of ecstasy.'

Vishnu Sharma, a postgraduate law student in his thirties, attended one of the early lectures at Conway Hall. He grew up in an orthodox Hindu family in India, but was sceptical of swamis who came to the West, because in his experience they were usually interested mainly in making money. He had noticed the Hare Krishna chanters on Oxford Street, and thought they were probably on drugs – definitely not the sort of people a law graduate should mix with. But a Jewish friend of his, a fellow student who had attended the lecture the previous week, assured him that this teacher was different from other swamis. So Vishnu agreed to come along and see for himself.

He saw the teacher enter the hall and noticed his aura of spiritual absorption and power. He sensed that he was deeply serious about what he was doing with these young people. When the teacher spoke Vishnu noticed that he only talked about Krishna, quoting from Vaishnava scriptures like the *Srimad-Bhagavatam* and the *Bhagavad-gita*. At the end of his lecture, in responding to questions, Vishnu thought the teacher gave perfect answers. He decided that this swami was here to give something important, and in the following weeks he attended all the lectures.

Most of Vishnu's days were spent studying law at the British Library just round the corner from Bury Place. One day when he was free he looked in at the temple to see how the construction was going. There he made friends with Mukunda and Shyamsundar, and offered to help them by passing out leaflets among his colleagues.

One night after the lecture Prabhupada came to Bury Place to see the progress. He found Shyamsundar working away to get the temple ready. This made him extremely happy.

As the lecture series continued the audience began to dwindle. By the sixth week only fifty people attended. That night the kirtan was more wonderful than ever. Halfway through it Prabhupada shifted into a new melody and tempo. Gurudas and Yamuna looked at each other in amazement, as they all danced round and round the stage with him. Afterwards Mukunda and Gurudas apologised for the small audience and asked Prabhupada about the new melody. 'I did something to keep the people entertained,' was all he would say.

Word spread among the Hindu community that Prabhupada was at Tittenhurst, lecturing there daily. Some of the Hindus had heard him speak at Conway Hall; others had met the devotees during the year and kept in touch. Each week a few families made the pilgrimage out to Tittenhurst to hear him lecture and afterwards to visit him in his room to ask his blessings.

Among the pilgrims was Kedar Nath Gupta and his family. He had come from North India and settled in England fifteen years earlier. Now he ran a grocery store in North London, helped by his wife, and they were raising three sons. He and his wife had both been brought up in Vaishnava families to worship Radha and Krishna, so they quickly established a rapport with Prabhupada and invited him to their home. When he came to visit them they prepared a feast and performed arati to their Radha-Krishna deities. Prabhupada was pleased and encouraged Mr Gupta to help the London mission by gathering support from the Hindu community. After that the Guptas visited Tittenhurst regularly, and before long Prabhupada agreed to initiate the whole family as his disciples, naming them Kshirodakshayi Das, Kirtima Devi Dasi, Sandipani Muni Das, Karanodakshayi Das, and Chaturbhuja Das.

OXFORD TOWN HALL, 30TH OCTOBER 1969

Prabhupada's guru, Bhaktisiddhanta, had wanted Krishna consciousness preached in Oxford, so at Prabhupada's request Mukunda arranged a speaking engagement there. The devotees had already been to Oxford in June when they had chanted on a college lawn. A large crowd of students had linked hands and danced round them in a circle, barefoot in the grass, singing Hare Krishna. When they had reported their success to Prabhupada he had written saying, 'I shall request you that your next attempt shall be to establish a centre in Oxford, where I have heard you have successfully performed kirtan.'[3]

Encouraged by the good reception they had received on that first visit, Mukunda booked Oxford Town Hall, which had a large concert hall. Every day for a week before the programme a party of devotees went up to chant in the streets and hand out leaflets publicising Prabhupada's visit.

The hall filled with several hundred people. It had a vaulted ceiling, ornate galleries on three sides, and a large orchestral stage with a grand concert organ whose upright pipes formed a backdrop. Prabhupada took his place on a raised cushion, his Radha-Krishna deities beside him on a table. Mukunda mounted the steps behind to the organist's seat and played the instrument with professional ease. The thunder of the organ drowned Yamuna's voice and harmonium, but Prabhupada evidently liked it, for he danced with abandon, his robes swaying and his arms extending upward with open hands, as if imploring mercy from on high. The combination of the organ and Prabhupada's graceful dancing made it an unforgettable occasion.

Prabhupada lectured for an hour, and the many questions that followed extended the programme until after ten. He was happy, because the questions were serious and philosophical.

'London is for the mass, Oxford is for the class,' he said afterwards.

'These are the future leaders who can transmit Krishna consciousness. Our next temple after London should be here.'

Following their musical success with the 'Hare Krishna Mantra', the devotees, under their stage name Radha Krishna Temple, became a popular act. Their agent booked them to perform at major venues, such as the Marquee Club in Wardour Street and the Hammersmith Odeon, where they shared the bill with Quintessence, a band of musicians who followed a Hindu guru and included mantra chanting in their repertoire. Most notable were two appearances on BBC's flagship entertainment show, Top of the Pops, where they mimed to their recording. The resident dance troupe were Pan's People, pretty girls whose role was to dance provocatively. On the insistence of Gurudas, they dressed in saris for the performance, and both the dancers and the audience loved it. Top of the Pops, with its mass youth audience, introduced the Hare Krishna mantra to millions of young people.[4]

An invitation came from Amsterdam for the Radha Krishna Temple to appear on Dutch TV's version of Top of the Pops. When Prabhupada heard of this he said he wanted to go with them. Mukunda asked the organisers if their spiritual master could come and say a few words. They were hesitant, but eventually agreed to give them a five-minute slot: three minutes for chanting and two minutes for speaking. Mukunda informed Prabhupada that he would only be able to speak for two minutes. Was it worth a whole day's travel, including return flights? Prabhupada was undeterred.

'Two minutes is enough. I can explain the whole philosophy of Krishna consciousness in two minutes.'

They flew to Amsterdam and were shown to a stage set that had been spray-painted to look like an Indian temple. Again the dancers, who turned up in miniskirts, happily agreed to change into saris. When the devotees' turn came, the stage manager pumped dry ice onto the stage, almost hiding the chanting devotees so that Prabhupada, on his raised seat, seemed to float serenely on a mystical cloud. After the chanting he delivered a perfectly timed two-minute summary of Krishna consciousness, checking his watch to make sure he didn't run overtime.

'Chanting the Hare Krishna mantra is the process of God realisation recommended by Lord Chaitanya Mahaprabhu for this age. It is the universal medicine for human society. It is so simple even a child can do it,' he began, and explained that *bhakti-yoga,* devotional service to God, established a personal link between the soul and Krishna, the ultimate source of all life. 'When you chant Hare Krishna, Krishna dances on your tongue. This is recommended for everyone: to chant the names of the Lord.'

The broadcast went out live all over Holland. Afterwards, as they waited in the airport lounge for their flight, Prabhupada was buoyant. He rested his hands on his cane and smiled lovingly at his disciples.

Near the end of October Ishan was working in the kitchen of the main house, where John kept an upright piano. John came in and started chatting. They were both musicians, so they had something in common. To amuse them, John sat at the piano and started to sing Hare Krishna. As he played he spontaneously switched styles between mantras, trying out variations on the melody in different idioms – jazz, blues, folk. They were both enjoying themselves, with Ishan singing along, when Yoko came in.

'Please, John, I have a headache. Can't you stop that and come upstairs?'

By this time they had been guests of John and Yoko for nearly two months and were beginning to feel it was time to move on. Prabhupada was impatient to see the new temple open at Bury Place, and he no longer felt he had any reason to be staying in the countryside. He had a worldwide movement to organise, and his place was in the city.

John called at the cottages to speak with Mukunda. He had often assured the devotees that he liked having them there, but they knew that others in his household were less keen. After all, the devotees were receiving many callers and their numbers were increasing. Moreover, the work that had kept them so busy when they had first arrived was now mostly done. John explained to Mukunda that although he would willingly let them stay as long as they wanted, he was under pressure. So it was agreed they should go soon.

Work at Bury Place was taking longer than expected. Prabhupada wanted to speed things up, so he decided the devotees should move into the upper floors at Bury Place, while he would stay close by in a rented apartment to oversee the final preparations. Mukunda found a place for him on the second floor of Farley Court, a block of flats opposite the London Planetarium near Baker Street.

Meanwhile Mukunda and Gurudas were still trying to finalise planning permission for 7 Bury Place to be used as a place of worship. Their neighbour, Mr French, had lodged a protest against the change of use. He was disturbed by the sound of early morning kirtans coming through his basement wall. Solicitors were engaged. The devotees, courtesy of George, were represented by the celebrity barrister Lord Goodman, and Tom Driberg wrote letters in their support on his parliamentary notepaper. A meeting of all parties was arranged, with representatives from the council present to supervise a noise test. In the soundproofed temple room Kulashekara played the *mridanga* while readings were taken. The temple's sound insulation passed the test. Mr French's objection was overruled, and the temple was granted planning permission.

All this pressure was weighing greatly on Mukunda's shoulders, and Prabhupada saw he needed more help. He wrote to his disciple Tamal Krishna, who was running the Los Angeles temple, calling him to London.

> I think Mukunda is a little bit strained managing all the affairs. The most important thing before us immediately is to organise a nice Samkirtan party here in London for daily work.... I would advise you for some days to come here.[5]

Tamal Krishna was excited to receive this call from Prabhupada. He had first met the devotees in San Francisco in the spring of 1968. Prabhupada had given him initiation just before the London-bound group had left, and Tamal had fond memories of them. In Los Angeles he had proved himself to be an exceptional organiser, and now he looked forward to joining them and serving Prabhupada in London.

At the beginning of November, as the devotees were preparing for their departure, a storm swept through the south of England, buffeting the tall trees at Tittenhurst. Prabhupada had made friends with many of these trees on his walks, stopping to touch their leaves and appreciate their shelter. The storm felled several of the larger trees and brought down many branches. One large branch crashed onto the cottage roof and made a hole right above Prabhupada's room.

'This is a sign that we should go now,' he said. 'We must leave within twenty-four hours.'

The next morning, before getting into the car, he walked out alone to say goodbye to the trees of Tittenhurst Park.

CHAPTER 7

Radha and Krishna in Bloomsbury

BAKER STREET, 3RD NOVEMBER 1969

The day of the move a cold wind blew. Prabhupada wrapped himself in his warm winter coat, and Trivikrama travelled with him, carrying his deities. They arrived at the Baker Street flat, and while they carried his things up from the car Prabhupada sat patiently in an armchair, chanting on his beads. The large living room was carpeted and fully furnished, with a low table and cushion specially for him. He directed Trivikrama to place his deities in a cabinet with sliding doors that stood along one wall. Purushottama came in and stood the tambura beside him, so he reached for it and began to vibrate its strings.

'Bhaja sri krishna chaitanya,' he sang softly with his eyes closed.

Trivikrama sat at his feet, absorbed in listening. Prabhupada opened his eyes and looked down.

'Oh, you like?'

Before Trivikrama could answer Janaki burst in after climbing two flights of stairs.

'Where do you want this lamp, Prabhupada?' she cried breathlessy. She had finally started to call him by his new name.

'On my table next to the picture of Prabhupada.'

Both Trivikrama and Janaki looked at him in surprise. They had never heard him use that term to address his spiritual master.

'Yes,' Prabhupada smiled, 'I too have my Prabhupada.'

It was still early morning, and beneath them the city was coming to life. Underground trains pulled into Baker Street station, and thousands of workers hurried up from the platforms and onto the streets. Red double-decker buses pulled up to carry them to their places of work. Prabhupada was back in the city where he belonged.

Later that morning he wanted his head shaved and called for Dhananjaya. The young man worked with care – Prabhupada had warned him to avoid shaving off his *sikha,* which he protected with a hand over his crown while Dhananjaya shaved round it. He saved particles of Prabhupada's hair and stored them with the other mementos he had been gathering – a discarded glove, one of Prabhupada's old shirts, and a piece of cloth from his *dhoti.*

Tamal Krishna arrived on 11th November, and Mukunda brought him straight to Bury Place to meet Prabhupada. When Tamal saw his master after a four-month separation it seemed to him, not for the first time, that his presence illuminated the room. He also noticed how relaxed Prabhupada was, surrounded by his small group of London devotees.

'How is everything at our Los Angeles temple?' Prabhupada enquired, and Tamal gave his report.

'Here there is very good prospect for our preaching. Things are going on nicely, and at all our meetings hundreds of people join us in chanting and dancing.' He turned to address Mukunda and the other devotees in the room. 'Now that Tamal is here with his good experience in organising sankirtan, all of you work together to develop it more and more. Chalk out the long-term programme for our World Sankirtan Party so that after London we can take Krishna consciousness to every country.'

Tamal Krishna was a man of action and a natural leader, who took it for granted that he had been called there to organise them all. He called meetings and began implementing some of the lessons he had learned in Los Angeles, where Prabhupada had trained him in temple leadership over a period of many months. Soon he had reorganised the daily chanting party, set up an accounting system, and assigned new responsibilities. He appointed Malati as Prabhupada's cook and told Yamuna to stay at Bury Place to prepare for the arrival of Radha and Krishna. He trained Dhananjaya to be the temple commander at Bury Place, in charge of cleanliness and maintenance, and to take out the *harinam* party.

For the past six months a regular consignment of *Back to Godhead* magazines had been delivered to London – a quarter of each monthly printing – and they were accumulating in the basement of Bury Place. Tamal did as he had in San Francisco and Los Angeles, organising a determined push to sell the magazines alongside the *harinam* party on Oxford Street.

Prabhupada took his morning walks in Regents Park with Tamal and Dhananjaya. That November was unusually cold, bringing snow and ice to the park. He wore a pink woollen balaclava knitted for him by Yamuna, with a blanket wrapped over his *dhoti* and extra layers beneath his black coat. They walked with him the short distance from his apartment north toward the park, crossing its outer circle to enter the gardens at Clarence Gate. He walked quickly, steadying himself on the slippery pavement with his cane, and by the time they reached the crossing he was yards ahead. Not waiting for cars he crossed the road without hesitation, and waited smiling for them on the other side.

Entering the park between flowerbeds they walked toward the inner circular rose gardens. He pointed with his cane to the sheet of ice on the lake, on which ducks and Canada Geese congregated, unable to swim.

‘The nature of water is to be liquid, but now it has become solid. This is like *maya*.’ He broke a frozen puddle with his cane. ‘Similarly, the nature of our hearts is to be soft like molten gold, but now they have become hard. Just as the sun melts the ice, so the name of Krishna melts our hardened hearts.’

He strode onward, one hand in his bead bag as he chanted Krishna’s names and the other on his cane, leading his young disciples through the gardens. Poplar, chestnut, plane, and oak trees grew tall among well-kept lawns that sloped down to the water’s edge, where heron, geese, and ducks of many colours chattered and shuffled in the cold. Some of them had found a patch of unfrozen water under a weeping willow that overhung the lake. Prabhupada pointed with his stick.

‘They are sitting in the water beneath the tree. The Six Goswamis knew this art. In Vrindavan they used to shelter beneath the trees because trees give warmth in winter and shade in summer. The water there has not frozen because the tree is alive and its breathing gives out warmth.’

At the edge of the lake a man sat on a bench feeding the birds.

‘It is natural for one living entity to render service to another,’ Prabhupada said, ‘but only when this service is offered to Krishna do we become happy.’

The second moon landing was televised on 19th November 1969. Prabhupada had told reporters after the first moon landing in July, and again at Heathrow airport when he had entered England, that the moon mission was a waste of time and money. Privately, he disbelieved the whole thing and said it was impossible for humans to visit the moon. Nevertheless, he was curious to watch the events unfold, and he turned on the television at his Baker Street flat. The broadcast showed Apollo 12 with its two-man crew touching down in the Ocean of Storms. The ship stayed on the surface of the moon for twenty hours before returning to earth.

The day of the moon landing Malati was cooking for Prabhupada early in the morning. From the kitchen she saw that his door was ajar and peeped in. Prabhupada had arranged to sit to the side of the television during his massage. This enabled his deities to see the TV without him blocking their view. It was Dhananjaya's turn to be the masseur, which meant that while he worked he too could watch TV. Purushottama was also present.

As the moon landing proceeded Prabhupada kept asking Purushottama to describe what was happening. Prabhupada was teasing him; Purushottama had been unable to accept Prabhupada's assertion that the moon landing was a hoax. Prabhupada said this because the moon was described in the *Vedas* as a heavenly planet, open only to pious beings reborn in higher realms. In his view, it could not be reached by any mechanical means, no matter how sophisticated they were. As Dhananjaya massaged, he eagerly followed what was going on.

'So what is the news?' Prabhupada asked Purushottama.

'As soon as the capsule lands we will see the surface of the moon.'

Walter Cronkite was reporting from Cape Canaveral. The screen went fuzzy, like snow, then cleared, and Charles Conrad stepped down the ladder while the camera panned in front of him.

'They've landed in a crater and it's like a desert.'

'Can you see buildings or parks or people?'

'No, Prabhupada,' laughed Purushottama incredulously. 'There's no air or water, so how can there be life?'

'According to Vedic authority the moon is a heavenly planet full of varieties of life. The nectar called *soma rasa* enhances the pleasure of the inhabitants. Nothing on earth is comparable.'

'It's not like that. It's dry and lifeless,' replied Purushottama.

'Therefore this is not the moon,' concluded Prabhupada. 'They are somewhere else.'

Listening to this extraordinary conversation Dhananjaya's attention began to wander from the task of massaging Prabhupada's head. All of a sudden Prabhupada patted the floor in front of him. 'Come round and sit here,' he commanded. Dhananjaya sat where he was told, facing Prabhupada, who began massaging his disciple's head.

‘Like this.’ He squeezed so hard the young man saw stars. ‘Now get behind and do it properly.’

Dhananjaya returned to his post and tried his best to concentrate. The door to the kitchen opened a little wider.

‘Come in, Malati. We’re watching television. Come in. Sit down. They say they are going to the moon. Let’s watch the fun.’ For a while they all watched as Purushottama continued to insist that NASA was a respected government programme. Then through the open door to the kitchen Prabhupada saw that Malati had placed dirty milk bottles next to the deities’ silver tray.

‘You didn’t notice?’ She had no idea what he meant. ‘See where you have put the milk bottles. I am training you to be a *brahmana,* but still you haven’t learned.’

‘I’m sorry, Prabhupada.’ She hurried back into the kitchen.

‘This box has made fools of us all. Turn it off. They did not land on the moon.’ As Malati returned to her work in the kitchen he called after her. ‘Our Malati making *kachoris* and offering them to Krishna is far more significant than their so-called going to the moon.’

The day after he settled into the Baker Street apartment Prabhupada set the opening date for the new temple for 14th December. The building at Bury Place was tall and narrow – six floors (including the basement) with a central stairwell climbing the full height of the property, so that it was possible to stand on the top floor and yell down to someone in the entrance hall. Its new residents got plenty of exercise racing up and down the stairs as the pace of work increased.

The kitchen and dining room were in the basement, and the temple room was on the ground floor, its large arched windows opening onto the street. Above was Prabhupada’s room, with tall windows that admitted plenty of light. Next to it was a bathroom and a room for his assistants. The second floor was reserved for the women. Here Yamuna established a sewing and storage room for Radha and Krishna’s paraphernalia. The men’s quarters were above, and the office on the top

He wrapped himself against the morning chill with a black overcoat.

In September 1968 they found their first refuge at 80 Herne Hill.

Site of the former Arts Lab, 182 Drury Lane, where they chanted.

22 Betterton Street, where they made their home in November 1968.

7 Bury Place, home of the London Radha Krishna Temple, 1969–1979.

With their instruments they posed for a group portrait in front of Jagannath's altar. (Left to right, standing: Gurudas, Shyamsundar; below: Yamuna, Kulashekara, Malati, Mukunda, Janaki)

Below: At the Roundhouse they sat in a circle round a sacred fire, joined by many hundreds of chanters. Incense filled the air, and bells, drums, and guitars sounded from all sides to accompany their chanting.

In February the IT carried a photo of Mukunda, Gurudas and Shyamsundar (upside down) chanting in Hanover Square.

Photographed in February 1969 in their Betterton Street temple, Malati with Saraswati, Shyamsundar, and Gurudas.

George Harrison at home rehearsing, (below) with Mukunda playing harmonium.

Listening to the playback at Abbey Road Studios, 7 July 1969. George at his psychedelic harmonium, Yamuna seated in the centre, on her left Shyamsundar, and behind him Kulashekara. Malati kneels beside the gong.

Apple publicity shot for the 'Hare Krishna Mantra', taken by Gurudas at Abbey Road Studios. (Left to right: Mukunda, Yamuna, Pritha, Kulashekara, Malati, Shyamsundar, George)

Clive Arrowsmith's portrait of the Radha Krishna Temple, commissioned by Apple for the record sleeve of the 'Hare Krishna Mantra'. (Left to right, standing: Gurudas, Janaki, Tirthapada, Shyamsundar; kneeling: Trivikrama; seated: Digvijaya, Malati with Saraswati, Mukunda, Kulashekara, Ramatanu, Vishakha, Yamuna)

Above: The 'Govindam' single, released by Apple in March 1970.

Left: IT carried a full-page ad.

At the Sydenham Hill press launch George sat on the grass with the devotees, chanting and posing for photographs. To his left Dhananjaya looks on.

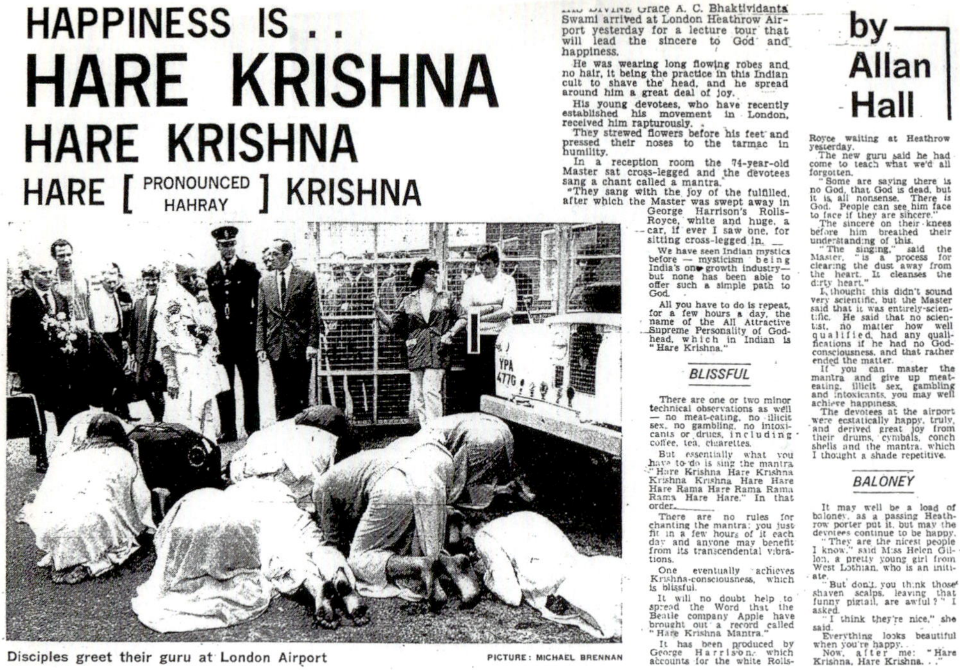

HAPPINESS IS . .
HARE KRISHNA
HARE KRISHNA
HARE [PRONOUNCED HAHRAY] KRISHNA

by Allan Hall

HIS DIVINE Grace A. C. Bhaktividanta Swami arrived at London Heathrow Airport yesterday for a lecture tour that will lead the sincere to God and happiness.

He was wearing long flowing robes and no hair, it being the practice in this Indian cult to shave the head, and he spread around him a great deal of joy.

His young devotees, who have recently established his movement in London, received him rapturously.

They strewed flowers before his feet and pressed their noses to the tarmac in humility.

In a reception room the 74-year-old Master sat cross-legged and the devotees sang a chant called a mantra.

"They sang with the joy of the fulfilled, after which the Master was swept away in George Harrison's Rolls-Royce, white and huge, a car, if ever I saw one, for sitting cross-legged in.

We have seen Indian mystics before — mysticism being India's one growth industry—but none has been able to offer such a simple path to God.

All you have to do is repeat, for a few hours a day, the name of the All Attractive Supreme Personality of Godhead, which in Indian is "Hare Krishna."

BLISSFUL

There are one or two minor technical observations as well — no meat-eating, no illicit sex, no gambling, no intoxicants or drugs, including coffee, tea, cigarettes.

But essentially what you have to do is sing the mantra "Hare Krishna Hare Krishna Krishna Krishna Hare Hare Hare Rama Hare Rama Rama Rama Hare Hare." In that order.

There are no rules for chanting the mantra: you just fit in a few hours of it each day and anyone may benefit from its transcendental vibrations.

One eventually achieves Krishna-consciousness, which is blissful.

It will no doubt help to spread the Word that the Beatle company Apple have brought out a record called "Hare Krishna Mantra."

It has been produced by George Harrison, which accounts for the white Rolls-Royce waiting at Heathrow yesterday.

The new guru said he had come to teach what we'd all forgotten.

"Some are saying there is no God, that God is dead, but it is all nonsense. There is God. People can see him face to face if they are sincere."

The sincere on their knees before him breathed their understanding of this.

"The singing," said the Master, "is a process for clearing the dust away from the heart. It cleanses the dirty heart."

I thought this didn't sound very scientific, but the Master said that it was entirely scientific. He said that no scientist, no matter how well qualified, had any qualifications if he had no God-consciousness, and that rather ended the matter.

If you can master the mantra and give up meat-eating, illicit sex, gambling and intoxicants, you may well achieve happiness.

The devotees at the airport were ecstatically happy, truly, and derived great joy from their drums, cymbals, conch shells and the mantra, which I thought a shade repetitive.

BALONEY

It may well be a load of baloney, as a passing Heathrow porter put it, but may the devotees continue to be happy.

"They are the nicest people I know," said Miss Helen Gillon, a pretty young girl from West Lothian, who is an initiate.

"But don't you think those shaven scalps, leaving that funny pigtail, are awful?" I asked.

"I think they're nice," she said.

Everything looks beautiful when you're happy.

Now, after me: "Hare Krishna, Hare Krishna. . ."

Disciples greet their guru at London Airport

PICTURE: MICHAEL BRENNAN

Prabhupada's arrival at Heathrow airport, as reported in *The Sun*, 12 September 1969.

In front of the waiting press, he chanted with abandon.

Saraswati saw him and ran out to catch hold of his hand (watched by Devaki and Malati).

Prabhupada stayed in two small rooms at the garden cottage.

His door would be open for anyone to come and talk informally.

George arranged with John and Yoko to speak with Prabhupada.

Pattie, Yoko, George, Shyamsundar, and John sat together for the feast.

Early in the morning, as daylight broke through the mist at Tittenhurst, Prabhupada walked under the dew-dripping trees.

The gallery, originally a music room, had a high ceiling and good acoustics. John Lennon let them use it as their temple while they were staying at Tittenhurst.

November 1969 was unusually cold, bringing snow and ice. He took his morning walks wearing a pink woollen balaclava knitted for him by Yamuna.

Each morning Prabhupada walked in Russell Square, just round the corner from the British Museum.

A large crowd filled Oxford Town Hall. While Mukunda played the organ to accompany the chanting, Prabhupada danced gracefully, his robes swaying.

At Conway Hall in Holborn, he lectured weekly, his first public talks in London. Then he led kirtan and the devotees danced on the stage.

In Amsterdam airport he rested his hands on his cane and smiled.

Prabhupada's first talk at Conway Hall was 'Teachings of the *Vedas*'.

He unveiled the deities to reveal Radha and Krishna's pale beauty enhanced by intricately painted jewellery and robes edged with filigreed gold leaf.

In those last few days of 1969 his room was never empty.

He sat on his new *vyasasana* for the first time and softly chanted.

As the new girl from France listened to his lectures, she found that, although she had difficulty understanding spoken English, she clearly understood his every word.

On Sunday 14 December Radha and Krishna appeared in London. There followed six days of feasting, during which people crowded in to see them.

The day he left he gave away the sweaters and scarves he had accumulated in the last four months, and everyone went to the airport to see him off. To Prabhupada's right are Malati and Kshirodakshayi, to his left Pritha and Mondakini. Jyotirmayi is on the right of the picture squeezed between Shyamsundar and two unidentified *brahmacharis*.

The sankirtan party in Hyde Park – they went out chanting three times a day. (Left to right: Harivilasa, Purandar, Tamal Krishna, Mondakini, Malati, Jyotirmayi, unknown, Yogeshvara, Ilavati, Jaihari, Yamuna, Devadatta, Dhananjaya, Umapati, Shyamsundar)

Yamuna sewed a new set of deity clothes, dark blue with silver and gold trim, for the feast of Sri Advaita in mid-February. That day they had a wonderful festival.

floor, along with a small room for Gurudas and Yamuna. In November the renovation work was far from finished, with sawdust and tools everywhere, but the devotees moved in anyway.

Yamuna's first task was to decorate and finish Prabhupada's room so he could move in as soon as possible. She chose blue – the colour of Krishna – as the dominant colour. She fitted the windows with dark blue velvet curtains that reached from floor to ceiling, and Prabhupada's seat had a pillow, bolster and cushions, all in matching blue velvet. She painted the walls and woodwork white. She brought in a low table to serve as Prabhupada's desk and placed shelves for his books beneath the windows on either side of his seat. His bed, simply constructed from a wooden board on six legs, went behind the door. She provided another small low table for his meals, and to heat the room she found a traditional gas fire, which she painted blue.

PUBLISHING KRISHNA BOOK, 14TH NOVEMBER 1969

With only a few weeks to go before the temple opening Prabhupada came daily to Bury Place to see the progress. Shyamsundar was busy.

'I'm sorry for all the noise, Prabhupada.'

'No need to apologise. Noise means something is coming,' he said.

Shyamsundar was racing to finish the building on time, but he was running out of money. Although they still had no deities, he had designed an altar to hold a large marble slab. He had hinted to George that he had no marble and George had volunteered to pay for it. He had a sculptor friend, he said, David Wynne, who would take them to his marble dealer and help choose a suitable piece. The night before they were to go, Prabhupada stayed late at Bury Place, upstairs in his room, while Shyamsundar was working downstairs. Everyone else had gone to bed. Prabhupada called for Shyamsundar. On his desk some documents lay in a pool of light.

'So, you are going to see George tomorrow?'

'Yes, Prabhupada. We're going to choose the marble.'

'I have one request. This is the completed manuscript for our *Krishna* book. See these?' He spread out a collection of large transparencies.

Shyamsundar studied them; they showed exquisite paintings illustrating the pastimes.

'Our artists have painted more than fifty pictures. These transparencies just arrived today from Boston. For months I have been waiting for these. Now we are ready to publish but we don't have the funds. We have now two books – *Bhagavad-gita As It Is* and *Teachings of Lord Chaitanya*, and soon *The Nectar of Devotion* – but we really need this *Krishna* book. It is very important. I want you to ask George to pay to publish this book.'

Shyamsundar froze. He tried to explain that to ask this of George was not a good idea. 'The way I've always worked with George is I've never asked him for anything. I wait until he volunteers. That's why we've been so successful.'

'Yes, I understand.'

'How much will it cost?'

'Nineteen thousand dollars.'

'Prabhupada, that's a lot of money. I really don't think. . . .'

'You can just tell him this is my request,' Prabhupada reassured him. 'Krishna will help you. You will see.' Shyamsundar always completely trusted Prabhupada, but this suggestion filled him with doubt. Nevertheless he resolved to do his bidding.

The next day as planned they chose a piece of yellow sienna marble, richly veined with ochre and cream and weighing about half a ton, and three smaller blocks of blue granite for the steps in front of the altar. All the time Shyamsundar dreaded asking the question. What would he do when George said they were just like all the rest?

The day ended at David Wynne's house in Wimbledon, where they had dinner with his family. During the meal Shyamsundar put off the inevitable moment. Outside the sky darkened, and in the distance could be heard the rumble of approaching thunder.

At the end of the meal came a pause in the conversation as they sat round the table in mutual satisfaction. Shyamsundar would have to leave in ten minutes, so he gathered his courage.

'George, Prabhupada wants me to ask your help. He has finished the manuscript for a wonderful book telling all the stories about Krishna, and his disciples have painted the most beautiful illustrations for it – more than fifty of them. Now he wants to publish. He asked me to ask you personally if you would pay for the printing.' George looked back in surprise.

'How much is it?'

'It's nineteen thousand dollars, George.'

George looked shocked. He had got them a recording contract, recorded their chant, helped them get their building, just paid for the altar, and now he was being asked for what was a great deal of money, even for him. He sat in stony silence.

Seconds ticked by as the sound of the storm grew louder. Suddenly, with a crash, a bolt of lightning struck just outside the house and the lights went out. For a few moments they sat in darkness, then the lights came back on. To his relief Shyamsundar saw that George had a huge grin on his face.

'After that, what can I say?' It seemed Krishna had helped just as Prabhupada predicted.

A few days later, at Prabhupada's invitation, George came in a humble mood to talk about the book. He explained how people regularly asked for his money. Prabhupada listened to his concerns with sympathy, then showed him the paintings, and George spent a long time going through them one by one. When he learned how much the book meant to Prabhupada, he gave up all resistance.

'I love these people,' he told him. 'I would rather be with them than anyone else. I live in two worlds – my associates and friends in the music world and my Krishna friends. I would rather be with the Krishna people all the time.'

'You don't need to do that,' answered Prabhupada. 'Simply keep Krishna in your heart and realise that everything you're doing is for him.' George felt a real love for Prabhupada.

'Should I become your disciple?'

'No, carry on in your own way and glorify Krishna through your music.'

Before George left he agreed to write a foreword for the *Krishna* book.

'George is more than my disciple,' Prabhupada told Shyamsundar later. 'He is my very own son.'

Prabhupada had much to accomplish. He was pushing to get his core books written and published, laying the foundation teachings of Krishna consciousness for generations to come. That very day, preserving George's anonymity, he wrote to his trusted editors at the newly formed ISKCON Press in Boston.

> Here some respectable friend has promised to publish my book, *KRSNA*, in two parts. The manuscript is also ready. So I want to take up this work immediately...[1]

> The size should be 7" × 10". Please give me the actual expenditure for printing 10,000 Krishna books, four hundred pages including fifty colour pictures. It is essential for me to know this because the friend who wants to publish this book should be informed about the cost of production within a week.[2]

George fully intended to write the foreword, but when it came to putting pen to paper he faltered. He just could not find the words. Friends were criticising his affiliation with the devotees, and he was uncertain about publicly attaching his name to the book.

'Why should anyone buy it just because of *my* name?' he asked Shyamsundar. 'Suppose they don't like me? They might be put off.' But he had given Prabhupada his word. So three months later, when the deadline could no longer be avoided, he turned to Shyamsundar for help.

'Help me write it, Shyam,' he pleaded. 'I want to make sure it's right.' The two collaborated on a simple statement inviting the reader to experiment with Krishna consciousness. George added his signature at the bottom.

'ALL YOU NEED IS LOVE (KRISHNA),' he wrote, then 'HARI BOL' and his signature dated 31/3/70.

As a result of Prabhupada's determination and George's generosity, and with much hard work in Boston, *KRSNA, The Supreme Personality of Godhead* was printed in two volumes in Japan the following year.

The work totalled 750 pages and had over one hundred gorgeous, full-page colour paintings.

FINDING KRISHNA, 2ND DECEMBER 1969

Yamuna had been praying for large Radha and Krishna deities ever since she had seen some at the Hindu Centre when she had first arrived in London a year earlier. She still remembered her first sight of them. She had been led into a back room where a pantheon of three-foot-high marble deities were arranged around three sides of the room. The sight staggered her. The instant she saw, in the midst of the crowd of divine forms, Radha and Krishna resplendent in white marble, she knew they must have deities like them for their London temple.

She convinced the others that they should start a fund-raising campaign. They placed collecting cans for the new Radha-Krishna temple in all the offices on every floor of India House, home of the Indian High Commission in London. Once a fortnight someone would empty them, but after several months they had only collected £42, which she kept in a safe place. Then one day the van broke down and Shyamsundar insisted she hand the money over to pay for its repair.

Yamuna was crestfallen and wrote to Prabhupada about her desire for the deities. He said never mind, Krishna would come, so she kept her mind set on them.

That summer Mukunda was sent eighteen-inch wooden Radha-Krishna deities, carved by Gaurasundara in San Francisco. But they were plain and unadorned, and Yamuna thought them rather crudely made. Nevertheless, up to late November they were the only Radha-Krishna deities they had.

Now Yamuna was preparing for the deity installation, which was only weeks away. At that time, their plan was to go ahead and install Jagannath, Subhadra, and Balaram. Yamuna had given up hope of white marble Radha-Krishna deities. Prabhupada suggested they cast Gaurasundara's wooden deities in bronze, and Mukunda was planning to do that in time for the opening. However, neither Prabhupada nor anyone else was really happy about this solution. So they put out word across the Hindu community of London that they were searching for deities of Radha and Krishna, and if anyone knew of any they should telephone. They gave Janaki's number, because she was always near the phone.

In Germany 'Hare Krishna Mantra' had been riding high in the charts. A call came from their agent, who wanted the Radha Krishna Temple to tour Germany, including a visit to the Star Club, the famous Hamburg nightspot where seven years earlier the Beatles had started on their road to fame. As well as promoting their record and earning money it would be an opportunity to visit the Hamburg temple and help the devotees there. Tamal was excited to go because this would be the start of the wider assignment given him by Prabhupada to push on the sankirtan movement in the capitals of Europe. At first, when he heard about the trip, Prabhupada considered going himself to install the small Radha-Krishna deities he had kept for just such an eventuality – the ones that Yamuna had painted for him at Tittenhurst. Then he decided that his presence was needed in London, so he deputed Tamal Krishna and Yamuna to conduct the installation on his behalf.

That summer in Los Angeles, on 23rd June, Prabhupada had installed the movement's first Radha-Krishna deities. Tamal Krishna had been there and observed the ceremony, in which the small brass images were bathed and dressed for the first time before being permanently installed on the altar. Now Prabhupada went through the procedure with them – Tamal would perform the fire ceremony and Yamuna would bathe and dress the deities.

The group left for Germany with Radha and Krishna on 20th November, crossing at Dover. Their first stop was the Star Club in Hamburg. They found the place run down and dirty, but they set up an attractive altar on the stage with a framed poster of Gopala Krishna, and sat in front of it beneath the glare of the spotlights. The audience, sitting with drinks on their tables in the darkened dance hall, must have found the devotees, with their flowing robes and exotic instruments, a curious act in such a setting. Yet they warmed to them and liked their music. By the end some of the patrons were chanting and had even gone to the dance floor to gyrate to the mantra. After their two performances, though, the devotees were glad to leave.

The next day they met up with their brothers and sisters, including Kulashekara and Vishakha, at the Hamburg temple, and together they toured universities and clubs in Munich, Frankfurt, and Kiel. In each city they chanted on the streets and sold copies of the German *Back to Godhead.* Their stage appearances earned them enough to make the trip profitable.

While they were away, Prabhupada continued the search for deities. He wrote to Gaursundara, who was working to start a centre in Hawaii. He was the one who had carved Mukunda's wooden deities. He told him about the German expedition.

> Just now they have got four days in Germany. More than one half dozen devotees have gone there, and they will also install the Radha-Krishna murtis. What did you do with the murtis you received from Calcutta?[3]

The high point of their tour was a concert in the Krüger Club, an old dance hall in Kiel. More than a thousand young people crowded into the dilapidated ballroom expecting a three-hour concert. The devotees were apprehensive, for they only knew three songs. A German devotee, Suchandra, introduced the audience to the Hare Krishna mantra, asking them to repeat it after him. Soon, with the benefit of their large banner with the mantra written on it, they had the whole audience chanting. The same thing happened as had occurred previously at the Avalon in San Francisco and the Royal Albert Hall in London: the entire assembly erupted into ecstatic chanting and dancing. So eager was the audience that they wouldn't let the devotees stop, and again and again insisted on an encore. At the end of each extended kirtan, when the devotees bowed to the floor to say their customary closing prayers, the audience imitated them by dropping to the floor and bowing down, then got up and asked for more. After three hours the devotees were exhausted. They signed many autographs and excused themselves, leaving a record of the Hare Krishna mantra playing over the sound system to cover their exit.

They returned to Hamburg for a grand festival to install the deities. Tamal Krishna performed a fire sacrifice as Prabhupada had taught him, and Yamuna bathed and dressed Radha and Krishna and supervised the setting up of the altar. Thus, on 23rd November, Europe's first Radha-Krishna deities were installed in Hamburg. Kulashekara and Vishakha took up the daily worship, and the London group returned to England. ISKCON now had two temples where Radha-Krishna deities were worshipped.

However, Radha and Krishna had still not appeared in London and Prabhupada was deeply concerned. It was just two weeks before the scheduled installation, and Shyamsundar had yet to start building the altar. Yamuna had only a vague idea of Shyamsundar's plan, and no measurements with which to start sewing deity clothes, so she put her energies into sewing for Jagannath. When the slabs of marble were delivered she was puzzled: Shyamsundar was planning an altar for much larger deities than anyone expected.

Then Janaki took a phone call. A Hindu gentleman named Goyal called to say he had three-foot-tall white marble deities of Radha and Krishna at his home which might be suitable for a temple. He wanted Prabhupada to come and see them. Janaki told Mukunda, who drove to Mr Goyal's house with Tamal Krishna. There they saw the most perfect images of Radha and Krishna they had ever set eyes upon. Krishna had a bluish cast and fine vertical lines on his forehead. Radha smiled by his side. They rushed back to Baker Street to tell Prabhupada.

'Bring me my coat,' he said.

With Shyamsundar driving and Tamal Krishna and Mukunda riding in the back, Prabhupada set off in the temple van to Mr Goyal's house in Stratford. The East London Hindu Centre had ordered deities from India, but the tip of Radha's finger had been chipped in transit. According to orthodox Hindu tradition this meant they could not be worshipped. Mr Goyal, the temple secretary, had them at his home.

They were shown into the living room. There in the corner stood the deities, covered by cloth. Mr Goyal wanted to reveal them straight away but Prabhupada sat in a relaxed mood and began a long and cordial conversation with him and his family. They talked in Hindi and soon they were laughing, while Prabhupada's disciples sat in silence. An hour went by and Prabhupada's foot started vibrating up and down, which happened when he got excited. All at once he was telling one joke after another and they were all laughing together. Suddenly he got up.

'Let us see them,' he said, and led the way across the room.

The cloth was removed. Shyamsundar gasped, but Prabhupada betrayed no emotion.

'Do you think your temple can use them?' asked Mr Goyal.

'Yes, I think we can,' replied Prabhupada in a noncommittal way. Then he turned to Shyamsundar. 'Can you lift Krishna?' And to Tamal, 'Can you lift Radha?' They each took hold of the figures and raised them carefully. They were solid marble and extremely heavy, but the two young men appeared to lift them easily.

'Then each one take and we'll go. Thank you so much.'

Mr Goyal appeared to be changing his mind. 'We will bring them round to the temple in a few days,' he stammered.

'That's all right, we can manage. We have our own transport,' said Prabhupada. 'Shyamsundar, Tamal, take them out to the van. Go on, go ahead.'

Mr Goyal anxiously watched Krishna leaving as Prabhupada kept talking in Hindi. All of a sudden they were outside, carefully placing the deities in the back of the vehicle and climbing in with them, while Shyamsundar closed the doors and got in the driver's seat. Prabhupada emerged from the house in a convivial mood, shaking hands with Mr Goyal and smiling.

'But wait,' Mr Goyal was protesting.

'It's alright, we will look after them,' Prabhupada assured him, and he too got into the van.

'Now drive,' he ordered Shyamsundar.

Off they went, Tamal and Mukunda clutching the deities to make sure they didn't fall over. Shyamsundar drove until they were out of sight, then Prabhupada told him to stop. He got out, went round the back, and opened the doors. There in the road he bowed before Radha and Krishna, palms together, and recited prayers from the *Brahma-samhita*.

'*Govindam, adi purusham, tam aham bhajamy,*' he sang softly. 'Now Krishna has come.'

They were stunned. How had this happened? As they carefully drove back Prabhupada was thoughtful.

'Prabhupada, I think you have kidnapped Krishna,' Mukunda ventured at last, breaking the silence. Prabhupada chuckled.

'In my householder days I had a scheme to borrow a lot of money from the bank, but the bank manager refused. So I spoke to him for a long time and convinced him. He said, "Mister De, you should have been a politician."' They all laughed.

At Bury Place, Yamuna was waiting for their return, watching from Prabhupada's window. She saw the van pull up and the rear doors fly open. Out climbed the devotees carrying the deities. Prabhupada followed, as they brought them upstairs to his room. He entered, saw Yamuna waiting, and beamed at her.

'Your marble Radha and Krishna have come. Put them in the corner,' he gestured. 'Cover them with cloth.' Then he sat down with a huge smile on his face, eyes sparkling.

'Krishna wanted to come here all along. He has played a great trick. We were searching everywhere for him, but he was here waiting for us. Mr Goyal made so much effort to bring Krishna here for his Hindu Centre, but all the time Krishna wanted to come to us. This chip on Radha's finger was just Krishna's trick.' And he told them the story from the *Mahabharata* of how Arjuna had chosen Krishna and Duryodhana had chosen Krishna's army. Krishna had tricked Duryodhana so that he could be with his devotee Arjuna.

He instructed Yamuna to put a curtain around the deities. 'I will give you a key to my room. Only you will come in here. Now you prepare everything.' Then he went back to his apartment at Baker Street, and Yamuna started to sew the outfits.

Even while temple preparations were going on, calls kept coming for the Radha Krishna Temple to perform. The next day, Wednesday 3rd

December, the devotees topped the bill at a student concert in Queen's College, in the centre of Regents Park.

Prabhupada wrote letters to his godbrothers in India proudly announcing the imminent opening of the London temple. His first letter was to Sridhar Maharaj, his old friend and godbrother, who had all along encouraged his mission in the West. His letter emphasised how the temple fulfilled the long-cherished desire of their own Prabhupada, Bhaktisiddhanta Saraswati.

> Srila Prabhupada desired that a temple should be established in the centre of London, so you will be pleased to know this is going to take place on the Odana Shasthi Day, December 14th, in a 5-storey house situated in one of the most important quarters of Central London, in the vicinity of the British Museum and London University. It is very, very respectable quarters, and we have invited many hundreds of people, both Indians and Europeans, in this ceremony which will continue from the 14th till the 21st of December 1969. I am submitting herewith our humble invitation for your blessings.[4]

In his letter he also asked Sridhar Maharaj to help him acquire land in West Bengal. Even though he was on the brink of a historic step forward in London, he was not content to rest: he was meditating on his ambition to establish a major centre for his movement in its spiritual homeland, Mayapur, birthplace of Sri Chaitanya. And his plans did not stop there. He had five sets of brass Radha-Krishna deities waiting to be shipped from India. Once Radha and Krishna were installed in London he planned to go straight to Boston and install them there too.[5]

Work at Bury Place intensified. In the basement kitchen they were preparing for seven days of feasting. On the ground floor Shyamsundar worked flat out on the temple ceiling. Everyone implored him to simplify his design, but he insisted that the temple be both an expression of Krishna devotion and a cultural statement. Prabhupada backed him up. From their top floor office Gurudas and Mukunda sent out invitations and called their contacts in the media. They managed to book a BBC news team for the big day. Tamal visited Hindu supporters to raise the extra funds needed to finish everything and stage the opening. Trivikrama led out the daily *harinam* and increased the sales of magazines.

In the sewing room on the second floor Yamuna confronted the task of dressing the new deities. Radha and Krishna already had exquisitely detailed clothes carved and painted on them, and she had no idea how else they should be adorned.

'Dress them as in the Brijbasi prints,' Prabhupada told her, referring to the traditional Hindu posters. 'Bring me five saris in different shades of yellow and gold and I will show you.' She hurried out to find the saris. He selected two that were sympathetic in colour and showed her what to do. 'Krishna should wear a *dhoti,* shirt, and shawl, and Radha should wear a pleated skirt, blouse, and veil.' She bought costume jewels and buckram and made crowns similar to the ones already carved on the figures, with matching necklaces, bracelets, and ankle bells.

In the last week before the installation devotees were so caught up in service that they slept no more than a few hours a night. Their energy came from sheer exhilaration as they neared their goal.

Shyamsundar was put in charge of repairing Radha's hand. Through George he asked for help from the sculptor David Wynne, who came and made the repair. On the morning before the installation, workmen came and laid a deep purple carpet in the temple room – another gift from George. Shyamsundar put the marble altar in place. The yellow sienna formed the main slab, mounted two feet off the floor on blocks of redwood, and the three oblong pieces of granite lay in front as steps. Behind the altar he lined the wall with plain redwood panelling, the natural wood contrasting with the highly polished marble. Above the main altar he fixed a two-inch-thick redwood shelf, firmly supported by two sturdy columns, to bear the three Jagannath deities. Dark purple curtains were hung in front of the altar to divide it from the main room, and four spotlights were installed to illuminate the place where Radha and Krishna would stand.

Shyamsundar created a unique seat for Prabhupada, round like the pad of a lotus. He constructed it in solid redwood finished with broad strips of polished brass that curved around its tiered base. With a circular back upholstered in ochre-red velvet it stood to one side of the altar, giving Prabhupada a view of Krishna on his right and the worshippers on his left. By the time evening approached all was in place, except the deity umbrella, which would be suspended from two more columns that were to stand either side of Krishna. Shyamsundar promised that the overnight crew would install these.

When all was ready, on the eve of the installation, Prabhupada moved from Baker Street to his new room at Bury Place. He called everyone to meet in the temple for a special kirtan to invite Radha and Krishna to come. Flowers and candles were arranged on the marble altar and the lights dimmed. Each devotee knew he or she stood at the edge of a historic moment. They began chanting and waited for Prabhupada to arrive.

Prabhupada entered and sat on his new *vyasasana* for the first time. Mukunda garlanded him with white chrysanthemums. The devotees came forward one at a time to offer chrysanthemum petals at his feet, then place a flower on the marble where Radha and Krishna would stand.

Prabhupada closed his eyes and softly chanted the *mangala-charana* prayers before leading them in kirtan. This was the first time he had chanted in the new temple. Candles burned and incense sanctified the atmosphere. The building site was transformed into a magical place, ready for Krishna.

The kirtan flowed gently like the Ganges, soothing away their exhaustion. They felt like a family, with Prabhupada as father, who had struggled together and were on the verge of fulfilling a wonderful dream. This was what he had wanted all these years, ever since his spiritual master had expressed his hopes for a temple in London. When the kirtan ended, Prabhupada went to the altar, placed his own flower on top of his disciples', and bowed down with them.

After Prabhupada had gone upstairs to his room, they began their last nightshift, clearing away the remaining dust and wood shavings, decorating the redwood walls with flowers sent over by Apple, and starting to prepare the feast. In the early hours of the morning they thoroughly cleaned the temple and altar while Shyamsundar set in place the columns and umbrella. He was exhausted from weeks of lack of sleep. After staying up all night he disappeared upstairs to collapse into a deep slumber.

THE TEMPLE OPENS, 14TH DECEMBER 1969

As Shyamsundar was closing his eyes, a cold December dawn broke over London. The Sunday morning streets were empty save for a few pigeons and the occasional taxi driver on his way home. A BBC broadcasting van drew up outside the temple, and engineers began running cables into the building to power their lights and cameras. Soon a trickle of visitors started, and by ten the temple room was full of expectant guests.

In front of the closed curtains a printed cotton cloth had been spread over the carpet and on it were arranged two round stainless steel trays in which Radha and Krishna were to stand, a pink satin cushion beside them for Prabhupada, and a raised square bed of earth for the ceremonial fire. Assistants brought in bowls of honey, ghee, yoghurt, and milk. Chanting began as more guests squeezed in until the small room was packed. With the kirtan in full flow, Radha and Krishna were carried in, with Prabhupada following behind. The deities were positioned on the two trays, their forms hidden beneath creamy satin.

The freshly timbered temple, brightly lit by BBC floodlights, smelled of redwood sap mixed with incense, and the distinctive sandalwood aroma that Prabhupada always brought with him. The hues of his saffron robes and golden skin matched the heavily grained panels and pillars. At his side stood Radha and Krishna, the same height as his seated form.

He began with a short address, then unveiled the deities to a collective intake of breath. Krishna's upheld hands awaited his flute, while Radha held a lotus flower in her left hand and raised her right hand in blessing. Their pale beauty was enhanced by intricately painted jewellery and robes edged with filigreed gold leaf. As the devotees chanted, Prabhupada began to bathe them. Yamuna supplied the honey, ghee, yoghurt, and milk, which he poured alternately over Radha, then

Krishna. The liquids mixed as they flowed down the divine forms and collected at their feet. When the trays were full he wiped their forms, cleaning away the bathing liquids with warm water, then towelled them dry and garlanded them with fresh flowers. Next he bordered the small bed of earth first with fruits and flowers, then with sticks of burning incense, and built the sacred fire in the centre using splinters of wood fuelled by ghee. He carefully regulated the dancing flames while at the same time chanting Sanskrit prayers, one word at a time, so that everyone could repeat them after him.

The temple filled with smoke as the fire began to die down, and he directed the curtains to be parted momentarily so that Radha and Krishna could be carried through to the altar. As Purushottama and Tamal Krishna carefully manoeuvred Radha and Krishna into position, Prabhupada and Yamuna followed them through into the altar area and closed the curtains behind them, leaving all four of them together in the confined space.

At that moment, as Radha was being set on the altar, her bearer's elbow nudged one of the columns that supported the canopy. The column had not been fixed securely. It began to topple, and with it, the canopy. In an instant Prabhupada saw everything. With one hand he swept the candlesticks and arati paraphernalia from the bottom step, placed his foot on the step, and caught hold of Radha's raised right hand while with his other hand he held the column firmly in place. This happened almost before anyone else noticed the danger. Yamuna turned to see Prabhupada's mouth frozen in grim determination. Tiny droplets of perspiration had broken out on his brow. Just as the canopy began to slip Tamal Krishna caught it and calamity was averted.

Prabhupada ordered Tamal and Purushottama to leave. His eyes were blazing but his voice was steady and controlled. 'And take these with you,' he commanded, referring to the two loose columns and the canopy.

'Now dress them quickly,' he said to Yamuna, then left the deity room and went upstairs. During all this time the devotees in the temple room were conducting a roaring kirtan, and the crisis passed without anyone noticing.

Yamuna dressed the deities as fast as she could, then blew the conch to announce that Radha and Krishna were ready to be seen. To a tumultuous roar she swept open the curtains for the first arati. Guests stood on tiptoe to catch a glimpse of Krishna's smile and receive Radha's blessings. After a long kirtan a sumptuous feast was served to all.

So on Sunday 14th December, the feast of Odana Shasthi – the day when Jagannath puts on his winter clothes – Radha and Krishna appeared in London. As Prabhupada decreed, there followed six days of feasting, during which the curtains were kept open all day and people crowded in to see London's new Radha-Krishna temple.

Shyamsundar, hidden deep in the loft, slept for two days, then emerged refreshed. Only then did he hear how his altar had almost collapsed. He was devastated and went in to see Prabhupada.

'I tried my best. I'm sorry.'

'Never mind. Radha and Krishna didn't want a canopy anyway.'

Prabhupada could not be angry. He knew how hard Shyamsundar had worked. Even when Prabhupada was displeased with his disciples and occasionally reprimanded them, they felt his words more as a caress and a sign of love than as a punishment. He knew they had given their lives to serve him, so in the end he always forgave and encouraged them.

Outside the temple a large sign announced RADHA-KRISHNA TEMPLE (LONDON). Beneath it, beside the front door, Prabhupada instructed Mukunda to fix a brass plaque acknowledging Shyamsundar's dedication. It read: THIS TEMPLE WAS BUILT BY THE HARD LABOUR OF SHYAMSUNDAR DAS.

On the day of the installation, two French girls arrived with the small group of devotees who came from Paris. Monique was a nineteen-year-old student of ethnology at the Sorbonne. Since childhood she had prayed to God every night by all the Christian and Jewish names she knew to protect her and her family. Now, with her two school friends, Joelle and Evelyne, she was at university searching among the religions of the world for a truth that would satisfy her. The three of them were reading widely in Buddhism, Taoism, Shamanism, and the *Vedas*. Their readings had convinced them that they needed a guru, so they had been saving up to go to India together. Then they met Suridas. He and Umapati were early New York disciples of Prabhupada, now preaching in Paris. The two girls noticed that Suridas had a long lock of hair hanging down at the back of his head and that he was reading books about Krishna.

'I have a spiritual master,' he told them.

'Oh! We are looking for a guru.'

'My guru is Bhaktivedanta Swami. There is a book – the *Srimad-Bhagavatam*. Just by opening it you become completely liberated from material existence. And there is a mantra – Hare Krishna. If you chant it liberation is guaranteed.' Suridas invited them to the American Centre, where the devotees were holding weekly meetings. There the girls learned to chant and heard Umapati lecture. They thought the devotees were like angels, and they started chanting all the time. So it was that Monique and Joelle travelled with the devotees to London, hoping to meet a genuine guru. If Prabhupada turned out to be the one they were looking for, they had promised Evelyne they would come back and tell her all about him.

Monique walked into the crowded temple at noon, dressed for the first time in a sari. She found it a magical place, full of incense and singing. When Prabhupada came back down and entered the room she instinctively bowed down with the others. On her knees with her forehead to the floor she noticed right beside her two golden feet. Raising her head she looked up and saw Prabhupada. He appeared to her like the emperor of the world, yet humble – these two qualities together, humility and greatness. He sat on the *vyasasana* and began to chant Hare Krishna. He glanced straight at her and she felt him look into her soul as if he knew her better than she knew herself. It was an overpowering experience and she couldn't help the tears of both joy and sorrow that welled up from deep inside.

Each morning Prabhupada took his walk in Russell Square, just round the corner from the British Museum. Gurudas made sure everyone got a turn to go with him. A day or two after the installation he selected Monique and Joelle. It was December, and they followed close beside him beneath the bare plane trees in the cold dawn air. He stopped and looked directly at Monique. What would he say, she wondered – would she know he was her guru?

'Are you cold?' He gave a knowing smile.

It was a trick, she thought. Her esoteric reading had told her this was how a guru would test his disciple. Yet Joelle thought, 'He is worried that we are cold – that means he cares.'

That afternoon Yamuna arranged for the two girls to join some other guests in Prabhupada's room.

'What is your name?' he asked Monique. She was confused.

'I don't have a name,' she answered, thinking she had no spiritual name. Prabhupada laughed.

'Your parents did not give you a name? Don't worry, you will get a nice name.' She knew he understood her, and she felt accepted as his daughter. But his teaching of a personal God frightened her. She had learned from her books not to be attached to forms, either Krishna's or her own. What drew her, though, was that she liked to chant. When she chanted she felt bliss. She was becoming deeply attached to Krishna's names.

Gradually, as Joelle and Monique listened to his lectures they began to understand that they had nothing to fear. And Monique noticed something strange: it was usually difficult for her to understand spoken English, but when he lectured she clearly understood his every word. Could this be her guru? She had to know.

Something else was strange, too: it seemed he could read their minds. This was the first time either of them had encountered the philosophy of a personal God – previously they had been attracted to Buddhism. Now faced with these new ideas they had so many questions they were too shy to ask. Yet somehow, even before they voiced them, he understood and answered their questions. One by one, all their doubts about Krishna were cleared.

They asked each other, 'Do you think he's our spiritual master?'

'Maybe he is, but what about the personal approach to God?'

One day after the lecture a guest challenged Prabhupada. 'There is no God. Krishna is not God – we are *all* God!'

Suddenly Prabhupada was angry. He shouted the man down. Monique and Joelle were shocked. A holy man didn't get angry, they thought. Filled with fresh doubt they considered leaving. But the next morning Prabhupada invited them to his room. He asked them about themselves, how they were doing. He wanted to give them something to do, some service for Krishna.

'Do you know how to type?' he asked Joelle, who happened to be an expert typist. He asked if she would like to help type the French translations of his books. That meeting changed their minds. They saw that he cared about them and wanted to help them. They decided to stay for good. Afterwards they heard that Prabhupada had told Yamuna not to let the argumentative guest return because he was disturbing the devotees. They felt protected, and they gave themselves heart and soul to helping the temple.

For five days Monique and Joelle had Prabhupada's association, and on the sixth day were to be initiations. He had said in one lecture that initiation was the beginning of spiritual life. Nervously the two of them went to his room.

'I would like to start spiritual life,' ventured Monique, afraid to ask directly for initiation. He laughed and laughed.

'But you are already living spiritual life. You are sweeping the floor. You are washing the pots.' She was dismayed – she thought spiritual life would be more mystical than that.

He told Tamal Krishna, 'We should initiate these two girls. They are like flowers blowing in the wind.'

'They've only been here five days,' Tamal replied. 'Let me train them first.' Prabhupada deferred to him.

By the day of Prabhupada's departure Monique knew without doubt that he was her spiritual master. She feared she had lost her chance for initiation, but Tamal assured her it would not take long. She and Joelle resolved to stay at the temple, study, and practice, so that soon they could be initiated.

In those last few days of 1969 Prabhupada's room was never empty. A succession of visitors came – George brought friends, delegates arrived from the Anglican Church, Tom Driberg brought parliamentary colleagues, and Hindus with their families came to pay their respects.

The opening of the London temple marked a new phase. Suddenly the devotees were famous in an international city. Prabhupada considered London the central city of the world, a steppingstone from which to expand to other cities in Europe and beyond. He had already sent Kulashekara and Vishakha to Hamburg. Within a month he despatched Tamal Krishna to Germany and Paris and Tirthapada to Sydney.

Now that his immediate task in London was accomplished, he was confident to leave the temple in the hands of his married disciples.

'I find that my disciples combined together, husband and wife, are doing this preaching work so nicely,' he wrote on the eve of his departure from London. 'I am especially proud how my householder disciples are preaching Lord Chaitanya's Mission. This is a new thing in the history of the Samkirtan Movement.'[6]

Trivikrama had remained a staunch *brahmachari* and had continued to massage Prabhupada, a task which brought him ever closer to his teacher. One evening he listened to him lecture in front of Radha and Krishna on the role of the guru.

'The spiritual master is the representative of Krishna,' Prabhupada said.

Trivikrama had heard him say this before, but this time it was different: he was reminded that the person he massaged every day and felt so close to had a significance beyond his comprehension. Puzzling over this, he watched Prabhupada speak, his golden features shining under the spotlight against the ochre shadows of the redwood temple.

Trivikrama was transfixed by a vision of Prabhupada as Krishna's divine mouthpiece. The next day when he came to massage Prabhupada he wanted tell him what he had seen, but he couldn't find the words.

'I very much liked your lecture last night, Srila Prabhupada.'

'Oh? What part did you like?'

'When you said you are the representative of Krishna.' Prabhupada seemed to appreciate what he wanted to say.

'You also can represent Krishna,' he said in a matter-of-fact way. 'When you say "Krishna says" or "Prabhupada says" you are acting as Krishna's representative.'

Yet Trivikrama felt he still had so much to learn. One day a quarrel broke out on the stairs outside Prabhupada's room. One man shoved another and voices were raised.

'You heard this fighting?' Prabhupada exclaimed when Trivikrama came into his room. 'It is not at all Vaishnava, this demand to have your way regardless of consequences. A devotee is just the opposite – he is always humble.' He looked sharply at Trivikrama. 'I don't want you ever to fight with your godbrothers. Is that clear?' Trivikrama felt these words keenly: he knew he had an assertive nature and that Prabhupada wanted him to keep it in check.

As Prabhupada's final days in London slipped by, Trivikrama wanted to go on being his servant forever. He would like to have travelled with him, but he knew that was not going to happen. His service had already been promised to another devotee, Upendra, who was waiting in Boston.

'Srila Prabhupada, Purushottama says you're not going to be needing me when you go.' Prabhupada said nothing. So it must be true, thought Trivikrama. Usually so self-assured, he now felt uncertain. He put on a brave face.

'Well Prabhupada, I never met Upendra. Is he a nice devotee?'

'Yes,' Prabhupada smiled, understanding Trivikrama's feelings, 'but not as nice as you.'

These words stayed with him. He knew Prabhupada felt real affection for him, for the person inside that few people saw. These past three months had convinced him of that, and he felt a great debt of love.

Although Prabhupada would leave him here in London, he vowed he would never leave Prabhupada.

On 21st December Prabhupada was booked to fly to Boston. They would all feel his absence terribly, but things would carry on. They were planning another record with George and new adventures to open more temples across Britain and Europe.

The day he left, everyone was to go to the airport to see him off. Only Yamuna would stay behind to serve the deities. In his room Prabhupada gave away personal things, gifts such as sweaters and scarves that he had accumulated in the last four months. While the devotees waited for him in the van outside, he came down the stairs and went into the temple to say goodbye to Radha and Krishna.

There Yamuna waited alone, her heart pounding. He came in and stood before the deities who had come to him so unexpectedly. For a long time he looked at the beauty of Krishna's moonlike face and shining eyes, as Yamuna stood by. Then he stretched full length on the floor. At last he turned to her. He had taught her all she knew, and now he was leaving and she must carry out his teachings. She was distraught. But he gave her a promise. 'If you follow the instructions I have given you, you can go back to Godhead in this life.' Her eyes filled with tears as he turned and left.

CHAPTER 8

Call to India

After the installation of Radha and Krishna, Yamuna felt as if her feet hardly touched the ground. From two in the morning, when she rose to chant, until late at night when she put Krishna to sleep and closed the shrine for the night, she was busy seven days a week. The new girls could be of little help at first, for they had much to learn before they could receive the brahminical initiation necessary to enter deity service.

Shyamsundar and Malati moved in with George and Pattie to stay at their new country house, Friar Park in Henley-on-Thames. Janaki and Mukunda lived in Hackney. This left Gurudas and Yamuna to run the temple. Prabhupada had told them that the temple president should act like a father and his wife like a mother, and that's how they worked, caring for the young devotees as if they were their own family and fostering a spirit of love and trust in the temple community. He had done the same for them in San Francisco.

At the Arts Lab the previous year a seventeen-year-old Irish boy, Thomas Hegarty, had learned to chant Hare Krishna in the kirtans led by Yamuna. He and his older brother had been through a troubled upbringing in a succession of foster homes. Now they were living and working in London. Tom's overwhelming interest was the mystical, which he avidly read about whenever he could. He explored London's alternative spiritual groups and chanted Hare Krishna, but he missed Prabhupada's visit. One day in mid-January he was led to the temple.

On Portobello Road, amid the market stalls, Dhananjaya noticed the untidy, long-haired teenager watching the devotees with fascination. He spoke with him and learned he had no home of his own – he was crashing with friends.

'Why not stay with us?' suggested Dhananjaya, and he persuaded Tom to collect his few belongings and come with him to the temple. The next morning, having slept on the floor in the ashram, Tom asked Dhananjaya to shave his head.

Tom's tough upbringing made him a natural ascetic, and he found life in the austere men's quarters much to his liking. This was what spiritual life was meant to be, he thought. The rooms were bare, they slept on the wooden floor sharing a few blankets, the men's shower was a mere pipe projecting a jet of cold water, they even shared their clothes – and they chanted and served all day. He delighted in it all.

In Paris, waiting for her friends to return from London, Evelyne had continued to chant Hare Krishna and visit the devotees. When one of them told her that her friends would not be coming back she was devastated. She had set her heart on going with them to India. She wondered what they had found in London to make them change their minds. Then one day Monique came to find her. She arrived on Evelyne's doorstep and begged her to come with her back to London. Evelyne was hesitant, but her mother urged her to go.

'If you don't find out for yourself you will regret it all your life,' she told her.

So Evelyne went with Monique to the London temple. She had

missed the chance to meet Prabhupada, but by hearing about him from her friends and reading his books she learned to have faith in him, and she applied herself to the process of Krishna consciousness. Yamuna looked after all three friends like daughters, and passed on to them the devotion she had for Prabhupada by constantly talking about him and repeating the things she had heard him say.

For the new devotees life was exciting. There were hardships – the women, like the men, had to sleep on the bare floor until Shyamsundar built them bunks from the timbers of the old Rathayatra car – but Monique came to realise that even the simplest thing, like washing pots, was fulfilling when done to please Krishna.

Under Yamuna's guidance she and her friends wrote to Prabhupada requesting initiation. In February each of them received a letter from him addressed 'My dear daughter'.[1] He gave Monique a name, as he had promised he would. She had wanted to be named after a river, as Yamuna was, and to her joy he named her Mondakini, the goddess of the Ganges. Joelle had been attached to the impersonal white light before she had discovered Krishna, and Prabhupada named her Jyotirmayi, after the effulgent light from Krishna's body. He gave to Evelyne the name of the earth goddess Ilavati, which made her happy because she had always felt herself a down-to-earth person.

Umapati came over from Paris on a short visit and spoke with Evelyne. He had been attracted to Evelyne from the start. Now that she had received some training and been initiated he proposed to her. She accepted his offer and returned with him to Paris.

Not long after she left, her two friends in London were given second initiation, qualifying them to serve the deities. Jyotirmayi was assigned to help Digvijaya in the kitchen, while Mondakini became Yamuna's assistant and learned from her the art of deity worship.

Prabhupada stayed in constant touch with his disciples by letter. Not a week went by without at least one of them hearing from him.[2] He urged them to keep up their spiritual practices and to remember their duty to train the new members to do the same. 'I think Lord Chaitanya is planning a situation which will help us in pushing the Krishna Consciousness movement throughout the whole world,' he wrote to Shyamsundar. 'I therefore request you all to chant Hare Krishna mantra very rigidly sixteen rounds a day and thus be fixed up in your spiritual strength. Then everything will come out successful.'[3]

To Gurudas he wrote, 'Please see that the prescribed routine of temple activities is followed according to schedule, and all the members are chanting rounds daily sixteen.'[4] And to Yamuna: 'Advanced life in Krishna Consciousness means one should be always very much anxious to calculate whether every moment of his life has not been utilised in devotional service. This is called feeling of being afraid for misusing time ... Try to realise it yourself and teach the method to all your younger brothers and sisters.'[5]

The sankirtan party went out three times a day – morning, afternoon, and evening. Every morning they chanted the length of Oxford Street, and in the afternoons they went either to Oxford Street again or to one of the other major shopping streets, such as Kensington High Street or King's Road in Chelsea. In the evening some of them went out a third time, to Theatreland for the nighttime crowds.

This pattern of street chanting was set up by Tamal before he left for Germany. He insisted on them wearing a uniform shade of saffron, dancing in time in two swaying lines with the women in the middle. As the party proceeded slowly down the street the magazine sellers would move alongside, giving out *Back to Godheads* and incense sticks and accepting donations.

At night, when they braved the crowds converging on Piccadilly Circus, they had to contend with the police, who seemed intent on preventing them from performing their sacred duty. Frequently devotees were arrested and even held overnight in police cells. They learned to defend themselves in court, where magistrates usually dismissed their cases or let them off with a light fine. Once, when Tom was arrested, he lectured the policeman so movingly that the officer paid his fine for him.

One evening in Piccadilly Circus, at the end of a long day, Jyotirmayi fainted. Her friends were uncertain whether it was due to exhaustion or because she was in ecstasy from the chanting.

'I see you chanting in rain or snow,' George told them one day when he visited the temple. 'Always chanting up and down Oxford Street. Just seeing you there convinces me of Krishna consciousness.'

In the evenings when they came in from the streets Yamuna would have hot milk and bananas waiting for them, with special prasadam from Krishna's plate. Then Gurudas would sit up and tell stories of Prabhupada at Tittenhurst or the early days in San Francisco, or read to them from the still unpublished *Krishna* book manuscripts.

Daily classes educated the young devotees in the philosophy of Krishna consciousness and deepened their faith. Chanting Krishna's names, speaking of Krishna, reading about Krishna: there was no time to think of anything but Krishna.

One of Tom's duties was to scrub the kitchen floor. Yamuna had told him that cleaning Krishna's kitchen was as good as cleaning Krishna's altar. As he cleaned, meditating on her words, he felt so close to Krishna that once he ran outside with raised arms and shouted to the heavens, '*Haribol!*'

Tapes of Prabhupada's songs played all day. Devotees constantly talked about him. Gurudas distributed photos of Prabhupada, printed in his darkroom where he stored his collection of thousands of negatives.

Prabhupada's room on the first floor of the temple was kept exactly as he had left it, with fresh flowers on his desk and incense burning. No one could pass his door without remembering him. Because he was so present in everyone's thoughts, and because they were always striving to serve him, they felt he was still with them in the temple.

Yamuna found that Krishna's clothes no longer fit. Prabhupada wrote that she must have fed Krishna so well he had put on weight. Mondakini believed this to be true. When she helped Yamuna she felt she was personally serving God at last. This was the antidote to her impersonal ideas of merging into the white light, which were now giving way to constant thought of Radha and Krishna. She had needed deity worship to realise that God was a person.

With the girls' help Yamuna sewed a new set of clothes, dark blue with silver and gold trim, in time for the feast of Sri Advaita in mid-February. That day they had a wonderful festival, with the deities wearing their new outfit. Again the temple was packed, and they ran out of space to serve the feast. George brought five magnificent flower arrangements to decorate the temple. During the feast he consumed so many bowls of Yamuna's sweet rice that he eventually cried for her to stop refilling his bowl.

The musical collaboration with George continued, and in March the second Radha Krishna Temple recording – the 'Govindam' song they had rehearsed the previous year – was released by Apple and sent to Prabhupada. When it arrived in Los Angeles he asked that it be played in the temple before his morning lecture. In front of all the devotees he sat and listened and was unexpectedly overwhelmed. Tears started from his eyes, and when the music finished he sat silent and motionless except for a slight shivering. The devotees watched as a long moment passed before he opened his eyes and repeated the words of the song, '*Govindam adi purusham tam aham bhajami.*' He wrote to Shyamsundar, 'The record is so nice that I am playing it at least once in a day and it is giving me transcendental pleasure with tears in my eyes.'[6]

For a second time the Radha Krishna Temple had a single in the top twenty, and renewed bookings. One of their tours took them to France, where they stayed at a small country hotel outside Paris to record a TV feature and were filmed miming to their record in the open fields. The highlight of their French tour came when they chanted on stage at the Rainbow Festival near Amiens. A huge audience joined in – they all seemed to know the words of the Hare Krishna mantra – and afterwards surrounded the devotees asking for autographs and more chanting.

Around this time George decided to accompany them on an overnight dash to Paris to promote Krishna consciousness. He called a press conference at the Paris Ritz to speak about Krishna. But he had miscalculated. This was the first time a Beatle had visited Paris since 1964, and he was mobbed by reporters whose only interest was to find out whether the Beatles were breaking up. Outside, fans besieged the building. He felt trapped. Unable to speak about what really mattered to him, he escaped with the press in pursuit, and not a word about Krishna was ever reported.

In June they flew to Sweden with several famous rock groups for the Festival of the Midnight Sun, where Lena Engvall overcame her stage fright to speak in her native Swedish to the vast crowd, telling them about Krishna.

At the end of the summer Lena was initiated. She had been coming regularly to the temple, helping in the kitchen, and chanting with the devotees outside, but she was still working as an au pair. As soon as her six-month contract was up she said goodbye to the children she had been caring for and moved into the ashram. She was initiated with the name Lilashakti. On the same day Tom became Tribhuvanatha.

With the other devotees, they were regularly staying out late to chant in the nightclubs. People liked the devotees' chanting but were too distracted to hear their message, so the late nights were discontinued. The royalties from Apple and the appearance fees dwindled. They were no longer pop stars, and were forced to depend more and more on magazine sales and donations for their survival.

On 25th February the temple in Los Angeles moved into a large former church and set of community buildings on Watseka Avenue. Prabhupada declared this to be ISKCON's world headquarters and made it his base, where he would work on his books and train his leaders.

He told Mukunda he wanted the same in London: a large building that would establish the London temple on a par with the temple in Los Angeles. He recalled a redundant church they had seen on their visit to Oxford, and urged Mukunda to find out if it was available. He wanted centres opened in Manchester, Birmingham, Liverpool, and all over Europe. His letters kept reminding the devotees of his plan for a World Sankirtan Party. He asked the original devotees who had founded the London *yatra* to do what they could to strengthen and extend the movement into Europe, and then come with him to India in early 1971.

'We shall travel all over India with Samkirtan Party and thereby we will recruit many Indian sympathisers for this movement,' he wrote to Gurudas.[7] 'I shall ask you to go there with your wife and preach Krishna Consciousness among the Indian community. Sometimes you desired to go to India, and Krishna will fulfil your desire.'[8]

To Mukunda he wrote, 'The purpose of World Samkirtan Party will be to establish a centre in each and every city and village of the world. Why not first of all start a centre in Paris and a few other centres in Germany, and then think of the World Samkirtan Party?'[9] His ambitions for Lord Chaitanya's movement were summed up in a letter he wrote at this time to Umapati in Paris:

> My only hope is that even if I die these missionary activities will go on. And to keep yourself on the standard spiritual strength, please do not neglect the sixteen rounds chanting and follow the regulative principles. Try your best, and Krishna will help you in all respects.[10]

Shyamsundar embarked upon a second London Rathayatra. This time he made sure the chariot was sturdy. 'As strong as a warship,' he told Prabhupada, and in July the parade went without a hitch. Devotees gathered from across Europe, and at Prabhupada's suggestion used the opportunity to discuss plans for opening new temples. The popularity of their records in many countries, especially in Germany and Czechoslovakia, and the many letters they were receiving from fans, encouraged them to think boldly, as Prabhupada kept urging them.

> Just make a very rigid plan for opening centres in every nook and corner of the European countries.[11]

Prabhupada had looked forward to meeting them all again at Rathayatra in London, but instead he attended the Rathayatra in San Francisco. He wrote to encourage Shyamsundar, saying the best way to be together was through service in separation.

> Let us meet by samkirtan. I do not feel separation from my Guru Maharaj when I am engaged in his service. His pictures give me sufficient strength. To serve the spiritual master's word is more important than to serve him physically. Please try to open as many branches as possible in European countries.[12]

In August Prabhupada's plans were suddenly disrupted by a crisis of trust. He had come to suspect some of his American leaders of disloyalty. He reassigned some to travel and preach as *sannyasis,* and increased the managerial responsibility of others. On 28th July he constituted a twelve-man Governing Body to manage ISKCON, and created the Bhaktivedanta Book Trust to carry forward his book publication. After doing this he announced his intention to retire and devote himself to writing, and unexpectedly left Los Angeles, bound for India.

He stopped for three weeks in Tokyo to negotiate book-printing contracts, and reached Calcutta on 29th August. Two weeks later he called Yamuna, Gurudas, Shyamsundar, and Malati to come to India and assemble with a dozen other devotees to form his World Sankirtan Party. They made hasty preparations to leave London.

At Friar Park, as Shyamsundar was packing his things and preparing to say goodbye, George was putting the finishing touches to his first solo album. He had been working since May on recording the songs for *All Things Must Pass,* some of which were deeply influenced by his Krishna consciousness. He had told Gurudas that he didn't want to make 'nonsense records' any more. Prabhupada had suggested he sing about his feelings for Krishna, and in February wrote to him a theme based on one of his own favourites songs, *Hari Hari Biphale:* 'My dear Lord, I have simply wasted my human form of life … I fully surrender unto you. Please do not reject me as I have no other shelter.' In this mood of humility, George wrote 'Hear Me Lord', in which he asked forgiveness for 'those years when I ignored you' and help 'to love you with more feeling.' Prabhupada particularly wanted him to write in a mood of longing for Krishna in separation. In response he wrote what was to be his most popular song:

My sweet Lord, I really want to see you
I really want to be with you
I really want to see you, Lord
But it takes so long, my Lord

The chorus combined the Alleluia mantra with the Hare Krishna mantra, emphasising the one God with many names. His album, *All Things Must Pass,* was released in November, along with the single 'My Sweet Lord'. Within a week both records topped the charts in Britain and America.

Ever since Prabhupada had first talked about going to India in 1967, Yamuna had been preparing for this moment. She and Gurudas came on the expedition to London as part of that journey. Establishing the London temple had been the high point in her life, but now he was calling her to India and she would go wherever he led. She had trained Mondakini to look after the deities, so she passed her sacred responsibility to Mondakini and Lilashakti.

Prabhupada also called for Shyamsundar and Malati, with Saraswati, now two years old. But he asked Mukunda and Janaki to stay in London to oversee the temple.

After a frantic two weeks of preparation the World Sankirtan Party made a rendezvous in Brussels with a party of devotees who had travelled from America. Now twenty-strong, they flew to Bombay where Prabhupada joined them after a few days for the start of his Indian adventure.

Bereft of his closest friends, Mukunda found his new burden in London a heavy one. Janaki, lonely without her sister, fell into depression. Mukunda, at heart a musician, had borne so many responsibilities for Prabhupada since joining him in 1966. Now he needed time for himself and his wife. He asked Dhananjaya to become temple president, promising to come regularly to give advice, and withdrew from the day-to-day management.

So much had happened in the last two years. Now, overnight, the temple became a quieter place. The children of the fifties had left. For London's children of the sixties a new era was about to begin.

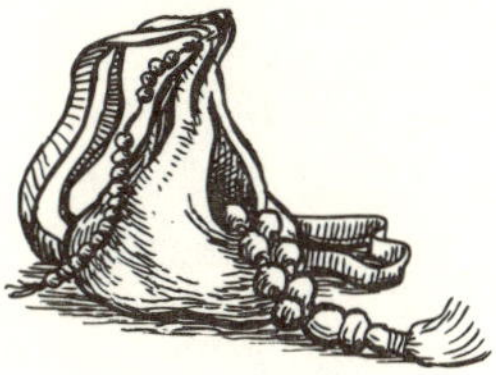

BOOK THREE

Growing Community
1970–72

CHAPTER 9

Youthful Temple

Winter turned to summer, and the young temple at 7 Bury Place filled with hopeful souls, most of them barely twenty years old, come to dedicate their lives to the service of Krishna. The kitchen, always short of money, strained to feed the growing family, and regular begging rounds kept them from starvation. Twice a week before sunrise two devotees wheeled an ancient trolley through narrow streets, past Betterton Street where the first temple had been, to Covent Garden Market. By five in the morning the market was already humming with activity. Here they competed with nuns from nearby convents in begging from stall to stall.

'Hey, Krishna! We got summat for yer.' Half mocking, half in affection, stall-holders called them to take a box of cauliflowers or a sack of potatoes, usually produce they couldn't sell.

The flower market, housed in its ornate cast iron Floral Hall, was the same. The flower sellers were friendly, and donated wilting blooms or bunches of greenery. The devotees set money aside each week to buy new flowers for garlands: if all they could beg was a consignment of rotten apples, they might live on stewed apples all week, but Radha and Krishna were offered fresh garlands every day without fail.

Despite this unreliable supply of ingredients, the kitchen did its best to maintain the high standard of cooking for the deities that Yamuna had learned from Prabhupada and faithfully passed on.

She and the other founding devotees who had gone to India were greatly missed. The community became further depleted when Digvijaya, one of the first English devotees, left to open a temple in Birmingham with his wife Pritha – Prabhupada wanted his married disciples to go to new cities and start centres – and when Lilashakti was sent to help in Hamburg. They also lost Dhananjaya, their newly appointed president and the oldest member of the temple, when he unexpectedly left to take charge of the small Amsterdam centre. Dhananjaya was replaced by an American devotee named Murari, who had come from San Francisco. None of this diminished the steady influx of new members. Among the ones who joined during the winter months were Pam, Serena, Jill, Jeff, Nicolas, Ian, and Milan.

Pam Borden came to London's cold winter from the sunny beaches of Hawaii. Searching for a deeper meaning in life she had moved from California to Hawaii and joined a group of suntanned young American men and women who followed a young yoga teacher named Sai. They lived near the beach and learned from him to chant Hare Krishna and follow Prabhupada's teachings. Pam became Sai's disciple and was named Gopala. In September 1969, Sai had surprised everyone by surrendering himself to Prabhupada. He disbanded his yoga group and instructed his followers to join ISKCON temples. Four of them, including Gopala, were sent to England, arriving at the Bury Place temple in December. Gopala found the austerities of the ashram and the long winter nights a trial, but she was comforted by the friendship offered her by Janaki and the excitement of being in London.

The day Gopala arrived she accompanied a party of devotees through Soho to meet George Harrison at a recording studio in Dean

Street. There they spent the evening adding tracks to songs already recorded by Yamuna and Mukunda. Gopala watched as George led proceedings from the control booth, with Mukunda as music director, putting the finishing touches to the Radha Krishna Temple album, soon to be released by Apple.

Gopala was determined to become Prabhupada's direct disciple. Within weeks of her arrival she wrote to him and asked for initiation. He wrote back, extendering her name to Bala Gopala and accepting her as his disciple. Before long she married Dhananjaya, who proposed to her while he was visiting from Amsterdam. In May the couple exchanged marriage vows in front of Radha and Krishna, with Mukunda conducting the fire sacrifice.

Bala Gopala phoned her parents in California to tell them the good news.

'But do you love him?' her mother asked anxiously.

'We love everybody, mom,' she replied innocently. They visited Dhananjaya's parents in Scotland then returned to Amsterdam, where she devoted herself to her new role as wife of the temple president.

Serena was the only daughter of a respectable middle-class family in Wimbledon. Her father was a quantity surveyor and a Freemason, who had always given her everything she wanted. From childhood she had felt a psychic connection to all living things, beginning with the wildlife in her garden.

At fourteen she discovered Eastern spirituality and became a vegetarian. She began to read books on Buddhism and Taoism, and dreamed of one day joining a Zen monastery in Japan. After leaving school she took a job at BBC Radio 1, where she made friends with famous DJs and attended rock concerts.

She was influenced by one of George Harrison's songs. 'Without going out of your door you can know all things on earth. Without looking out of your window you can know the ways of heaven,' he sang, straight from the Book of Tao.[1] She met members of the rock band Quintessence. They chanted on stage, using mantras accompanied by Indian-influenced music and dance. She learned to chant and dance with them. Then she met the devotees. First she saw them on television, then on Oxford Street. She started going to the temple for the Sunday feasts, and came more and more whenever she could.

Just after her eighteenth birthday Serena handed in her notice at work, left a note on the kitchen table, and ran away to the temple, bringing from home her potted plant and a little Indian table as a gift for Prabhupada's room. It was a sacrifice to give up her friends, her music, and her freedom, but she believed she had no choice: this was her spiritual duty, and would benefit her parents even though they were losing her. Once in the temple, she loved to go out chanting and learned to cook for Krishna.

Jill grew up between Tanzania, where her father was a government scientist, and boarding school in Oxford. As soon as she was old enough to leave school, she rebelled against her middle-class upbringing and sought the company of Oxford's hippie crowd with their radical politics, drugs, poetry, and jazz. She was a striking red-haired beauty, surrounded by admiring men, but inside she agonised over the meaning of life, forever asking, 'What is the point?' She became fascinated by Indian culture and philosophy, with its emphasis on the search for truth, and found some solace in yoga and George Harrison's music. She moved south to a hippie commune on Eel Pie Island in the Thames near Richmond. There she saw the hippie ideal, which had started as a dream of love and peace, corrupted by greed and money. She watched as her friends tried to force their way in upon the truth with hallucinogenic drugs, and concluded the attempt was artificial and premature since none of them were ready to understand it, let alone live by it. She went to the Isle of Wight concert, where she heard George Harrison introduce the Hare Krishna mantra to a huge gathering. That marked a turning point for her. A packet of Spiritual Sky incense directed her to the temple: it bore an invitation to morning meditation and a Sunday Feast. She came in search of answers, without her friends because they refused to accompany her. What she heard while sitting at the back of the temple during the Sunday lecture felt so right that it filled her with relief. At last she was getting answers to her questions about life. She concluded that she must have experienced Krishna consciousness in a previous incarnation. A month later she exchanged her hippie life for the temple ashram.

Nicolas Riddihough, from Birmingham, went to public school then art college. His search for truth led him to Canterbury where, in the shadow of the Mother Church of English Christianity, he founded an experimental art studio and tried to follow the ideals of Jesus. In London he had seen devotees chanting in Portobello Market and been fearful of their purity and divine rapture. With this haunting impression his interest in spiritual life grew. One of his friends taught him to chant Hare Krishna, and he visited the London temple, where he bought a copy of Prabhupada's *Bhagavad-gita As It Is*. Back in Canterbury he studied the book and knew he had found his spiritual guide and the knowledge he had looked for all his life. Soon afterwards, in January 1971, he joined the temple, bringing with him his savings of five pounds – which he handed over to fill the temple van's petrol tank on the day he arrived. At the age of twenty-six he was older than most of the others, and quickly became known for his bold preaching.

Ian Keill came to London after graduating from university in Edinburgh. He avidly read about mysticism and bought the incense made by the devotees. He also saw the invitation on the incense packets and thought of going one day to find out what it was all about. In a hippie shop he came across a copy of the *Krishna* book and was drawn to its beautiful paintings. He went to the temple and got some chanting beads. As soon as he started chanting, Krishna consciousness became real. He read a collection of Prabhupada's lectures published in a small booklet, *Krishna Consciousness: The Topmost Yoga System*. In a single night he found he understood more about life than through all his other reading put together: for the first time a spiritual book made sense.

Ian began coming to the temple every evening and dancing wildly during arati. After hearing the classes and getting to know the devotees, it wasn't long before he decided to move in with them – on the birthday of Lord Chaitanya. For a while he commuted from the ashram to his job as a factory production manager and donated his income to the devotees. But the temple incense business, then in its infancy, needed a manager, and with his manufacturing experience and dependability he was the best one to take it on. So in April he quit his job, gave away his possessions, and started running the business. From the temple he would drive all over the country, selling incense to local shops. The income was small but critical to the struggling community.

Milan Talukdhar was a Bengali man from Prabhupada's hometown, Calcutta. His father had paid for him to come to London to study engineering, but his real interest was spiritual life, and he was neglecting his studies. One day, after visiting the British Museum, where he liked to look at the statues and paintings of Krishna, he happened upon the temple. He was surprised to see, on the doorstep, a saffron-robed devotee polishing the brass door handle. He was familiar with the saffron dress of a *sadhu* in Bengal, but here in London it was to him an astonishing sight. The devotee was Jeff Coker, who had recently joined. Jeff invited him in and showed him Radha and Krishna. To Milan's eyes the devotees, with their bright and welcoming faces, seemed like divine beings, and he started to visit early each morning.

His father was pressuring him to return to India, and he feared disappointing his family. Then one of the devotees showed him a passage in the *Bhagavad-gita As It Is* where Prabhupada had written that one who surrenders to Krishna is freed from all other obligations.

'This is your culture,' the devotee urged him. 'Why don't you come and live with us and be a *brahmachari*?'

That evening Milan took a *Back to Godhead* magazine home to his bedsit, and when his fellow lodgers were asleep brought it out to read. It smelled of incense and its fragrance spread throughout his room. In the night he pondered the question put to him and felt a spiritual thrill.

At the temple Mondakini befriended him and made sure he always had prasadam. One day he brought her a small bunch of daffodils to offer to Krishna. It was all he could afford, but she appreciated his gift very much, and told him it was his duty to join the temple. So, feeling a little fearful, he took the plunge. His first day was spent out chanting with the devotees, and ended with them being chased by the police.

'Don't worry. Just depend on Krishna,' they laughed. 'He will look after us.' Milan found he believed them: his fears had vanished. Next morning he agreed to have his head shaved, and when he came down to the temple dressed in a *dhoti* all the young men and women, seeing in him an authentic Bengali devotee of Krishna, spontaneously broke into chanting and dancing. He felt he had joined a family, with Prabhupada as his father.

Digvijaya and Pritha were in Birmingham without any help, so it was decided to send Milan to assist them in preaching among the local Hindu population. There he spent many hours on his own trying to sell *Back to Godhead* magazines in the city centre, without much success. The temple was in a large haunted house in the suburb of Handsworth, at the deserted end of a street awaiting demolition. Sometimes, when he was there alone, he could hear a child's laughter, yet when he turned he saw no one. He chanted Hare Krishna and felt no fear.

One of the people Milan met on the street in Birmingham was Virasingham Kumarakonasingam, an Indian student from Malaysia studying at the local college of technology. Virasingam bought a magazine from Milan. The two made friends and Virasingam started visiting the Birmingham temple. He bought books, studied the philosophy, and helped with the chores, contributing toward the temple's upkeep from his meagre student allowance. One weekend he travelled with Milan down to London, where he too met Mondakini. She gave him a string of japa beads and taught him to chant. He saw how happy the devotees were and he sang and danced with them, wishing he could join the temple.

After Dhananjaya had gone to Amsterdam in November the temple was left in Murari's care, but Murari needed help. Prabhupada heard this and wrote to Mukunda, urging him to resume his responsibilities.

> I want that you and your good wife Janaki will develop the London temple, as it is one of our most important centres. London is the most important city in the world and as you originally opened this branch, it is my desire to see it come to full blossom under your expert management.[2]

Mukunda returned to being president, and Janaki agreed to help too, coming in daily with her husband to work with the young women in the temple. The biggest challenge Mukunda faced was the temple budget, which seemed to be in permanent crisis now the Apple royalties had diminished to almost nothing. A small daily income came from sales of magazines and incense. Morning and afternoon devotees would chant on Oxford Street, or further afield in Chelsea, Kensington, or Hampstead. On Saturdays they usually spent the whole day at Portobello Market among the crowds of shoppers and tourists, chanting, with incense burning, and offering magazines for a few shillings. But despite the sankirtan party's best efforts, rent was owing and utility bills were unpaid.

In the midst of these financial pressures the temple van, purchased with earnings from recording contracts, was repossessed. News reached Prabhupada of its loss, and in March he wrote to Mukunda again.

> I am very sorry to inform you that the London management is not going on nicely. I have received so many unfavourable reports.[3]

Mukunda tried to stay positive in the face of this rebuke. He had already begun looking for a larger temple, and despite the financial trials he continued his search. The idea had taken shape, encouraged by Prabhupada, to acquire land for a temple in Regents Park. It was based on the slender hope that the British government might be willing to make a plot available for a Hindu temple as they had done for the Regents Park Mosque. So Mukunda continued his efforts to keep the devotees inspired, pay the bills, and look for a new temple.

Then suddenly, one bright morning in May, came a terrible shock.

While devotees were busy with their services, a former associate of the temple named Robert, mentally unstable and wearing a flimsy silk *dhoti,* came to demand money. Mukunda, in his office upstairs, was in no mood to part with precious funds and tried to reason with him. White-faced, the man left the room and went down to the temple, coming before Krishna with a bunch of dead flowers. Mondakini had just finished performing arati. She saw his pale, tormented features and the dead flowers in his hand – he had taken them from a cemetery – and told him they could not be offered to Krishna. She closed the altar curtains and hurried downstairs with the tray of arati things, briefly leaving him alone with the deities before coming back to lock up.

On his own in the temple room, Robert fell prey to his unstable mind and suddenly ran at the altar, throwing himself headlong at the exquisite marble forms of Radha and Krishna concealed behind the curtains. The weight of his body sent them crashing against the back wall with a sickening thud that reverberated through the building. Downstairs Mondakini heard the devastating sound and raced back upstairs.

Tribhuvanatha was in the hall, chanting his rounds, but the assault was over in a flash and he could have done nothing. The attacker, terrified by his deed, fled past him barefoot into the street and was last seen disappearing into the West End crowds. In the temple, with infinite care and sorrow, devotees carried the broken forms of Radha and Krishna upstairs and laid them on Prabhupada's bed. They sent urgent word to India asking guidance. What were they to do?

In Calcutta a telegram landed on Prabhupada's desk. He had just returned from a week in Australia, where he had installed Radha and Krishna deities in a tiny storefront temple, entrusting them to the care of young, inexperienced devotees. He read with alarm how Radha and Krishna in London, also in the care of inexperienced devotees, had been attacked. He knew the London temple had not been going well and needed help – now more than ever. But he was in the midst of a crowded preaching schedule in India and was soon to fly to Moscow, and there was nothing he could do from this distance. He sent back a telegram.

'The deities should be nicely repaired and replaced on the altar,' he replied, and he resolved to visit London as soon as he could.[4]

For three days life in the temple stood still. The altar, centre of everyone's devotions, was bare like an empty house save for a small picture of Radha and Krishna ominously framed in black. With tears devotees offered prayers, wondering who could be to blame for such a terrible event and if they would ever see Krishna again. Upstairs, Nicolas, trained as a sculptor, worked intently to restore Krishna's broken form.

Then, as suddenly as it had fallen, the darkness lifted. Radha and Krishna returned to their altar and the storm passed. They seemed more merciful than ever, their delicate beauty tinged with a new fragility and softness.

Prabhupada had spent nearly a year traversing India with a growing band of Western devotees, laying the foundations for centres in Bombay, Delhi, and Calcutta and major temples in Vrindavan and Mayapur. He had completed a short tour of Southeast Asia and Australia and flown to Moscow on 20th June to spend four days there as a guest of the Soviet Academy of Sciences. This was to be his only visit behind the Iron Curtain, and it would have momentous consequences.

Now he headed west. The London devotees hoped he would visit them on his way to America, and their hopes were raised when on 12th June he wrote to say he would be with them for the London Rathayatra, scheduled for 4th July.

To: Mukunda, Nara Narayana, Jeffrey Coker, Ian, Mondakini, Aditi, Tribhuvanatha, Jai Hari, Sananda Kumara, Vivienne, Neville Carr, Nicolas, Charlie, Serena, Ranchor, Pratejas, Philip, Jill, Nigel, James Gavin Statt, Devadatta, Draupadi, Dhruvananda, Devaki, John, Jim, Greg, Jaya Jagadisha, John

My dear sons and daughters,

Please accept my blessings … You will be glad to know that very soon I am coming to London, and will be there for participating in the Rathayatra festival … You write to say that you are expecting 50,000 people to participate in the festival this year. That is very encouraging. All of you work very fervently to make the festival a grand success and Krishna will surely bless each and every one of you.[5]

With their spiritual master's promise in mind, the devotees bent their efforts to the enormous task of preparing for the festival. Their biggest challenge was how to build a chariot without any money. The two previous London chariots had been built by Shyamsundar, but neither of them had survived: they had been broken up after each festival because there was nowhere to store them. This year, they were to be helped by Nara Narayana, an expert carpenter who had built chariots for the San Francisco Rathayatra several years in a row.

Nara Narayana arrived from California late in May and took charge of the construction. Because of the shortage of money, he planned to use recycled timber gathered from scrap yards and demolition sites. With energy and passion he recruited a team of assistants. In a parking lot behind St Pancras railway station, in the appropriately named Phoenix Road, London's third sacred chariot rose to the skies.

The biggest construction challenge the crew faced was to build and assemble the seven-foot wheels. Each wheel required six men to lift it, and had to be bolted onto the chassis' steel hubs, a difficult and dangerous operation. Living on a diet of chapatis and dal, fortified by much singing and chanting, and driven on by Nara Narayana's raw enthusiasm, Nicolas and the rest of the construction crew exulted in the challenge and laboured long hours.

There seemed no end to Mukunda's trials. Janaki had become desperately unhappy and was spending most of her time at home, alone in a foreign city without her friends and without Prabhupada to encourage her. Unable to tolerate her situation any longer, she left her husband and returned to her family in America. Mukunda was torn between love for her and duty to the temple. In the midst of preparations for the festival and for Prabhupada's arrival, he decided he must save his marriage. With a heavy heart he handed over charge of the temple to Tribhuvanatha and followed Janaki to America.

Tribhuvanatha, though only eighteen years old, seemed to have the maturity of a man twice his age. But he was thrown in the deep end. On his first day in charge he answered the door to an official from the gas company who had come to turn off the supply for nonpayment.

'Please don't cut us off,' Tribhuvantha begged. 'I promise we'll pay if you just give us a few more days.' And somehow the money was found.

Another day the landlord, who had not been seen for months, came to demand three month's back rent – four hundred pounds. He gave Tribhuvanatha until the following day to find the money. That very evening a former member of the temple, Ramatanu, arrived unexpectedly from Brazil on his way to India.

'I had a dream,' he said. 'Krishna told me to give you my savings,' and he wrote out a cheque for the full four hundred pounds.

Bailiffs came to assess the temple's assets. The only items of value they could find were the deities, which they estimated at three hundred pounds. Tribhuvanatha advised them, without exaggeration, that if they were to attempt to remove Radha and Krishna from the temple he could not be responsible for their safety. They left empty-handed.

Hearing of Prabhupada's impending visit, devotees all over Europe made plans to come to London. The Hamburg devotees packed up everything and travelled with their Radha-Krishna deities. On the way, aboard trains and ferry, Lilashakti kept up their worship, cooking and offering arati just as she had done for them in the Hamburg temple. From Amsterdam came Dhananjaya and Bala Gopala with a group of devotees. The temple quickly filled to capacity and beyond, with devotees sleeping in every available space, even on the landings. The cramped conditions and lack of facilities added to the excitement and air of expectancy.

Nara Narayana thought the *vyasasana* Shyamsundar had made for Prabhupada was too small, so he decided to build a new one.

'Prabhupada is spiritual master of the universe,' he said. 'At Rathayatra, when he addresses the crowds in Trafalgar Square, he must have a suitable throne.' So saying he ripped out Shyamsundar's well-proportioned redwood seat and built a replacement so large that the finished product was barely able to fit inside the small temple room. Vasudeva, the German artist, softened it by embellishing the base with gilded panels painted with a delicate frieze of peacocks.

A week before Rathayatra, news arrived that Prabhupada had reached Paris. With mounting excitement the devotees in London made final preparations for the festival and for his arrival. But at the last moment they heard he had flown on to Los Angeles to attend the San Francisco Rathayatra instead.

The devotees were disappointed. They now had no idea when Prabhupada would come to London – or whether he would come at all that year. But remembering what he had told them they staged their Rathayatra without him. It turned out to be a memorable occasion. Nara Narayana's chariot performed well and safely delivered the deities of Jagannath, Balaram, and Subhadra to Trafalgar Square, where a feast was distributed to the crowd. The afternoon culminated when, with Jagannath installed on the plinth beneath Nelson's Column, the devotees performed the drama of Lord Narasimha, in which Vishnu saved his devotee Prahlad. At the climax of the play Dhananjaya, dressed as the lion-headed Narasimha, leapt onto the stage and rescued his devotee to the accompaniment of triumphant chanting from all present.

In pride of place throughout was the huge throne, upon which sat a large framed portrait of Prabhupada, symbolising his spiritual presence. Nara Narayana added a final exuberant touch: a pair of gilded plastic elephant heads rescued from a Selfridges window display decorated the two arms of the throne.

The devotees' disappointment was not to last for long. Prabhupada stayed in Los Angeles for two weeks, and while he was there he wrote to say that he would soon be in London.

> My dear Tribhuvanatha,
>
> Please accept my blessings and offer the same to all the boys and girls there who have worked so hard to make Rathayatra festival in London a grand success … Presently I am in L.A., and by the middle of this month I

shall be going to NY. From there, you will be glad to know, I will be going directly to London.[6]

This time his plans didn't change. After a further two weeks in New York, on 2nd August 1971, he flew to London.

CHAPTER 10

The Master Returns

That Monday evening devotees travelled out from Central London by tube and bus to gather at Heathrow Airport. Most had never been to an airport before, and it took them a while to find their way to the international arrivals hall. Only Malati, who had just returned from India ahead of her husband, had any experience of air travel. She was also the only one to have met Prabhupada in person. The youthful temple president, Tribhuvanatha, led the thirty or so young men and women in chanting. They began singing loudly with drums and *kartals,* but the airport officials silenced them, so they sat quietly counting their beads.

They learned that Prabhupada's plane was delayed. An hour passed, then another, and they struggled to stay awake well beyond their bedtime. Their colourful robes and the men's shaven heads provoked the curiosity of onlookers. Sometime after eleven they saw a blur of saffron through the frosted glass separating them from the customs hall. Someone called out, 'It's Prabhupada!'

Devotees jumped to their feet, and their chanting, cymbals, and drums resounded through the terminal building. Blinking eyes turned in time to see a kindly, elderly monk, his eyes sparkling and his face lit with a broad smile, emerge followed by two young travelling companions.

Afterwards, most of the devotees reported seeing his small figure shine with a golden light as he advanced through the doors. His smile seemed to radiate joy and love, and he appeared to float as he walked toward Tribhuvanatha, who had been chosen to offer the first garland. When for the first time in his life he beheld his spiritual master, Tribhuvanatha was stunned. The floor-length garland hung motionless in his outstretched hands as Prabhupada walked right past him.

'His smile was oceanic. It just knocked me out,' was all Tribhuvanatha could later recall. In a moment he came to his senses and ran after Prabhupada, adding his garland to the others already being piled around Prabhupada's neck. On all sides, before the astonished public, devotees were falling to the floor and picking themselves up to leap into the air. As they did so, their faces shining with tears, they scattered flower petals in his path.

Encircled by his disciples and followers Prabhupada moved through the terminal and was ushered to a waiting car. Aravinda, the servant who had accompanied him from New York, loaded his baggage into the boot, and soon the car was on its way with Prabhupada, his travelling secretary Shyamsundar, and his Sanskrit editor Pradyumna. Left behind at the airport the young devotees milled about in confusion, looking for Prabhupada, who had seemed to pass through their midst all too quickly. Once they realised he had left, their only thought was to return to the temple to be with him.

At Bury Place more devotees waited. Some stood outside watching for his car and carrying yet more garlands. Others were in the hall and on the stairs. Among them was Nicolas. For six months he had faithfully served in the temple and bowed every morning before the picture of the author of the *Bhagavad-gita As It Is*. He needed to see for himself the person in whom he was trying to place his faith. Would Prabhupada be all he hoped for?

Well after midnight the sound of chanting signalled Prabhupada's arrival. The door opened and Nicolas saw him framed in the entrance. As all around him people bowed to the ground, Prabhupada stepped calmly forward, smiling radiantly while flower petals rained upon him. Nicolas watched him closely and was reminded of how his father used to come home in the evening, turning his key in the front door. Prabhupada entered the temple room and walked up to Radha and Krishna. He had not seen them in one and a half years and had been gravely concerned for their safety. He looked at them for a long time in silence.

'Do they have enough flowers?' he asked Malati, then added, 'They should have more jewellery. Radharani should be covered with jewellery.'

He bowed to the floor before them and turned to the back of the temple, where he paused in front of the enormous *vyasasana*.

'This is too big,' he remarked, and a look of dismay appeared on Nara Narayana's face. But he mounted the huge seat and looked around at the youthful faces crowded on all sides.

'I am so happy to be back with you in London.' He closed his eyes for a moment. 'Actually we are not in London, we are in Vaikuntha, the spiritual world. Wherever the name of Krishna is chanted, that is Vaikuntha.' He smiled and everyone responded '*Jaya!*'

'Last month I was in San Francisco, where the Rathayatra festival was gorgeously performed, and I spoke before a crowd of ten thousand. Now you have performed Rathayatra here in London also, and I so much appreciate how you have all worked sincerely to make it a grand success.' Then he spoke of their beautiful Radha and Krishna, who had suffered such a severe attack. 'Radha and Krishna have come to live with you. They are so kind, to let you look after them. Be very careful; do not become proud.'

Briefly he repeated the basic philosophy of Krishna consciousness, just as he had done countless times in his books. There was nothing new to say. This was what drew his young followers to him: his message was simple and never changed. Serve Krishna. Chant Krishna's name. 'This Krishna consciousness is so simple you will miss it.'

Nicolas, having observed Prabhupada's modest self-composure and heard his straightforward words, concluded that he was genuine. Prabhupada had passed his test. Here was someone in whom he could place his faith.

In his room, Prabhupada found everything as he had left it – the simple wooden bed in one corner, his clothes rack in another, his rocking chair, and his familiar desk beneath the window. He settled into the cushions behind his desk and the room quickly filled with devotees – many had just arrived back from the airport. Someone brought in a large tray of *kachoris*. Prabhupada tasted one.

'Who has cooked?' he looked round the room.

'Mondakini, Prabhupada. She has been working very hard.' Malati extolled her godsister, who was hiding at the back of the room. All eyes turned to find her.

'My favourite. My mother used to make them for me. You have made them very nicely.' Prabhupada's eyes settled upon Mondakini, smiling with recognition. He remembered her from the days after the installation in 1969. She blushed, and everyone felt happy. It was as if by appreciating her service he was appreciating them all.

'Now distribute,' he requested, and the *kachoris* were shared around the room until everyone had eaten something.

'Our main business is to chant the holy name of Krishna. Everybody is more or less engaged in sinful activities, so we have to be very kind and patient. A young woman who is newly married cannot expect a child immediately. If she patiently serves her husband she will have a child in time. So be patient, chant Hare Krishna, and rest assured the result will come.'[1]

All sat spellbound and the room fell silent.

'It's late and we're all tired,' Prabhupada smiled. At this signal the devotees bowed and filed out. They were satisfied. Their master had come to share the same roof with them for a few precious weeks, and he was pleased with their efforts. That meant Krishna was pleased.

During the first few days of his stay in London Prabhupada remained in his room, translating the *Bhagavatam* and answering letters. Two concerns were uppermost in his mind: his translation work and the project to build a temple in Mayapur. He had recently completed the long-awaited purchase of land close to Sri Chaitanya's birth site, and he wanted the project started. But within a few days he fell ill. For months he had been constantly touring; now his body needed rest. Not that he was in a mood to rest – he wanted to use every moment in Krishna's service, and so many people were depending on him.

Shyamsundar was awakened in the night by Prabhupada calling his name. He sat up so quickly that he knocked his head on the bunk above before running into Prabhupada's room. He entered to find him stumbling toward the door and was just in time to catch him in his arms. Prabhupada's face was grey and he was gasping for breath and shivering uncontrollably. Shyamsundar carried him to his bed – his body seemed to weigh nothing – and covered him with blankets.

'Don't call a doctor,' Prabhupada gasped. 'Make a paste of black pepper and put it on my forehead.' Shyamsundar called Malati, who ran down to the kitchen and made the paste. Then he applied it and stayed by Prabhupada's bed.

'I still have so many things to do,' murmured Prabhupada. 'I have my plan but Krishna has his. Man proposes and God disposes. We must have a plan, but in the end it is all up to Krishna.'

As Shyamsundar listened, his spiritual master's breathing became regular and he fell into a deep sleep. Shyamsundar went upstairs. It was three o'clock in the morning, nearly time for fifty young men and women to start their day. Soon they would rise, wash, clamber downstairs to the temple, and sing their way through their early morning worship. He told them not to get up and to remain silently upstairs so they would not disturb Prabhupada. While their spiritual master wrestled with his fate, they fell back to sleep and the building remained clothed in silence.

Around eight in the morning, Prabhupada awoke refreshed. He got up and insisted on going about his usual business. By midday he was ready to eat, and after lunch and an afternoon rest he was almost his normal self, carrying on as if nothing had happened. But for the next few days he seemed fragile.

'I was sick for four or five days,' he wrote. 'Now I am a little better, but the disease is prolonging in a different way. I cannot sleep at night for more than two hours and during the day I sometimes am feeling some dizziness. Otherwise everything is alright. I am chanting Hare Krishna as usual and writing my books regularly.'[2]

One night a devotee who had been working after midnight returned from chanting his rounds while walking in the empty streets. All was quiet as he rounded the corner into Bury Place, but he saw the lights in Prabhupada's room blazing into the night, and from outside in the road he distinctly heard Prabhupada's voice. The realisation dawned that he was hearing his spiritual master dictate his translation and commentary of the *Srimad-Bhagavatam*. He tiptoed up the stairs, anxious not to be heard, but he couldn't resist pausing on the landing outside Prabhupada's door, hardly daring to breathe, to listen to his voice. He heard a few words, then a pause, then a few words more, then another pause. In between was the click of the Dictaphone. A long silence was followed by another passage. Prabhupada cleared his throat, then more silence. He and Prabhupada were the only ones awake. He could hear the sound of devotees sleeping, breathing heavily, snoring, turning in their beds. He felt uncomfortable, as if he were an intruder eavesdropping on a sacred act of divine inspiration. Suddenly he feared Prabhupada and crept up to bed.

The memory haunted him. While everyone slept, practically the whole city of London, his spiritual master stayed awake to translate his books. All day he was under pressure to run his society, but at night, the one time he could have peace, he was doing his most precious work.

The day after Prabhupada's arrival he was surprised to see a small Indian *brahmachari* offering his respects outside his room. It was Milan.

'Where are you from?'

'I'm from Calcutta,' replied Milan in Bengali.

'Come into my room.' Milan followed him in and Prabhupada

beckoned him to sit near. For a while they conversed in Bengali, Prabhupada speaking with a relaxed familiarity that made it seem to Milan that he had known him all his life. Prabhupada learned that Milan had attended the same Scottish Churches College in Calcutta where in 1916 Prabhupada had studied English, Sanskrit, Economics, and Philosophy.

'Every day come to my room and sit with me. Whatever I say you do.' He spoke as a grandfather would. When he heard that Milan was serving in the kitchen, he told Tribhuvanatha that he wanted Milan as his personal assistant.

From then on Milan received favoured treatment. He was called regularly into Prabhupada's room to draft the reply to a letter, to sit in on a conversation, or to accompany him to an outside engagement. On one such outing Prabhupada took several devotees with him to visit a wealthy Hindu family who lived in a flat overlooking Regents Park. While the family cooked for their guests Prabhupada sat in an armchair ringed by disciples, who sat on the floor, with members of the family and their friends looking on. He led everyone in chanting Hare Krishna, then he looked around the room until his eyes fell upon Dhananjaya.

'Stand up and say something about Krishna consciousness,' he commanded, and Dhananjaya self-consciously enunciated some of what he had learned over the last two years. After a few minutes Prabhupada thanked him and turned to Milan, indicating that he should do the same. Embarrassed and confused, the little Bengali man, who had only been in the temple for a few months, stood up and stammered a few words.

'Alright,' Prabhupada nodded his appreciation. 'Now chant.' Dhananjaya took up the *mridanga* and led the chanting for a few minutes until the meal was brought in and served.

The next day Prabhupada called for Milan. He handed him a copy of *Easy Journey to Other Planets,* the first book he had published, in India in 1961, and asked Milan to translate it into Bengali.

'I want it before I leave London,' he said. 'I will teach you how.' Every few days after that he checked on Milan's progress, correcting his mistakes and giving him encouragement.

Prabhupada's door was open to any who wanted to see him, especially after four in the afternoon. 'In the old days the student had to go to the forest in search of a guru, but now guru has come to you,' he said in one of his classes. However, most of the young devotees were too shy to go into his room unless they were invited. They feared they might be distracting him from his work. The senior American devotees were less inhibited. They often spent time with Prabhupada, and if he went anywhere they went with him. Shyamsundar, though, tried to arrange for other devotees to have opportunities to be with their guru, and involved them in services that brought them closer to him.

'We must begin designing our temple in Mayapur,' Prabhupada announced one day to Shyamsundar. 'We need drawings to send to India. Find some men to help.'

Shyamsundar recruited Nara Narayana, whose skill in construction was proven and who was expected to go on to Mayapur to help on the actual building. The German artist Vasudeva, who was visiting London, was also asked to help. And he called for a young English devotee who had experience as an architect and knew how to make plans and elevations. They gathered in Prabhupada's room to be briefed.

For several afternoons Prabhupada led wide-ranging discussions on his ideas for the proposed Mayapur centre. The plot was a narrow strip of land amid cultivated fields beside the Ganges, in the heart of Bengal close to the historic town of Navadvipa. He wanted to create an international headquarters for ISKCON, a place where people from all over the world could stay to study Vaishnava tradition in depth and imbibe the culture and way of life of the followers of Sri Chaitanya. He was thinking on a grand scale, and outlined plans for four large ashram buildings alongside a massive new temple.

Gradually designs took shape on the drawing board, but a major obstacle would be Mayapur's unstable environment. The land was a flood plain composed of layers of silt between the confluence of two large branches of the lower Ganges, the Bhagirathi and the Saraswati. Special precautions would have to be taken to make stable foundations and flood-proof buildings.

He had very specific solutions in mind. The buildings should stand on plinths to raise them above the flood level, supported on modern raft foundations. He wanted to combine this with traditional Bengali materials, and called for the excavation of clay close to the site to bake huge numbers of bricks. He estimated how thick the walls should be relative to the height of the main temple, and his estimate was confirmed when an Indian structural engineer came to volunteer his professional advice.

One day he took his Mayapur construction team to visit Westminster Abbey and told them that he wanted the interior of the temple to resemble the inside of the abbey. Outside they posed for a group portrait, taken by a tourist photographer, with the abbey behind them.

Each morning the design team accompanied him to discuss ideas on his walk round Russell Square.

'How high are those buildings?' he asked, pointing to a well-proportioned Georgian terrace on the north side of the square.

'About forty feet, Prabhupada.'

'Our temple should be as high as those,' he said, and the design team pondered his words. The next day he again pointed, this time to the Russell Hotel.

'What about that one – how high is it?' he asked.

'Nearly a hundred feet,' came the reply. The Russell Hotel was an impressive, ten-storey Victorian edifice.

'Then our temple should be *that* high,' he said, and the devotees laughed, catching his mood. By the third day, as he passed beneath the Russell Hotel he stopped and turned to his companions.

'Actually, our temple should be as tall as we can make it. At least three times as high as this.' The devotees were stunned.

'That's three hundred feet, Prabhupada!'

'Can it be done?'

'Yes, Prabhupada!' declared Nara Narayana.

And so it was accepted. Prabhupada's wish would override all obstacles. Somehow, even on a flood plain, it would be done.

A young Frenchman had recently started coming to the temple. His name was Serge. He had come from Paris to further his career as a computer programmer, an exciting profession then in its infancy. His skills were in big demand in the City of London. He had already met devotees in Paris, and now when he met them again in London he was attracted to their company. They had answers to life's important questions, and it seemed to him they were occupied with more significant things than the mere pursuit of material success. He tried bringing his friends with him to the temple, but they didn't share his enthusiasm. Gradually he left their company and spent more and more time helping the devotees. One morning he went with Mondakini to Covent Garden Market and was shocked to see her gather rotten vegetables from the refuse tip. He had not realised the devotees were so poor. He paid for ten bags of the best potatoes and had them delivered to the temple at once.

Prabhupada heard about this act of generosity and asked to meet him. That same afternoon Serge entered Prabhupada's crowded room, expecting to meet a grand and lofty master. Instead he found a simple man sitting on the floor. He seemed friendly and approachable. The first thing Prabhupada did was to give him a sweet, pausing as he did so to look around the room.

'People may come to the temple and they might not listen to what we have to say, but at least if they have prasadam they will be saved,' he said.

These words puzzled Serge at the time, but later he took the simple lesson to heart: prasadam has the potency to heal the soul.

That evening Prabhupada came down to give a lecture. Devotees and guests squeezed into every available space to hear him speak. When the time came for questions, Serge, unable to find space in the room, stood in the crowded hallway peering round the door. A dilemma burned in his mind. He had two sons, but he and their mother were separated. One boy lived with her and the other with Serge's mother in Paris. He wanted to stay in London with the devotees but he needed to ask Prabhupada's advice – and was scared by what the answer might be. Urged on by those beside him he nervously cleared his throat.

'Your Divine Grace, I have been visiting the temple for a while, and for the last few days I have stayed here with the devotees. They are wonderful people. But I don't know what to do. I feel pulled away to my family in France.'

'You have left behind the company of crows and come to live among swans,' said Prabhupada. 'This means you are becoming swan!' Serge was taken aback. Was Prabhupada comparing his family to crows? He decided he must be talking not about Serge's mother and son, but about the mundane world in which they lived, a world at odds with the life of a devotee.

'Save yourself first. Then you can save your family,' Prabhupada concluded, and Serge understood. First he should learn to practise spiritual life, then he would be able to help his family. He decided to stay with the devotees.

That summer the Bury Place temple filled to bursting, and during Prabhupada's lectures was quite unable to accommodate the devotees and guests. It was as Prabhupada had said from the start: the building was too small. Following the success of the new Los Angeles temple, which was housed in a converted church, Prabhupada looked with great interest at unused churches that dotted London. On his way to or from outside engagements he would point out various buildings. Serge was often the driver on these occasions, with Prabhupada beside him and Shyamsundar in the back. He would drive carefully, conscious of his precious load.

'Go faster,' came Shyamsundar's voice from behind.

'Drive slowly,' said Prabhupada.

Once they drove past St Pancras church, which stood on the junction of Woburn Place and Euston Road. Although the church was in use, it looked uncared for. It was built in the classical Greek style, with a large portico and magnificent lanterned tower. It appealed very much to Prabhupada. He said he would like a temple in London like that. From that time on, he made the search for a larger temple in London a priority.

One day Shyamsundar had been to look at a redundant church in Kensington. He was walking back to the tube station when a young woman dressed in hippie clothes ran up to him. She was in a distressed state, and pleaded with him to take her to the temple. Her name was Carol Kandler. She was a well-educated and intelligent young woman who had dropped out of university and left the security of her home in Manchester to come south. She wanted to find out what life was all about. Until recently she had held a responsible job with BBC Television, but she had abandoned it to hitchhike round Europe with a friend. On her travels she had picked up books on mysticism, including a little *Bhagavad-gita* which she always carried with her. In it she had read that she should be detached and seek a spiritual master. She had learned to chant the Hare Krishna mantra with George Harrison's record 'My Sweet Lord', and she had seen devotees around town. Now her travelling companion had gone to Israel and she was in crisis, intensified by the dose of LSD she had just swallowed. At this critical moment she saw, just across the street, Shyamsundar in his flowing robes. He looked to her eyes like a rescuing angel. Shyamsundar was a compassionate soul, and she soon persuaded him to take her back to the temple. On their way, riding on the underground train, he was disconcerted to find that she insisted on sitting at his feet on the floor of the carriage.

The two reached the temple and Carol stayed for the rest of the day, trying to make herself helpful, although she was hardly in a state to be of any use. She had been praying to find a guru, and now she believed she had been led to one, so when evening came and it was time for her to leave, she begged to be allowed to stay in the temple, the only place she wanted to be. Shyamsundar spoke up for her and she was allowed to remain. Within a few days she had sobered up, and from that day on she never left the temple.

In his small room adjoining Prabhupada's, which he shared with two others, Shyamsundar dreamt of producing a book on philosophy. He wanted to explore how the Western philosophers he had read as a student stood up to the scrutiny of Krishna consciousness. He suggested to Prabhupada a series of dialogues in which he would put forward their ideas and Prabhupada would respond, allowing Shyamsundar to record and publish the discussions. Prabhupada liked his proposal, so they started at the beginning, with daily sessions on Plato and Socrates.

During this time the secretary of Mensa became a regular caller at the temple. Mensa is a club for the super-intelligent, and Pat Fitzgerald was keen to match his wits with Prabhupada. The two had long philosophical discussions, and soon became friends.

'The love propensity is being misplaced in this material world. It should be placed in God. Then love would be perfection,' expounded Prabhupada to Pat one afternoon in his room. 'For example, to pour water on the leaves of a tree is simply a waste of time, but if you pour water on the root, then the water is distributed. Similarly, if you love God, your love is distributed to everyone. If people take this movement seriously, how to love God, then human society will be first-class.'

'May I suggest you have already made a contribution from India, which is almost the antithesis of pouring water on the root,' responded Pat mischievously. 'We get leaves from India, we pour water on them, and we make that delicious drink tea, which is used to inculcate the brotherhood of man.'

Prabhupada laughed, but he was not to be deterred from his purpose. Patiently he discussed the intricacies of Vedic philosophy with Pat while guests listened and Shyamsundar recorded their conversations.[3]

George was away from London during Prabhupadaıs visit, helping Ravi Shankar make a film called *Raga*. It was about Ravi Shankar's life and music, and due to have its world premiere in New York in the autumn. When Prabhupada had passed through New York at the end of July, George had been in the midst of staging his historic Concert For Bangladesh, the first charity rock concert of its kind. Shyamsundar had gone to see him at his hotel, and arranged for prasadam for his crew. George was bringing together one of the biggest ever line-ups of rock stars, including Bob Dylan, who came out of a year's seclusion specially for the occasion, and the already legendary guitarist Eric Clapton. Ravi Shankar would also perform. George had shown Shyamsundar the jacket he would wear for the concert: round the collar were embroidered the words of the *maha-mantra* in tiny Sanskrit characters. He told him he would like to have the audience chant Hare Krishna with him, but it wouldn't go down well with some of his musician friends.

George had strolled onto the stage in front of 40,000 people in Madison Square Garden on 1st August and greeted Shyamsundar, seated in the front row, with 'Hare Krishna'. He had opened with 'My Sweet Lord', then launched into 'Awaiting On You All', in which he invited everyone to chant 'the names of the Lord and you'll be free.'

The concert raised nearly a quarter of a million dollars for UNICEF to help children in Bangladesh. Afterwards George had told Shyamsundar they should do something like this for the temple in London.

'You're too crowded in that place,' he said, and that had been the beginning of him helping to get a bigger temple.

Prabhupada's birthday, which was the day after Krishna's birthday, fell on 15th August that year. This was a day for honouring not just Prabhupada but all gurus in the line of Vyasa, author of the *Vedas*. In the temple Prabhupada asked his newly initiated disciples to stand up and speak about the significance of the spiritual master. One by one they stood in front of their guru and spoke a few words.

The following day he initiated fourteen new disciples. Among the initiates was Serge. When he came forward to receive his beads Prabhupada smiled broadly. 'Ah! You have decided to remain a swan,' he said with pleasure. 'Your name is Sudurjaya, "One who cannot be conquered" – by the crows.'

Prabhupada chanted in turn upon each initiate's beads, one round at a time, while everyone chanted with him. He was grave as he accepted his young charges, and one by one they were called forward to make their vows and receive their names. Nicolas was named Mahavishnu, Ian became Birasingha, and Jeff was named Sukarma.

Serena was nervous when she knelt to collect her beads. 'Your name is Devamaya,' he said. '*Deva* is God and *maya* is energy. When the mind is with Krishna it is in *devamaya*.'

Jill was called up. She had been so happy at the temple, feeling that she had joined a family. The things she had read in Prabhupada's books had all been confirmed when she had met him in person: he lived exactly as he taught – as she imagined Jesus had. She felt his power, yet at the same time she felt his affection, as if he were her father. She came up nervously and bowed.

'Your name is Jijñasi, which means one who is always enquiring about the absolute truth.' Everyone laughed, because she had the reputation among them as the one who was forever asking questions. Prabhupada silenced them.

'No, this is not funny. It is a very serious business. One cannot begin spiritual life until one starts to enquire.' She felt protected by his fatherly concern.

Next came Milan.

'Your name will be Subhaga, which means "fortunate".' Then he explained to everyone, 'His father sent him to study, but his actual education he is getting – Krishna consciousness. Therefore he is most fortunate.'

When the last young man came up, Prabhupada listened as he nervously promised to abstain from the four sinful activities – meat-eating, gambling, intoxication, and illicit sex. Prabhupada looked serious.

'So, which one do you like the best?' The young man blushed, and with a reassuring smile Prabhupada gave him his beads.

That day some were to receive their second initiation. This meant Prabhupada would personally teach each disciple the words of the *gayatri-mantra* and show how to count the mantras. The process required the guru to whisper the words of the mantra in his disciple's ear. It was a moment of intimacy between guru and disciple. Bala Gopala, visiting from Amsterdam with her husband Dhananjaya, came into Prabhupada's room, and he called her to sit beside him. She was so overwhelmed that when he asked her the name of her husband, her mind went blank and she couldn't answer. Nevertheless, she left his room in deep bliss.

Outside his door, sitting halfway down the stairs, waited Lilashakti, carrying a bunch of yellow roses, which she had been told were Prabhupada's favourite. His servant called her in, then left the room. After receiving her flowers and placing them on his desk, Prabhupada told her to hand him a book, *Teachings of Lord Chaitanya,* from the nearby shelf. He asked if she had read it. She nodded.

'Did you like it?'

'Yes, but I found it difficult to understand.'

'Oh. If you don't understand, then ask the older devotees. But while I'm here you can come and ask me.' He showed her how to chant Gayatri and as most devotees did, she got it wrong and he corrected her. After they were finished she quietly took her leave.

While others wanted to be noticed, Lilashakti preferred to keep in the background. She was at her happiest performing simple tasks, like washing Prabhupada's dishes, ironing his clothes, and, now that she had second initiation, learning to serve on the altar.

Another day she was cleaning his room with one of her sisters. The three sisters were identical triplets, with blond hair and blue eyes, and youthful Swedish beauty. Lilashakti and Ulla, visiting from Sweden, were busy vacuuming his rug and dusting the shelves when Prabhupada walked in unexpectedly. He stopped short. He had been told of the three identical sisters, but had not seen any of them together. The two girls dropped their cleaning things and fell to the carpet in obeisance. When they looked up they were surprised to see that he was amused. Seeing these sincere and simple-hearted identical sisters serving so willingly together, he threw back his head and laughed and laughed.

Jijñasi was another of the women who cleaned his room. She was conscientious and loved the opportunity to be close to him, even though when she cleaned he would be out on his morning walk. On a few occasions, though, he came back early. Whenever he did she would offer her obeisances and start to leave.

'No, you carry on cleaning,' he would say. When that happened she would be so acutely self-conscious working in his presence that she trembled with nervousness. Her favourite time was later, when she washed his saffron socks. They had the aroma of sandalwood, and she felt blessed, as if she were touching his lotus feet.

Bala Gopala learned to cook for Prabhupada that summer. In his triple-tier cooker, which travelled with him wherever he went, she prepared vegetables, dal, and rice. Once the cooker was set up and simmering on the stove in the temple's basement kitchen, she would sit on the stairs just out of sight of his room, waiting to hear him emerge for the noon shower which always followed his massage. That was the signal for her to add the rice to the cooker and start the chapatis, so that in exactly twenty-five minutes, when the rice was done and the first chapati hot off the flame, he would have chanted his noon Gayatri and be ready to eat. She would carry the meal up to him personally and then supply hot chapatis one at a time, rushing up and down the two flights of stairs from the basement.

Mondakini had the service of preparing his fruits, which he would have after waking from his afternoon nap, around four o'clock. She went to great lengths to obtain special fruits, such as mango or strawberries, and combine four or five varieties into a fruit salad, along with a sliced-up orange and freshly squeezed juice, and black pepper and salt on the side of the plate. Each day she carried a fruit tray up to Prabhupada, and sometimes he would talk with her.

'So, Mondakini, you're not married yet? You didn't find anyone good enough for you? Don't worry, Krishna will find someone.'

Yamuna had wanted her to marry one of the men in the temple, but all she wanted was to serve Prabhupada. When she was near him she felt that Krishna was there too. So she had decided against marriage, and to discourage proposals she dressed in old saris and tried her best to look melancholy.

One morning she wanted to do something extra for Prabhupada, so she made time to go out on the street and sell magazines. She met an interested young man.

'Take this magazine by my spiritual master,' she told him, 'and all your questions about spiritual life will be answered.' He took it happily, and she went back to the temple and brought Prabhupada his fruits. When she entered his room he looked at her closely.

'Thank you very much, thank you very much, thank you very much,' he repeated three times. He didn't say thank you like that every day.

The young man who had met Mondakini was Paul Barrow. He had grown up in Northern Ireland in a stable, middle-class family, with parents who encouraged his curiosity about the world and his sense of adventure. After finishing his A-levels he took time out to follow the hippie trail to Morocco and other North African and Middle Eastern countries. For three years he pursued this exotic life, then at twenty returned to Britain to take up the offer of a place at the University of St Andrew's. While in London he had been stopped on the street by Mondakini, and bought the *Back to Godhead* magazine, which he took with him on one last journey to stay with a friend in Canada. His friend gave him a copy of Prabhupada's *Bhagavad-gita As It Is,* which he read avidly. Passing through New York on his way back to London, he was captivated by the sight of a large party of devotees chanting on Fifth Avenue. He bought another magazine from them and read it through the night on his transatlantic flight. By the time his plane touched down his mind was made up to go the London temple, whose address he found in the magazine.

Paul came in and sat in the temple room. In the evening Prabhupada came down to lecture. Paul saw his delicate feet as he took off of his slippers at the door, and noticed that he seemed to float across the room to the huge seat. He thought he looked very scholarly, yet surcharged with an electrifying presence.

A few days later he heard him lecture again and decided to join the temple. Kulashekara, just back from working at ISKCON Press in Boston, took Paul under his wing.

Mondakini continued serving Radha and Krishna, but she longed to do something adventurous for Prabhupada. She knew he wanted his disciples to preach, and she had heard him say in a lecture that the perfection of life was when your spiritual master asked you to do something and you did it without hesitation. So she prayed to Krishna that Prabhupada would ask her to do something difficult so that she could reply 'Yes!'

During Prabhupada's recent visit to Moscow he had preached to a young Russian student of philology, Anatoli, whom Shyamsundar had met on the street and brought to their hotel room. After hearing from Prabhupada for three days and nights, Anatoli had been convinced of Krishna consciousness and accepted initiation, secretly taking the name Ananta Shanti. Prabhupada and Shyamsundar had discussed ways to stay in touch with him and to supply him with books, and one idea had been to find him a foreign wife, who could then visit him from the West. This would allow him to communicate with the outside world. Ananta Shanti was the only Hare Krishna devotee behind the Iron Curtain, and Prabhupada wanted to do whatever he could to encourage him.

One day Mondakini entered Prabhupada's room with his afternoon fruit. Prabhupada smiled at her. Shyamsundar was also there.

'Mondakini?'

'Yes, Srila Prabhupada?' She was expecting him to ask her to get something from across the street.

'Would you like to go to Russia and marry a boy to help spread Krishna consciousness?' The memory of her prayer flashed through her mind. She replied without hesitation.

'Yes, Srila Prabhupada!'

He smiled broadly and asked Shyamsundar to make all the arrangements.

It had been Shyamsundar's idea: a French girl stood the best chance of avoiding suspicion in Soviet Russia, and if the boy agreed to marry her she could visit there freely. Shyamsundar asked Sudurjaya, who had studied Russian, to give Mondakini a crash language course. They used to sit on the landing outside Prabhupada's door, and two or three times a day, when he emerged, they would bow, feeling privileged to be serving him in this way.

Shyamsundar asked Lilashakti to stay in London and take over Mondakini's service as *pujari* to Radha and Krishna. She was fearful because she had seen Mondakini working so hard with so little support that it made her cry. But Lilashakti knew Prabhupada wanted unmarried girls to be *pujaris,* so she surrendered to the new responsibility.

Not long afterwards, Lilashakti had just finished offering Krishna his lunch and was alone with Radha and Krishna when Prabhupada walked unaccompanied into the temple.

'Has the food been offered?' he enquired. She nodded, and he put out his hand. 'Then give me some prasadam.'

She had been taught not to serve food from Krishna's plate, but Prabhupada was the one who made the rules, so she offered him the whole plate. He took a morsel and popped it into his mouth. He seemed to be acknowledging her service and encouraging her.

One morning in class not long before Mondakini was due to leave for Russia, Prabhupada asked her to chant a Sanskrit verse. But she was too shy. 'She's going to Russia to preach,' he laughed, 'and she's afraid to speak a few lines of Sanskrit.'

A few weeks later, though, she bravely departed, first to France to get her visa and visit her father, then with a group of French tourists by train to Moscow to see the Bolshoi Ballet. When she reached Moscow she found a tall, thin young man waiting in the snow outside her hotel.

'Is your name Monique?'

Ananta Shanti was polite and sensitive, but she felt lost with him. He had with him a beautiful girl, and he seemed to know very little about Krishna. Somehow they made friends, and over the next few years she went to Russia many times, although marriage never became a serious consideration. Encouraged by her brief visits Ananta Shanti found the strength to pioneer the Hare Krishna movement in Russia, and Mondakini met people there who were ready to sacrifice everything – their freedom and even their lives – for the sake of spiritual knowledge. This mission to Russia became her heart's service to her guru.

One evening Prabhupada gave a talk in the temple packed with devotees. An Indian woman who came regularly stood up.

'Can you see God?' Her tone was mildly challenging.

'Yes. Everyone can see God. You cannot see?' Prabhupada looked straight at Radha and Krishna on the altar. '*Here* is God!' The devotees laughed for sheer joy, seeing Krishna as if through Prabhupada's eyes for the first time. Then he looked again at his questioner.

'Why you cannot see? Do you *want* to see God?' She looked down and said nothing, then slowly shook her head.

'Therefore you cannot see,' he said gently. He didn't need to elaborate any further. She bowed and sat down.

Virasingham came from Birmingham on the coach, paying the fares for two devotees to come with him. The night of their arrival Prabhupada came down to lecture.

When everyone offered their obeisances Virasingham remained standing: before he bowed down he needed to see if this was a genuine *sadhu* or not. He listened to the lecture carefully and was deeply affected by what he heard. After it was over guests began to leave. He wanted to stay, but was told he was not allowed to until he became a regular visitor, so he slept on a bench at the railway station, where the police kept moving him on.

Next morning he was back at the temple by six. Mahavishnu took him upstairs to have a shower, and gave him a clean saffron *dhoti* to wear. This time when Prabhupada came into the temple Virasingham's mind was free from doubts. With a full heart, he bowed down.

The first time Robert Housden saw Prabhupada was when he gave a public lecture in Hampstead. Robert had a job making clothes for pop groups. One day on Kensington High Street he bumped into a devotee.

'You don't have to smoke dope to get high, you know,' said the monk, giving him a magazine. A few days later Robert heard the same words repeated when he met another devotee, this time in a carriage on the underground. The words stayed with him as a challenge to the way he lived.

Robert was preoccupied with the spiritual search. He used to visit St Paul's Cathedral in the City of London, where he would kneel beneath 'Light of the World', Holman Hunt's painting of Jesus knocking at the door of the human heart, and there he would pray to meet a true Christian.

He started work for the Simon Community, helping to run a hostel for London's homeless in Kentish Town. One night on the street nearby he met four devotees who were walking to the temple, five miles away, because they had missed the last train home. They seemed to be glowing. He offered them a room for the night. They lay down on the bare floor, with no bedding and only their shawls for warmth. At five in the morning when he got up to find them, he was told that they had left hours ago.

He couldn't forget them, so he visited the temple, where he bought a *Krishna* book. At the end of each chapter it was written that the reader would be liberated. A few weeks after buying the book Robert heard that the book's author, the founder of the Hare Krishna movement, would be giving a talk at Hampstead Town Hall.

The event was publicised with posters on the underground, showing a prophetic figure with his arms outstretched in an ecstatic pose, radiating beams of light emblazoned with the words PURE LOVE OF GOD. The figure was a depiction of Prabhupada, and the design was executed by a devotee-artist and hand-printed in day-glo inks on donated paper using an improvised silkscreen press upstairs in the temple. A friend of the devotees paid to display two hundred of these handmade posters along the platforms of Central London's tube stations.

Robert went along to hear Prabhupada speak, bringing with him the director of the hostel. On the way from the tube station they passed a strange sight: a group of monks in saffron robes were struggling to carry an enormous throne up Haverstock Hill – the temple van had broken down. Robert and his companion entered the hall, sat at the back, and watched as the throne arrived and was heaved onto the stage. A kirtan began and the hall filled. Prabhupada arrived and took his seat on the throne. After leading some more chanting he began his lecture. Robert's friend was uncomfortable – he was a committed Christian – and during the talk he lit up a cigarette. Prabhupada paused.

'Someone is smoking. Stop it.'

The smoker extinguished his cigarette but his ego was hurt. As he listened to the lecture, delivered with uncompromising directness, his discomfort increased. At one point Prabhupada warned that a person who lived like a dog would become a dog in the next life. A man in the audience stood up and interrupted. 'What's wrong with dogs? I wouldn't mind being a dog.'

'Then you have my blessings,' responded Prabhupada.

Robert's companion had heard enough. He got up to leave, gesturing for Robert to leave too. But Robert was struck by Prabhupada's authority and stayed put as his colleague disappeared.

When Prabhupada had finished and made his exit, Robert considered the experience. The person he had just listened to had left a deep impression on him. He wondered if his prayers had been answered and he had found the true servant of God he had always prayed to meet. As he pondered, the devotees fanned out among the audience to preach and sell *Krishna* books. Robert admired their passion – he had always wanted to dedicate himself like that – heart and soul to God's service. He believed he had found a channel through which to do it.

Close to the temple, opposite St Pancras railway station, was the old St Pancras Town Hall. There Prabhupada gave another lecture. It was a warm summer evening as the devotees strolled over from the temple, chattering excitedly through the Bloomsbury streets. At the hall they started a rousing kirtan either side of the empty *vyasasana,* and built to a crescendo for Prabhupada's arrival.

He lectured on the importance of human life as an opportunity to realise God. When he had finished Shyamsundar invited questions.

'Why are you wearing so many rings?' challenged a hippie.

Prabhupada turned away and left Shyamsundar to answer. He explained that Prabhupada wore two rings given to him by his followers, which had no value to him except as tokens of love. One of them was Janaki's treasured gift. After that evening, Prabhupada told Syamasundara that at public lectures he would take no more questions.

Several devotees were gathered in Prabhupada's room, while outside a group was preparing to chant on Oxford Street. Somebody dropped a pair of *karatals,* and the brass cymbals crashed to the pavement. Prabhupada got up to see from his window. In the street the devotees saw him gazing down on them, a look of fatherly affection in his eyes. His look made them determined to go out and please him by singing Krishna's names and selling magazines. He turned back to the devotees sitting round him in his room.

'Sri Chaitanya Mahaprabhu will personally protect them,' he said.

John Grant was among the ones in his room that day. As a boy in Glasgow he had loved to serve as an altar boy at his church, but at school he used to get into trouble. Glasgow was a violent place – you either joined a gang and fought, or other boys fought with you because you were not in a gang. John found an escape when he saw the *Radha Krishna Temple* on television singing 'Hare Krishna Mantra' on Top of the Pops. That was how he learned to chant Hare Krishna.

At seventeen he hitchhiked to London, where he tasted what the world had to offer, made friends, and thought he had discovered love. But after three years in a relationship and the birth of a daughter, the love was gone and he found himself alone. Disillusioned with life, he remembered how he had several times met Hare Krishna devotees and how they always seemed so happy. He found his way to the temple, where he stood hesitating on the front step. The door burst open and there was Tribhuvanatha with a *mridanga* round his neck.

'I've come home,' said John. He was just twenty.

Now, barely six weeks later, he was one of those accepted as a disciple of Prabhupada. He was given the name Kishor.

Every morning around six Prabhupada went for his daily walk. He first entered the temple to pay his respects to Krishna, and brought to life those few devotees drowsily chanting on their beads who were waiting to see who would accompany him. Shyamsundar would select a few lucky ones, usually no more than three or four. They would follow Prabhupada at a brisk pace as he walked the short distance, past the British Museum and up Montague Street, to the tree-filled gardens of Russell Square. The park was created in 1802 on the grounds of the demolished Bedford House. At one end a large statue of the fifth Duke of Bedford, who had laid out the square, stood on a towering plinth. A pigeon usually sat on its head.

'This is material life,' Prabhupada laughed. 'After so much labour for money and prestige, his reward is to stand in a public place with the pigeons passing stool on his head.'

One morning Kishor joined Prabhupada's walk and asked a question. During his years of confusion before he had come to the temple, he had acquired one special possession: an Indian poster of Krishna standing among trees on the bank of a river beneath the full moon, smiling and playing his flute. He used to chant for hours in front of that picture and feel himself in the spiritual world. Under Krishna's feet had been the name 'Murli-Manohara'.

'Srila Prabhupada, one of Krishna's names is Murli-Manohara. Could you tell us what this means?' Prabhupada stopped and closed his eyes for a moment. Kishor could tell by his smile that he had appreciated the question.

'*Murli* means flute, and *manohara* means beautiful. So when Krishna takes his flute he is even more beautiful.' As he said this Prabhupada looked deep into Kishor's eyes.

In early September Prabhupada made plans to fly to Mombassa, Kenya. He had been invited there to recuperate from his recent bout of ill health in a house by the seafront. A party went ahead, consisting of Nara Narayana, Pradyumna, and Bhavananda, recently arrived from New York. They would prepare the place for him and plan a major public event in Nairobi the following week.

In those last few days in London the temple was quiet. The devotees from Germany, Holland, and France had returned to their countries, and of Prabhupada's American retinue only Shyamsundar and Aravinda remained to look after his needs. This provided an opportunity for the London devotees, who numbered less than twenty, to come closer to Prabhupada. Shyamsundar arranged for them to spend time with him either in his room or on walks in the fine September weather.

On one morning walk round Russell Square, a few shy young devotees accompanied Prabhupada. He chanted on his beads while they obediently followed him, chanting on theirs and trying to think of good questions, which they knew he liked them to ask – that was how they would learn. Just as they were about to leave the square Mahavishnu thought of a question. He picked a rose and ran over to offer it to his guru.

'Prabhupada, when a worm is cut in half, what happens to the soul?' It was a trivial question, hardly worth bothering his spiritual master with. But more than knowing about the worm's soul, he needed to know that his own soul was recognised and cared for. Gently holding the rose, Prabhupada stopped and looked at his young disciple.

'Another soul takes the opportunity and enters,' he said gravely. It was the only time he spoke on the whole morning walk, but it was enough for Mahavishnu. Prabhupada had taken his question seriously.

On the last day of his visit to London, he called Subhaga and told him he must finish his translation by nightfall so he could take it with him. Subhaga confessed that this was impossible, so Prabhupada told him to finish as soon as he could and to send it to him in India.

When a few weeks later Subhaga sent his manuscript, Prabhupada corrected it in his own hand and returned it, with a note to say that it was 'eighty-five percent alright' and he should continue.

On 10th September, the morning of his departure, Carol heard that Prabhupada was leaving. Since moving in she had worked hard in the temple. Now, recovered from her psychedelic haze, she realised she didn't know him at all, and feared she had missed her chance. Mondakini was crying, everyone was upset. Carol ran out to the van and piled in with the others to go to the airport.

At the airport by the departure gate, they sat on the floor, surrounding Prabhupada, anxiously watching his face as he quietly chanted on his beads. He called Tribhuvanatha over and spoke a few words of encouragement to him. Kshirodakshayi arrived with his family and garlanded Prabhupada with carnations interspersed with ten-pound notes. Hearts beat faster as the minutes ticked by until the call came for Prabhupada's flight. Wanting to keep him with them, but knowing he must go, his disciples followed him to the gate and bid a tearful farewell.

The following day Carol sent him a heartfelt letter, carefully inscribed in her very best handwriting, expressing her regret at having been too bewildered to appreciate his presence, and her hope that he would be her spiritual master forever. He wrote back from Nairobi.

> My dear Carol,
>
> I beg to thank you very much for your letter.... I have read the headline prayer. It is nicely written, correctly spelled, which shows that you are a very intelligent girl and you can use your talent and intelligence for serving the Lord. Young boys and girls are sometimes agitated in mind but if we follow the regulative principles and chant Hare Krishna mantra regularly the onslaught of material nature can be checked.... By the grace of Lord Chaitanya things have been reduced to a very simple operation: by chanting Hare Krishna, Hare Krishna, Krishna, Krishna, Hare Hare/ Hare Rama, Hare Rama, Rama Rama, Hare Hare.[4]

She was afraid she might not see him again, but his letter showed that he had accepted her, and as good as initiated her into the chanting of Hare Krishna. Reassured, she devoted her talents to serving Krishna in the London temple. Along with her spiritual brothers and sisters, she prayed that Krishna would protect her spiritual master as he travelled the world, and bring him back to London soon.

CHAPTER 11

Expanding Mission

By the time Prabhupada's stay in the summer of 1971 came to an end the young community was infused with new energy. However, money was short. With Dayananda's arrival from America this began to change. He had trained as a U.S. Marine before serving as president of the Los Angeles temple. Prabhupada wrote expressing his confidence in him and in his wife Nandarani. 'Our London centre is very important … try to develop [it] to the best of your capacity. I am sure that now London temple is in the right hands.'[1]

Supported by these words Dayananda expanded the sales of *Back to Godhead* magazines and *Krishna* books, and built up the temple's incense business, while Tribhuvanatha, with his youthful dedication and contagious enthusiasm, inspired the devotees.

As the sense of stability grew, the way opened for a new phase of expansion. The Birmingham centre had already been opened, and the same pioneering spirit that had brought the original six founding devotees to London now inspired a new wave of British devotees to beat their drums on the streets of Cardiff, Manchester, and Edinburgh.

Prabhupada, having rested in Kenya for a month, returned to India with renewed vigour. There he pushed his disciples, among them Shyamsundar, Malati, Gurudas, and Yamuna, to start three major temples: Bombay in the west, Vrindavan in the north, and Mayapur in the east. Life in India was austere and progress was beset by obstacles, but Prabhupada's energy was undiminished in even the most trying circumstances. He encouraged his disciples to be the same in fulfilling his vision. 'I have built the skyscraper skeleton,' he wrote, 'now you all intelligent American and European boys and girls fill in the spaces nicely in good taste.'[2]

Heartened by the movement's progress in India and around the world Prabhupada exhorted his young followers in Britain to preach fearlessly.

> Empires come and go, so many huge empires and lands and properties all vanquished, just like the British Empire. Present our philosophy nicely, and they are very intelligent people, they will understand and appreciate. By becoming Krishna conscious, no more need for wasting time acquiring this or that to expand our economy. Every Krishna conscious man should know for certain that this material world simply has no use for us. With every step there is danger and so many anxieties. No gentleman should want to live here in this material world. Preach to the Britishers very strongly in this way.[3]

In response to their efforts, a steady stream of young men and women came to join them. In Manchester devotees became a daily sight on Market Street, chanting and selling magazines. When they first appeared they were a sensation, and drew a crowd so large that it had to be dispersed by the police.

Pauline McCurry, from Knutsford in Cheshire, was studying engineering at the University of Manchester. She was on her lunch break when she was stopped by Mahavishnu carrying several *Krishna* books in his shoulder bag. Pauline was devoted to Jesus; her fervour was such that she persuaded her whole family to be baptised, and organised a family reunion for the occasion. Now, encountering a new form of devotion, she studied this unusual young man, and found herself buying a *Krishna* book from him. She took it home and read it wide-eyed. For the first time she appreciated that God was truly a person. On the back of the book was a picture of Prabhupada laughing, his eyes alight with joy. She felt a strong connection to him. Confused, she went to church to ask Jesus what she should do. As she sat praying a beam of sunlight shone through the stained glass image of Christ directly onto the *Krishna* book in her lap. She took this as a sign, and began visiting the temple.

There she made friends with Devamaya, who answered her questions and taught her to cook vegetarian food. She met lots of people on her visits, good people with whom she wanted to spend more time. One night she saw Prabhupada in a dream. He stood on the opposite bank of a river, surrounded by dancing devotees, inviting her to cross the river and join him. This vision impressed itself upon her so deeply that as soon as she passed her eighteenth birthday she said goodbye to her family and moved in with the devotees to share their small ashram in Salford, across the river Irwell from Manchester.

Not far from the temple in Salford lived a young Muslim girl named Nagma Mir, who had run away from her family in Burnley to stay with her older sister. At home in Burnley she had been brought up to be strictly religious. She felt isolated as the only Pakistani girl in her school, and at home she felt that her parents were forcing her to live a life she didn't want. They allowed her no freedom and had already chosen her future husband. There had to be a better life than this, she thought, and prayed to Allah every night to guide her to freedom and happiness.

When her older sister left home, Nagma packed her bag and followed her to Salford, where her sister put her up in her apartment. They saw the Hare Krishna devotees regularly when they went to Market Street. Nagma wanted to be happy like them: they seemed to possess something special. She bought one of their booklets, but found it hard to understand.

One fateful night after a traumatic scene at a party she found herself alone on the streets of Salford. Her sister had gone off her with the keys to their flat. Frightened and upset, she wandered the streets during the small hours, feeling lost and abandoned. All her life she had prayed for freedom and happiness. Why were her prayers not being answered? As dawn broke and her despair deepened she passed a launderette on Langworthy Road and saw inside two otherworldly figures dressed in saffron robes. They looked to her almost divine, their faces shining. They were in fact two devotees doing the temple laundry. She went in and sat beside them, mute with fear. They could see she was distressed and invited her to the temple. The minute she stepped through the temple door she felt safe, as if she had come home. They gave her breakfast and a place to sleep. Pauline looked after her and dressed her in a sari. Nagma didn't understand their philosophy, but she recognised their warmth and humanity, and above all their happiness. She knew her life had taken a new path, and at last she believed Allah had answered her prayers.

Tony and Stephen also joined the Manchester temple. Anthony Paget grew up in Manchester. As a student he became a long-haired and confused rebel, seeking answers to life through music and drugs and propounding his ideas to anyone who would listen and help him make sense of them. A friend gave him a copy of *Back to Godhead*. The painting on the cover fascinated him: Krishna was walking through the Vrindavan forest surrounded by white cows and brightly dressed cowherd boys. The forest seemed luminous, lit by a soft pink sky. Tony was irresistibly drawn to the magazine. He read Prabhupada's article, which described how modern youth were frustrated, resorting to intoxication, and becoming lost in an impersonal void. Reading it he felt he had at last found someone who understood what he was going through. A few days later he had an overwhelming sense of the presence of a guiding force in the universe and felt the urgent need to understand more. He came to the temple, which to him appeared as a solid island in an ephemeral world. There the devotees made him feel at home, and he entered the ashram, where he eventually sacrificed his long hair.

Stephen Perry was on a spiritual odyssey. He grew up in Preston, where he had been a sensitive child always searching for the truth about life, God, and the soul. At school he could get no satisfactory answers and felt restless. When he was twenty he won a place at Bristol College of Art. Away from home for the first time, surrounded by open and enquiring minds, he felt his life open out. Art was for him a window through which to explore the world of spirit. Yet inevitably in an art college in 1970, LSD was everywhere. Under its influence he entered a spiritual struggle in which he glimpsed higher truths but felt shadows drawing around him. In the darkness he found strength in George Harrison's songs. 'Beware of *maya,*' sang George, and offered Stephen a guiding light that helped him find shelter in a deeper truth and give up drugs.

Stephen moved back home to be with his family. One day his sister came in with the Radha Krishna Temple record – 'Hare Krishna Mantra', with 'Prayers to the Spiritual Masters' on the 'B' side. He played that 'B' side over and over. He had never heard a sound like it. It took his breath away. He left home again, this time in search of a spiritual teacher. First he went to Scotland, to the recently established Tibetan Buddhist centre, Samye Ling. Not finding what he was looking for there, he hitchhiked to Manchester. A single ride took him all the way to Piccadilly Gardens in the city centre, where he arrived just in time to meet a party of devotees gathering on a bench to have lunch. They welcomed him to share their meal and afterwards took him back to their temple.

That night he stayed with a friend, and dreamt that night that he was chanting Hare Krishna. Next day he walked across Manchester, with his guitar and sleeping bag, back to the temple. He moved in, and a few days later, while chanting with the devotees at Bickershaw Pop Festival, he felt something vast open inside him and had a glimpse of the beauty of Krishna's name. That was enough to persuade him to stay.

Sally Anne Bourne grew up in South London where she did well at school. She had plenty of opportunity to explore life, but could find nothing that satisfied her. While her friends were going out with boys, her search for answers led her to church where she talked with the priests, to books about the occult, and to learn yoga. But none of these held her interest. Her mother asked her what was the matter. 'I don't know,' she said. 'I just can't find what I'm looking for.'

In Brixton Market she met a devotee and bought a *Back to Godhead* magazine. She went through it from cover to cover. It made more sense to her than anything she had ever read. She looked at the photo of Prabhupada and felt she had never seen anyone with a face so wise, serene, and loving. She told her mother she was going to the London temple for the Sunday feast, saved up her money, caught the bus from Streatham, and followed her street map to the temple door. But she was scared to enter. Then some devotees arrived and invited her in. Lilashakti smiled and beckoned her into the temple room to sit down. When the curtains opened and she saw Radha and Krishna, she knew she was home. After that she went there whenever she could. She lost interest in school. She was only fifteen, though she looked much older, and when she missed one of her exams her mother gave her an ultimatum: 'Either give up the temple and focus on your exams, or take your things and go.' Sally packed her overnight bag and walked all the way to the temple. Bala Gopala, recently returned from Amsterdam, welcomed her into the ashram and looked after her as if she were her daughter.

In Birmingham Virasingham, who had returned to college after seeing Prabhupada in the summer, was becoming daily more involved with his local temple, sacrificing his meagre allowance to help to keep the centre afloat. One day he appeared at college wearing a *dhoti*. His lecturer talked to him about the importance of finishing his course, but for Virasingham it was too late: his heart was already with the temple. He went to London and, tearfully remembering his father, who had had such high hopes for him to have an engineering career, had his head shaved and took his place among the devotees. His sister was studying in London. One day on Oxford Street she saw her brother chanting with the devotees. She hurried up to him. 'My brother, what are you doing?' she cried. Realising his secret would now be exposed to his family in Malaysia, Virasingham brought his sister to the temple in an attempt to explain his choice. To his relief she was profoundly touched by the experience. She helped him break the news to their family and herself became a regular visitor to the temple.

At the end of Prabhupada's 1971 visit Kulashekara had gone to open a centre in Cardiff, taking with him Paul Barrow and Sukarma. The three of them had received Prabhupada's personal blessings and his garland before setting off. Kulashekara was a natural communicator and a talented musical performer who easily drew an admiring crowd. They arrived in Cardiff at a time when young men were experimenting with psychedelic experiences. The devotees offered a spiritual alternative, based on chanting, dancing, and feasting, and their numbers soon grew. Among those who joined them were three friends: Chris, Ian, and Jeffrey.

Christopher Murphy began life as a devout Catholic altar boy. When, at the age of fourteen, he missed Sunday mass, his father beat him. Disillusioned, he decided to try being an atheist. He joined the merchant navy to see the world. In the middle of the Atlantic he had a change of heart when his ship was caught in a hurricane – it was the most terrifying experience he had ever had. He found himself praying, and that was when he realised he still believed in God.

Back home, he wandered through several jobs, tried to live the hippie dream, and read all Lobsang Rampa's books on Tibetan Buddhism. One day he saw the devotees singing Hare Krishna on Top of the Pops. He bought George Harrison's *All Things Must Pass* and the *Radha Krishna Temple* album and played them continuously. In the spring of 1971 Tribhuvanatha and a group of devotees visited Cardiff and sang on stage at the college union, and Chris was the first to talk with them.

'You're not that body!' Sukarma had told him, poking him in the chest. All that Chris had read about the spirit suddenly became real to him. He bought a *Gita* and read it straight through twice, then started praying to Krishna to send the devotees back to Cardiff.

By the time Kulashekara arrived at the end of the summer Chris was waiting for him. He put him up in his tiny flat, along with Paul and Sukarma. As a result the landlord threw him out, and Chris had little choice other than to join the devotees. Two weeks later, his head shaved, he was singing with them on the street every day. By Christmas he was at the temple in London.

Ian Cheverton was well-known among the alternative youth in Cardiff. Unlike many of his friends he held a steady job as a chemical engineer at British Steel. In his spare time he sang in a band and pursued his main interest, studying Eastern philosophies and chanting mantras in the hope of uncovering the mysteries of God and the universe. He had a wide circle of friends who respected him as an authority on spiritual matters. When he met Kulashekara and chanted with the devotees, he felt a kinship with them, and after they left Chris's flat, he helped them find their own place. Before long he decided to join them. After spending one last Christmas at home with his parents, making his peace with them round the tree, he moved into the temple.

Jeffrey Davies grew up on Barry Island in South Wales. All his life he had been a spiritual seeker, and had read widely in Buddhism, Chinese religions, and Hinduism. He even read the *Bhagavad-gita* as a schoolboy and from it developed an attachment to Krishna's name. He learned to chant Hare Krishna at the Glastonbury Festival in 1970 by listening to the rock group Quintessence chanting on stage.

One day in Cardiff he met a young Welsh devotee named Graham (who later became Gunarnava) and started visiting the ashram. He bought a copy of Prabhupada's *Teachings of Lord Chaitanya* in a high-street bookshop and read two hundred pages in one day. By the time he reached the end he was a devotee of Krishna. In the early hours of the next morning he rolled up his sleeping bag and hitchhiked to the temple.

Another young man who went to the Glastonbury Festival was Geoffrey Warman, from Swindon, who had just completed a degree in

Geography. Like many of his generation his experiences with psychedelic drugs had drawn him to Eastern mysticism, and in the course of his reading he had discovered Krishna and the *Bhagavad-gita*. He came across a pile of *Back to Godhead* magazines at a friend's house and read them through one by one. The articles, whether by Prabhupada or his followers, captured his interest. He wanted to chant Krishna's name, which sounded to him clear and pure after the confusion of sounds he was used to hearing in hippie pads. His friends thought him deluded, but they let him take the magazines with him and he studied them for weeks before finding his way to the London temple, where he was greeted with lots of chanting and fed continuous plates of prasadam. He bought the two volumes of *Krishna* book and carried them home to Swindon.

In his room he made a simple altar with a picture of Radha and Krishna and instituted his own daily routine, based on what he had seen at the temple, of chanting, reading *Bhagavad-gita As It Is*, and offering his food to Krishna. He even invited friends round for feasts on Sundays. He got a cleaning job at a factory, and saved his earnings to give to the devotees in London when he went to visit them. Over a period of six months he prepared himself to exchange his secure life at home for the uncertainty of living in the temple. When the time came his mother begged him not to go, but his mind was made up. He moved into the London temple on Lord Chaitanya's birthday in March 1972.

Jeffrey Cargill was born in Jamaica into a middle-class family who raised him to be a good Christian. When he was very young he wrote a letter to God saying, 'I want to see you in this lifetime.' His mother emigrated with him to England when he was twelve and enrolled him in the local school in Stepney Green, East London, where he excelled. Influenced by Rastafarianism he turned vegetarian. He also became a student of Marx. He enrolled in the Young Socialists, but when he realised that Marxism contradicted his religious instincts he gave it up.

After finishing sixth form he decided not to go straight to university – first he wanted to find a spiritual path. He spent time with the Jesus People, then explored the alternative scene in London. That summer, 1971, he saw the devotees celebrating Rathayatra, and followed them back to Bury Place. On the steps stood Manohara, a Hindu friend of the temple. 'Here you will find the absolute truth,' Manohara predicted, and Jeffrey did. Three months later, while his head was being shaved, he resolved that whatever it took he was determined to see this through to the end.

During his early days in the temple he had difficulty accepting the worship of Krishna's deity form – he had been brought up to regard such worship as idolatry. After examining the practice and studying the philosophy behind it he concluded that to make personal offerings to God in this way was profound and meaningful. So he overcame his doubts and worked hard for Krishna.

As these and other young men and women settled into life at the temple that winter and spring, Prabhupada travelled ceaselessly across India – north, south, east, and west. Shyamsundar, accompanied by Malati and little Saraswati, went with him as his secretary, typing his letters to disciples all over the globe. In November Prabhupada lectured for ten nights at Delhi's Connaught Place, in the heart of the city, inside a huge marquee in the central gardens. Attendance surpassed all expectations, numbering over half a million. Prabhupada's stock was high, and many came forward during those days to help his mission.

He went to Vrindavan, where he received a hero's welcome in his former home and was given land in the groves on the edge of town upon which to build a temple. In Bombay he negotiated the purchase of a twenty-acre, palm-filled plot near Juhu Beach, by the Arabian Sea, where he planned a 'Hare Krishna City'.[4] In Mayapur, West Bengal, on Sri Chaitanya's birthday in February, he laid the cornerstone for the new temple. A week later in Vrindavan he concluded the transfer of land and held a ground-breaking ceremony, leaving instructions with Yamuna and Gurudas to stay there and build a beautiful temple for Krishna and Balaram. At the end of this whirlwind of activity

Prabhupada in his room at 7 Bury Place.

Morning and afternoon, devotees chanted on Oxford Street, or further afield in Chelsea, Kensington, or Hampstead. (Left to right: Tribhuvanatha, Ranchor, Jaihari, Sukarma, Bhushakti, Trilokanatha)

At the Hindu Centre, Prabhupada told his audience to offer respect even to an ant, because Krishna is in the heart of every living entity. (Left to right: Kshirodakshayi, Aravinda, Pratejas, unknown, Vishvadharini, Shyamsundar, Jijñasi, Prabhupada, Ratimanjari, Vidyabhadu, Vasudeva)

'We are preaching love of God,' Prabhupada told Sister Mary. 'It doesn't matter what religion you are following. We simply want to see that you have love for God.' (Left to right: Svati, Rebatinandan, Sister Mary, unknown, Kshirodakshayi, Suchandra, Shivananda)

'atiently he discussed the intricacies of Vedic philosophy with his guests.

Every day he lectured from the first two chapters of *Srimad-Bhagavatam*.

Above his head hung a silk parasol fringed with pearl-like beads. To his right he could almost reach out and touch Radharani. His devotees could now see Krishna and their guru in one glance, as if they were together on the same altar.

Milan received favoured treatment, being called regularly into Prabhupada's room, or to accompany him to an outside engagement. (Left to right: Nara Narayana, Shyamsundar, Prabhupada, Milan [Subhaga])

Every morning around six o'clock Prabhupada went for his daily walk.

Prabhupada, Pattie Boyd, George, and Dhananjaya, photographed by Shyamsundar at Friar Park in 1972.

Outside Kshirodakshayi's house, Jaihari opens the car door.

Shyamsundar took Prabhupada to visit a redundant church near Sloane Square.

In St James's Park they passed a man asleep on a bench. 'These people are rich, but they have to sleep in the park,' commented Prabhupada. 'But Krishna consciousness is so powerful it can change a person's destiny.'

In Kensington Gardens by the pond, Prabhupada commented, 'The pond is dangerous for us, but for these ducks it is safe because they have taken shelter of the water. If we take shelter of Krishna, we will always be safe.' (Rebatinandan holds his staff; behind Prabhupada on his right is Narendra, on his left Partha; the others are visiting from Amsterdam)

The Hindu Centre was packed with devotees. On Prabhupada's right is Nanda Kumar and the young Animisha, to his left in yellow is Devamaya.

Kshirodakshayi booked an old wooden mission hall in Wembley. Prabhupada, sitting on the small stage, gave a short lecture to the crowded room.

He began an initiation ceremony. At the end of the programme he addressed the audience with a few words of Hindi. His disciples could not understand, but he praised them, saying how well they were doing in devotional service and how they were helping him spread Krishna consciousness. (Prabhavishnu sits on stage on the left of the picture; in the centre Bhajahari casts grains in the fire)

Prabhupada boarded the large *vyasasana* mounted on the front of the car. This was the fourth Rathayatra, but Prabhupada's first, in London. As the procession slowly got under way, he rode below Lord Jagannath but just above the heads of the crowd, grave and serene amid the pageant and music.

Amidst all this, Prabhupada sat calmly, his head held high, surveying the multitude of Jagannath's devotees.

'Ladies and Gentlemen, thank you very much for coming here and participating in this great movement. The purpose of this movement is to cleanse the heart.'

When Prabhupada spoke, a hush spread across Trafalgar Square. His voice echoed from the imposing façades, carrying his message into the heart of London.

In Glasgow, at Woodside Hall, Prabhupada gave a short lecture on the *Bhagavad-gita,* keeping it simple but powerful. Afterwards the audience began to applaud, first one, then another, until the whole auditorium was standing in ovation and cheering.

Prabhupada spoke to the modest crowd of devotees and temple friends. Among them were four ten-year-old local boys, dressed in their Sunday best, who bowed along with everyone else. 'Krishna is God, and God is great. Philosophy means to know how God is great.'

In Edinburgh, the temple room was brightly-painted and spacious. The floor was deep blue, the walls yellow and pink and hung with large oil paintings of Narada Muni and Sri Chaitanya, and there was the familiar old London *vyasasana,* which in this high-ceilinged room no longer seemed so huge.

One day he took his Mayapur construction team to visit Westminster Abbey and told them he wanted the interior of the Mayapur temple to resemble the inside of the abbey. (Left to right: Bhavananda, Aravinda, Shyamsundar, Prabhupada, Nara Narayana)

Shyamsundar summed up Prabhupada's achievements when he wrote, 'At last we have got huge projects at Mayapur, Vrindaban, and Bombay. All the lands are acquired, arrangements made, and everything by Prabhupada. But only a few of us are here to struggle with an immense task of developing these three places.'[5]

Not pausing to rest, Prabhupada embarked on his second major world tour. Leaving India via the Pacific route, stopping in Australia, New Zealand, and Hawaii on the way, he arrived in Los Angeles by the middle of May. There he halted, wishing to concentrate on his writing. For twenty months he had kept up a relentless pace. Now he needed to reduce the pressures upon him of managing his rapidly growing society. For this purpose he had already created a governing body, known as the GBC, with the hope that its members would take the burden of management from him. Yet still, most of his time was taken up with management. His need for relief became a regular theme of his letters during the first half of 1972.

> Our Society is growing very rapidly all over the world, and the burden of administration is taxing me too much and taking too much time.[6]
>
> I am now old man and inclined for philosophy and translating.[7]
>
> I am feeling the tendency more and more to retire behind the scenes for translating work, and I want to turn over the management of everything to the GBC and other senior leaders among my disciples.[8]

These pressures of expansion were being felt in London. With new members joining all the time, and a stream of travellers passing through between America and India, the Bury Place building was hopelessly inadequate. The need for a larger temple was clear. Dayananda had located a large Methodist hall in Holborn and was bidding for it. The asking price was more than £200,000 – well beyond the devotees' means – but Prabhupada encouraged him.

Mukunda and Janaki were now living in Portland, Oregon, close to their old hometown. Prabhupada wrote to them about the importance he attached to developing the London temple:

> You are both some of my first disciples, and because of you so many others came, so I am always remembering you fondly. Practically it was you who started our two most important centres. [Dayananda] has requested you to return to London to help him in getting that huge church in the most important quarter of the most important city in the world. [He] is confident we can raise the money in England, because George and his friends are offering to help very enthusiastically. [London] is the best place for us. It will be the most grand headquarters for ISKCON in all the world, and I want to get that place very very much.[9]

Basing himself in Los Angeles for two months to concentrate on his writing, Prabhupada asked Dayananda to fix a date for him to attend the London Rathayatra.[10]

A significant addition to the London community came in early 1972 with the arrival of Rebatinandan. He had joined the San Francisco temple in 1968, a month after his cousin Vishnujana and just after the London-bound pioneers had departed. Later he went to India as part of Prabhupada's World Sankirtan Party. He was an energetic man with a talent for philosophy, debate, and charismatic leadership. In recognition of his dedication to preaching Prabhupada had awarded him the order of *sannyasa* and told him to preach wherever he went. Rebatinandan Swami arrived in England to find a temple crowded with young devotees eager to learn from him. It was an atmosphere in which he flourished both as a teacher and a kirtan leader. His plan was to travel round the universities and teach students about Krishna consciousness. Prabhupada wrote to him with approval.

> I am very much pleased upon you for taking up the matter of preaching work in England … I think your idea to canvass the youth groups and colleges is good proposal … England is the best field in the world for distributing our books, as good or better than USA.[11]

While Rebatinandan was touring with a small crew of men, the Bury Place basement was piled to the ceiling with unsold *Krishna* books. When they had been printed in Japan the previous year Prabhupada had ordered a quarter of the print-run to be sent to London. The stock took up half the basement room where the devotees ate their meals. It filled them with dismay: how were they to sell that many books?

Dayananda did his best to push *Krishna* book sales and raise money for a new temple. He bought a van, filled it with books, and took devotees out on the road to sell them door to door and on high streets. The boxes of books steadily reduced all through winter and spring, until at last they were gone. Supplies of *Back to Godhead* magazines, also shipped from Japan, were intermittent. While finances diminished, Dayananda soldiered on. His wife Nandarani, feeling neglected and with nowhere to raise their two small daughters, decided to return to America. At the limit of his capacities and deserted by his family, Dayananda resigned his post to follow them back across the Atlantic.

Dhananjaya came with his wife Bala Gopala and took over as president. They had served in Amsterdam for over a year, after which they had visited Bala Gopala's family in California. While visiting the temple in L.A., Dhananjaya had learned how to sell *Krishna* books. Dhananjaya's relaxed management style was welcomed in London, and despite continuing money problems the devotees did well under his guidance. Rebatinandan regularly led kirtans, taught the devotional songs he had learned in India, and inspired the devotees with his bold teaching style.

A letter arrived from Prabhupada for Carol and Chris, naming them Sarvamangala and Bhajahari. Paul, who had been with Kulashekara in Cardiff, was given the name Prabhavishnu. He had spent the winter helping in the Paris temple, and while there had received his initiation letter from Prabhupada. Even as he was initiating these new disciples, Prabhupada counselled his leaders not to add too quickly to their numbers.

> Now we have got so many students and so many temples but I am fearful that if we expand too much we shall become weakened.... Just like milk, we may thin it more and more with water for cheating the customer, but in the end it will cease to be any longer milk. Better to boil the milk now very vigorously and make it thick and sweet.[12]

Despite this counsel the devotees were so excited about Krishna consciousness that they wanted to tell everyone about it. Paul returned to London to help with the book distribution. He was a natural leader and took up this new challenge with determination. When more *Krishna* books arrived, many eager hands came forward to distribute them. Mahavishnu discovered that if he went inside the carriages on the London Underground, holding aloft a *Krishna* book and announcing that it would save the reader from suffering repeated birth and death in this world, he was able to find purchasers. He started selling five or even ten books a day.

Sudurjaya took charge of the incense business. He rented a four-storey building in Hoxton Square, painted its façade pink, yellow, and blue to match the colours of the incense packet, and recruited devotees and friends of the temple to work there when they could, as a service to support the temple. He played tapes of devotional music, provided nourishing lunches, created an atmosphere of happy industry, and ferried his workers to and from the temple in a blue Transit van bought for the business.

A date for Rathayatra was set, finances were getting healthier, talk of a new temple abounded amid general optimism. Svayambhur took time out from building the *rath* car to build a new *vyasasana*. He made a smaller throne, in scale with the small Bury Place temple room, to fit at the front of the temple beside the altar, so that Prabhupada could be next to Radha and Krishna again. Peter, who had just joined, was trained in upholstery. He went out into the West End and returned with a length of green velvet, several gold trims, and a pair of delicate sequinned peacocks. On the eve of Prabhupada's arrival he worked through the night to give the new *vyasasana* a handsome finish, while others made last minute preparations.

Sarvamangala sat with a group of friends in the sewing room making decorations for the temple. Her special project was a floral banner spelling out the words 'Jaya Gurudeva,' which she planned to hang across the width of the building beneath the second-storey windows. Full of excitement, they awaited Prabhupada's imminent arrival.

CHAPTER 12

The Best Rathayatra Ever

At the airport, while Geoffrey arranged chairs in the VIP room and nervously anticipated his first meeting with his guru, Sudurjaya and Jaihari stood out in the arrivals hall. Suddenly they were shocked to come face to face with Prabhupada standing in the middle of the busy concourse. Accompanied by Shyamsundar, Pradyumna, and his new servant Nanda Kumar, Prabhupada was looking around to find who had come to meet him.

'*Jaya* Prabhupada!' sang Sudurjaya, raising his arms in greeting.

'Where are my devotees?' asked Prabhupada.

Sudurjaya tried to explain. He and Jaihari had planned a high-profile reception. They had booked the VIP lounge, Jaihari had invited the press, Svayambhur, Mahavishnu, and Geoffrey were busy setting up the big old *vyasasana*, a book display, and arranging prasadam for the journalists, and the devotees would arrive from the temple in about an hour.

'Srila Prabhupada, we weren't expecting you for another two hours. The devotees are still at the temple.'

'Then let's go,' said Prabhupada decisively. But first he wanted to see the reception they had arranged. Jaihari led the way. Reaching the lounge Prabhupada saw the waiting *vyasasana* and sat down on it. He asked if there was anything to eat. Nanda Kumar made him up a plate and as Prabhupada ate, Geoffrey watched spellbound, while Svayambhur and Mahavishnu crouched behind the *vyasasana,* holding it together because it had not yet been fully assembled. Prabhupada asked his servant to fill his tiffin, then got up and followed Sudurjaya to the temple van, leaving the three *brahmacharis* and Jaihari amid the remains of the press conference.

As Sudurjaya drove with Prabhupada beside him on the front seat the thought struck him that he must phone the temple. He pulled in beside a red phone box and made the call. A woman's voice answered, and when he said, 'Prabhupada's coming,' she said, 'Yes, I know,' and hung up.

He phoned a second time.

'You don't understand,' he spelled it out. 'Prabhupada will be there in twenty minutes.' As they crawled through the Knightsbridge traffic it began to rain. 'Where are my devotees?' Prabhupada asked Sudurjaya again, as if he doubted they would be there. The London devotees were never far from his thoughts. They were so young and inexperienced. So were all his disciples, but in London particularly they lacked experienced leadership even though they were at the heart of his international movement and living in the city he regarded as the most important in the world. He had flown through the night from New York, where he had only stayed for five days, because he was determined to witness the London Rathayatra.

The van rounded Russell Square. Lookouts posted by Dhananjaya relayed the message to the temple that Prabhupada was arriving. The rain stopped, and just as the clouds parted and sunlight flooded the scene, Sudurjaya switched on the headlamps and turned into Bury Place. Over a hundred chanting devotees crowded the short street. They surged forward as Sudurjaya came slowly to a halt outside the temple.

Tribhuvanatha stepped forward and opened the passenger door. As Prabhupada emerged Tribhuvanatha offered him a garland of French gardenias that reached almost to the ground. He saw how Prabhupada's face lit up at the sight of his disciples, and fell at his feet. Clouds of rose petals drifted down from the upper windows. Prabhupada beamed, his hands joined in acknowledgement of the love that surrounded him. Something remarkable happened that day: many devotees claimed they saw a dazzling light shining from Prabhupada. It was clear he was not an ordinary person.

'My, he really is a holy man,' gasped Nagma. Her faith had been wavering in the face of the rigours of temple life, but they were forgotten when she saw a golden aura around Prabhupada's head and shoulders.

Ian too saw a golden glow that he concluded was a spiritual effulgence; he also saw in Prabhupada a grace of movement that astonished him.

Jeffrey Cargill knelt in the road. He too saw a distinct halo around Prabhupada's head, 'more dazzling than the sun', and it seemed to him that Prabhupada's feet did not touch the ground. None of them spoke of what they had seen until years later.

Sarvamangala saw him look up and smile at her banner. This year she was able to see Prabhupada clearly, and her heart opened to him as her eternal spiritual master.

He made his way inside and stood before the deities, approving their dresses and quietly giving instructions to the *pujaris*. He took his new seat and expressed his gratitude for their welcome, asked how everyone was, then went up to his room. Shortly he called for Peter and Svayambhur.

'Did you make the *vyasasana*?' he asked them. 'I like it very much. Now I want two more – one for Lord Brahma and one for Lord Shiva.'

Three years earlier he had said that Brahma and Shiva had been present at Conway Hall, although no one else had seen them. Now he wanted seats made for them. He said the seats should be identical to the one made for him, but smaller so they could fit beside the main altar, on either side of Radha and Krishna. That same evening Peter and Svayambhur made them.

Prabhupada came down for his morning walk. After offering prayers to Radha and Krishna in the temple, he was driven in the van, with a dozen men and women squeezed into the back, to St James's Park. Now he was with them their life was complete. They felt safe. Whatever happened, whatever appeared to go against them, he would know what to do.

When he returned to the temple he took his place on the new *vyasasana* and began the class. A silk parasol fringed with pearl-like beads hung above his head. His seat was so close to the altar that he could almost reach his hand out and touch Radharani. His devotees could now see Krishna and their guru in one glance, as if they were together on the same altar. On either side of the deities he noticed the new miniature seats.

'Very nice. You should know that Lord Brahma and Lord Shiva come here every night for the evening arati.'

He called for the new edition of his *Srimad-Bhagavatam* – Canto One, volume one – which had just arrived from New York, its cover illuminated with a new panoramic painting of the spiritual sky. This was the first time the devotees had seen the book. To mark its appearance he began from the first verse, teaching them how to chant the Sanskrit verses. He nodded to Pradyumna, his Sanskrit scholar, who led the chanting. First Pradyumna recited one word at a time, then one line at a time, and then Prabhupada asked the devotees to take turns leading the recitation. A few faltering attempts were made. He explained how by repeating the verses like this before the class they would soon learn the words and their meanings.

That first morning he looked over his glasses at his young charges as a father looks at his children. He saw Radha and Krishna, the supreme truth, beside him, while in his lap was the *Bhagavatam,* also the supreme truth. Patiently he explained the truth to his children while they struggled to stay awake. Seeing their heads nodding he sometimes corrected them. He needed them to learn self-discipline both for their own sakes and for the sake of his movement. But he also accepted that they were doing their best.

'It is very important to rise early,' he remarked one morning during the class, then added with a wry smile, 'but even though we rise early in the morning, sometimes we compensate at other times.'[1]

Outside the British Museum on his way to Russell Square in the early mornings, he had passed long queues that snaked round the outside of the museum, waiting to see the Tutankhamun exhibition. They were prepared to wait for hours to see the mummified body of an ancient Egyptian king. He was amazed.

> When we install deity, actually the eternal form of Krishna, nobody offers obeisances. In the British Museum, they are standing in queue to offer obeisances to a dead body. It has no value, but they are wasting time there. But here, if they are invited, 'Oh, they are worshipping idols, why should I go there?' This is called illusion.[2]

Wanting his disciples to depend on Krishna, he drew a lesson from the park. That morning they had seen flocks of waterfowl sitting undisturbed by commuters hurrying through the gardens to work. He saw in the ways of birds and animals the intentions of an intelligent creator, teaching humans how to live.

> The swans and ducks in St James's Park, they don't worry what to eat, but they are getting their eatables. They don't go to office, to factory. Even the swans and ducks, what to speak of human beings? Even a small duck and swan, he has got everything ready there in St James's Park. He does not go to Downing Street. Why don't you study? If a swan is provided with all the necessities of life, why I shall not be? I am so much developed human being. Why I am so much busy in economic development?[3]

If his disciples would trust in Krishna, he assured them, all their needs would be supplied. The steady growth of ISKCON – a growth based entirely on their collective faith – was proof to him of Krishna's providence. He gave them an example from his personal life:

> In due course of time, everything, whatever you require, it will come. In my childhood we heard so much about London city that I was desiring, when I shall go to London? Now in due course of time I am walking in London. So Krishna has provided everything for you. Don't worry.[4]

He had high expectations for his British disciples, whose predecessors had built an empire.

> British nation was very powerful nation. So I request you, all English boys and girls present here, now you become greater than your forefathers by taking this Krishna consciousness that will make you more spiritually powerful. You can render service to the humanity through your family, your nation.[5]

Every day he lectured from the first two chapters of *Srimad-Bhagavatam*. He spoke on the opening verse for three mornings, then each day he covered one or two verses. Patiently, day by day, he explained the foundations of the science of Krishna consciousness. After the lectures, rousing kirtans were led by Prabhupada's servant Nanda Kumar, who sung with a strong, youthful voice and set a driving rhythm with his rock-style drumming.

Nagma struggled to understand much of what Prabhupada said, but she was captivated by his mood of devotion and the conviction in his voice. As he left the temple room each day she rushed to be the one to help him into his slippers. He never failed to smile as she did so.

Each morning after the lecture Tony hurried upstairs with the precious reel of recorded tape and transferred it onto a cassette, the latest technology, to be sent to America. There it was added to the archive of Prabhupada's lectures, and copied for distribution throughout the society.[6]

Early on the first morning of Prabhupada's visit Nagma stationed herself outside his door. She sat there trying to chant on her beads while wrestling with the confused impressions in her mind from seeing Prabhupada for the first time. Part of her still felt she couldn't handle living in the temple and must escape to live again with her sister, and part of her wanted to stay there with Prabhupada. He came out of his room and saw her shivering with cold and nerves.

'You're cold,' he said.

'Pardon?' she couldn't understand what he said. Bala Gopala told her that Prabhupada was telling her she was cold.

'No, I'm not,' she protested. She was freezing, but she didn't want to move from that spot.

'Give her a shawl,' he told Bala Gopala. Later he called Nagma into his room.

'So, are you going to stay?' She had not told anyone she was thinking of leaving, but he seemed to know. He asked about her family. She told him they didn't know where she was.

'Then you must contact them and tell them you are here.'

He said he was very happy to have a Muslim disciple. She was too young to understand, but she knew he was kind to her and that he listened when she spoke. She wanted to please him and to give him something in return. So she made up her mind to stay.

Bala Gopala organised a rota so the women could take turns to sit outside Prabhupada's door. Once, when she was sitting there, Prabhupada saw her and commented to his servant.

'Just see,' he said, 'she is sitting there looking like the goddess of fortune.'

When Bala Gopala heard that she felt wonderful. She always felt encouraged by the way Prabhupada treated her with such kindness and consideration.

Sarvamangala and Ramadevi took turns sitting outside his door. One day after using the bathroom he asked Ramadevi to bring him a towel. She dashed upstairs to the sewing room, where she had some of Krishna's towels drying. After Prabhupada dried his hands and returned the towel she kept it for herself, replacing Krishna's towel with a new one bought using her own money. She treasured the one Prabhupada had touched as a reminder of that day.

Another time, when Sarvamangala was sitting there, he sent his servant to invite her in. She sat in the corner of his room while he spoke to his guests, thrilled just to be in his presence.

Prabhupada's male disciples were not always as considerate toward the women as he was, and life for the women in the temple could be tough. They had very little private space and felt that the men discriminated against them. For example, sometimes at meal times the women had to wait until the men had been served; on Prabhupada's walks they were expected to trail behind the men; in the temple room they stood at the back.

It hadn't always been like that. In the early days in London the women could stand where they pleased; then they stood on the right while the men stood on the left. By 1972, after some of the men complained of being distracted by having to see them, the women were forced to the back. It was as if the men were *making* themselves dislike the women because they knew they had to give them up. Prabhupada did not approve. 'If the men are agitated they should go to the forest,' he said. But their behaviour often went unchecked and was a cause of tension in the community.

Living so close to Prabhupada, some devotees would wait on the stairs just to catch a glimpse of him when he emerged from his room. He didn't seem to mind, even when he was dressed only in a cloth wrapped round his waist, crossing to his bathroom.

He noticed and appreciated the smallest detail, as Peter discovered. He was appointed as a regular guard on the landing outside Prabhupada's door. Peter was a natural choice because of his forbidding appearance. Before joining the temple he had cultivated a tough image, but underneath he was a gentle person who loved to read. While on guard duty he absorbed himself in the new *Srimad-Bhagavatam*. Mostly, the only time he would see his guru was if he emerged to visit the bathroom. As Prabhupada passed, Peter would offer obeisances. It only took Peter a few days to read the first volume of the *Bhagavatam*. Just at the moment he finished the book Prabhupada's door opened and Nanda Kumar handed him the second volume.

'Prabhupada said I should give you this one to read.'

The next time Prabhupada came out of his room he nodded his approval to Peter and told him he needn't bow down every time he saw him. After that he bowed first thing each morning, and thereafter continued reading Prabhupada's book.

Some wealthy Hindu businessmen visiting from India came to see Prabhupada. He called for Jeffrey, his black disciple, to sit in the room with him while he spoke to them. As he explained how he was training his disciples to be *brahmanas,* they looked askance at Jeffrey, who to their caste-conscious eyes was an inferior.

'Here in the West people have become degraded,' Prabhupada said. 'They are enjoying sense gratification without restraint like hogs enjoying stool.' His two smartly-dressed guests nodded their agreement.

'And from across the water come some bigger hogs from India, who also want to enjoy this stool.'

After saying this, Prabhupada calmly asked their help to fund a new temple. They laughed nervously, seeing the sparkle in his eyes. This guru, they realised, would not flatter them for their wealth.

Prabhupada called for Subhaga, wanting to see how far he had progressed with his translation work. Subhaga was surprised when Prabhupada remembered exactly where they had left off. How could his memory be so precise? During his stay Prabhupada insisted on keeping Subhaga nearby both in his room and on morning walks so he could examine his knowledge.

'How would you translate "Krishna consciousness" into Bengali?' asked Prabhupada on a walk, then supplied the answer: 'The correct phrase is *krishna-bhavanamrita,* as used by Vishvanath Chakravarti Thakur.'

Sally enjoyed working in the temple. Her sunny disposition and hard-working nature meant she was always kept busy. Bala Gopala assigned her to help Malati cook Prabhupada's lunch. When his empty plate came down she was given it to wash. One day she saw to her satisfaction that it was licked clean – every grain removed. But one small bowl was upside down. Beneath it Sally found half a *gulabjamun*. She was sure he had hidden it specially for her. She stepped outside the kitchen and ate it.

Every morning when Prabhupada went out for his walk, Sally helped the other women clean his room. His Mysore pure vegetarian sandalwood soap was replaced, carpet vacuumed, sheets changed, everything dusted, flowers renewed, fresh garlands laid out, so that he returned to find a sparkling room.

Prabhupada kept a tin of sweets for guests behind his seat. His cleaners noticed that sometimes he left one or two sweets out on his desk, but they didn't dare touch them. Then one day there was double the amount. They decided he must have left them there for a reason – everything he did was for a reason – and that he must have meant them for his cleaning crew, so they took them. After that he regularly left them sweets.

Each morning they tried harder than the previous day. They began decorating his landing with flowers. One day when he returned from his walk he was greeted by a joyful all-female kirtan. From the front door they had lined his path with flowers. Along the hallway, up both sides of the stairs, and all the way to his door – every inch was edged with flowers. Slowly he climbed the stairs, smiling with delight, as above and below him they sang their hearts out. He had been gone for less than an hour, but the women had a festival for his return.

During his daily morning walks Prabhupada mostly chanted quietly on his beads while up to a dozen devotees chanted with him. Sometimes, however, he would answer their questions or comment on what he saw around him. For variety Shyamsundar took him to different parks: Russell Square, Kensington Gardens, Hyde Park, Regent's Park, or St James's Park.

In St James's Park they passed a policeman rudely waking a man who had been asleep on a bench. There seemed no reason in a wealthy country like England for anyone to sleep out in the open, yet it was a common sight.

'These people are rich, but they have to sleep in the park because their karma cannot be changed,' commented Prabhupada. Then he added, 'But Krishna consciousness is so powerful that it can change a person's destiny.'

On another morning in the same park they saw a young lad asleep. He looked like he must have spent the night there. 'By good fortune they can all come to Krishna consciousness,' Prabhupada said as they passed.

Bhajahari, walking behind Prabhupada, heard this and wanted to know more. Why had the devotees been fortunate where others had not? How was it that he had achieved this rare opportunity to walk with a pure devotee? He plucked up his courage and asked Prabhupada.

'Srila Prabhupada, I understand from reading your books that nothing happens by chance. When you said, "By good fortune they can come to Krishna consciousness," what did you mean?'

Prabhupada walked on in silence. A minute passed before he stopped and raised his cane, turning to look right into Bhajahari's eyes. '*We* are their good fortune!' he said.

Rebatinandan Swami, walking beside Prabhupada in Kensington Gardens, brought up the previous day's news. The American Secretary of State, Henry Kissinger, had been photographed in a nightclub with a bare-breasted girl. Prabhupada was scornful. 'They cannot control their own senses, so how will they control the world? These rascals are simply interested in sense gratification.' Turning to his *sannyasi* disciple he advised him, 'Sense desire is like an itch. Just tolerate it and it will go away.'

Passing the Round Pond, the party surprised some sleepy ducks, which scattered over the water. 'The pond is dangerous for us,' commented Prabhupada, 'but for these ducks it is safe because they have taken shelter of the water. If we take shelter of Krishna we will always be safe.'

The swans along the edge of the pond were less easily intimidated. Extending their long necks and flapping their wings, they appeared menacing, blocking the way. Some of the devotees flinched, but Prabhupada showed no fear and the swans retreated.

'The animal kingdom is under nature's laws,' he said. 'These ducks and swans act according to their natures and they get a certain amount of happiness and distress. We humans, who work so hard, also get happiness and distress according to our destiny. So where is the advancement of human civilization?'

In Russell Square a building was being demolished. 'They can create and they can destroy, but they cannot maintain,' commented Prabhupada. 'That is the difficult thing. Therefore Vishnu is the maintainer.'

'Prabhupada, a sage once had no alternative but to eat meat,' one devotee said.

'I would rather die.' He pointed to the hedge. 'Just eat green leaves: they have chlorophyll in them.'

On one walk Shyamsundar took Prabhupada to see a fine church in Kensington. The party of devotees followed him into the porch, where some of them began removing their shoes. As they were about to enter, to everyone's surprise a priest appeared and told Prabhupada to take off his hat. While a few of his disciples went inside the church barefoot and looked around, Prabhupada remained in the porch with his hat on.

'They have everything upside down,' he said as they left. 'They want us to remove our hats but keep our shoes.'

In Hyde Park Tony asked a question. Ever since he had visited the Manchester temple with his friend, something had puzzled him: why had he joined yet not his friend, who had seemed the keener of the two? He formulated his question and respectfully placed it before his spiritual master.

'Prabhupada, why is it that when two people come in contact with Krishna consciousness, one takes it up and the other doesn't?' Prabhupada stopped and considered for a moment.

'When someone is materially fatigued he can take up Krishna consciousness.'

Tony thought he understood, but wondered whether he was sufficiently tired of the material world. Would he be drawn back to it? Then Prabhupada spoke again.

'One becomes materially fatigued by associating with devotees.' With these words he answered Tony's unspoken doubt.

Each morning during the walk Prabhupada's servant went in search of a willow twig for him to use as a toothbrush. On one occasion in Regent's Park the servant returned pursued by a park attendant, who accused him of breaking a twig from a tree. It seemed a trifling matter, and Prabhupada was not impressed.

'Your country has plundered wealth from all over the world, and now you will not allow us to have even a twig from your garden?' The attendant was taken by surprise and backed away without a response, leaving the twig in the servant's hand.

Prabhupada walked on in silence, chanting quietly on his beads through the damp grass and crisp, early-morning sunshine. His disciples followed, committing to memory whatever they had heard.

Returning home in the temple van, with half a dozen devotees in the back, he sat on a brightly coloured blanket in the front seat. As clouds of incense billowed from the dashboard, he sang softly of the spiritual world, '*Chintamini prakara sadmasu …*' Krishna's abode is built with spiritual gems.

Robert Arnold, an assistant manager for the Midland Bank, was a regular visitor to Prabhupada's room. He was a genial man in his fifties, who appeared distinguished with his grey curling locks and proud Scottish bearing. He and his wife Mary became devotees in an unusual way.

One Saturday afternoon, while they were visiting the antiques market on Portobello Road, a devotee accosted Mr Arnold and tried to sell him a magazine. Mr Arnold took exception to the intrusion – he did not like having his time wasted with what he considered superstitious nonsense. In strong language he told the devotee where to go. His wife was shocked at his behaviour and made him apologise and buy the magazine. At home he looked through it and was surprised to find it made good sense. At her suggestion they visited the temple to make a donation to the cause.

So began an unlikely friendship between the Arnolds and the devotees. When Prabhupada came, Mr Arnold offered his services as chauffeur and soon formed a deep attachment for 'Your Divine Grace', as he always addressed Prabhupada.

One evening the couple called in on their way to a Highland Ball, he in a tartan kilt and she in a flowing evening gown. Mr Arnold sat awkwardly on the floor in front of Prabhupada, his legs crossed in a position not becoming a man wearing a kilt.

'You are wearing a skirt,' Prabhupada observed with a polite smile, pronouncing it 'skart'. 'Wouldn't you be more comfortable sitting on a chair?'

Mr Arnold laughed in agreement, and to everyone's relief a chair was brought. He brought a cheery atmosphere to his meetings with Prabhupada, and Prabhupada found his knowledge of banking and commerce a welcome asset. He asked him to advise Dhananjaya on finances and to help with the project to buy a new temple.

An unexpected guest came to see Prabhupada, whose visit prompted a discussion about the practice of chanting God's name. Sister Mary was a Carmelite nun who lived in a small community just round the corner from Bury Place. She was devoted to praying on her rosary, and she always carried with her a set of large wooden prayer beads. She had seen devotees chanting on their beads and become curious. Then one day she met Nanda Kumar outside the temple and he invited her in to meet his spiritual master.

Sister Mary followed Nanda Kumar into Prabhupada's room. When he offered his obeisances she spontaneously followed his example, touching her head to the floor. She was dressed in a full-length grey habit tied at the waist with a cord, from which hung her rosary beads. Her head was shrouded in starched white cloth beneath a black veil. She took her seat on a cushion directly in front of Prabhupada, encircled by devotees, and began by asking if he was trying to make converts.[7]

'We are preaching love of God,' he answered. 'It doesn't matter what type of religion one is following. We simply want to see that he has love for God.'

'How do you know who is a lover of God?'

Prabhupada cited Sri Chaitanya's poem *Shikshastaka,* which

described his feelings of love for Krishna. 'Every moment is like twelve years. I am crying torrents of rain. I find everything vacant without God,' he translated. 'Like Jesus Christ, Sri Chaitanya sacrificed everything. That is love of God. You may follow any religious path – it doesn't matter. The method is simple: chant the holy name of God. We don't say you chant Krishna. If you have got any name, God's name, then chant that.

'A simple thing, to chant the name. God has become so kind. These people are being taught. They have got this bead bag. I have also got. Hare Krishna, Hare Krishna, Krishna Krishna, Hare Hare/ Hare Rama, Hare Rama, Rama Rama, Hare Hare. Where is the loss? And where is the want of time? I am sitting here and now I am talking with you. As soon as I finish I shall chant Hare Krishna.'

'Do you find the chant goes on in your heart?'

'Yes, why not?'

'It goes deeper and deeper?'

'Yes. Everything we hear, it goes to the heart.'

'I am doing that, saying, sometimes, a little prayer.'

'If you repeatedly chant, it will always remain in your heart. Chant constantly Hare Krishna, Hare Krishna, Krishna Krishna, Hare Hare/ Hare Rama, Hare Rama, Rama Rama, Hare Hare. It remains in the heart.'

Prabhupada then asked about her own prayer.

'I pray, "Lord Jesus Christ, son of God, have mercy on us." '

'That's nice,' he agreed. 'Very good.'

Sister Mary was not used to sitting on the floor. She shifted on her cushion and clasped her knees together in front of her. Tilting her head to one side, she concentrated on Prabhupada's words as he continued to speak.

'Now, by praying it is expected one should have the mercy of God. So what is the test that one has got the mercy of God?'

'The mercy of God is the love of God, isn't it?'

'That's it!' Prabhupada was full of approval for her answer. 'God and God's name, or God and God's son, they are the same. So whether I am in touch with God's son or God's name, I am in touch with God.'

Having reached a profound level of agreement, they went on to discuss the method of chanting.

'It is very difficult to think of God,' she admitted, wanting to know what to do with her mind while chanting. Prabhupada explained the importance of a blameless life.

'It's not difficult. One can chant the holy name of the Lord if one is free from sinful activities.' This brought him to the benefit of being vegetarian. She continued to listen, as other guests and devotees joined the conversation. Rebatinandan, sitting beside her, interjected his own lengthy explanations and she heard him patiently. She even helped explain devotional life to a reporter who had found his way into Prabhupada's room. After an hour she excused herself, but before she left Prabhupada appealed to her.

'The whole world is suffering for want of God consciousness. It is the duty of all religious sects to teach this simple art of chanting Hare Krishna, or any other name you have got. Let us cooperate.'

Sister Mary rose and thanked Prabhupada, and Nanda Kumar showed her back to the front door. She went home to her religious sisters and was not seen again at the temple. However, the devotees did not forget her visit. They had learned that Prabhupada's aim was not to convert people from other faiths. Instead he encouraged them to love God regardless of what faith they professed, and to chant God's name, whatever name they had. In the following days his meeting with the Christian nun was the subject of much discussion in the temple.

Not all Christians were as open-minded toward the devotees as Sister Mary. Daily on the streets they met with suspicion and sometimes outright hostility from people claiming to follow the Bible. Sometimes the devotees debated with them, but mostly they walked away. Prabhupada had taught them that they should not preach to those who were unwilling to hear because that would only encourage them to disrespect Krishna. On one occasion, however, Rebatinandan was given no choice.

The devotees had arranged a lecture for Prabhupada at Kensington Town Hall, an imposing Victorian assembly room on Kensington High

Street.[8] Posters had been put up and leaflets distributed, and a good crowd showed up.

Prabhupada spoke for nearly an hour about the purpose of human life.

> Human life is meant for austerity. People are pursuing sense gratification, and the result is confusion and frustration. If we want happiness, we must purify our existence, otherwise happiness in this material world is an illusion. Our true nature is that we are eternal souls. Therefore we are teaching Krishna consciousness all over the world. Lord Chaitanya gave us a simple method: chant Hare Krishna, Hare Krishna, Krishna Krishna, Hare Hare/ Hare Rama, Hare Rama, Rama Rama, Hare Hare. Then, when our heart is cleansed, we will see our true self.[9]

He finished and waited for questions from the audience. A young man near the back stood up and introduced himself. He spoke in a strident voice.

'I'm a Christian. Lots of what you just said is disputed in the Bible. The word of God as described in the Holy Bible I hold very sacred. Today I have witnessed blasphemy against God.'

Peter, sitting on the stage near Prabhupada, heard these words with indignation and had to be restrained from jumping down among the audience to silence the man. The speaker was allowed to continue, and he finished by demanding that Prabhupada tell him what God he claimed to represent.

All turned to hear how Prabhupada would answer this challenge. Instead of responding he motioned to Rebatinandan Swami to reply. With some reluctance the tall young *sannyasi* stood up and gathered himself before the microphone. He had no idea what he would say. He started by reciting a prayer to his guru. Then he found the words.

'My spiritual master has asked me to answer this question. We follow the Vedic literatures, among which we include the Bible. Lord Jesus Christ teaches in the Bible that you love God first, with your whole heart and soul, and then you love your neighbour as yourself.'

'I do ...' began the young man, but Rebatinandan was warming to his task now, and his words came like a torrent.

'If you love your neighbour as yourself, then why are you killing? This civilization claims to be Christian, yet they are slaughtering so many animals and constantly slaughtering each other in wars and in the streets. Killing, killing, killing. Jesus said, "Thou shalt not kill," and you are killing. Killing the animals, killing each other. It is a society of dogs and cats, fighting and killing. My spiritual master is giving love of God to the world. Jesus said, "Hallowed be thy name, my Father," and we are hallowing the name of the Lord. We don't even ask you to say Krishna. You can say Jehovah or Yahweh. Just chant the names of God, purify your heart, and develop love of God. Then you will stop killing and slaughtering each other.'

He finished, trembling with emotion. The young Christian also appeared shaken. Rebatinandan had acted as a lightning rod for the collective frustration the devotees felt toward the sort of Christians who harassed them. His response had not been to just one man: he had demolished the whole preposterous argument of those who attacked them in the name of God and yet killed God's innocent creatures. Prabhupada smiled with satisfaction at his disciple's decisive words, and the devotees rose to their feet to cheer.

'Now chant,' instructed Prabhupada, and Rebatinandan led a stomping kirtan. While the young Christian made a subdued exit, the devotees were so happy that they were dancing on the chairs.

The next morning at the end of Prabhupada's walk they all scrambled into the van. Prabhupada turned round in the front seat to look at them. 'Henceforth you should all be able to answer like Rebatinandan did last night.' For several days afterwards he praised 'our Rebatinandan Swami', who knew the proper way to defend Krishna consciousness.

Two more lectures were organised for Prabhupada, one at the Commonwealth Centre in Kensington and one at the Hindu Centre in Grafton Terrace, Hampstead. The Hindu Centre was where the devotees had been made welcome when they first arrived in London in September 1968. The hall was packed, men and women crowding round Prabhupada's feet to hear him speak.

At one end of the hall was a large painting of Brahma, Vishnu, and

Shiva. Prabhupada had always taught his disciples to worship Krishna and not to divert their attention to the numerous demigods of the Hindus, but when he saw this picture he offered his respects.

'A devotee of Krishna offers respect not only to Brahma, Vishnu, and Shiva but even to an ant,' said Prabhupada, 'because Krishna is in the heart of every living entity.'

After the lecture Shyamsundar showed a slide show of Prabhupada's progress through India. Photographs, taken by Gurudas, showed him addressing large crowds, visiting temples, walking in Vrindavan, and meeting with important people. Among the slides was a picture of a beautiful pair of white marble Radha-Krishna deities.

'These are the deities we worshipped for ten days in our *pandal* in Delhi.' There were gasps of admiration from the devotees. 'Since then they have been kept in storage. Now they are coming here to be installed at the Edinburgh temple.' The admiration turned to cries of *'Haribol!'*

Prabhupada had already mentioned these deities to Dhananjaya and told him that if he could find the money they could come to England. Dhananjaya had persuaded Dr Shah, who came to the temple every evening to see Radha and Krishna, to pledge five hundred pounds, and immediately advanced this sum to Gurudas in Delhi through the Reserve Bank of India. The next day Prabhupada advised Dhananjaya to wait until he actually had Dr Shah's money in his hand before sending anything to India. It was too late: Gurudas had already received Dhananjaya's payment and was shipping the deities from Delhi.

The deities arrived at the bonded warehouse in Heathrow cargo area and devotees went to fetch them. When the crates were opened, they saw the delicate white marble figures, with their finely painted features, in perfect condition. Back at Bury Place they carried their precious cargo up to the sewing room, where Radha and Krishna remained covered with white cloth. No one knew what would become of them, and they remained there in storage for the next nine months.

When he learned that Krishna was on his way Prabhupada drew his own conclusion: 'If Krishna wants to come, no one can stop him.'

Two years earlier, while staying at John Lennon's place, Prabhupada had initiated Kshirodakshayi Das, his wife Kirti Dasi, and their three sons. Kshirodakshayi had emigrated to London from his native New Delhi in the early 1960s, and opened a small grocery store in North London. Since his initiation he had served Prabhupada from his home, and then for more than a year he had gone to join the mission in India, where he had helped to establish the Vrindavan project. Now he was back in London with his family and had asked Prabhupada if he would come to his house to install his deities of Radha and Krishna. Prabhupada agreed, and went there, along with a group of devotees.

Kshirodakshayi lived above his shop in Dollis Hill, and the only route to his living quarters lay through the shop, past shelves stocked with groceries of all kinds. Prabhupada presided while his servant Nanda Kumar performed the ceremony, then an elaborate feast cooked by Kirti was served to all.

Prabhupada told Kshirodakshayi that he should regard his deities as expansions of Radha and Krishna at the Bury Place temple. Since this was the case, whatever donations he received for their worship – from friends or guests – should be passed on to Dhananjaya for the service of the main temple. He further told him that now his home was a temple of Radha and Krishna he would no longer be able to sell nonvegetarian foods in his shop. Kshirodakshayi was left with a double challenge: he would have to change his business *and* give money to the temple.

After Prabhupada left Kshirodakshayi managed to do both: he converted his grocery to a launderette, and while his family ran the laundry and he worshipped his deities, he helped the temple enrol ISKCON Life Members from among the Hindu community of North London.

A week after Prabhupada arrived in London he went to Reading, on the Thames, west of London, where Mr Prajapati, a friend of the temple, had booked a small church hall and organised a programme for his Hindu friends and their families. A contingent of devotees followed Prabhupada out, bringing the *vyasasana* in a van and setting it up at one end of the hall. Chairs were arranged for the guests, and about twenty devotees sat on the floor round Prabhupada. After the talk, while the devotees cleaned up and drove to Mr Prajapati's house, Prabhupada went to visit George Harrison, who lived nearby, then returned later to rejoin his disciples at the Prajapatis' home.

It had been a busy day and none of the devotees had eaten. When his host asked Prabhupada what he would like, he modestly requested a glass of hot milk. His host pressed him to have more, so Prabhupada agreed to some puris. Before long the modest snack had grown to a fifteen-course meal.

'You have tricked me,' Prabhupada laughed, as his host served the feast not only to him but to all his disciples. Some of them were reluctant to eat so late, but Prabhupada insisted they should eat everything.

'We are just devotees of prasadam,' he said, as they were fed more and more, and the meal carried on until after midnight. Devotees were so tired they fell asleep there in the house, but Prabhupada insisted they wake up to return with him to the temple in time for the first morning arati.

Rathayatra day, 16th July, dawned bright and clear. By mid-morning the new *rath* car stood by Speaker's Corner on the north side of Hyde Park. It had been built by Svayambhur, and was bigger and stronger than the previous year's model. From its pinnacle forty feet above the ground a long pennant, inscribed with HARIBOL, rippled in the breeze. Devotees, after walking the length of Oxford Street, began to gather round it. Soon their kirtan, with drums and cymbals, echoed across the park, bringing a crowd of onlookers. The Jagannath deities arrived and were carried up onto the platform, ten feet off the ground.

Prabhupada boarded the large *vyasasana* mounted on the front of the car. This was the fourth Rathayatra in London but Prabhupada's first. As the procession slowly got under way he rode below Jagannath but just above the heads of the crowd, grave and serene amid the pageant.

Lilashakti and Bala Gopala, whose service was to care for Jagannath, rode on the platform above Prabhupada, feeling overwhelmed by his proximity below them. Next to them stood Rebatinandan Swami, pounding on his *mridanga* and singing into a microphone, setting the pace for all the devotees to follow. Either side of him on the platform men danced above the crowd.

Amid all this, Prabhupada sat calmly, his head held high, surveying the multitude of Jagannath's devotees. He saw the procession stretching several hundred yards ahead, bordered by colourful flags and led by a group of Hindu devotees holding aloft a large red banner announcing 'Jagannath Ki Jai'. Behind them four men marched stoically under the weight of a heavily-built set of steps designed to carry Prabhupada up to his seat and onto the plinth of Nelson's column. The steps bobbed along amid a sea of heads, a curious burden of love.

Halfway to Trafalgar Square the procession waited momentarily while Prabhupada disappeared into a hotel lobby to use the facilities. The police grew restless, but he soon re-emerged to resounding cries of '*Haribol!*' and resumed his place. The procession continued smoothly and, two hours after leaving Marble Arch, reached its destination. Trafalgar Square was tightly packed with devotees and tourists as Prabhupada carefully climbed down the steps. Looking round, he asked for his bodyguard, Peter, who came running though the crowd. Again Prabhupada disappeared, with Peter clearing a path through the throng. There followed an anxious few minutes during which no one seemed to know where he had gone.

This was Peter's special moment – when he was relied upon to conduct his spiritual master down into the maze of subways beneath the square to the public conveniences. Thinking ahead he dispatched two men with enough pennies to book several cubicles, then stood guard in the subway to ensure his master's privacy. Soon Prabhupada was back in front of the crowds. The scene at the base of the column created a striking tableau. In the centre, beneath the great bronze relief depicting the death of Nelson, the deities of Jagannath, Subhadra, and Balaram stood in a row inside their sculpted thrones. On their right Prabhupada settled onto his seat under the shade of his ornate parasol. All around these central figures rose a tide of devotees thronging the plinth, jostling for a view of their leader, their eyes fixed on him.

As Prabhupada began to speak a hush spread across the square.

His voice echoed from the imposing façades, carrying his unchanging message into the heart of London.

> Ladies and gentlemen, thank you very much for coming here and participating in this great movement. The purpose of this movement is to cleanse the heart. We have created so many problems in our life simply on the platform of misunderstanding. What is that misunderstanding? It is that we are accepting this material body as the self.
>
> I am born in India and therefore I am thinking I am Indian. You are born in England and therefore you are thinking Englishman. But we are neither Indian nor English; we are spirit soul, part and parcel of God.
>
> God is by nature joyful. Therefore as we are part and parcel of God our aim of life is to be joyful. We are searching for that joyfulness in material life, but that is not possible. Just as a fish, if it is taken from the water and put on the land, will never feel joyfulness, similarly we are spirit souls, and a spiritual being requires spiritual joy that is beyond the material senses. Therefore this Krishna consciousness movement is meant for purifying the senses.
>
> Beyond this material sky there is another sky which is eternal. Our only business is to transfer ourselves from this dark world to the world of light. This Krishna consciousness movement is trying to educate people how to transfer from the world of darkness to the world of light.
>
> We have dozens of books that you can read and understand. Otherwise you can simply chant the Hare Krishna mantra – only sixteen words: Hare Krishna, Hare Krishna, Krishna, Krishna, Hare Hare/ Hare Rama, Hare Rama, Rama Rama, Hare Hare. Please try to chant these sixteen words whenever you have time – walking on the street, travelling in the bus, or sitting alone. There is no loss, but the gain is very great.
>
> I am very thankful to you that you have given me your time. So please read our books and take advantage of this opportunity and make your life successful.[10]

After Prabhupada had finished speaking he gave initiation to twenty-two devotees right there on the base of Nelson's Column. They sat in two rows beneath the deities of Jagannath, Subhadra, and Balaram, and the ceremony was watched by several thousand.

One by one the initiates were called forward to receive their beads and their name from Prabhupada. Virasingham from Birmingham became

Brajendra Kumar, Tony from Manchester became Tribhangananda, Ian from Cardiff became Vichitravirya, and Mr and Mrs Arnold became Bhaktipramoda and Yashodamayi. Sally watched, wishing she could be among the initiates. She had been told she was too young and must wait another year (she eventually became Shailendriya). Altogether six women and sixteen men received new names. Next came the fire sacrifice.

The week before the festival Birasingha had been sent to ask permission to light a sacred fire on the day.

'You want to light a *fire*?' The police asked incredulously.

'Well, just a few candles,' he quickly assured them.

'Oh, a few candles? That's okay,' they replied.

Now a full Vedic fire ceremony was begun. Pradyumna chanted the mantras and lit the pile of wood in front of him, fuelled by ghee. Soon, on the 150-year-old granite steps, beneath the lofty gaze of Lord Nelson, flames were dancing merrily in the hot sun. A police inspector jotted in his notebook: Had this been part of the agreed-upon programme for the day?

While the flames died down and smoke drifted across the square, Prabhupada surveyed the scene with deep satisfaction. As a small child he had led Jagannath through the streets of his neighbourhood in Calcutta, which at the time was the capital of British India. Now, seventy years later, he had led Jagannath through the centre of London, given Vaishnava initiation to young Britons at the foot of Nelson's Column, and publicly spoken on behalf of his spiritual master, who had so wanted London to hear the message of Sri Chaitanya. It had been a momentous day. He described his satisfaction in a letter a few days later.

> We have celebrated a very, very nice Rathayatra festival here in London, and in the Trafalgar Square itself I initiated nearly 30 new devotees with fire yagna before 25,000 persons, mostly Englishmen. All in all, it was the best Rathayatra we have seen to date.[11]

Geoffrey Warman had been among those waiting to be initiated, but he seemed to have been forgotten. He was certain his name had been on the list. He had sat there as the names were being read out one by one, patiently waiting for his turn, but everything had concluded without him. Sitting there, with no beads and no name, he felt confused. He feared he wasn't qualified to receive this great fortune, that he couldn't cheat Krishna.

Then Dhananjaya asked him his new name and discovered he hadn't been given one, so he went and checked with Pradyumna, whose job it had been to supply Prabhupada the beads and names. No, Pradyumna assured Dhananjaya, everyone had been called. See, there were no more beads in his bag. But wait a minute, what was this? A string of beads labelled 'Geoffrey Warman' remained at the bottom of the bag. Pradyumna hurried to inform Prabhupada, who was just about to leave the square and return to Bury Place.

'Tell him to meet me in my room,' Prabhupada said as he descended from the plinth.

Geoffrey hastened back to the temple. Out of breath, he arrived at the front door and ran up the stairs to sit down and wait outside Prabhupada's room, trembling nervously.

'You can go in now,' said Shyamsundar as he emerged, leaving the door ajar for Geoffrey.

Hesitantly, Geoffrey entered and found himself alone with his spiritual master. In Prabhupada's calming presence, his apprehension melted away. Prabhupada sat beneath the window holding Geoffrey's japa beads in his hands. He finished chanting on them and handed them to him.

'Your name is Janananda, one who gives bliss to all people,' he said. Then he opened a tin beside him, and took out a sweet and dropped it into Janananda's outstretched hand.

In the days that followed Prabhupada gave second initiation – *gayatri-mantra* – to several disciples. Mahavishnu, still recovering from his exertions to help build the *rath* car, came to see him, conscious that he had not yet succeeded in removing all the paint from under his nails. When he arrived Prabhupada was on the point of going out, already on his feet and wearing his overcoat. He looked down at the young man.

'Repeat after me,' he began, still standing up, and led him through the verses of Gayatri, showing him how to count on his fingers. As he did so he looked with surprise at the paint on Mahavishnu's nails.

'You want to be a *brahmana*?' He put out his own hand for comparison. 'Just see.'

His fingers were soft and translucent, his nails pale like ivory. Mahavishnu's heart sank. What could he possibly say?

Prabhupada paused in thought, then with a shrug of his shoulders draped the sacred thread across Mahavishnu's chest. It was his chosen duty, he seemed to be saying, to accept and educate disciples and offer them to Krishna.

Pauline had spent the first two weeks of Prabhupada's visit convalescing in a Manchester hospital with a burst appendix. As a result she had missed everything. Now she arrived at the temple with her mind set on one thing: to find Prabhupada and be initiated by him. Outside his room she quizzed his servant Nanda Kumar.

'Do you know where Srila Prabhupada is?'

'He's in here.'

'Can I go in and see him?'

'No. He's resting and then he'll eat.'

'But you don't understand. I missed my initiation because I was in hospital. I need to get initiated. I was hoping I could go in and see him.'

'Well, you're lucky. I'm Prabhupada's servant. When he wakes up I'll tell him.'

She told him her name was Pauline and that she was from Manchester. 'I've been recommended for initiation by my temple president, Ranchor. Would it be alright if I could be initiated today?'

'Well, I don't know if it will be today,' Nanda Kumar replied cautiously, 'but I'll call you as soon as I know.' She was persuaded to go upstairs to the women's quarters and settle in as best she could.

The next afternoon Nanda Kumar called Pauline into Prabhupada's presence. Shaking with fear she came in and sat down while Prabhupada remained at his desk, absorbed in work.

'This is the girl who has been in hospital, Srila Prabhupada.'

Prabhupada looked up.

'Are you better now?'

She could hardly understand his accent.

'I'm f-fine now.'

'Come closer.' He lifted a string of beads from his desk and handed them to her. 'I will call you Ashtasakhi Dasi,' he said, looking straight into her eyes.

She felt a mist clearing and realised his accent seemed to have gone; she could understand every word he said.

'*Ashta* means eight and *sakhi* means friend. There is a *gopi* who is the dearmost friend of the eight *gopis* and she is called Ashtasakhi. I want you to be called Ashtasakhi Dasi and become the dearmost friend of all my devotees.'

She offered her obeisances and left in a daze, holding her beads. For half an hour she sat on the stairs outside his door, unable to move.

Nagma came down and asked what she was doing.

'I've been initiated and my name's Ashtasakhi Dasi, and Prabhupada said I'm to become the dearmost friend of all the devotees.'

Very early one morning Vichitravirya, who had just been initiated in Trafalgar Square, sat in the darkness outside Prabhupada's room. He had got up early because he wanted to chant japa in the magical hours before dawn at the door of his spiritual master. It was about two o'clock. He was taken by surprise when Prabhupada came out of his shower room. Seeing his young disciple bowing down to recite his obeisances, he waited for him to rise, then looked directly at him.

'Sincerity of purpose, that is what is required,' he said with gravity, and went into his room. Vichitravirya cherished these words, though he couldn't understand why Prabhupada had said them. This was the moment, so close to his guru in the night, that all his life he would never forget.

Two of the newly initiated young men heard that Prabhupada wanted British devotees to go to India to help construct temples. Since they both wanted travel and excitement, they decided to offer their services, and each came before him. Gunarnava entered first, feeling exposed by Prabhupada's penetrating gaze.

'Do you have any experience in building work?'

'Not really, no. But I want to do some service for you in India, and I could learn.' Prabhupada seemed satisfied.

'Yes, Krishna will help you.'

Then it was Smarahari's turn. He told Prabhupada he had learned technical drawing at school. Prabhupada nodded his approval. Neither of them had the skills he was seeking, but they were eager to learn and to serve. In them he saw unlimited potential, as he did in all his disciples. He released them from their temple duties and told them to prepare to go to India. Then he wrote to Jayapataka, in charge of building the temple in Mayapur.

> I am sending two first-class men from England, both of them have got good experience in engineering and building work. They are named Smarahari and Gunarnava. They shall be arriving very soon in India and you can train them to help you there full-time.[12]

Later that week Prabhupada flew to Paris for his second visit to France. Fifty devotees from France, Holland, and Germany gave him an emotional welcome when he landed at Orly Airport. During his stay in Paris he delivered a public lecture at the School of Architecture. His French disciple Jyotirmayi, who after joining in London had returned to Paris to translate his books, acted as interpreter. The next day he held an outdoor initiation ceremony in the Jardin du Luxembourg, beside the Sorbonne, Jyotirmayi's old university. Rain cut short the ceremony, which was completed the following morning at the temple, when around fifteen European devotees were given their new names. Prabhupada had planned to install deities of Radha-Krishna at the temple in Fontenay-aux-roses on the south side of Paris, but he postponed this to a future occasion.

Next he went to Amsterdam, where another public programme had been arranged. It was attended mostly by hippies, many of them intoxicated.

'In Europe the hippies have become so disgusted with material life and so degraded that they will not hear our philosophy,' lamented Prabhupada. 'They are simply mocking. It is better not to preach philosophy to them. Just get them to chant Hare Krishna.'[13]

While in Amsterdam he installed Jagannath deities. It was a stormy ceremony full of mishaps. Prabhupada did not conceal his dismay at finding the devotees unprepared and disorganised. Still, he went ahead with the installation, and all ended well.

From Amsterdam he returned via London to Edinburgh, arriving in Scotland on Saturday 29th July, two weeks after the London Rathayatra.

CHAPTER 13

Austerities in Edinburgh

The Edinburgh temple had been started the previous year by Kishor and Tribhuvanatha. The first foray into Scotland had been to Dundee, where in 1971 Devadatta and Draupadi, with their little son, recruited a young *brahmachari,* later initiated as Shambhunath. They fell on hard times and were reduced to sheltering in a derelict squat. Kishor and Tribhuvanatha relieved them and moved with Shambhunath to Edinburgh. There they chanted and sold magazines on Princes Street through the harsh winter. Meanwhile they searched for a suitable place for a temple, and eventually they leased the upper floors of Oddfellows Hall, a landmark building close to the city centre. Its Gothic façade was encrusted with heraldic beasts and gargoyles. Inside was a flea market on the ground floor, and upstairs, spacious rooms with a large meeting hall.

Reinforcements came, the rooms were cleared and painted, and a shower installed. This was paid for by Tribhuvanatha, who roved all over Scotland and the north of England on his scooter and sidecar selling Spiritual Sky incense.

A young girl from Edinburgh came to join them. Her name was Rosie Coburn, born in London but descended from Robert the Bruce. When she was eight her father died and she and her mother moved to Edinburgh, where she grew up as an only child.

Her cousin gave her a copy of the 'Govindam' single when she was sixteen. A year later her boyfriend Barney bought some Spiritual Sky incense and she was captivated by it. She started playing the 'Govindam' record over and over again until she almost wore it out. She would sing to Govinda, without understanding what she was singing, on her way to school, while washing her hair, smoking, rock 'n' rolling – the song was constantly in her head.

Then Barney left her, saying he was going to join the temple. She followed, looking for him, but he had already moved on. Kishor gave her something to eat and talked to her, telling her about Krishna consciousness. She was attracted to Prabhupada's picture, in which he appeared so kind. She loved the sacred food, and she liked to chant Hare Krishna. She spent two days helping Kishor sell magazines, returning home each day late in the evening. She was meant to be studying for her 'A' levels, and her mother lost patience. 'Either stay at home and go to school,' she told her daughter, 'or hand over your front door key and do what you like.' Rosie had no hesitation. She had just turned seventeen, and she went to stay in the London temple.

In June a letter arrived from Prabhupada addressed to Tribhuvanatha saying he might come to Edinburgh 'if you can arrange some big, big meeting for me to speak there and address the public at large as well as the students.' Prabhupada had a special interest in Scotland because he had been a student at the Scottish Churches College in Calcutta. There he had learned the Bible from Dr William Urquhart, a minister in the Church of Scotland, whom he later cited as a man of learning.

Once they heard of Prabhupada's willingness to visit Edinburgh, there was no holding back the devotees' enthusiasm to bring him there. They decided the best place for him to speak would be Glasgow, where people were more friendly toward them than in Edinburgh and where there were many Hindus. They booked Woodside Hall in Maryhill. Glasgow was a rough city and Maryhill a rough neighbourhood, but the hall was spacious and affordable, and Maryhill was home to a large community of Hindus and close to the University of Glasgow.

As soon as Rathayatra was over a group of devotees, including Sarvamangala and Rosie, went to Edinburgh from London to help prepare for Prabhupada's arrival. They decorated the altar, and in Prabhupada's room they hung curtains and made cushions, bolsters, and a rudimentary table and bed. They brought with them the large *vyasasana* from the front of the *rath* car.

Kishor and Tribhangananda printed a poster advertising Prabhupada's lecture, which they fly-posted around the centre of Glasgow under cover of darkness. Around midnight they were picked up by the police, held for a few hours, then released without charge onto the deserted early morning streets. They thumbed a lift with a milk lorry all the way to the doorstep of the Edinburgh temple, arriving just in time to hear the sounding of the conch shell for the first arati.

During those same small hours Rosie and Gangamayi were climbing over the gate out of Princes Street Gardens, dressed in saris and laden with freshly picked roses. Narrowly escaping detection they headed back to the temple and strung together a garland for Prabhupada.

Later that morning an excited crowd of devotees met Prabhupada at the airport. They scattered rose petals in his path and one of them stepped forward to offer him the garland. Still moist with morning dew, it reached down to his knees.

He arrived at Oddfellows Hall to the strains of 'Govindam' played over the market's sound system. With an effort he climbed the long stairway to the first floor and entered a brightly painted and spacious temple room. The floor was deep blue, decorated with a large pink lotus design, the walls yellow and pink and hung with large oil paintings of Narada Muni and Sri Chaitanya, and there was the old London *vyasasana,* which in this high-ceilinged room no longer seemed so huge.

Prabhupada spoke to the modest crowd of devotees and temple friends. Among the guests were four ten-year-old boys dressed in their Sunday best, who bowed down along with everyone else. There were also some inquisitive visitors from the Divine Light Mission, who had a centre opposite the temple. After Prabhupada's philosophical address one of them stood to ask a question.

'Why must God be philosophy?'

'Krishna is God, and God is great. Philosophy means to know *how* God is great,' replied Prabhupada. Then he asked, 'Would you prefer me to tell you fairy stories?'

Prabhupada's room was plain, with bare floorboards painted white, and his bed was a canvas camp bed. Even in July the building was cold, and his bathroom, with no hot water, was shared with the entire ashram. Yet although he disliked the cold he did not complain. He appreciated the austere simplicity of it all.

A press conference had been called, and several weary Scottish journalists arrived to sit in Prabhupada's room. They appeared sceptical, their questions challenging.

'Why have you come here? What do you hope to achieve?'

Prabhupada was unruffled. He answered them calmly, quoting the *Bhagavad-gita*, and soon they warmed to him.

'Edinburgh has *two* universities?' He complimented them on their beautiful city with its grand buildings. Then he turned the tables.

'So why your children are all becoming hippies and taking LSD?' They had no answer, and he began to expound the philosophy of Krishna consciousness.

'Do you know everything?' one of them asked with a hint of sarcasm. Prabhupada took his time to answer.

'Yes, perhaps it is true, since everything I say is from Krishna.'

That afternoon he sat in his room with his door open, inviting anyone who wished to come in and talk. He seemed relaxed. Prabhavishnu was in Edinburgh with his team of travelling book distributors, and they came in to see Prabhupada with his party. They showed Prabhupada the small Jagannath deities who travelled with them in their van, and Prabhupada readily gave his blessings, saying they should simply offer Jagannath incense and a flower whenever they could, change Jagannath's dress once a week, and continue distributing books. The Edinburgh temple could also install deities, he said, once they had a sufficient number of trained *brahmanas*.

Tribhuvanatha asked who could give the young devotees of Edinburgh the guidance they needed to progress in Krishna consciousness. They would need the association of exemplary devotees, he said.

'You become their good association,' was Prabhupada's reply.

The following morning, after a walk in the meadow, Prabhupada lectured in the temple room. His talk turned to prasadam and cooking for Krishna.

'Krishna would leave Radharani,' he said, 'but she is such a good cook he cannot go.' Rebatinandan Swami was in the kitchen preparing breakfast for everyone and heard Prabhupada's words. He emerged, tall and energetic, his hands dusted with chapati flour. Prabhupada was pleased to see him.

'I'm Kitchen Swami now, Srila Prabhupada,' he laughed, and they all laughed with him.

That afternoon Prabhupada went by taxi to Waverley station, where he boarded a train for the fifty-minute journey to Glasgow. Rebatinandan and a team of devotees went ahead to warm up the audience with a rousing kirtan while the stage was prepared and the *vyasasana* put in place. By the time Prabhupada arrived, an audience of over two hundred, young and old, Hindu and Scottish, awaited him.

He gave a short lecture on the *Bhagavad-gita,* keeping it simple and direct. He explained that the living being is an eternal fragment of God, and he emphasised Krishna's instruction to Arjuna to fight without attachment for victory or defeat, for the sake of serving God. At the end he called for questions.

Near the back of the hall an untidy young man with long hair and an unkempt beard stood up to expound and elaborate question. Prabhupada called him nearer so he could be heard. The man walked down the central aisle, speaking and gesticulating as he did so. Prabhupada called him still closer until he was right in front of the stage, just beneath Prabhupada, and in full view of everyone.

'I am God. We are all God. Everything in one,' he finally concluded.

'So? You have finished?' Prabhupada looked down over his spectacles. Silence filled the hall. Everyone waited to see how he would respond. His mood stiffened and he raised his voice.

'You think you are God? You are not God. You are dog!'

The young man stepped back, overwhelmed by the force of Prabhupada's response. He retreated all the way back to his seat under the gaze of everyone. The audience was taken by surprise and so were the devotees. Prabhupada had put the man in his place along with all those who thought they could be God. For a few seconds the hall was silent as everyone took in what had happened. Then someone in the crowd began to applaud, then another, until the whole auditorium was standing in ovation.

Devotees climbed onto the stage for a tremendous final kirtan, and many in the audience joined in the dancing. Children, who had been hanging around the entrance at the back of the hall, ran onto the stage and leapt up and down with the rest. They were fooling around, and one of the devotees was about to remove them.

'Let them dance,' said Prabhupada. 'They are devotees.'

The evening concluded with distribution of oranges cut into quarters – the only food the temple could afford. Prabhupada ate his fill while people crowded round him to ask further questions, and in high spirits he preached to them for a long time. At last it was time for him to leave. Beaming with pleasure he rubbed Tribhuvanatha's head with both hands.

'I am very pleased with what you have done. Now preach Krishna consciousness all over Scotland,' he told him.

Prabhupada and his party spent that night in a hotel at Glasgow Airport, where Tribhuvanatha tracked down a late-night snack of toast and hot milk for his guru. Then, early next morning, Prabhupada returned to London.

A few months later he wrote to Kishor, who succeeded Tribhuvanatha as temple president in Edinburgh.

> I liked that place in Scotland very much when I was there last time, and especially I saw that the Scotsmen were much inclined toward our preaching – but the weather was for me unbearable. I think by next summer they might have got a nice place in London, and because it is a little warmer there I may go and stay some time in London, and if there is opportunity I shall see Scotland temple also. Because you have worked so hard for Krishna, making all sacrifice without any personal selfish motive, therefore you are making such nice advancement in spiritual life. Thank you very much for helping me in this preaching work. May Krishna bless you more and more.[1]

Stephen had moved from Manchester to the London temple. His name had not been on the initiation list at Trafalgar Square, and he was waiting his turn. Others were also waiting, so when Prabhupada got back from Edinburgh he announced he would give further initiations at a hall in Wembley, North London.

Kshirodakshayi had booked the old wooden mission hall, hidden behind the houses near his home, for a week. Prabhupada agreed to present a series of nightly lectures on the *Srimad-Bhagavatam*. The programme was aimed at the local Hindus and advertised as a Bhagavat Sapta – seven days of *Bhagavatam* recital.

Stephen designed a poster to advertise it and took it to Shyamsundar for approval. Shyamsundar told him to show it to Prabhupada. With trepidation, Stephen knocked on his guru's door.

'Come in.'

Prabhupada was sitting beneath the window with sunlight streaming in behind him. Stephen felt exposed.

'Shyamsundar asked me to show you this.'

'Let me see.' Prabhupada reached across. His voice was patient and gentle. He held the poster in his hands and read it aloud from top to bottom.

'Thank you very much,' he said with approval, and returned it. Stephen was relieved that Prabhupada seemed to like what he had done and to be thanking him. He left grateful for Prabhupada's trust in him and trusting Prabhupada completely in return.

When the day came, the initiates – five women and eleven men – went ahead to the hall and, while Pradyumna and Nanda Kumar prepared for the fire sacrifice, did their best to clean the place up. But there was no time, and the hall soon began to fill with guests. Prabhupada arrived and, sitting on the small stage, gave a short lecture to the crowded room. Then he began the initiation. Stephen's name was called.

'Will you chant sixteen rounds a day?' asked Prabhupada.

'Yes, Prabhu,' replied Stephen, realising too late that he had addressed his guru as an ordinary devotee. Prabhupada took no notice.

'Your name is Sakshi Gopala,' he said, handing over his beads.

Peter came up.

'What are the four regulative principles?'

'No meat eating,' he began, but Prabhupada stopped him.

'That's alright. Your name is Padmalochana,' he said, and gave him his beads.

Nagma Mir from Salford became Nabhasvati; Jeffrey Cargill from Stepney Green became Jagat Bandhu; Jeffrey Davies from South Wales became Yaduvendu; and a serving member of the Queen's Guard, Frank, was given the name Abhimanyu after Arjuna's heroic soldier son.

At the end of the programme Prabhupada addressed the audience with a few words of Hindi. His disciples could not understand what he was saying, but he was praising them. He told the guests how well they were doing in devotional service and how they were helping him spread Krishna consciousness. Nabhasvati, the only one among his disciples who could understand Hindi, thought to herself how much he loved them all.

Prabhupada was not happy with the way the programme had been staged. The hall was small and dirty, with a lifeless atmosphere. He did not return, and for the remaining six days he asked Rebatinandan Swami to take his place.

The same July evening that Prabhupada had spoken in Reading he had gone with Dhananjaya and Shyamsundar to see George Harrison. As soon as his lecture was over, Prabhupada had emerged from the hall into the chill evening air.

'Is Your Grace feeling warm enough?' fussed Mr Arnold, tucking in Prabhupada's travel blanket. They drove slowly between copses of alder and willow and lush meadows full of cows settling down for the night beside the meandering River Thames.

Reaching Friar Park, situated on a hill overlooking Henley-on-Thames, they passed an ornate lodge and wound their way up the long driveway to halt beneath the turreted mansion that was George's home. George could not be found. In the fading light the four of them strolled around the gardens, then Shyamsundar, who knew his way around, showed them inside. He led them to the lounge where they settled amid the panelled walls and gathering gloom to wait for George.

Suddenly he burst in, bearing a big bouquet of freshly gathered flowers. He presented them to Prabhupada, then fell at his feet. Pattie followed him into the room and offered Prabhupada her greetings.

While the shadows deepened around them Prabhupada spoke about light and dark, of how this world of darkness was a place of death whereas the soul belonged in the world of eternal light.

As he talked, they moved to the subject of a new temple. A year earlier, after the Bangladesh concert, George had spoken to Shyamsundar about raising money for a larger temple in London. At the time Shyamsundar had not pressed him. Now, sitting here with Prabhupada, George wanted to make a firm commitment.

'The devotees should have somewhere like here,' he said indicating his home and its surrounding grounds. He promised that he and Shyamsundar would start looking for a suitable place right away, and he undertook to buy it for the devotees. It was a historic moment.

Soon Prabhupada took his leave, agreeing to meet again in a few days. The next day he wrote to Gurudas in Vrindavan and told him of his meeting with George and Pattie, including a special request on their behalf.

> Yesterday I met with George Harrison and his wife in their place at Henley, and they are both very much favourable. They want to stay with us for some time at Radha-Damodar temple this winter. I will tell you when.[2]

Prabhupada had lived at the Radha-Damodar temple in Vrindavan during the 1960s, and now Gurudas and Yamuna were staying there to look after his private rooms while they managed the construction of the Krishna-Balaram temple. For George and Pattie to be invited there made them part of Prabhupada's intimate family.

George was inspired by the fact that Prabhupada had come all the way to his home to see him. Afterwards, remembering the occasion, he wrote 'The Lord Loves the One', which became one of the songs on his *Living In The Material World* album. 'The Lord loves the one that loves the Lord,' he sang, 'and the law says if you don't give then you don't get loving.'

George looked upon Prabhupada as a person surrendered to the will of God. What was the point of battling for fame and fortune, he thought, if in the end death came to take everything away? Better to do something to please the Lord.[3]

Prabhupada had often spoken about getting a large place in Central London. George's idea was different: he wanted a rural setting for the devotees, where they could create a peaceful ashram, a haven of Krishna consciousness removed from the pressures of the city. Whatever the outcome, in the city or in the countryside, Prabhupada was determined that a new temple be found soon. He wrote to Gurudas in India,

> The Delhi deities have arrived safely. Presently we are looking for a large temple in London to install them, and I shall remain in London until we have got something.[4]

A few days later, Prabhupada accompanied George, Shyamsundar, and Dhananjaya to see a property near Windsor called Runneymede Farm. They tramped through woods and meadows to emerge in front of a

Georgian mansion. But the property was neglected and overgrown, and George was not impressed.

'This shouldn't be called Runneymede Farm,' he remarked, 'it should be Runnydown Farm.'

The next day George arrived unannounced at the temple to see Shyamsundar. He was out, so Nanda Kumar asked if he would like to see Prabhupada.

'No, no, I don't want to bother him,' he protested. But when Prabhupada heard he was there he wanted to see him. George removed his socks and entered. The first thing he did was prostrate himself full-length before his guru.

Prabhupada called him forward until George was sitting right beside him. Then he gave him a big hug, pulling his head to his chest and ruffling his hair.

'I am so pleased to see you. How is Pattie?' He spoke like a concerned father. They talked for a while, then George asked a question that had been on his mind. He wanted to know whether he should give up his music and join the temple.

'No!' Prabhupada said emphatically. 'You have a great gift. Just continue your music and Krishna will bless you. I will give you many ideas.' He took out a book of songs written by Bhaktivinoda Thakur, his predecessor guru, and went through some of them, translating them from the Bengali.[5]

That week George visited several times. One day he brought with him his mentor, Ravi Shankar. Ravi and Prabhupada laughed and joked in their native tongue, and as he had promised, Prabhupada gave George ideas for songs. Following this, George went to work on his *Living In The Material World* album. Later, when he published his memoir, he recalled how the album had been inspired. '*Material World* was the influence of A. C. Bhaktivedanta Swami,' wrote George, 'and the realising that we are not these bodies: we are in these material bodies in the physical world. No matter how good you are you still need grace to get out. You can be a yogi or a monk or a nun, but without God's grace you still can't make it.'[6] The title track of the album went to the heart of George's personal faith that kept him so close to Prabhupada. 'I'm living in the material world,' he sang. But he hoped to 'get out of this place by the Lord Sri Krishna's grace.'

After seeing 'Runnydown Farm' Prabhupada wrote again to Yamuna and Gurudas, describing his house-hunting, his time with George, and his feelings for George and for Britain.

> Today we are looking at a very nice place of 75 acres near London with Mr George Harrison, who has found the place and wants to have our ashram here. He is coming to see me daily and he is a very nice boy and I like him very much. If we get this place I shall make London my permanent world headquarters. Practically I am British by training, so I am also trying for dual Indian-British citizenship. I still remember that you both helped me very much by opening this London centre, and it is the most important centre in the world.[7]

As it turned out, neither Runnymede nor any of the places they saw that summer and autumn were right. But with nearly fifty initiated devotees added to their number since the start of the year, with the growing reach of the devotees across Great Britain, and with George's wholehearted backing, there was now an unstoppable momentum of expansion.

By the second week of August it was apparent that the search for a new temple would take some time. Prabhupada decided to go back to Los Angeles and rest for a while. He delegated the property search to Dhananjaya, who would work closely with George until they found the right place.

Prabhupada was now seventy-six years old. His flights to Paris and Amsterdam, then with hardly a break to Edinburgh and back to London – all in the space of ten days – in addition to conducting major initiation ceremonies in Paris and twice in London, the installation of Jagannath in Amsterdam, then the Glasgow lecture were all taking their toll. He wrote that after so much travelling he was feeling the strain. 'Now I am thinking to sit down for a while in Los Angeles for translating work.'[8]

He was booked to fly to L.A. on 14th August. He had stayed in London for six weeks, but when the day of his departure arrived it all seemed to come in a rush: one day he had been talking of staying until George found a property and the next he was in a hurry to go.

That morning he gave the class as usual, while downstairs Ashtasakhi and Mondakini prepared his breakfast. The class went on late, and Nanda Kumar hurried down to tell them he had no time to eat breakfast before leaving – could they pack him a tiffin for the journey? Then a last-minute caller arrived to see Prabhupada, and they were asked to unpack his breakfast. They rushed upstairs with his plate, hoping to serve him, only to meet him coming down the stairs and heading for the door. Mondakini started to cry. He just laughed. A crowd of devotees followed him, some of them in tears, as he got into Bhaktipramoda's car for the last time.

They crowded into whatever transport they could find and followed him to the airport. Others came from further afield. Gradually there assembled around him a crowd of men and women, sitting in the departure hall and sat around him on the floor chanting japa. They were trying to fix in their minds how Prabhupada looked, going back over the events of the last six weeks, recalling all they had heard. They wanted to remember forever what it was like to be with him now, sitting here at his feet. In body he was leaving, but in spirit they would keep him.

Nothing much was said, but a buzz of japa rose softly from the flock of devotees, gathered like petals around the whorl of a lotus flower. In their midst, seated in repose, wreathed in flowers, with his small white travel bag at his side and his hand in his bead bag, Prabhupada was completely at peace. He saw Rebatinanda Swami and beckoned him to come and sit beside him on the seat. From time to time he turned to him and exchanged a few words and a smile. Mostly he sat there looking round at his British disciples, appreciating this final moment with them, happy at what they had achieved together, at the new initiates, and at the imminent purchase of a substantial new temple. Now all that mattered was to chant Krishna's name. For him, that was all that ever really mattered. He had always said that.

The flight call came and Prabhupada stood up purposefully. With eyes ahead he walked calmly through the crowds of travellers, leading the way toward his departure gate. When he got there, he turned and waited as his disciples caught up behind him like a tide reaching its limit that can go no further. Alone he passed through the barrier and walked the remaining ten yards to a final gap leading to the transit area. Now he was the centre of attention not just for the devotees but for everyone within sight. Who was this small man, smothered in flowers and so self-possessed? The devotees were singing intensely, craning their necks for a last glimpse, joy mixed with sadness on their faces. One last time he turned, with an enormous smile, and raised his arms high.

Then he was gone.

BOOK FOUR

A House in the Country
1973–75

CHAPTER 14

Search for a Temple

TRAVELLING AND PREACHING

Through the autumn and into spring the following year, energy flowed through the devotees, inspiring them to go out on the road. This was the spirit of Sri Chaitanya's sankirtan movement – to take the name of God and the love of God to people wherever they were on the streets, in their homes, or in their colleges and universities. Dayananda had started this outward movement in early 1972 with the purchase of a large Transit van. This was inherited by Prabhavishnu, whose strength of character gave cohesion to a small band of dedicated book distributors. Among them were Mahavishnu, Janananda, Jagat Bandhu, and Vrajendra Kumar. They would live in the van, sleeping on top of their stock of books, and periodically return to base.

Hearing of his travelling party, Prabhupada wrote to Prabhavishnu with appreciation. His letter summed up his own approach to teaching Krishna consciousness during his never-ending travels round the globe, and recognised that the devotees in Britain were doing exactly as he had hoped they would.

> Go on in this way, stopping in every village and city … Distribute books, hold sankirtan procession, answer questions, give some leaflets or small informations freely, distribute prasadam wherever possible – at least some small thing – and if there is interest shown request the townspeople to arrange for speaking in their schools, or in someone's home or hall.
>
> Remain always without anxiety for destination and comfortable situations, always relying on the mercy of Krishna for your plan, just go on preaching his message and selling his books. I can understand it is not an easy matter to travel extensively over long period of time, without proper food or rest, and sometimes it must be very cold also. Still you are getting so much enjoyment, spiritual enjoyment, it seems like play to you. Because you are rightly understanding through your personal realisation this philosophy of Krishna consciousness, therefore in such a short time you have surpassed all the stages of yoga processes to come to the highest point of surrendering to Krishna.[1]

Even while they were on the road living in such a compact space, the travelling devotees followed a strict schedule of early rising, bathing (using a bucket of cold water at the roadside), studying scripture, and cooking prasadam. Whenever they returned to the London temple their energy raised the spirits of the ashram-dwellers.

In the spring Prabhavishnu led an expedition to Dublin, where they met with a good response, selling books and chanting on the street. At first they slept in their van, parked in the hills outside the city. Then they rented a bungalow on the bay, and on Sundays up to sixty people turned up to chant with them and share their feast.

Rebatinandan Swami led another travelling group touring the country's universities and colleges. Recognising the value of his work, Sudurjaya gave him a new car – a Hillman Estate – as a gift from the incense business. Rebatinandan wrote to tell Prabhupada of his activities, and received his warm endorsement. Perhaps Prabhupada was remembering Rebatinandan's dramatic words at Kensington Town Hall as he heaped encouragement upon his young shoulders.

> You are a good kirtan man, you can sing and play *mridanga* like anything. You are also good cook, expert philosopher and preacher, you are in the renounced order of life, having given up all thoughts of wife, family, and home. You are determined to assist me by training so many younger devotees in Krishna consciousness … therefore Krishna is giving you great strength and pleasure from working in this way. By this travelling and preaching in the schools, colleges, youth clubs, and selling books, I think you are accomplishing more good preaching than anyone. If you continue travelling and preaching in the British Isles, very soon the entire population will become devotees of Krishna. I am very much pleased upon you for helping me in this way. It is the highest achievement of this human form of life.[2]

Rebatinandan had with him a bright team of talented men. Vichitravirya travelled with him for two years, while Bhoumadeva arranged the programmes, hitchhiking two weeks ahead of the rest of his party and living out of a backpack. Another member of the group was Robert Housden.

After hearing Prabhupada speak at Hampstead Town Hall the previous summer, Robert had left his work in London to trek in the Pyrenees and ponder his future. While walking high in the mountains he had got lost, and for three days and nights wandered across stony peaks not knowing if he would get out alive. He had promised Krishna that if he survived he would join the temple. On returning to England he found that while he was away his father had died. He was ready to make a fresh start, and joined the devotees. Three months later, initiated by letter with the name Rohininandan, he was travelling with Rebatinandan.

Their driver was Paul Anderson, recently initiated as Partha. Paul grew up in the West Riding of Yorkshire. His family expected him to get a steady job and settle down, but his life took an unexpected turn when, while away at university in Guildford in the south of England, he experienced a spiritual awakening. He felt as if a door to another world had opened inside him. He began avidly reading books like the *Tibetan Book of the Dead* and Timothy Leary's *Politics of Ecstasy*. One day his girlfriend gave him a copy of Prabhupada's *Krishna Consciousness, the Topmost Yoga System*. Sitting in her flat he opened it at random and started to read. The book spoke to him with such clarity and honesty that by the time he had read just one page he knew he had found his teacher. He told his girlfriend what he felt.

'This is the person I'm looking for – this is the one!'

He started visiting the temple in London, where he made friends with Tribhuvanatha and Sarvamangala. He dropped out of university and went back to Harrogate, keeping in touch with the temple by letter. On New Year's Day 1972, after selling his record collection, he took the train to London to join the temple. He soon caught the attention of Dhananjaya, who asked him to give the morning *Bhagavatam* lecture. Although he had never spoken in public before and was shy by nature, he spoke with a new confidence and assurance. That summer he was among those initiated at the base of Nelson's Column, receiving his beads from Prabhupada with the name Partha.

With Partha as driver and personal assistant, Rebatinandan Swami and his team toured the country. At night they stayed with anyone they could find: young men with long hair were often willing to give them floor space for a night or two. They built up a network of contacts across the country, and at weekends they would stay with one of them and cook a Sunday feast, inviting their host's friends to a chanting session. These occasions and the college programmes were soul-stirring and inspirational, and through them a steady stream of young men and women were exposed to Krishna consciousness, some of them finding their way to the temples.

Hearing of the dedicated preaching of his disciples was a great encouragement for Prabhupada. More and more he spoke of reducing his travelling and handing the preaching work over to them. He wanted to free himself for the remaining years of his life to do what he now saw as his most important task: writing his books.

I am desiring now to stay six months of the year in Los Angeles and six

> months in Mayapur, spending my time solely for the translation of *Srimad-Bhagavatam* and other books, so that I may give them to you, my sincere disciples. So as far as possible, try to arrange preaching programmes with [*sannyasis*] as I prefer to remain now in the background.[3]

Yet no sooner had he written these words, in January 1973, then he was off again to Australia and New Zealand, and then to America. Whenever he seemed about to retire, he would be needed somewhere and would answer Krishna's call.

After Prabhupada's visit to Edinburgh, the temple continued for a while under Tribhuvanatha's leadership. He was helped by Kishor, whose tireless chanting and distribution of magazines on the streets of Glasgow inspired the devotees. Their numbers grew.

Rosie stayed on at the temple in Edinburgh and made peace with her mother. In November she was given her new name, Ramadevi, in a letter from Prabhupada. Now that she was initiated, she returned to the London temple to help look after Radha and Krishna.

Sheena Pawson came from York to join the Edinburgh temple. At a music festival she met a devotee who sold her a copy of *Teachings of Lord Chaitanya*. A few weeks later in Leeds, she got another of Prabhupada's books, the *Krishna* book, which she had seen displayed in a bookshop with the pages opened to show its brilliantly coloured paintings. She didn't have enough money to buy it, but the shop owner agreed to sell it to her at a reduced price. She loved the stories of Krishna, thinking they had the same flavour as stories of Jesus. Because she liked George Harrison she also bought the *Radha Krishna Temple* album. In her room at home she put the album sleeve, with its picture of Prabhupada, on the mantelpiece next to her *Krishna* book and sang along with the record. Beside them she kept an image of Jesus, for she believed that he also wanted her to chant Hare Krishna.

She gave all her belongings to OXFAM and hitchhiked to Edinburgh to join the temple, arriving just after Prabhupada's departure. Even though the temple was without money or comforts, she was happier there than she had ever been. Six months later Prabhupada initiated her by letter, giving here the name Shuchi, 'one with a pure heart.' She married Svayambhur, builder of the *rath* car, and they moved to a flat close to the London temple.

In late November 1972 Tribhuvanatha handed charge of the Edinburgh temple to Kishor and moved to Manchester to carry forward the preaching there in a rented house in Chorlton. He was joined by a handful of devotees, including Tribhangananda, Devamaya and her husband, and Ashtasakhi, who cooked for all of them. On Sundays they feasted, chanted, and danced with a houseful of guests.

Jane Cobon's father ran a sweet shop in Oldham, Lancashire, and brought her up to believe in a benevolent God who lived in heaven. If she was good and said her prayers, he told her, she could live with God forever when she died. Jane believed in love, and spent her youth searching for the ideal partner, the perfect loving relationship. She left home and went south to London, where she tried to find what she was looking for. But all her relationships left her feeling dissatisfied.

She spent time on her own, praying to Jesus and asking why some people were happy and others were sad. She wanted to know where she had come from and what would happen to her when she died. In 1971 she met a chanting party on Oxford Street – they seemed to her to stand out from the crowd, like angelic beings – and one of them gave her a magazine. Prabhupada's words told her that she was an eternal spirit, not her body, and that she could find eternal love only in relationship with God. She read the magazine over and over again. It made perfect sense, so she visited the temple.

At first she was afraid to walk in, but some other guests arrived and she went in with them. This was the summer of 1972. She was shown into a room upstairs where a saintly-looking Indian teacher in saffron robes was sitting on a cushion. She watched as a young man came in and bowed at his feet, then handed him a cup of water. She found the respect and love the monk showed his teacher remarkable. The teacher appeared perfectly self-composed. Although there were several guests in the room he sat silently, seemingly indifferent. He was not like anyone she had ever met: he was steady, secure, at ease with himself. He asked her name and where she was from and gave her a sweet. That was her first meeting with Prabhupada.

She went back to Manchester just as Tribhuvanatha was starting the new centre there, and began visiting the devotees and making friends with them. They taught her that Prabhupada was a messenger from the spiritual world who had come to teach them how to live. She took home books and beads, and began to follow all Prabhupada's instructions as if she were living in the temple. Her life was transformed, and she felt a deep spiritual consolation.

Jackie Carthy came from Preston. Born in 1956 as the oldest of six girls, she was bright and gregarious. She enjoyed school, but always felt there was more to life. In her free time she explored different religions and visited their places of worship, looking for people whose convictions she could share. When she was sixteen she heard a song from the *Radha Krishna Temple* album in a record shop. To her it was more than music – it was another world.

She met a devotee in the street and bought a copy of *Easy Journey To Other Planets.* Following the directions the devotee had given her she caught a bus to Manchester to visit the small temple in Chorlton. This was just before her seventeenth birthday, and it was the furthest she had ever ventured on her own. When she met the temple devotees and joined in their chanting she thought she had never experienced so much joy. What was the point of holding back, she thought, when she could be with them all the time?

She found the philosophy of karma a revelation – it explained why good things seemed to happen to bad people. She went out singing with them in Manchester, sewed book bags for them, read their *Krishna* book, and made friends with Jane. Once, she was so absorbed in helping at the temple that she missed the last bus home and had to seek shelter for the night in a police station. Jackie was determined to live with the devotees, so she left home and went to Edinburgh, where according to Scottish law seventeen-year-olds are adults. There she lived in the temple, sold books, and did the devotees' laundry.

In May 1973 Jackie was initiated by letter as Govardhan. In the same month Jane Cobon, who by then had moved in with the devotees, was initiated as Yashasvini.

In London, after Prabhupada left in early September, the search for a new temple continued in earnest. He wrote to Kshirodakshayi urging him to support the general effort.

> There in London we have such a big field for pushing on preaching work. These temples are just like oases in the desert for the conditioned souls to quench the thirst of their desire for real happiness.[4]

George Harrison took Dhananjaya to see properties – a health spa near Oxford, a convent near Virginia Water. He drove his Aston Martin with his hand in his bead bag. At traffic lights people recognised him, and he would raise the bead bag and say, 'Hare Krishna.' But whenever property agents saw who the buyer was they inflated their prices. So George decided Dhananjaya should continue the search on his own, and George went to America.

George was working on his *Living in the Material World* album, which would bring his Krishna consciousness into the open as never before. When it came out in June 1973, the single that accompanied it, 'Give Me Love (Give Me Peace on Earth)', went to number one on the U.S. charts.

Dhananjaya searched on. Prabhupada wrote to him with urgency.

> In order to expand properly all over the British Isles we shall require a big, big headquarters. Seize the iron while the fire is hot, my Guru Maharaj used to tell me. George is now convinced of our movement, he will pay, so why the delay and difficulty? I think you should very seriously and with a cool head apply yourself to getting that place as soon as possible, at least by the springtime.[5]

As soon as he received this letter, Dhananjaya heard about Piggots Manor, located in a small Hertfordshire village north of London. On a cold winter's day he and a friend climbed through a gap in the fence and peered across a frozen lake at a magnificent mock Tudor mansion set among ornamental trees in seventeen acres of gardens. The asking price was £220,000, which they knew to be within George's range. They made an appointment and were shown round by the owner, a woman who had bought the former nurses' training college from St Bartholomew's Hospital. Inside, the manor house was spacious; daylight flooded through leaded windows to illuminate oak floors and panelled galleries. The house was in two wings: a two-storey, high-ceilinged private residence with a grand oak stairway on one side, and a service wing on three floors with numerous smaller rooms on the other. Across a courtyard was an extensive set of outbuildings, including stables and a four-bedroomed cottage that looked out onto a walled kitchen garden, with paddocks and orchards beyond. The garden, full of redwood, yew, Scots pine, chestnut, and oak, enclosed a lake and lawns thickly bordered by rhododendrons. Set in the picturesque village of Letchmore Heath, close to the motorway, only fifteen miles from the centre of London, it seemed the perfect place to house the devotees and a temple for Krishna.

In the hallway Dhananjaya found a callbox, and phoned George. When George heard his voice he was already in a mood to be positive. He had just received a long letter from Prabhupada encouraging him in his devotional service.

> Great soul does not mean politician, or scholar, or famous musician, or scientist. No. Great soul is one who understands that Krishna is the cause of all causes and all that is, and then surrenders unto Him. You are doing that, therefore I say that you are a great soul, not because you have got some material name, fame or wealth. That will vanish at the time of your death, so what good it is? But because you are serving Krishna in devotional loving mood, therefore I say great soul.[6]

Prabhupada added at the bottom of his letter a note urging George not to delay in buying a property. He repeated the same words he had spoken to Dhananjaya: 'Strike while the iron is hot. If we delay the matter too long it may not remain a favourable proposition.'

Fortified by Prabhupada's urgent plea George was decisive. As soon as he heard how Dhananjaya liked the property, he authorised him to make a firm offer of £220,000 and told him to put the matter in the hands of his solicitors.

Three months later, in April, the purchase was finalised in the name of the Material World Foundation. George had just created the foundation to receive the profits from his forthcoming album, due to be released in the summer. It would channel funds to humanitarian causes for the relief of suffering in the material world. For the time being, the foundation gave ISKCON a lease at the token rate of ten pounds a month.[7]

With the purchase of the Manor came rapid changes. The pressure on space was quickly released as devotees flooded out to the new temple. However, although they could now chant their rounds in the long corridors and walk in the grounds of this opulent mansion, they had none of the resources necessary to occupy such an extensive property – to repair, decorate, furnish, or maintain it. The previous owner, before leaving, had stripped out even the doorknobs. Nothing but the bare surfaces remained.

Tribhuvanatha came from Manchester with a crew of helpers and set to work to turn the big empty house into a temple. The tasks seemed endless. Their diet was austere – porridge for breakfast, and dal, potatoes, and carrots for lunch – but their spirits were high.

It was Shyamsundar's idea to hire a helicopter for the glorious day at the end of May when Prabhupada flew in from Los Angeles to see the new manor house. There was no lack of transport to meet him at the airport. George was out of the country, but he sent a fleet of three coffee-coloured limousines with cream seats. Jaihari, unaware of George's gesture, had booked a top-of-the-line Mercedes. Shyamsundar, however, recently returned to England, went further than either of them, and on impulse rented a helicopter at Heathrow Airport.

He hadn't foreseen the weather, though. It turned overcast and stormy, and now he was riding beside his spiritual master inside the helicopter's small glass cabin, being tossed about like a ball in the wind. He felt ill and looked to see how Prabhupada was taking it. Prabhupada smiled broadly, assuring Shyamsundar he was fine, and looked down as they skimmed the treetops across Hertfordshire. The Manor, with its gardens, tree-lined lake, and turreted chimneys, came into view.

Prabhupada saw spread beneath him, on a lawn strewn with wild flowers, a joyous mass of young men and women leaping up and down. A light rain had begun to fall, but it hadn't dampened their spirits as they chanted Krishna's names. Looking up, Ramadevi saw the helicopter burst through the low clouds with a loud clatter. She cried out, 'Prabhupada's here!' Dashing across the grass, she slipped on the damp turf and fell headlong, but it didn't matter. Devotees were throwing themselves full-length in the wet grass. Rhododendron blossoms in full bloom, pink, white, crimson and purple, were being plucked and carried forward by eager hands, straight toward the path of the whirling blades.

The pilot saw his landing spot overrun and was appalled. He hovered, circling slowly, allowing Prabhupada a full view of the Manor while he waited for order to assert itself below. As the craft descended, the devotees saw that Prabhupada was waving to them. When at last he stepped onto firm ground, a little shaken, he turned to Shyamsundar with a wry smile.

'I don't think we'll travel like that again.'

The devotees lined up on either side, and he passed along their waiting avenue, up the sloping lawn toward the Manor. As he went, smiling his acknowledgement on either side, the two rows rippled as they fell one by one into the damp grass to offer flowers at their master's feet.

He went inside, entering through the conservatory that was soon to be the altar room, and proceeded to the makeshift temple. There he gave a short speech. He found difficulty lecturing: he had a severe cough, the weather was cold and damp, the building draughty and bare. In an improvised temple in the old billiard room, where they made an altar for Gaura-Nitai, he led the routine prayers, finishing with a special prayer of thanks – 'All Glories to George Harrison! All Glories to George Harrison! All Glories to George Harrison!' – to which everyone thrice responded, 'Hare Krishna!'

'We must be thankful to this good boy George Harrison,' he opened, 'that he has given us the facility of assembling in this nice house. We must give him all glories, and Krishna will bless him, more and more.' He went on briefly.

> Krishna is inconceivable. But to his devotees he is very easily attained. The *gopis* are village girls, uneducated, but Krishna is within their hands. Krishna, who is unapproachable by any other method, can be attained only by *bhakti* – by love and devotion, in service. He reveals himself by his causeless mercy, being pleased upon you. Therefore we should approach a person who knows the *bhakti* science, and by devotional service to Krishna and the spiritual master, all becomes revealed.[8]

'Thank you very much,' he concluded, and rose. Shyamsundar then took him on a tour of the ground floor rooms. At the bottom of the broad flight of stairs that led to Prabhupada's room waited a group of chanting devotees. Many of them were setting eyes on him for the first time, and were full of nervous apprehension. On the stairs waited Shuchi.

She had positioned herself on the landing halfway up, where she thought she could attract Prabhupada's attention. This was her first sight of her spiritual master and her expectations were high. She hoped to see the effulgence she had heard about and receive a smile of acknowledgement. She jumped up and down, waving her arms wildly in the kirtan as he walked past. But he seemed to take no notice.

After that her mind was beset with doubts. Instead of experiencing Prabhupada as a humble saintly man she saw him as stern and aloof. She dealt with this by avoiding getting too close to him. Instead she studied his books. Two years later in Nairobi, wiser and calmer, Shuchi found peace with Prabhupada when she presented him with a yellow rose and he looked straight into her eyes with gratitude. He carried her rose with him all that day in a way that made her believe that he did care for her after all.

Another devotee who saw Prabhupada for the first time was Richard Naismith. He was the son of a well-to-do family in New Zealand, where he had worked as a motoring correspondent. He went surfing a lot, but soon grew tired of his predictable life. He came to England on a journey of discovery, and along the way heard that the only serious spiritual group in London were the Hare Krishna devotees. At the London temple he learned to chant and was introduced to Dhananjaya, the temple president. They discovered they shared almost the same surname and were distantly related, which Richard took as a good omen. When Dhananjaya told him that Krishna Consciousness was the 'absolute truth', he believed him and joined.

Richard was among those waiting at the bottom of the stairs, and when Prabhupada came past he reached down and touched his feet. Usually Prabhupada was reluctant to allow this, but on this occasion he was in a magnanimous mood and accepted Richard's gesture of surrender. A few weeks later he initiated him as Raghubhir.

In his room the next day, when Prabhupada learned how much the helicopter had cost to hire, he told the story of a guru whose disciples showered him with gifts whenever he came to see them, telling him, 'All this is yours, master.' When the guru called for his purse, however, his servant told him it was empty. 'Where has my money gone?' he asked his disciples. They were surprised. 'Oh, but we spent it all on buying gifts for you.'

This story did not dampen Shyamsundar's enthusiasm to spend money for Prabhupada during the following weeks.

A professional photographer was there to capture Prabhupada's visit. Harernamananda was born in Germany, where he spent the sixties exploring every conceivable avenue of alternative knowledge. He got work as a U.S. Army photographer and lived comfortably, but with a growing feeling of emptiness. He took up yoga and realised that he was eternal and that there was a divine force behind everything. In 1971 he read Prabhupada's commentary on the *Ishopanishad* and learned how at the age of seventy Prabhupada had travelled alone to New York to spread this teaching. He became convinced that Prabhupada was a genuine teacher. He gave up his lucrative job and became his follower. When he first met Prabhupada a few months later in Paris, he saw with the eyes of a photographer that this man was extraordinary. The way he moved his hands, his expressions, how he held his head, his noble bearing – all these told him that Prabhupada was a very special person. At the ceremony in the Jardin du Luxembourg he accepted initiation, then started his service as a photographer for the Bhaktivedanta Book Trust.

That week at the Manor, each morning when Prabhupada came down to give the class, Harernamananda was there with his camera on a tripod. He had his lens focussed exclusively on Prabhupada's face. He wanted to explore it with his camera – to try to find his identity through photographs. Using an ultra quiet mechanism and super-sensitive film in the dark conditions, without a flash, he took ten or fifteen photographs per session for five days. On the last day he looked through his viewfinder and noticed that the image was brighter than on previous days. He couldn't explain this, because the lighting conditions had not changed, the day was as overcast as before, and the settings on his camera were the same. When he looked up at Prabhupada he saw why. His whole form was glowing. He guessed this was not something that he could photograph, and was not surprised when it didn't register in his pictures that day.

Because of Prabhupada's weak health his visit was low-key. He stayed in his rooms most of the time and received few visitors. Shyamsundar, Malati, and Mukunda were all now back in England. The three of them received firm instructions from Prabhupada to have everything ready for the summer, when he would return to open the Manor officially and to install the Radha-Krishna deities that had been kept in storage at Bury Place since the previous summer. After seven days at the Manor Prabhupada continued on to India, where he rested in Mayapur for the full month of June.

Devotees staying at the Manor travelled into London daily to sell magazines and books and to collect donations from the Hindu community. They introduced a Life Membership scheme, offering benefits to anyone willing to donate a regular sum to the temple. Kshirodakshayi was experienced at making members in India. He was helped by Partha, who exchanged his place on Rebatinandan Swami's team for service as the Manor's head cook and to help sign up Life Members.

The Manor needed a president. Tribhuvanatha was a likely choice, but he wanted to travel and preach as Prabhupada had asked him to do. Prabhupada had suggested Dhananjaya for the post but left the decision with Shyamsundar and Mukunda. They decided to appoint Bhajahari, with Mukunda working with him closely as advisor. Around the same time they asked Prabhavishnu to come back to England from Dublin and take charge of the Bury Place temple, leaving the Dublin centre under the care of Narahari.

Preparations were underway for a grand Rathayatra festival to welcome Prabhupada back. Jaihari sent him a letter of invitation signed by all the devotees, with an advance copy of the souvenir magazine prepared for the occasion. Prabhupada's health had improved, and he wrote back warmly.

> The collage of the pictures and the articles in the magazine *Rathayatra '73, London's Summer Festival,* has been wonderfully set up, and I very much appreciate it. I can understand from your attempt that you are doing something wonderful this year. So far my health is concerned, by the grace of Krishna, I have improved very much, about ninety percent. Offer my beloved blessings to all devotees who have signed the invitation album. I shall enjoy their company when I meet them.[9]

As the summer of 1973 unfolded, the devotees anticipated welcoming Prabhupada to his new temple in the Hertfordshire countryside.

CHAPTER 15

Dancing in Piccadilly

At the start of a glorious summer Prabhupada returned. The devotees had advertised so widely, proclaiming Rathayatra 'London's Summer Festival', that they really believed it was going to be the main event in London that summer of '73. Their optimism was boosted by Shyamsundar's confidence and verve, by the purchase of the Manor, and by Mahavishnu's good fortune.

Mahavishnu had inherited £11,000 from a favourite uncle, and with no other thought than to please Krishna he had told Shyamsundar the good news. The Society had no money to spend on Rathayatra because the Manor was draining its meagre resources.

'Then we'll put you in charge of Rathayatra,' Shyamsundar told him, 'and you can make it the biggest ever.'

Mahavishnu didn't hold back. He financed a brand new *rath* car, a full-colour souvenir magazine (the one that had so impressed Prabhupada), a lavish Rathayatra feast, an advertising campaign that had posters on two hundred London buses with stickers all over London, and decorations for Trafalgar Square that included large banners and a small forest of potted plants – even some palm trees. He then hired a film crew to record the event. His biggest purchase was an expanse of bright yellow canvas to be erected as a pavilion over large parts of Trafalgar Square. He saved the last thousand pounds, at Prabhavishnu's request, to buy a van for the book distributors travelling in Ireland.

Shyamsundar drove Prabhupada to London in a small orange car. The previous day Prabhupada had flown from Calcutta to London, and now, under the July sun, aged seventy-seven, he was about to participate in a two-mile procession to Trafalgar Square. Although he had rested in Mayapur all the previous month, he had yet to regain his strength. Shyamsundar feared he was overtaxing himself.

Prabhupada stepped out of the car and moved through the kirtan toward the front of Jagannath's chariot. It was bigger and stronger than any of the previous chariots, tall and well-proportioned. On the lofty platform with Jagannath were Lilashakti and Ashtasakhi, who would care for the deities, and Rebatinandan Swami, who would lead the kirtan. The devotees had placed a beautiful *vyasasana,* shaded by a golden umbrella, on the front of the car. Steps were placed beneath it to help Prabhupada ascend. He bowed before Jagannath, then looked at the magnificent seat waiting for him and shook his head.

'No. I am an ordinary devotee. I will go with the devotees in the kirtan party.' When they understood his choice, a great cheer went up.

He gathered around him the chief kirtan leaders with their *mridangas.* These tall young men, strong and agile, formed a circle, and inside it, wreathed in garlands, Prabhupada moved unencumbered. He walked forward and they moved with him. He halted and they halted. He raised his hands and they leapt. He beckoned with a nod of his head and they continued forward again. They spun and dipped as they danced, beating their drums with all their hearts. Every so often Prabhupada stopped and turned to look back at Jagannath with the look of a man in love. Then he raised his arms and jumped like a young man, as all around devotees lifted off the ground effortlessly, carried on a wave of exultation. All who witnessed the dancing were astonished.

The Scotland Yard inspector supervising the parade approached Prabhupada's servant, Shrutakirti. 'Your leader is causing too much disruption,' he said. 'Tell him to sit down on his seat so we can restore order here.' But how could Shrutakirti restrict his spiritual master? He did nothing, and the inspector approached him a second time.

'You have to tell him.'

Reluctantly he went up to Prabhupada.

'The police want you to sit on the *vyasasana*.' Prabhupada looked away and continued dancing as if he had not heard. Shrutakirti suggested the inspector tell Prabhupada himself, but the inspector decided against it.

On the way down Haymarket the heavy *rath* car gathered speed on the hill. The breaking system wasn't working properly, and the chariot was in danger of going out of control. The dancing devotees were unaware of the danger, but some of the policemen noticed.

'Who's in charge here? Who's in control?' they asked anxiously.

'Krishna's in control!' a devotee happily assured them, and returned to his chanting and dancing. The police later claimed that one of the car's wheels had briefly mounted the pavement, but fortunately nothing worse occurred.

Expecting that Prabhupada would soon need to rest, Shyamsundar had arranged for his car to follow closely behind. However, the longer Prabhupada danced, the more energised he became. After two hours they reached Trafalgar Square. Prabhupada was clearly enjoying himself. With the help of his cane he climbed the steps to the plinth and took his seat, shaded from the strong sunlight by the fronds of palm trees.

The square had been transformed into a festival village. A sound system had been installed and had been playing George Harrison and *Radha Krishna Temple* throughout the afternoon, so by the time the procession arrived the square was already full. Stalls had been set up for serving the feast, which devotees had been preparing for three days in the temple kitchens.

A highlight of the festival was to be a Vedic wedding ceremony around a sacred fire. After the unauthorised fire of the previous year the police had warned that if a fire was lit again there would be serious consequences. Yet someone lit a fire anyway. Govardhan, from Scotland, and her bridegroom Achintyarupa were married that day on the plinth of Nelson's Column in front of a thousand people.

Another surprise for the authorities was the pavilion, for which no permission had been asked or given. Its bright yellow canopies were lashed to the heavy stone bollards that dotted the square, and some minor damage resulted. These infringements would cost the devotees dearly in future years.

On his way back to the Manor with Shyamsundar and Malati, Prabhupada stopped for a rest and some refreshment at the Bury Place temple. While Malati prepared him a cooling mango drink, he went in to see Radha and Krishna. Sarvamangala was serving on the altar. She had volunteered to stay back during the festival, although she was sorry to be missing what had promised to be an unforgettable experience. The temple room was quiet and she was there alone when the door opened and in walked Prabhupada. He bowed to Radha and Krishna, and when he turned to leave she ran to the door to kneel at his feet and help him put on his slippers. She had always wanted to touch Prabhupada's feet but had never dared. Now she held them and felt how soft they were. Her wish was fulfilled. He smiled at her, then went up to his room.

When Prabhupada returned to the Manor that evening he slept for an hour, then got up as usual to translate through the night. It was as if he were not subject to the physical laws that governed ordinary people. His energy seemed to just go on and on.

The next day the front page of the *Guardian* carried a photograph of the *rath* car framed against Nelson's Column. The twin pinnacles appeared sidy by side with the caption, 'A Rival For Nelson.' Prabhupada was jubilant.

'Nelson was a hero. Now Krishna is going to be a hero in this country,' he said, and declared that Mahavishnu had spent his inheritance well.

CHAPTER 16

Krishna's Manor House

Prabhupada's rooms looked over the lawns and lake. Leaded windows filled the southern side of each room, flooding them with light and air. Through the panes he could see the gardens spread on all sides and the lake fringed with willow, pine, and oak, echoing with the cry of moorhens and the chatter of ducks.

His reception room was wide and spacious, large enough to accommodate fifty guests. The carpet was spread with cool, white sheets, Indian-style, and his cushions arranged so he had his back to the windows, framing him against the trees and allowing him a clear view of his guests. He sat on the floor as they did, behind a low table, with his harmonium on one side. Sometimes when he was alone he played the harmonium, accompanying himself while he sang to Krishna. Next door was his spacious panelled bathroom, where he took his morning massage, and beyond that his bedroom, its small balcony overhung by a magnolia tree whose large creamy blossoms scented the whole apartment.

The peace and orderliness of his surroundings and the well-being of the temples in England made a positive impression and his health quickly improved. He wrote,

> The place is very calm and quiet. It is sufficiently spacious also. I walk within the village daily in the morning along with devotees and it is very pleasant. I am holding morning class from 7–8 a.m. There are about 40 devotees living with me, similarly there are 30 devotees in 7 Bury Place. Sometimes I go there. Things are being managed there nicely.[1]

Each afternoon Prabhupada walked out into the grounds, with Shrutakirti carrying a blanket and a cup of water, and chose a spot beneath a tree or in some corner of the lawns. There he sat for an hour or more, chanting on his beads or hearing Shrutakirti read. All summer long, as the sun shone in a clear sky, devotees and guests gathered round him and he answered their questions, spoke philosophy, told stories, and laughed with them. 'When the sun shines,' he said, 'England is one of the most beautiful places on earth.'

First to come and see him was George Harrison. As soon as he entered Prabhupada's room he paid homage to his guru, full-length on the floor. He told him he was trying to chant sixteen rounds a day on his beads, but when he did he lost his desire to work at his musical career.

'That's alright. Just chant when you can,' replied Prabhupada.[2] After having lunch together, he showed George his rooms.

'This is actually your house,' said Prabhupada with gratitude.

'No, this is Krishna's house and these are your rooms,' protested George, and he promised his support to help expand the movement more and more.

A few weeks later George returned with some musician friends, among them Ravi Shankar's sister-in-law. George had written a song for her called 'Krishna, Where Are You?', which Ravi Shankar had set to music. It was a simple song, inspired by an idea Prabhupada had several times mentioned to George. They performed the song for him, sung by Ravi's sister-in-law.

'O Krishna where are you?' she sang. 'I am missing you.' The song ended with the emotional plea, 'Please come and wipe my tears and make me smile.'

'Yes, this is the proper mood,' Prabhupada said. 'Always searching for Krishna, not thinking that I have found him. Like the Six Goswamis – they were always asking, "Where is Krishna?" '

Prabhupada was working on his translation and commentary of the *Chaitanya-charitamrita,* the epic sixteenth-century poem written in classical Bengali and Sanskrit that tells the life and teachings of Sri Chaitanya. He had just published a preliminary instalment of the work, and he announced the book one morning in the temple, praising his Sanskrit editor Pradyumna, who travelled with him everywhere. Pradyumna was well liked by the devotees in England.

> I am very much indebted to Pradyumna because he very carefully edits and makes the thing perfect. My beloved disciple – I call him Pandit Mahashaya because he is doing the pandit's work – works very hard, and his wife helps him.[3]

The instalment was a slim paperback called *Lord Chaitanya in Five Features,* with a luminous painting of Sri Chaitanya on the cover by Prabhupada's disciple Muralidhara. This was the book that Shrutakirti read from each afternoon on the lawn.

One day he read, 'When the spiritual master sees his disciple making advancement he becomes very happy.' Just at that moment Shyamsundar came striding across the lawn from the cottage, where he and Malati had a room. He appeared excited and had come to Prabhupada to share his enthusiasm. Prabhupada's eyes lit up as Shyamsundar approached, and they talked quietly for a few minutes as others in the circle round Prabhupada looked on. Sitting among them was Partha, who had managed to free himself from the kitchen for half an hour. He liked Shyamsundar and recognised the easy friendship that existed between him and Prabhupada. It was an intimacy he could not hope to have with his spiritual master, although he longed for it. After a few comments from Prabhupada, Shyamsundar was off again, busy with his schemes to bring visitors to meet the leader of the Hare Krishna movement.

He and Mukunda were preparing for a weeklong festival to celebrate the Manor opening. To honour Prabhupada they wanted to name the new temple Bhaktivedanta Manor, and to introduce him to influential people. Shyamsundar knew that Prabhupada liked to meet and preach to leaders of society, and he was organising a series of days for religionists, philosophers, scholars, intellectuals, artists, and musicians. Invitations were being sent out, a concert stage was going up on the lawn, and he had ordered gilded chairs and dining tables. His plans captured Prabhupada's interest, and he wrote to Kirtanananda regretting that he would be unable to celebrate Janmashtami with his disciples in New Vrindavan, West Virginia.

> Syamasundara has arranged a gorgeous festival beginning 21st till 27th August. Here is the programme:
> August 21st: Chief guest, Indian High Commissioner
> August 22nd: Chief guest, George Harrison
> August 23rd: Ecumenical day, chief guest, Malcolm Muggeridge and representatives from all faiths.
> August 24th: Young people's day, advertised 4 days before the event on all young people's programmes on BBC radio. At least 5000 young people expected to come.
> August 25th: Businessman's Day, chief guests Mr. Toyoto, and Baron Rothschild
> August 26th: Neighbour's Day, chief guest Graham Hill
> August 27th: Intellectual's Day, chief guest, D. Wayne, William Burroughs, Professor Alister Hardy.
> So please excuse me because I shall not be able to come there. When I return to America I will come there.[4]

During the actual event, the only one of the these persons who came was the Indian High Commissioner, though Sir Alister Hardy and the racing driver Graham Hill later came privately to meet Prabhupada.

'If only you would believe that Krishna is God,' Prabhupada said to his disciples as he looked round the room one morning during his lecture, 'then all your problems would be solved.' Prabhupada had never been an easy guru, one who would allow his disciples to drift along comfortably. He required them to examine their faith daily and be ever alert. For him, Krishna was all – there could be no doubt in the matter. For his disciples, however, perhaps only one thing was clear: Prabhupada was their all, the light that guided their lives. Their faith and hope rested in him.

Prabhupada began each morning class by singing *Jaya Radha-Madhava,* a song about Krishna in Vrindavan. The devotees had not heard it before, and it thrilled them to sing it back to him as he closed his eyes, completely immersed in the chant.

In London the previous year he had started lecturing from the first verse of the *Srimad-Bhagavatam*. Now at the Manor he started the *Bhagavad-gita* in the same way. Verse by verse, illuminating the story with his observations and anecdotes, he led them through the first chapter and on into the second. Day after day he set the scene for Arjuna's search for spiritual truth, presenting the dilemmas of material life and giving his young disciples practical and spiritual advice.

The room that served as a temple was large enough to fit everyone yet not so large as to lose its sense of intimacy. Prabhupada sat on his raised seat of blue and red velvet facing Gaura-Nitai, who stood on the stage at the opposite end. A skylight in an ornate arched ceiling shed natural light on the scene, while a broad expanse of windows gave onto dew-laden lawns and shrubs. It was a perfect setting for early-morning devotions: an English country garden room.

As Prabhupada lectured, Yashasvini felt his powerful presence and found that no matter how many people were in class he always seemed to say something just for her, something she needed to hear.

> When we see a person, we see only the senses. We do not see the director of the senses, the mind. The director of the mind is the intelligence and the owner of the intelligence is the soul. The intelligence comes from Krishna, who is within your heart. Not only your heart, he is also within the atom. The more you become purified the more you can get direct instruction from Krishna.[5]

In the rainy season, so many plants and creepers float on the river. Similarly we are floating on the waves of *maya*. Sometimes we are drowning, sometimes we are on the surface, sometimes on this shore, sometimes on the other shore; sometimes I am master of a kingdom, sometimes I am a dog; sometimes we are gathered together like so many straws, sometimes we are thrown asunder. We are assembled here exactly like that. No one is your father or mother or sister.[6]

The guru can save you by his instructions, but you have to take them seriously. My body, my family, my nation, my community, my philosophy, my politics – they cannot save me. They are all temporary, they come and go. My father and my mother, who protected me when I was a child, have gone away. Now who will protect me? Krishna will protect you always.[7]

A devotee is ready to excuse even the greatest enemy. But if you insult a devotee, Krishna does not excuse. Therefore be careful not to insult a devotee. A devotee may excuse, but Krishna will not excuse. He cannot tolerate an insult to his devotee.[8]

In the material world we are always puzzled. When something better is proposed to us – that we take to Krishna consciousness and be happy – we think, How will this help me? Therefore it requires a little time to understand. Krishna does not force. He says, surrender unto me, but he does not force. He has given you a little independence and he will not touch it. Otherwise there is no difference between a living entity and a stone. You will have to understand with love, 'Yes Krishna, I shall surrender.' This is Krishna consciousness. You must voluntarily agree. You must understand very nicely, with love. When you work for Krishna with love and enthusiasm that is pure Krishna consciousness.[9]

Devotees from the London temple took turns driving out to the Manor for the class. Others made the pilgrimage on foot to hear their spiritual master speak, first catching the train to Radlett, then walking through quiet country lanes alive with birdsong.

One day the kirtan was filled with a mystical energy. The roomful of devotees lifted into the air as one, weaving a spontaneous ballet. Tribhuvanatha played his *mridanga,* almost in trance, and his eyes met Prabhupada's in an exultant exchange of emotion between father and son.

Ramadevi came from London whenever she could, riding in the back of the temple van and bringing a garland for Prabhupada. She had heard he liked garlands to be light, so she went early to Covent Garden flower market, where she bought fresh blooms: small fragrant stock, brightly-coloured sweet peas, and blue cornflowers. In the back of the van she threaded these into delicate garlands.

One day they arrived late – Prabhupada had already started his lecture, and there was no opportunity for her to pass the garland forward to him. Malati, always a good friend, reassured her, 'Don't worry, after the class I'll take you up to Prabhupada's room and you can give it to him then.'

Once outside Prabhupada's room she hung by the door, wanting someone to take the garland from her. Prabhupada sat across the room, about to eat his breakfast. He beckoned her over with a reassuring nod, and held his head up waiting for her garland. As she put the flowers around him her hand brushed his ear. The softness of his skin startled her. The rest of the day she couldn't forget it. That afternoon she saw him walking out onto the lawn and realised he was still wearing her garland. It looked as fresh as the moment she had placed it round his neck. She felt a sudden rush of emotion, knowing her efforts had been appreciated.

The task of recording Prabhupada's daily lectures was given to Mohan. The previous year, as Mike Gulley, he had met the devotees in Manchester and bought Prabhupada's *Easy Journey to Other Planets.* He read the book slowly, meditating on each page, and it made a lot of sense to him. When he finished he walked the five miles to the temple in Salford. There he bought a set of beads and a bead bag, and after that regularly made the same journey on foot in the early mornings, while chanting. He felt himself sailing as he walked, carried by the holy name, and the miles passed unnoticed.

Mike bought more books by Prabhupada, and whatever questions he thought of were answered. He bought the *Radha Krishna Temple* album and danced to it in his room at home. After a few weeks he came to accept Krishna consciousness as the truth and Prabhupada as his guru. He played the record to his friends but was surprised that they didn't appreciate it. That's when he realised that the only thing left for him to do was to live in the temple and serve Krishna.

When Prabhupada came to London the previous summer Mike heard him speak on the first chapter of *Srimad-Bhagavatam*. Then he was asked to help at the Edinburgh temple, and it was there that his future direction emerged. He was not comfortable with going on the street to distribute books or chant, although he did it for Prabhupada. The reason was that he was shy. One day he volunteered to stay back to fix a broken drum. That led to other maintenance jobs, and he gained a reputation as a man who could fix anything. He was initiated as Mohan by letter in February 1973.

When the Manor was acquired he was given the job of installing electrical wiring. One day he was crawling beneath the temple room floorboards to fit cables when he heard Prabhupada walking directly above the spot where he was concealed. This made him very happy.

During the lectures Mohan sat next to Prabhupada's *vyasasana,* operating the sound system and recording the lecture. After the lectures he took the reel-to-reel tapes to the top of the stairs, where he had a small storage cupboard for his equipment. There he copied the lectures onto cassette tapes and sold them at cost to devotees. He took pride in doing his work well because he was helping Prabhupada preach.

Mohan became Prabhupada's personal technician in England. Whenever Prabhupada needed help with any of his equipment, such as his Dictaphone, he called for Mohan.

Prabhupada said he would install the Radha-Krishna deities on Janmashtami, which fell on 21st August that year. That gave six weeks for Shyamsundar to prepare the new temple room and for Malati to supervise the sewing of seven deity outfits. But they had no money.

George helped by paying for three slabs of pink Italian marble for the altar. Shyamsundar based his designs for the altar and *vyasasana* on the House of Lords, because when Prabhupada had visited the Lords' chamber two years previously he had praised its style.

The Manor was adorned with several ornate carved oak fireplaces. One was in the alcove Shyamsundar intended to use for Prabhupada's *vyasasana,* one in the reception room, and one upstairs. These would, in Shyamsundar's estimation, make perfect material to work with. He told Svayambhur to dismantle them and use the parts in the new temple. The new *vyasasana* began to emerge, modelled on the Queen's throne in the House of Lords. Instead of the royal coat of arms it was to be decorated with the lotus emblems of Vishnu. Prabhupada left these decisions in the hands of Shyamsundar – the Manor was his project – but when George heard about the demolition of the fireplaces he was shocked.

Upstairs, two artists were at work. Gopala was the flute-player for Quintessence, the band who chanted Hare Krishna at their concerts. He was also a brilliant painter. He had done the art for the Quintessence album covers: a portrait of Krishna seated in meditation in the Himalayas, and a psychedelic vision of Jesus radiating a multicoloured web of light. Now he was painting a life-sized portrait of Prabhupada standing beside a lake fringed with willows and attended by a peacock and a swan.

Sharadiya was at work in another room. She had joined Prabhupada in San Francisco in 1967 along with her brother Krishnadas. Krishnadas had gone to Germany to pioneer Krishna consciousness, and she had hoped to come to London with the original six devotees but had been too young. Now she was expecting a baby, and with her husband she had come to England to be with Prabhupada at the Manor. Each morning she heard his lecture, then held his slippers at the door while he put them on and handed him his cane: this simple service felt to her like the perfection of her life. Even though her baby was due in a matter of weeks, she eagerly accepted from Shyamsundar the challenge of painting a portrait of Sri Chaitanya and his four associates. Working in the room next to Prabhupada's, she put her heart and soul into a large, powerfully-conceived oil painting.

Both her painting and Gopala's were to hang in the new temple room.

Mahavishnu was building Prabhupada's throne according to Shyamsundar's design, helped by Sakshi Gopala. Padmalochana, who had just returned from a year in India, upholstered the *vyasasana*, incorporating four gold lotuses into the design. While the devotees worked, Prabhupada came daily to see their progress, speaking with Svayambhur, the construction team leader. Occasionally he allowed the construction workers to touch his feet. When he saw the finished throne he was surprised.

'What is this, a seat for Lord Shiva?' he joked with Shyamsundar.

With just a few days to go before the installation, he passed through the temple room on his way out to his walk.

'So, you will be ready?'

'Yes, Prabhupada, we'll be ready,' came a chorus of voices.

'You will never be finished,' he said, and walked off laughing.

Everyone was working flat out to prepare for the festival. One morning on his walk Prabhupada asked for the temple president, Bhajahari, but he was not present. When Prabhupada returned from his walk he sent someone to find Bhajahari. He had to be woken up. In a panic he dashed into the shower, dressed, and ran down to Prabhupada's room. He found his guru sitting in his rocking chair chanting his rounds and dived to the floor in front of him.

'So, you cannot rise in the morning?'

'Well, Srila Prabhupada, I was up with Mukunda until two in the morning, planning the Janmashtami festival.'

'Even if you take rest at two in the morning you must get up for *mangal-arati*.'

Not long after this incident Bhajahari noticed that Shyamsundar, who lived in the cottage, was himself not getting up early to chant with the devotees. He spoke to Rebatinandan, who said they should bring it to Prabhupada's attention. They went into Prabhupada's room, Bhajahari feeling a little nervous. Rebatinandan started to explain. As soon as Prabhupada understood why they were there he looked at Bhajahari.

'You should not criticise a superior Vaishnava,' he said severely, and to Rebatinandan, 'Tell him to leave.'

Bhajahari ran from the room, mortified. Whatever was said after he left, he heard nothing of it.

Two weeks before Janmashtami Prabhupada flew to Paris. The devotees in Paris had moved to a smart new building close to the Arc de Triomphe. Prabhupada installed large marble deities of Radha and Krishna, initiated ten new disciples, and gave the *gayatri-mantra* to seven more. He was received at the City Hall in the presence of the mayor, and met the head of the Roman Catholic Church in France, Cardinal Danielou.

The devotees asked Prabhupada to name the new Paris deities. Having explained that people in India looked to London for education and to Paris for enjoyment, he said, 'Radharani is beautiful, just like a Paris girl, and Krishna has come here to find out this most beautiful of the *gopis*. So his name is Paris-ishvara, "controller of Paris".'[10]

After six days in France he returned to the Manor. Having named Krishna in Paris, he agreed to name Krishna in London, calling him London-ishvara, 'controller of London'.

Shyamsundar issued emergency instructions. The construction crew were neither to sleep nor chant their rounds; otherwise, the temple would not be finished in time. The workers were uneasy – they were already missing Prabhupada's daily lecture. Now they were being asked to forsake their chanting as well. Shyamsundar assured them that Prabhupada approved of this dispensation, and one day in his *Bhagavad-gita* class Prabhupada was heard to say, 'On the field of battle, Arjuna did not chant rounds,' which some took as his tacit assent.

Svayambhur built Radha-Krishna's altar with parts of the fireplace surrounds and timbers from the *rath* car. George, having bought three massive slabs of rose-coloured marble, stored them in his greenhouse at Friar Park. On the day before the installation a gang of devotees transported them over and heaved them up onto the supporting framework.

The top slab, on which Radha and Krishna were to stand, was five feet from the ground. The deities would be reached by twin flights of solid wooden steps built on either side of the altar. Shyamsundar's design included a Gothic-style screen supporting a pinnacled canopy behind the altar. It was modelled on the screen that stood behind the royal thrones in the House of Lords. The final coat of gold paint was applied with only hours to spare. What the finished altar lacked in artistry it made up for in devotion. Its symbolism was inescapable: Krishna and his consort Radha were king and queen.

Sakshi Gopala stayed up all night to apply the final coat of gold paint to the *vyasasana*. Early in the morning, crouched on the seat meant for Prabhupada, paintbrush in hand, he nodded off. Suddenly he awoke to find the temple deserted and the garden door wide open – the very door through which Prabhupada usually left for his morning walk. A devotee came in.

'Has Srila Prabhupada just been through?' asked Sakshi.

'Yes.'

'Did he see me on the *vyasasana*?'

'Yes, of course.'

'What did he say?'

'He saw you sitting there sound asleep and he laughed.'

The finishing touch to the temple room was the chandeliers. Prabhupada had suggested them. Shyamsundar chose a pair of the most expensive ones he could find and wrote out a cheque with no idea where the money would come from to cover it. The temple room looked magnificent.

On Janmashtami morning, 21st August, devotees came from Dublin and Paris – a few even came from America – to witness Prabhupada install Radha and Krishna in their new home. In the kitchen Partha, now head chef at the Manor, prepared the feast. He enjoyed the challenge of gathering donations, going to the shops, ensuring that everything was on time, and seeing that the devotees enjoyed good quality prasadam.

Shyamsundar had invited many important guests, chief of whom was the High Commissioner of India. Through the course of the day nearly a thousand people visited. As Partha's feast took shape in the kitchen, punctually at ten o'clock in the morning Prabhupada came down the stairs.

He wanted the ceremony to be a simple one. His main requirement was the chanting of Krishna's names. He had, however, specified one ingredient beyond those collected for the usual fire sacrifices. This one was entirely new to the devotees: *pancha-gavya*, five products from the cow.

In the paddock a small family of cows had recently arrived, cared for by a devotee cowherd and his assistant. Prabhupada was happy now they had land for cows. Krishna loved cows. The devotees made a sign above the barn entrance that said, *Europe's First Cow Protection Programme*. Prabhupada wanted them to buy enough land for a hundred and fifty cows, and to make their own yoghurt and ghee and sell it to visitors. He called the Manor grounds New Gokula, 'home of the cows', and gave the deities of Radha-Krishna the names Radha-Gokulananda.

Since everything about the cow was deemed pure, he asked the cowherd men to provide milk, yoghurt, ghee, dung, and urine for the installation ceremony. These five substances were to be applied to Radha-Gokulananda's forms before they were bathed with rose-scented water.

In the middle of the temple room a low platform had been made, and on it the deities stood in large steel pots. Beside them containers held the *pancha-gavya*, and in front were flowers, fruits, and grains, together with sticks of wood for the sacred fire. Prabhupada proceeded with the bathing ceremony while the growing crowd chanted and danced. Those who had been working nonstop through several days and nights did their best to stay awake. Mahavishnu was determined not to succumb to sleep. In the kirtan he jumped, fell asleep in the air, collapsed on the floor, then got up and tried again. It kept happening, but he fought to stay awake.

The bathing over, Prabhupada dried the deities. He dabbed at Radha's cheeks with a soft cloth, touching her as he would a real person. Then Radha and Krishna were carried to the altar, where behind closed curtains they were dressed for the first time. When the curtains reopened the temple came alive with their presence. Radha-Gokulananda stood high up on their altar, dressed in pink and gold and wreathed with greenery and flowers. Prabhupada spoke to his young disciples, telling them, in less than twenty minutes, of their great fortune to have witnessed the appearance of Radha and Krishna that day in their midst.

> There is a planet in the spiritual world. This material world is only one fourth of God's creation. Beyond this is another sky, the spiritual sky. If you want to go there you will have to penetrate seven layers of material coverings, then you will reach the spiritual sky. There are many Vaikuntha planets. Above them all is Goloka, the planet full of cows which is Krishna's personal abode. In Goloka he is tending cows, and somewhere he is dancing with the *gopis,* but still, although he is there, he is everywhere. He is within your heart. Not only there – he is within the atom.
>
> Krishna is everywhere. If you are a devotee you can catch him – and he is ready to be caught. If you want to catch him, he comes forward ten times more than you. He is so kind. Where will you find him if he is everywhere? This deity worship in the temple means he has very kindly accepted a form which you can handle.
>
> The atheist will say here is a form made of marble. But if Krishna is in the atom, why not in the marble? The marble itself is Krishna. Krishna can accept your service through this marble, through water, through fire. Why not? Just like as soon as you touch the sunbeam, you touch the sun.
>
> Never think, 'Here is a statue.' No, here is Krishna personally. He is so kind that he comes before us in a way just suitable for our vision. Honour him and respect him, and be cautious not to neglect his worship. Be very clean. Rise early in the morning, take your bath, perform *mangal-arati,* chant Hare Krishna mantra, read scriptures. It is a great opportunity to serve Krishna, as the *gopis* are serving in Goloka. You can dress Krishna, offer him prasadam, chant his glories. In this way remain twenty-four hours engaged in Krishna's service, and gradually you will find how you are advancing in spiritual life.

After the fire sacrifice in the middle of the room came the first worship. Prabhupada went into the deity room to say the prayers for offering a feast to Krishna. Then he performed the arati, assisted by his servant Shrutakirti and the *pujaris* Malati, Bala Gopala, and Sarvamangala. Devotees crowded across the front of the deity room, craning to see Prabhupada and Krishna together. When the arati was over, Prabhupada beckoned them to follow him and led them around the back of the altar. Three times he circumambulated Radha and Krishna, pausing each time in front of them to turn in a circle. As he went round and round he mingled with his disciples, great and small, and danced alongside each of them, man, woman and child, churning the ocean of devotion, until all conception of time and space dissolved. They felt themselves lifted to another dimension, to an eternal moment where they were all together in Prabhupada's dance of love.

Finally he gathered them in front of Radha-Gokulananda and lifted his arms. They leapt effortlessly up and down, as if on a cushion of air. Here was the spiritual world he had just described: they were in it – the sound, the vision of Krishna, the companionship of love. Everything was there.

The day after Janmashtami was Prabhupada's seventy-eighth birthday. In the morning, after receiving flowers and spoken offerings from his disciples, he addressed them in the temple room, now presided over by Radha-Gokulananda. He began by addressing them as 'sons and daughters', and spoke some memorable words.

> I am very much hopeful that even if I die my movement will not stop. These nice boys and girls have taken so seriously. Bhaktivinoda Thakur wanted European and American people to understand and take part in Lord Chaitanya's movement. My Guru Maharaj attempted to send his disciples to the Western world. He invited me also. At our first meeting he asked me to preach.
>
> At that time I was a young man of twenty-five and still a householder. I should have joined immediately but I could not. But it was in my heart that it is to be done. So better late than never. I wasted so much time, I can understand that, but I did not forget. I was simply finding out the opportunity how to do it.
>
> By the help of my disciples this movement is gaining ground and I

have to thank you. It is all due to you. It is your credit that you are helping me in executing the order of my Guru Maharaj. This movement will go on. Nobody can stop.

Whatever little success I have got is because I do not present anything created by me. The bona fide spiritual master will not manufacture.

To become spiritual master is not a very difficult thing. You will have to become spiritual master. You, all my disciples, every one, should become spiritual master. It is not difficult. It is difficult when you manufacture something. But if you simply present whatever you have heard from your spiritual master it is very easy. If you want to become over-intelligent – to present something, to interpret something, to make some further addition or alteration – then you will spoil it. Simply present as it is. Remain always a servant of your spiritual master and present the thing as you have heard, then you will be spiritual master.

Go door to door. Simply say with folded hands, 'My dear friend, my dear brother, you surrender to Krishna.' Take up this process of being spiritual master and your life will become perfect. Thank you very much.[11]

After the lecture a large birthday cake in the shape of a temple was brought in. It stood on the platform in front of Prabhupada's *vyasasana* during the closing kirtan, decorated with coloured icing sugar and two tall domes, one of laddu and one of marzipan. The cake was the work of Devamaya.

'I don't want to eat a temple,' Prabhupada said when he saw it, and Devamaya was afraid she had done something wrong. Then he added, 'I want to build one.'

He had seen that the new temple room, though much larger than the one in London, was still not big enough. He wanted a temple built in the Manor grounds and called for Devamaya's husband, who knew something of architecture. Prabhupada told him what he had in mind: the temple would cover the two tennis courts, and above it would be several floors of ashrams for devotees and guests. The tower, he said, would rise thirty storeys. His architect disciple, lacking Prabhupada's visionary faith, advised him that such a tall building would never be permitted in the village of Letchmore Heath. Prabhupada asked how tall the temple could be.

'Maybe forty, perhaps fifty feet – as tall as the pine trees.' Prabhupada shrugged and modified his proposal to a fifty-foot tower.[12]

He asked that the cake be brought to his room, and then asked his architectural adviser to give him a slice of the dome.

'It's made of solid marzipan, Prabhupada. It will be very sweet. Are you sure you want it?'

Prabhupada's eyes lit up. 'Oh, yes! I would like that.' And he sat at his desk and ate the large piece with satisfaction.

During the day more crowds came. Prabhupada sat in his room with a few disciples and told stories of how he had set out on his mission from India to the West. He looked down on the lawn from his window and saw chairs and tables, set with plates and cutlery, awaiting the feast that would be served to the guests. He recalled how eight years earlier in Calcutta his godbrothers had organised a function in his honour on a wealthy man's lawn, at the eve of his departure for America. As guest of honour he had sat at the head of the table but had not known in which hands to hold his knife and fork.

'You don't know how to hold your fork and knife and you are going to teach in the West?' a godbrother had asked him incredulously.

'I am not going to teach them how to hold a fork and knife!' Prabhupada had replied with vehemence. 'I am going to teach them how to forget that!' Remembering the occasion now he laughed heartily with his disciples.

As the afternoon wore on guests mingled on the lawn. Prabhupada watched the results of Shyamsundar's labours indulgently. He had no wish to take part, but he applauded the industry and energy of his disciples. As daylight faded hundreds of lamps, strung from the trees, lit the scene.

The call came for Prabhupada to go down and speak to the guests in the temple. Immediately he rose, and for the third time that day donned his chadar, took his cane, and solemnly descended to take his place on the *vyasasana*. This was Vyasa-puja, the day when the spiritual master receives honour from his disciples, and Shyamsundar had asked him to give a public discourse.

Tonight's subject matter is, What is guru? If this room becomes dark we cannot see. Similarly in this material world we are all in darkness. Therefore there is need of sunlight. But there is another world where there is no darkness, where there is no need of sunlight. Guru's business is to lead the disciples from darkness to light, to bring the torchlight of knowledge and release the disciple from the sufferings of ignorance.

Although hundreds and thousands of *acharyas* have come and gone, the message is one. The same message as expressed by Krishna five thousand years ago when he spoke *Bhagavad-gita.*

The postman delivers the letter without change. That is guru. Guru cannot be two. The postman may be different but the message is the same. Krishna says, 'Think of me, become my devotee, worship me, offer your obeisances to me.' The same thing was spoken by all the *acharyas*. And we are also speaking the same thing. We do not interpret Krishna's words.

Krishna says you learn from the guru by surrender. Find such an exalted person where you can willingly surrender. Before taking a guru, first study to see if you can surrender there. And the guru also studies if you are fit to be a disciple.

No more death, no more old age, no more disease. Guru's responsibility is to guide the candidate to immortality, back to home back to Godhead. Thank you very much.[13]

One day Mukunda and Bhajahari were walking with Prabhupada round the lake when they heard the magical sound of a flute drifting across the water. It was Gopala, the artist, playing in his studio, his open window overlooking the gardens. Bhajahari was enchanted.

'Prabhupada, even in the material world the sound of the flute is so wonderful. I can't imagine what Krishna's flute must sound like.' Prabhupada opened his eyes wide and told a story of Krishna playing his flute and calling the *gopis*. As he spoke he became animated and acted out the parts. Then he spoke directly to Bhajahari.

'I want you to make an island in the middle of this lake. On it build a temple, and in the temple put Garbhodakshayi Vishnu with the lotus flower growing from His navel, and Lord Brahma. Then you can have boats so that guests can go round the island and chant.'

All summer long, as the sun shone in a clear sky, devotees and guests gathered round him on the Manor lawn. He answered their questions, spoke philosophy, told stories, and laughed with them. 'When the sun shines in England,' he said, 'it is one of the most beautiful places on earth.'

'The place is very calm and quiet,' wrote Prabhupada. 'It is sufficiently spacious also. There are about 40 devotees living with me.' (Left to right around Prabhupada: Harernamananda, Padmalochana, Pradyumna, Bhajahari, Charanaravinda, Sarvamangala, Svati)

He donned his chadar, took his cane, and descended to the temple.

Prabhupada on his seat with Shivajvara in front.

The room that served as a temple, where Prabhupada lectured on *Bhagavad-gita,* was large enough to fit everyone, yet not so large as to lose a sense of intimacy.

While they worked Prabhupada came daily to check their progress, speaking with Svayambhur, the construction team leader. (Behind Prabhupada are Shrutakirti and Mahavishnu)

Prabhupada proceeded with the bathing ceremony, while a growing crowd chanted and danced. (Left to right: Manu, Kishor, Sakshi Gopala, Anakadundubhi, Pradyumna, Mondakini, Rebatinandan, unknown, Rasamandala, unknown, Tulasidas)

He performed the arati.

As he went round and round he mingled with his disciples, great and small, so that he danced alongside each of them.

Prabhupada spoke to his young disciples, telling them of their great fortune to witness that day the appearance of Radha and Krishna in their midst.

Finally he gathered them in front of Radha-Gokulananda, and lifted his arms.

Prabhupada wrote Sir Alister Hardy a seven-page letter, wanting him to appreciate the wisdom of the *Bhagavad-gita.*

Every day, hour after hour, Prabhupada spoke about Krishna to guests in his rooms. He could talk about Krishna for as long as they were willing to hear.

Each afternoon he walked out into the grounds, with Shrutakirti carrying a blanket and cup of water, and chose a spot beneath a tree or in some corner of the lawns. There he sat for an hour or more, chanting on his beads or hearing Shrutakirti read.

Prabhupada welcomed young mothers with children to sit with him, and many were the hours they spent on the lawn. (Here he is with Bhaktikishori, with Shivajvara in the background)

Every day, before the village was awake, Prabhupada and his disciples followed the lane between sleeping cottages and hedgerows. (Left to right: Karanodakshayi, Shyamsundar, Shrutakirti, Subhaga, Prabhupada, Himavati, David Lawrence, Kishori, Sakshi Gopala)

Usually he crossed the great wheat field that stood between Letchmore Heath and the hamlet of Round Bush, following an old path to the Aldenham parish church.

As they crossed the field Prabhupada stopped. 'Krishna is called Yogeshvara, full of mystic power,' he said. 'Each living entity has a little of his mystic ability.'

There was competition to come on his walks, and each morning a group would be waiting downstairs. Conversation was prompted by questions from devotees. (Left to right: Vrindavani, Jaya Lakshman, Bhadrakrishna, Mohan, Shrutakirti)

Whenever he travelled into London Prabhupada would visit Radha-Londonishvara. 'Every time I come here the deities are beautifully dressed,' he told Lilashakti.

Prabhupada arrived tired but happy to see his devotees. They crowded excitedly into his room, overjoyed to see him again so much sooner than they had expected.

Bhajahari began to execute this plan. He got as far as cleaning the lake before he was replaced as president. The island Prabhupada wanted was never created.

Working in the gardens one afternoon, Jaya Lakshman rounded a corner pushing a wheelbarrow and came face to face with Prabhupada sitting with some devotees. He hesitated, wondering if he might come and join them. Prabhupada looked up.

'Carry on with your work,' he told him.

Jaya Lakshmana's first sight of Prabhupada had been the previous year in Kensington. As Geoffrey Davies he had dropped out of university to search for a solution to the problem of material suffering. He saw Prabhupada interviewed on television and heard him speak at Kensington Town Hall, then at the Commonwealth Institute. In the Institute's big auditorium Prabhupada's voice echoed, talking of souls as eternal servants of Krishna. Then he chanted the *maha-mantra*. Geoffrey was profoundly moved. After the lecture he and his girlfriend went back to Bury Place and stayed overnight. Next morning when he had heard Prabhupada's class he decided this was the man he was looking for. Prabhupada's whole demeanour embodied the ideal person whom Geoffrey wanted to follow. From that day he and his girlfriend studied the *Gita* and eventually joined the temple. Now they were initiated, as Jaya Lakshmana and Govatsa.

That day Jaya Lakshmana continued his work in the garden. But not long afterwards he got his chance to sit with Prabhupada, though only briefly. He was in bed with flu when his parents came to visit him. He got up, still weak, and led them to the garden to meet the man who had changed his life. Respectfully they sat down.

'How fortunate you are to have a son who has taken up Krishna consciousness,' Prabhupada said, and spoke to them about devotion to Krishna. Jaya Lakshmana's father listened thoughtfully, but his mother wanted to question what Prabhupada was saying.

'Surely there is only one God,' she began, and her son, knowing how his mother loved to argue, and feeling embarrassed, laughed nervously.

'You can go now,' Prabhupada told him, and continued to speak to the parents without their son. After hearing him for some time they got up to leave, and Jaya Lakshmana came to see them to their car.

'I have never met such an intelligent man,' declared his father, assuring his wife that their son was in good hands. Wishing Jaya Lakshmana well, they left.

Prabhupada did not encourage devotees to stop their work and come and sit with him, but he welcomed young mothers with children and devotees such as Bala Gopala, who had sewing to do for the deities and who could sew while she sat with him. She made a point of keeping her handstitching for these occasions, and many were the hours she was able to spend on the lawn with him. Another was Svati, whose two-year-old son Shivajvara became the object of much affectionate teasing from Prabhupada. Sometimes he imprisoned the boy's hand, then with an indulgent smile released him to run to his mother. Once when leaving the temple after morning class, followed by a retinue of devotees, he took Shivajvara with him, holding the boy's little tuft of hair as they walked along together, both of them smiling. He began to pull on his hair, and the boy looked uncertain, then he pulled more and Shivajvara looked worried. Eventually, Shivajvara was on the verge of tears when Prabhupada stooped down in front of him and tickled him under the chin until he laughed. Then Prabhupada laughed with him.

CHAPTER 17

Many Meetings

Every day, hour after hour, Prabhupada spoke about Krishna to guests in his rooms. Sometimes they asked questions and engaged in active discussion, sometimes they just listened – and he could talk about Krishna for as long as they were willing to hear. He always had time for whoever would come. He told Shyamsundar that as long as interesting and influential people came to talk with him he would stay at the Manor. Shyamsundar put out the word among the devotee community that everyone should be on the lookout for such people to invite. He hoped to keep Prabhupada in England for many months. His strategy worked, as was clear when Prabhupada wrote to Karandhar, urging devotees everywhere to follow Shyamsundar's example:

> Important men are coming to meet with me in the evening for discussion of Krishna consciousness. I have talked with a very famous sculptor, a teacher of a boys' college, and today George Harrison is to visit. Shyamsundar

> is arranging for visits by many other famous men. Wherever I shall go now this policy of important men being invited to talk with me about our Krishna consciousness movement should be implemented.[1]

Prabhupada called for Subhaga to come from Bury Place and stay at the Manor while he was there. Prabhupada liked Subhaga's company because he, being a well-educated Bengali *brahmachari,* was helpful in receiving Indian guests and fluent in Bengali: whenever Prabhupada wanted to cite a verse from the *Chaitanya-charitamrita* Subhaga could find and recite it.

A succession of learned men came to see Prabhupada. The meetings were not always comfortable for them, since he was determined that they should hear what he had to say and was willing to debate with them when necessary. Often the discussions became one-sided, with eminent professors listening in silence as he expounded Vedic philosophy. Among them was Sir Alister Hardy who, after a distinguished career as a marine biologist, had founded in 1969 the Religious Experience Research Unit at Oxford University. He was the same age as Prabhupada, an enlightened scientist looking for spiritual answers beyond the boundaries of conventional thought. They had a cordial meeting but found little to agree on. Prabhupada liked Sir Alister, and wrote him a long letter, wanting him to appreciate the wisdom of the *Bhagavad-gita.*

> Dear Sir Alister Hardy,
>
> I beg to thank you for your coming here yesterday evening, we had very nice talks on religious experience, and I have studied your replies to my questions very carefully.
>
> My first question was, 'What is the problem of human life?' So I have already explained, the problem is that at the present moment there is no proper understanding of God …

Over the following six typewritten pages Prabhupada developed his argument that the problems in human society were due to a lack of God consciousness, before concluding,

Therefore for right understanding we are advocating that people take advantage of this institution, International Society for Krishna Consciousness, by hearing about God from authorized books like *Bhagavad*-gita and *Srimad-Bhagavatam* which were directly spoken by God himself, therefore making the whole thing most scientific and practical.

I hope that we can again meet and discuss this important matter further. I hope this letter meets you in good health.

Your ever well-wisher,
A. C. Bhaktivedanta Swami[2]

Another distinguished scholar was Arnold Toynbee, famous for his writings on the sweep of world history. He was interested in how Eastern culture influenced the West. Because of his advanced age – he was eighty-five years old – Prabhupada went to his London home. Toynbee received Prabhupada with courtesy but had little inclination to enter discussion. Instead he simply heard in polite silence, nodding his agreement with whatever Prabhupada said.

Lord Brockway, whom Shyamsundar had met at the House of Lords, was more forthcoming. Born in Calcutta in 1887, Fenner Brockway was a pacifist who went to prison in 1916 for his opposition to Britain's part in the First World War. He was a lifelong champion of freedom and democracy and had campaigned in the 1920s for Indian Independence. His political career began in the House of Commons in 1929, and he was made Lord Brockway in 1965. From the House of Lords, even in his eighties, he continued to campaign for peace and justice. He came in July to meet Prabhupada in his rooms at the Manor, and began by informing him that although he did not belong to any established religion, he was a lifelong vegetarian.[3]

'I believe in the spiritual basis of the universe,' he explained. 'The great moments of inspiration are when you feel you belong to all of life, from the beginning of time, now, everywhere.'

He listened for half an hour as Prabhupada expounded the philosophy of the *Bhagavad-gita*. 'Without the centre point of God consciousness, we cannot substantiate the idea of universal brotherhood,' said Prabhupada. Prabhupada then spoke about the importance of preparing for the next life.

Lord Brockway kept an open mind about whether there was such a thing as life after death, but of one thing he was sure: 'If there is a form of life after death, the best preparation for it is service to one's fellow human beings in our present life.'

'Yes, but we must know what kind of service we shall give,' said Prabhupada. 'Real suffering is because people have forgotten God.'

Lord Brockway did not agree.

'Belief in God is not enough. Service to the world today means an understanding of the causes of war and the causes of poverty, and seeking an end to them.'

The chief cause of suffering, said Prabhupada, was repeated birth and death, and the remedy for this was to study the science of the soul. 'Simply try to get out of this dangerous position and go back to home, back to Godhead,' he concluded.

'Well, I've listened and I think I understand. Now I have to think about it,' was Lord Brockway's response. Prabhupada was not discouraged.

'Yes. Therefore we are trying to make men like you interested. People in Western countries are intelligent, especially the British. They have very good opportunity. So my request is that let us study this philosophy and science, and if possible, introduce it to human society.'

'Well, I don't want to keep you. It has been very, very kind of you.'

'It is very nice to associate with you,' returned Prabhupada, giving him a garland of roses while Malati brought in a specially prepared meal. Although the two men held quite different views, when it came to the treatment of animals they were in complete agreement.

'They talk of universal brotherhood but send poor animals to the slaughterhouse.'

'Oh, I agree. I'm a vegetarian.' With that Lord Brockway left, promising to return with his wife.

In a secluded enclosure beneath a blossoming lilac tree on the north side of the Manor, a small audience gathered in a circle on the grass around Prabhupada to witness what was expected to be a challenging discussion. A newly initiated devotee, Mahadeva, formerly Michael, had brought his mother and her theological adviser to the Manor. She was worried that the devotees were leading her son astray, and had asked to be introduced to the movement's leader so she could examine what sort of man he was. She blamed devotees for luring her son away from university. Michael had received an expensive education at Stonyhurst Jesuit College, so to help her state her case she brought with her a senior Jesuit priest.

Mahadeva's mother confidently voiced her opinion that university education was essential for the good of society.[4] 'Where would we be without our scientists? Without our doctors?' she asked boldly. Then, addressing Prabhupada with respect, 'Father, I can see you are a cultured man. But I am very distressed that none of the boys here continue their education at university. What is going to happen to them when they are older? They will have no talents like you.'

'This education for eating, sleeping, mating, and defending is not sufficient for a human being,' responded Prabhupada. 'Simply money-making education will not satisfy anybody. Education means to understand God. People must learn how to love God.'

'But the Jesuits taught Michael how to love God,' protested his mother, and the Jesuit priest spoke up in support.

'That's our main purpose,' he said. 'We train young men and women for success in this world but above all for success in the next, which means union with God. That's top priority – following Christ's words, "Seek ye first the kingdom of God." All other things are of very minor importance. That's how Michael was taught at Stonyhurst.'

'Yes, we are going to almighty God when we die,' continued Mahadeva's mother with conviction. 'We don't have to worry – everybody who believes in God and leads a good life in this world.'

'Then the question arises, what is a good life?' responded Prabhupada.

'Obeying the commandments of God,' the Jesuit answered with assurance.

'The commandment is thou shalt not kill,' pointed out Prabhupada.

Evidently the Jesuit had been expecting this line of discussion, and he immediately objected that if Prabhupada meant it was wrong to kill animals, then it was also wrong for the devotees to kill potatoes. Prabhupada stuck to his point.

'I have asked this question to so many people: Why are you killing innocent animals although it is prohibited to kill?'

'We kill animals because we need food.'

'If you can eat grains, vegetables, and milk, why should you kill animals?'

'There are many vegetarians today – you are not the only ones,' said Mahadeva's mother, coming to her priest's defence.

'Good,' replied Prabhupada. 'That will make them less sinful. Then they will be qualified to go to God when they die.' There was a pause while the priest considered this statement.

'Would you say, then, that if I didn't eat meat I would be less sinful?'

'Yes, that is our philosophy.'

'So, if I give up bacon and sausages …'

'You will become pure.'

'That's very interesting.'

A truce seemed to have been reached. More discussion followed, but Prabhupada's guests were subdued and soon got up to leave.

'Thank you for coming,' said Prabhupada. 'Our only proposal is that you try to love God. God is one; He is neither Hindu nor Muslim nor Christian. God is God. Let us love God.' On this point all agreed.

'I wouldn't have given my life to him fifty-two years ago unless I loved God,' confirmed the priest.

'That is understood. You are a brahmin,' assured Prabhupada. The Jesuit priest rose to his feet and expressed his gratitude.

'Well, thank you very much, father, for letting us talk and for letting us listen to you.'

'You are fortunate you have got so nice son. Please give them prasadam.'

'Thank you,' Mahadeva's mother said warmly as she turned to leave. 'Thank you very much.'

'Give up material enjoyment, give up liberation,' concluded Prabhupada. 'Krishna says, simply surrender to me. That is all. This is real love.'

David Wynne had no pretensions to being a philosopher. He was a well-known sculptor and friend of George Harrison and shared George's interest in Eastern spirituality. He had become friendly with Shyamsundar, whom he knew as Sam, and when he was invited to come and meet Prabhupada he welcomed the opportunity. He had recently won a commission to model the Queen's head for the new fifty-pence coin, and had just been with her.[7]

Shyamsundar informed Prabhupada that he had given the *Gita* to David, and that the Queen had looked through it while sitting for her portrait in his studio.

'Tell Prabhupada what she said about it,' he urged David.

'She said how marvellous to be able to give all responsibility to Krishna.'

'Yes, that one has to learn. The sentiment is very nice,' agreed Prabhupada. 'Just fitting from a royal. She is after all favoured. She has taken birth in the royal family. She is not ordinary woman. Her intelligence must be extraordinary. What exactly did she say?'

'How marvellous it would be to completely trust Krishna – what a relief to be able to pass all responsibility to him.'

'Krishna is ready. But the thing is, from our side Krishna expects something. He reciprocates. If you fully surrender to Krishna, then Krishna takes full responsibility. If you keep some reservation, Krishna keeps some reservation.' David listened as Prabhupada went on speaking.

'You are a famous sculptor because Krishna is helping you,' he told him. 'He is sitting in everyone's heart. He says, "Do like this." Everyone is being guided by Krishna.'

'One can feel this very much when one is trying to make a piece of sculpture,' said the artist. 'It feels impossible, as if one can't do it.'

'Yes, Krishna is guiding you.' Prabhupada paused. 'But at the present moment he is guiding you according to your whims, "You want to do this – alright, do it." When you will agree to act according to the whims of Krishna, that is perfection.'

'How does one agree to this?'

'You have to learn the process. Arjuna wanted to act according to his whims. This was the problem. Then he heard *Bhagavad-gita* and agreed to act according to the whims of Krishna, and the whole picture changed. Same Arjuna. Same fighting. Same battlefield. Everything same. But still everything is changed. The consciousness is changed. This is Krishna consciousness. Externally nothing is changed. Internally this change is required.'

'So one doesn't have to give anything up?' Shyamsundar prompted Prabhupada.

'No. Arjuna was a fighter and he remained on the field, but his consciousness was changed. This is perfection.' Prabhupada held up a copy of the *Bhagavad-gita As It Is,* showing the illustration on the cover. 'Just see the picture, how Krishna is guiding Arjuna. Krishna is holding the reins, helping from without and from within – from within as Supersoul and without as spiritual master. He is ready to help you both ways. Krishna is so kind. Nobody can repay. In every birth, in every kind of body, he is with me saying, "Just turn toward me." '

David was moved by what he heard and made a surprising admission.

'When I was a small child my mother told me that the *Bhagavad-gita* was the most important book in the world. But soon afterwards she died. I was very unhappy, but I gained great comfort then from the *Bhagavad-gita*.'

'Oh, you are fortunate.'

They shared prasadam, and at the end of the afternoon Shyamsundar got ready to take his friend home.

'How do you like our philosophy?' asked Prabhupada.

'I admire it very much. One can tell a little bit about your teaching by the people one knows who were taught. I know Sam and George, and they've changed. George has gained enormously in spiritual steps. Now he is wise as well as clever.'

The village policeman came to meet Prabhupada. As part of his job he took it upon himself to act as a liaison between the devotees and the village. There had been complaints about noise during their festival, and also about a devotee who had been chanting loudly in the doctor's waiting room. He wanted to assure the devotees that they had done no wrong.

Prabhupada said devotees should be considerate.[8] 'We may take pleasure in chanting Hare Krishna loudly, but others may not. When you go to others' places, simply chant in such a way that only you can hear. Not that you have to advertise yourself.' He demonstrated chanting the *maha-mantra* softly, almost under his breath.

'You know what they call me?' the policeman said. 'They say I'm Harry Krishna on this side, and Harry Edwards on the other side. I live just across the road,' he explained. 'So they joke that on one side my name is Harry Edwards, and on the other side my name is Harry Krishna. My name is Harry Edwards, you see.'

'A good name,' laughed Prabhupada. 'When somebody is disturbed he can say, "I am calling Mr Harry."' Everyone laughed as Harry elaborated further.

'In the morning when I ring up the station they say, "Ah, Harry Krishna," and I say, "Hare Krishna to you." So really, you've achieved your object without them knowing it.'

'Yes, yes.' Prabhupada laughed. 'All over the world, when people see us, they chant Hare Krishna.'

Harry ended by giving Prabhupada his assurance that he was always ready to be of assistance.

'If there's anything you need to ask me ...'

'You are always welcome,' said Prabhupada. 'When we are in difficulty, we must take shelter of you.'

David Lawrence taught religious education in a nearby school and planned to produce a schoolbook about Krishna consciousness. He had come for Prabhupada's blessings and advice. For five minutes he read out an outline of his proposed book. Prabhupada listened with interest.[9]

'If you, as teacher, present Krishna consciousness among your students, you will give the greatest service. This opportunity should be given. Especially your English nation. In India we have very good respect for the English nation because the British Empire meant unity of human beings all over the world. The politicians spoiled it, but that unity can be revived again if you come to this Krishna consciousness movement. So kindly awaken your students' dormant Krishna consciousness.'

The teacher had many questions, and he listened as Prabhupada taught him that the first principle of Krishna consciousness was to understand that the living entity is spirit soul. Once one had grasped that, explained Prabhupada, one could begin to understand one's relationship with God.

'The teacher must realise that he is not this body. *Bhakti-yoga* begins when one is purified from the bodily concept of life.'

David told Prabhupada that George Harrison's new album, *Living in the Material World*, had profoundly affected some of his pupils. One boy even said it had given him a religious experience and that he had prayed along with the record. One track in particular, he said, had influenced them – something to do with the light of the world.

'Oh, yes,' Prabhupada remembered. 'What is that song? "I have changed ..."?'

'Yes,' said Shyamsundar. 'He says his friends all criticise him for the change, but he doesn't care.'

The song they were remembering was called 'The Light that has Lighted the World'. In it George described the change he had undergone and how some people seemed to regret it. He sang that he was grateful to those who were free, who gave him hope while he was 'looking to see the light that has lighted the world.'

'He is not the loser,' observed Prabhupada. 'He is gainer. That he can understand.'

'Please tell George how his music has affected them. I am sure he would like to know,' said the teacher. 'Thank you very much for giving me your time.'

Prabhupada thanked David Lawrence for his interest.

'Come any time and ask any question. If you can introduce the study of *Bhagavad-gita* among your students – oh, it will be a great service.'

Donovan was one of George's musical acquaintances. They had been together in Rishikesh learning Transcendental Meditation. Donovan's songs had regularly made the charts on either side of the Atlantic for the last ten years. He arrived to meet Prabhupada on the day planned by Shyamsundar for famous musicians – he was the only famous musician who came. He brought with him his girlfriend and his old buddy and musical partner, Gypsy Dave. He sat close to Prabhupada, right in front of him, with the others a little way off. Straight away it was evident that whereas Donovan was keen to listen and learn, his friends didn't want to be there. As Prabhupada spoke Donovan was drawn in and a real connection was apparent. The young woman, seeing the effect Prabhupada was having on Donovan, looked worried, as if she feared losing him. At a certain point in the discussion Prabhupada mentioned that money could be used for Krishna and so become spiritualised.

'But money can't be spiritual,' she protested, speaking for the first time.

'How do you know what is material or spiritual?' asked Prabhupada, looking her in the eye. She was unnerved and so was Gypsy Dave. They both got up, saying it was time to leave.

'I'm sorry, I've got to go now,' Donovan apologised as they led him away. 'I'll come again.'

Allen Ginsberg, fresh from India, came to chant for Prabhupada. He had brought his small harmonium with him.

'You are still chanting Hare Krishna?'

'Yes. Can I chant for you?'

Prabhupada agreed, and Ginsberg began to chant Om, singing the mantra on successively lower notes. Prabhupada leaned back on his cushions and listened as Ginsberg's voice descended. The chanting finished and Prabhupada smiled. Devotees started coming in. Prabhupada told them all to join in kirtan. Allen Ginsberg began again on his harmonium, this time chanting Hare Krishna to a tune of his own and leading them all. After a while Prabhupada turned to one of the devotees and asked him to take over the lead. The tempo increased, and the devotees became animated. Finally, Prabhupada brought the chanting to a close.

'Chant whatever you like, Allen, but keep chanting Hare Krishna. As long as you chant Hare Krishna, everything else will be alright.'

CHAPTER 18

Living With Prabhupada

Every day Prabhupada walked on footpaths through the surrounding fields. Early, before the village was awake, he and his disciples followed the lane between sleeping cottages and hedgerows. Usually he crossed the great wheat field that stood between Letchmore Heath and the adjoining hamlet of Round Bush, following an old path that led to the parish church in Aldenham. Or he would be taken in a car a short distance so he could walk round Aldenham Reservoir.

There was competition to come on his walks, and each morning a group would be waiting downstairs. One morning Yashasvini was among them. She had run there hastily, barefoot and without a coat. Prabhupada stopped in front of her.

'You are coming on the walk?'

'Yes,' she replied with embarrassment.

'You are not properly dressed,' he said, and walked on.

She panicked, not understanding that he spoke out of concern that she would not be warm enough. Fortunately a friend helped her find her shoes and coat, and she followed, running to catch up.

Shyamsundar often prompted a discussion, or sometimes a younger devotee, feeling bold, asked a question. Once Prabhupada was reminded of a story from his youth.

'Srila Prabhupada, can you tell us about the time you climbed that tower in Calcutta?' someone asked. Prabhupada was reluctant to talk about it, but was persuaded.

'Among my student friends I was considered the leader,' he began. 'They were staging a protest, and they wanted someone to climb to the top of the Victoria Memorial and fix the national flag of India. But no one dared to do it, so they asked me.'

'Did you climb it, Prabhupada? Did you climb all the way to the top of the dome?'

'Yes,' he said nonchalantly.

'You were so brave, Srila Prabhupada,' said Malati.

'I am *still* brave!'

Sakshi Gopala loved being with Prabhupada on his walks. It was an exceptionally dry summer that year, and the water in Aldenham Reservoir was low, exposing the cracked bed along its banks.

'At the end of the universe there will be no rain,' said Prabhupada. 'Then there will be devastation by fire.'

Another morning Sakshi Gopala ran down the lane to catch up. On this day only two other devotees had accompanied Prabhupada – Patita Uddharan and Jaya Lakshman. The group walked up the hill, following the road round to the far side of the fifteen-acre field, then returned across the field toward a clump of Scots pines by the gate back into the lane. Prabhupada stopped chanting on his beads.

'Krishna is called *yogeshvara,* full of mystic power, and each living entity has a little of his mystic ability. For example, Krishna can eat with any part of his body, and there is a living entity who can eat with his feet. Which is that?' He waited for an answer, then pointed with his cane to the pine trees. 'See the tree? He eats with his feet.' He walked on. Then he spoke again.

'A frog also has mystic powers. Bury him in the ground and he will not die.' He seemed to know that Sakshi Gopala was a keen naturalist.

'But Srila Prabhupada, a frog needs to breathe through his skin.'

'No, he has yogic power,' insisted Prabhupada. Sakshi Gopala later read that frogs could survive underground with neither food nor oxygen for very long periods.

As they entered the lane and turned left, retracing their steps to the Manor, Prabhupada talked of how scientists promise to make life in the laboratory. 'They cannot do it,' he said, and laughed as he thought of a story.

'A village potter set his pots in the sun to dry, then lay down to sleep. He dreamed of how he would make many pots, sell them, buy more clay, and sell more pots – until he could afford an assistant to do all the work for him. If the assistant didn't do as he was told, he thought, he would kick him. In his sleep the potter kicked and accidentally broke his pots.' Prabhupada laughed aloud at the foolish potter. 'The scientists, who imagine they will one day produce life and who make promises they cannot fulfil, are like this potter.'

As he laughed he looked into Sakshi Gopala's eyes and they laughed together. Sakshi Gopala imagined the whole world laughing with them.

Tribhangananda was another who on a morning walk experienced the transforming effect of a look from Prabhupada. He was close by when Prabhupada began to talk of yogis coming to the West and telling their followers they could become God. He compared them to glowworms in the night.

'What is the use of so many stars when a single moon can light up the whole sky?' he said, looking Tribhangananda straight in the eye. He felt profoundly touched by Prabhupada's gaze, which seemed to penetrate his soul.

Rohininandan was near the back on a day when there was quite a crowd. As they followed the lane through Letchmore Heath, they passed a sign saying 'Horticultural Show'. Prabhupada stopped and asked what it meant. In the silence that followed Rohininandan spoke from the back.

'Srila Prabhupada, I think *horticulture* means growing fruit and vegetables and flowers.' Prabhupada turned to face him.

'You think? You do not know?' Rohininandan suddenly became the centre of attention. He felt his face going red. Prabhupada tapped his cane repeatedly on the ground to emphasise his point. 'You *think*? You do not know?'

Rohininandan was confronted by two things: Whatever Prabhupada said, he knew, and most of what Rohininandan said, he didn't know. It was a humbling experience for him.

Prabhupada wanted devotees to come to India. It was easier for those with British passports to stay there because they didn't require visas, whereas American devotees could usually only stay for six months at a time. One Sunday he called a meeting in his room for all those willing to go, and Tribhangananda attended. The room filled up with hopeful young men. Prabhupada asked for a bowl of grapes, blessed them by passing his hand over the bowl, then asked Shrutakirti to distribute them. There were not many to go round and Tribhangananda got only a few.

'So you will go to India?' asked Prabhupada, looking round the room.

Tribhangananda wasn't at all sure he could manage India. He had heard how austere it was, but he found himself volunteering anyway. Feeling anxious about what lay ahead – and hungry – he ate his few grapes. Unaccountably his anxiety evaporated and with it, his hunger – so much so that even hours later when the Sunday feast was served downstairs he didn't feel like eating it.

It was customary for a disciple to offer a gift to his guru after being initiated. Tribhangananda wanted to offer something following his Gayatri initiation, but he had no money. Shrutakirti advised him to write Prabhupada a letter instead. After agonising for two hours he produced a short note: 'I can't beg in the village because I don't want to give people a bad impression of your mission, but I really appreciate your kind gift of giving us back our spiritual lives.' He gave the note to Shrutakirti, and word came back that when Prabhupada read it he had said, 'His humility is his good qualification.'

When he heard this Tribhangananda understood that Prabhupada had accepted him, despite what he perceived to be his own failings. He was filled with relief and gratitude.

In the days following Janmashtami Prabhupada gave first initiation to nine women and sixteen men. A succession of second initiates were called to his room to receive their *gayatri-mantra*. For many of them it would be the first time they had exchanged words with Prabhupada, and they were nervous at the prospect of being alone in his presence.

Before Ramadevi went in she was given a piece of paper with the words of the mantra printed on it. She didn't want to cheat by seeing the words before she had heard them from her spiritual master, but she was unable to help herself seeing one word in the last line: *puspabanaya*, 'flower-arrow'.

She went in and sat next to Prabhupada. Was she chanting her rounds, he wanted to know? She said she was, and she handed him a five-pound note as an offering. He showed her how to count the mantras on her fingers, then led her through them word by word. On the last mantra, when he got to the word she had seen, he paused and looked up, hand on chin, apparently searching for the word. 'Ah! *Puspabanaya*,' he said with a twinkle in his eye.

Govardhan, like her fellow initiates, did her best to make her fingernails presentable for when Prabhupada would show her how to count the mantra on her fingers. She went in and bowed down to recite the Sanskrit prayer of respect to her guru. She understood every word – she had always been good at languages – and couldn't help smiling with joy. When she looked up she saw that Prabhupada was smiling back at her. He patted the floor beside him in a fatherly way, indicating that she should sit close, then looked at her slip of paper, which had the seven lines of the *gayatri-mantra* written out. It was faded – a copy of a copy of a copy – and the words were difficult to read.

'It requires transcendental eyes,' he commented, putting her at ease.

Then gravely he showed her how to count, and she repeated each line after him.

Mohan came in and repeated the words after Prabhupada. Even though he was following them from the printed paper, he got confused. 'Sorry, could you repeat that please?' Prabhupada looked mildly amused as he repeated the word. Mohan felt a fool, but he also felt that Prabhupada was kind to him and accepted him as he was.

Nabhasvati had learned from Lilashakti how to count on her fingers and had practised in preparation for her initiation. While she waited nervously on the landing Malati gave her a bunch of yellow roses to offer to Prabhupada. She took them in with her, and after bowing down, knelt by the door.

'Come closer,' he said gently, then seeing the roses in her hand he asked, 'Are those for me?'

She had forgotten she was holding them and handed them over. He showed her how to count on her fingers and asked her to do as he had done. But she couldn't do it – despite all her practice she got confused. He showed her again and this time she managed.

'So, how is everything with you?'

'I'm very happy. I wanted to be happy, and now I am.'

'You will always be happy so long as you remain in Krishna consciousness.'

Afterwards she ran out to find Malati.

'Prabhupada says I'll always be happy if I stay Krishna conscious!'

Nabhasvati had moved to the Manor to learn how to sell Prabhupada's books. Each day she went out with a group of devotees and spent long hours on high streets convincing people to take a book home to read. Her high spirits and happy demeanour made her good at it. At the end of the day, exhausted but satisfied, she would come and chat with Malati and her friend Shyamsundari, a young English woman who was helping Malati with the deity worship.

Most evenings Prabhupada crossed the corridor from his room and looked in on Malati to ask about progress with sewing the deity clothes. If Nabhasvati was there he would talk to her too.

'Oh, you have been on sankirtan?'

'Yes, Prabhupada.'

'Thank you very much.'

When Malati cooked Prabhupada's supper of puris with *halava* and hot milk, she let Nabhasvati carry it in to him. He liked the puris to be freshly puffed, so Nabhasvati ran in with them one at a time, hot from the wok. Laughing, she would tell him about her day: how many books she had sold, how much she had collected, who she had spoken to.

'Let him eat in peace,' Malati admonished her, but Nabhasvati's cheerful ways were irrepressible, and Prabhupada always seemed interested to hear what she had to say.

He regularly walked the corridors and looked into rooms to check how things were going. Was the cleaning being done? Was the worship on time? Were the devotees eating well? Once Nabhasvati heard him ask why the devotees were not getting milk. She felt he cared for them like a father.

Whenever he travelled into London, Prabhupada would visit the Bury Place temple to see Radha-Londonishvara. Many of the devotees stationed there went out daily on book distribution, headed by Prabhavishnu, the temple president. They were dedicated to serve Prabhupada's special wish to see his books widely read. During his stay at the Manor Prabhupada wrote to his publishing director in Los Angeles.

> There is no doubt about it, to distribute books is our most important activity. The temple is a place not for eating and sleeping, but as a base from which we send out our soldiers to fight with *maya*. Fight with *maya* means to drop thousands and millions of books into the lap of the conditioned souls. Just like during wartime the bombs are raining from the sky like anything.[1]

This letter was circulated round the movement. It reinforced the sense of urgency and dedication among the book distributors. Alongside their book-distributing brothers, the women at Bury Place served as *pujaris*, maintaining a high standard of worship for Radha and Krishna.

When Prabhupada came to London he always wanted to see the deities. One afternoon, when most of the devotees were out on book distribution, he arrived to find just the two *pujaris*, Lilashakti and Ashtasakhi. Lilashakti knew that he liked shiny, glittering outfits, so she had designed and made a dress for Radha-Londonishvara with green polyester satin covered in sparkling white and gold sequins, combined with a gold lamé backdrop. When he entered she opened the curtains for him, even though the temple was closed for the afternoon. He stopped in the middle of the room and raised his arms.

'Aahh!' He was so pleased with the way Krishna looked.

She hadn't dressed the deities to her own taste – by Western standards this style was gaudy – but she knew this was the way Prabhupada liked them. She watched as with folded hands and eyes full of devotion he gazed at Radha-Londonishvara, dazzling in their silver and green. She could see that he was looking not at statues but at real personalities. 'Every time I come here the deities are beautifully dressed,' he told her.

Another time he arrived in the evening while Ashtasakhi was offering arati. The *pujaris* had decorated the altar with extra flowers and given Radharani a bouquet to hold. While Ashtasakhi was offering the incense to Radha and Krishna she heard outside the cries of welcome for Prabhupada, then the kirtan grew louder as he came indoors. With shaking hands she turned to offer incense to the picture of Prabhupada that usually stood on his *vyasasana* and saw that he was sitting there in person. She was unable to check her tears. Devotees were leaping high in the air chanting Krishna's names. They leapt so energetically that the floor was shaking, which in turn made the altar shake so much that Radha and Krishna trembled as if they themselves were dancing. As Krishna moved, his crown slipped on his forehead, and Ashtasakhi stretched forward to reposition it. At the close of the arati she blew the conch shell as Prabhupada recited the closing prayers and everyone bowed down. Just then there was a clatter from the altar. Radharani's bouquet had fallen to the bottom step, dislodging some of the pictures. Ashtasakhi picked it up and handed it to Prabhupada. As she did so she saw his face shining with tears. As soon as he finished the prayers, and still holding the flowers, he went upstairs without speaking.

Prabhupada decided to celebrate Radhashtami, Radha's birthday, at Bury Place. The night before the festival, Lilashakti and Ashtasakhi sat up together sewing tiny beads on Radha's new silver and pale pink skirt. 'Does anyone ever notice how much hard work goes into sewing on these sequins?' wondered Ashtasakhi.

Prabhupada asked that the new devotees be introduced to him, and one by one they stood as their names were called. He asked them what books they were selling and which titles the people liked best. Then he sang a song to Radha that began *radhe jaya jaya madhava dayite*, and gave a lecture about her qualities.

> Krishna is pleased through Radharani. In Vrindavan all devotees address one another, '*Jaya* Radhe.' They know that anyone who comes before Radharani to serve Krishna, she becomes so pleased, she immediately recommends, 'Oh, here is a devotee of Krishna, better than me.'
>
> Therefore we should worship Radharani first. Instead of offering one flower to Krishna, you just put it in the hands of Radharani. 'My mother Radharani, mother of the universe, if you kindly take this flower and offer it to Krishna.' Radharani will say, 'Oh, you have brought a flower?' It will be very much appreciated by her.
>
> Pray to Radharani: 'Kindly be merciful and tell about me to your Krishna.' Krishna is Radharani's property. Worship Radharani very nicely and be happy.[2]

When his lecture was over Prabhupada added, 'Radharani never forgets a single thing a devotee does for her, even to the most insignificant sequin,' and he pointed to Radha's skirt while looking at Ashtasakhi. 'She will say to her beloved Krishna, "*He* Krishna, look at this nice devotee."'[3]

A book launch was organised by Jaihari for new editions of Prabhupada's books. Most significant of these was the long-awaited unabridged edition of *Bhagavad Gita As It Is*, recently published by Macmillan. The publishers agreed to hold the book launch at Dillons bookshop in Oxford Street near Marble Arch. Along with the new *Gita* were to be presented the full set of BBT books, now numbering eleven hardback titles: six volumes of *Srimad Bhagavatam,* the two volumes of *Krishna* book, *The Nectar of Devotion, Teachings of Lord Chaitanya,* and *Sri Isopanisad* –these last three with redesigned covers in bright colours. In addition to these eleven was a pocket-sized paperback trilogy of *Krishna* book.

Prabhupada showed interest in the arrangements for the day, particularly the food. Ashtasakhi proposed to make biscuits and cupcakes because these were what the press would be familiar with. He disagreed; he wanted *gulabjamuns.*

'But Prabhupada,' she protested, 'they're so sticky!'

'Yes, I know,' he said with a big smile. So she stayed up all night making enough *gulabjamuns* for two hundred people and left them to soak in sugar water in a large stainless steel pot. In the morning, with Ramadevi and Lilashakti, she ferried them to the bookshop in a London taxi, in the process spilling syrup on the taxi floor.

A crowd of reporters showed up, and in radiant mood Prabhupada delivered a powerful appeal.

> In *Srimad-Bhagavatam* is the description of this Age of Kali. People will live short lives, disturbed by lack of rainfall, scarcity of food, and over-taxation, and they will flee their homes and go to the forest in desperation. But in this age there is one great hope: if one chants the holy name of Krishna – Hare Krishna, Hare Krishna, Krishna Krishna, Hare Hare/ Hare Rama, Hare Rama, Rama Rama, Hare Hare – one becomes gradually purified from the contamination of this age and goes back to the spiritual world.
>
> In the *Bhagavad-gita* and *Srimad-Bhagavatam* that spiritual world is described. Everything is there. Each and every human being is a spiritual being, not this body. The mistake of the present civilization is that everybody thinks I am this body: I am American, I am English, I am Indian. These are all illusion. There is no education on this point. Human beings can be educated to revive their original consciousness.
>
> We chant from street to street, city to city, to awaken this spiritual consciousness by the transcendental vibration. When we chant Hare Krishna mantra a few people can hear, but these books are a bigger vibration, which can go from country to country, from continent to continent.
>
> Our Krishna consciousness movement has begun distributing this

important literature. We have translated about twenty books, here before you, and our aim is to present sixty books.

If the publishers and booksellers help us, then people will be benefited. We have come to this bookseller's office to request. Our appeal is that all booksellers, all publishers, may come forward and cooperate with us to distribute this transcendental literature. They will find something sublime and they will be benefited. Thank you very much. Hare Krishna.[4]

Several reporters came to speak with him afterwards, and as he answered their questions Prabhupada ate *gulabjamuns*. He repeatedly asked for more, and by the end of the meeting, to Ashtasakhi's joy, he and Pradyumna had consumed a dozen between them. Prabhupada was not the only one to enjoy the *gulabjamuns*. Next morning the *Times* published a favourable review, giving special mention to the 'mind-blowing sticky brown sweets'.

The devotees at Bury Place saw less of Prabhupada than their brothers and sisters at the Manor. One day, however, came a special opportunity. Sometimes Prabhupada accepted an invitation from a Life Member to visit his home. When this happened he brought his disciples with him, and the Hindu family would honour them all by serving a feast. Since the devotees did not have much money and ate very simply, these occasions were an opportunity for them to enjoy a good meal as well as to be in Prabhupada's company in an informal setting away from the temple.

'Come with me in the van,' Prabhavishnu called to Ramadevi and Ashtasakhi one evening. 'We're going somewhere special.'

Without explanation he drove them to a large house in North London. They entered a large sitting room to find Prabhupada on a raised cushion, addressing a crowd of around fifty Hindus and devotees from the Manor. Shyamsundar introduced them.

'Here are your daughters Ashtasakhi and Ramadevi, from Bury Place temple.'

'Oh, very good,' nodded Prabhupada, and returned to his talk. Afterwards the hosts announced that prasadam would be served in the next room. While the Manor devotees pressed forward, eager to eat, the two young women quickly made small plates and returned to be with Prabhupada, who was eating alone in the sitting room. He called them close, insisting that they sit right at his feet. The cooking was to a high standard, and while he was eating he taught them how one of the preparations was made. As he spoke he carefully picked out the onions and placed them to the side of his plate while explaining how to boil the chickpeas and make a tomato sauce with ginger. They watched him eat with his characteristic grace and economy of movement, using just two fingers and not spilling a drop.

'Just by smelling, a good cook will know every ingredient and spice,' he told them.

When it was time for Prabhupada to leave they followed him to his car. He waited as devotees, carrying plates of prasadam, hurried out.

'We can't leave without Pradyumna,' said Prabhupada. 'Where is he?' No one seemed to know.

'He will be where the food is. Go and get him.' Ashtasakhi rushed to the kitchen, and there he was, surrounded by the cooks. He came out to the car loaded with prasadam, and Prabhupada laughed aloud as he handed in boxes and plates to the devotees in the back seat.

'This is for me to have tomorrow. I can't eat so much late at night because I won't be able to get up in the morning.'

'What will you do that's so important in the morning?' Prabhupada teased him. 'Eat when you're hungry and sleep when you're sleepy.'

With Prabhupada still laughing, they drove away.

A devout Hindu named Krishnadas came to visit Prabhupada. He was from the Punjab, where he had been brought up by his Vaishnava grandfather to be a preacher of Krishna consciousness. When he left school he found a Vaishnava guru and was initiated with the name Krishnadas. Under his guru's direction he trained as a teacher and worked for twelve years in government schools, where he was soon promoted to headteacher.

Whenever he could, Krishnadas travelled around India with his guru to help him preach. In 1966 his guru asked him to go to England to preach to the British Hindu community. Life in London was hard, but he settled his family and, in between earning a living, preached in Hindu homes. In 1972 devotees knocked on his door in Woolwich in southeast London. He was astonished to see them. He thought they must have been sent from heaven. How could Westerners be persuaded to give up meat-eating and intoxication and to chant Krishna's names? Whoever their guru was, thought Krishnadas, he must be a person of exceptional spiritual strength.

At Rathayatra he saw Prabhupada dance and was convinced that he possessed a spiritual body to show such determination and energy at his advanced age. After visiting the temple, Krishnadas wrote to Prabhupada asking if he could meet him. Prabhupada replied that he would be happy to see him whenever it suited him to come. The next Saturday he knocked on Prabhupada's door and Mukunda invited him in.

Prabhupada asked where he was from, what his work was, and who was his guru. Then he preached to the preacher and asked him to join with his disciples.

'We already have so many temples, so with us you will have greater opportunity to preach,' he said.

Krishnadas was hesitant and said he could not leave his guru. Prabhupada replied that he was not asking him to leave his guru.

'We belong to the same lineage – both of us are in the Brahma *sampradaya,*' he reasoned. Krishnadas was proud of being a Punjabi, who would never acknowledge defeat, but he surrendered to Prabhupada's superior power and agreed to seek his guru's permission to join him.

That was not all. Prabhupada proposed that Krishnadas become a *sannyasi* – that he renounce his family, as Prabhupada himself had done, to dedicate the remainder of his life exclusively to teaching Krishna consciousness. For two hours they discussed Prabhupada's proposal, and at the end Krishnadas accepted everything. From then on he looked upon Prabhupada as his *shiksha* guru, the one who gave him spiritual instruction. In time, he promised, when his sons were a little older, he would free himself from his family obligations, and when he did, he would regard Prabhupada as his *sannyasa* guru.

'I will accept you as my *sannyasa* disciple,' promised Prabhupada. Krishnadas offered his obeisances and took his leave. He had come to see Prabhupada as a householder, but left feeling himself a *sannyasi* in all but name.

He wrote to his guru, who was at the Birla Temple in Delhi, and received his blessings to join Prabhupada. Six months later, despite some resistance from his family, he moved into the Bury Place ashram. At forty-two years old he became the elder of the temple community and dedicated himself to preaching Krishna consciousness.

Dhananjaya had been president at Bury Place, where he played a key role in finding and purchasing the Manor. Once devotees moved into the Manor, it was his hope that he would be asked to manage the project. When it became apparent that this was not to be, he and Bala Gopala decided to make a fresh start somewhere else. Dhananjaya went to see Prabhupada and proposed they go to Rome to pioneer a centre there. Prabhupada was pleased with the suggestion – he was always keen to see new temples opened. He said if Dhananjaya and Bala Gopala could find a house in Rome, he would come and stay with them and help them to establish a temple.

Opening the centre in Rome was the hardest thing Dhananjaya and Bala Gopala had ever done. Without money or friends, or any knowledge of the Italian language, they found a house and made a start. Three months later, when Prabhupada heard the good news, the letter he sent them made all their efforts seem worthwhile.

> The transcendental bliss I have derived from hearing the news is not measurable within the three dimensions. I thank you very much for your humble service and I pray to Krishna to always protect and bless you.[5]

Then, just as he had promised, he came and stayed with them and helped them lay the foundations for the Hare Krishna movement in Italy.

Two disciples in Sweden, Vegavan and Ajita, with their wives, Padmavati and Krishnapremi, invited Prabhupada to visit them at their temple in Stockholm. Prabhupada stayed with them for five days, meeting college professors and lecturing three times at the University of Uppsala.

At one student gathering he surprised everyone by choosing as his subject the four social divisions of Vedic society. He described these social divisions as made up of first-class, second-class, third-class, and fourth-class men.

'God consciousness does not mean that I shall be happy and let others go to hell. Therefore the first-class men must be there in society, who are firmly convinced about the existence of the Lord, to teach others.'

A student stood up and challenged him. 'Do you say you are a first-class man?'

'No,' Prabhupada said, 'I am a fifth-class man because I am servant of everyone else.'

Another student spoke up.

'Why do you say Krishna is God?'

'How do you understand God?' returned Prabhupada, and the student admitted that he didn't know.

'If you do not understand God, then I say Krishna is God. Take it from me.' The audience applauded, and Prabhupada ended, laughing, 'Alright, have chanting.'

Each morning in Sweden he went on a morning walk with the devotees, then gave a class on *Bhagavad-gita,* as he had been doing at Bhaktivedanta Manor.

After returning from Sweden, Prabhupada stayed for four more days at the Manor.

Mondakini had faithfully followed Prabhupada's order in 1971 to travel into Russia. With support from her regular visits, Ananta Shanti became more and more daring in his preaching of Krishna consciousness. She was based at the Paris temple, but after Prabhupada's visit to France she returned to serve him in London, where she spent much of her time cooking for him. She knew that he loved *kachoris,* so she took lessons from a Bengali woman in how to prepare the fried pastries stuffed with peas. The first time she brought in his lunch his eyes widened.

'Oh, these are *kachoris*?'

'Yes. I tried, Srila Prabhupada.' He was pleased to see her and pleased to see the *kachoris.* For the next month she cooked for him every day, trying different recipes and finding out what he liked best.

But Prabhupada did not forget her *kachoris.* When it was time for him to leave and resume his world travels he asked Mondakini to pack a lunch for him, and he listed many of the preparations she had cooked for him during his stay. Top of the list was *kachoris.* She was excited, and rushed out to buy ingredients. It was late, and she had to persuade one shop to open specially to serve her. Through the night she cooked. She got his tiffin, polished it until it shone, then packed it full. She stayed behind when he left for the airport: to say goodbye would have been too difficult.

The morning Prabhupada left the whole community crowded into his room to sit with him. Someone brought a plate of sweets, which remained on his desk while he spoke a few words. Mohan watched as Prabhupada reached out for one and delicately held it, forefinger extended, before popping it into his mouth. Now that Prabhupada had tasted them they were special. 'I want those sweets,' Mohan thought to himself.

Prabhupada got up to leave, and everyone crowded after him and also left for the airport. Mohan had to stay behind. There on Prabhupada's desk were the sweets. He took them and hid them in his maintenance cupboard, along with his tools and electrical gadgets.

Ramadevi at the Bury Place temple had stayed up all night hand-sewing a bead bag for Prabhupada, which Shrutakirti had asked her to make. The *pujaris* used to take turns to see Prabhupada at the Manor because one of them always had to stay on duty with Radha-Londonishvara. This time it was Lilashakti's turn to go, and she was waiting in the van about to leave for the airport. At the last minute Ramadevi ran out to give her the bead bag for Prabhupada.

But Lilashakti wouldn't take it from her. Instead, she hopped out and shoved Ramadevi into the van in her place, closing the door behind her. Before Ramadevi could protest the van drove off.

When she arrived at the airport Ramadevi tried to give the bead bag to Shrutakirti, but he wouldn't take it either. He insisted she give it to Prabhupada herself, pushing her forward with a grin.

'Yes?' Prabhupada looked up, and Ramadevi mumbled something as she gave him the bead bag, then bowed at his feet, feeling the tips of his toes touch her forehead.

'Thank you very much,' he smiled, and Ramadevi whispered her thanks to Lilashakti.

Devotees drove down from Edinburgh to see Prabhupada at the airport. They found him sitting in the departure lounge surrounded by his disciples. Mahavishnu, the Edinburgh temple president, had with him a picture of their Gaura-Nitai deities dressed in a tartan outfit. He gave Prabhupada the picture.

'Please take this Srila Prabhupada. These are our deities in Edinburgh.'

'This is for me?' Prabhupada spoke like a child and looked at the photo closely, seeming to be in another world.

Yaduvendu arrived with a group from Bury Place, chanting as they ascended the escalator. They entered the departure lounge causing a big stir, and gathered round Prabhupada.

Nabhasvati, feeling lost, sat at the back of the crowd of devotees on the airport floor. Prabhupada spotted her.

'Come and sit closer,' he said gently. She felt embarrassed, but came closer, grateful for the warmth he showed.

When his flight was called, bound for Bombay, he didn't get up straight away but sat smiling and looking at his disciples with affection. Eventually, seeming reluctant to leave, he stood up and walked toward the gate, followed by a great crowd. Padmalochana stayed close in his role as bodyguard. Ahead he spotted a drunken man standing in their path and kept his eye on him. As they passed the man raised his bottle.

'Cheers!' he said to Prabhupada.

'Hare Krishna!' said Prabhupada, smiling and tapping the bottle with his cane. To Padmalochana he added, 'Now he has started his devotional life.'

That night at the Manor, as the men were falling asleep tucked in their sleeping bags, Mohan went round to each of them carrying his tray of sweets.

'*Haribol,* wake up! Here's a special sweet from Prabhupada.' When he had been round to all of them, there were still a few left for himself.

CHAPTER 19

An Unexpected Visit

The London temple was in debt. It had accumulated a backlog of unpaid rent because the landlord could not be found, then without warning appeared and demanded full payment. Finances were so tight that the office phone had been cut off and the devotees had to rely on a single payphone on the stairs, which would ring and ring until someone came to pick it up.

There were debts at the Manor too. They owed $50,000 to Prabhupada's book fund, and the magnificent chandeliers, which Shyamsundar had bought and never paid for, had been repossessed. News of their loss reached Prabhupada in India and added to his concerns about Shyamsundar. Prabhupada had not heard from Shyamsundar since they had left England together the previous summer. For seven years Shyamsundar had served him ceaselessly, yet now he had left to find his independent fortune as partner in an Indian ruby mine. He hoped to become wealthy and do wonderful things for

Krishna, but first he would have to pay off the bills he had run up at the Manor and return money he had borrowed from Prabhupada.

The summer of 1973 was the last time Shyamsundar would be with Prabhupada. His rubies led him back and forth across India, Europe, and America for years but failed to make him any money. His warm and friendly presence was missed in England, not least by his friend George Harrison. He was also missed by Prabhupada, for whom, with his sense of adventure and ready wit and willingness to serve, he was like a son.

Prabhupada was in Bombay planning a marble temple for the Juhu land and directing Gurudas and Yamuna, who were labouring under difficult conditions, to build his longed-for temple and ashram in Vrindavan. He was also contending with growing rivalries between his senior disciples in America. This was not a new problem for him, but it was a source of worry. He had seen it all before in his youth, as he wrote to one of the rival parties:

> Our Gaudiya Math people fought with one another after the demise of Guru Maharaj, but my disciples have already begun fighting even in my presence. So I am greatly concerned about it.[1]

At the Manor, under the leadership of Mukunda and Bhajahari, devotees worked hard to sell books and maintain the big country house. For a while things were harmonious and Mukunda was able to report to Prabhupada that they were paying off their debt to the Bhaktivedanta Book Trust. Prabhupada wrote back,

> I am very much encouraged by the report of how nicely our books are being distributed. This is our main business all over the world. If you give full attention to this, there will never be any shortage of funds.[2]

One cold day in late November, Prabhavishnu, in charge at Bury Place, ran down from the office to answer the payphone. A devotee, on the line from Kenya, told him that Prabhupada was on his way to England. Prabhupada had left Delhi to attend a festival in Nairobi, but Kenyan officials, after making him wait several hours, had denied him entry.

Prabhupada arrived at the Manor tired, but happy to see his devotees. Just after arriving he wrote to Kirtanananda,

> I have come here at Bhaktivedanta Manor. I am feeling very much happy. Here everything is going on nicely. It has given me much pleasure.[3]

The devotees crowded excitedly into his room, overjoyed to see him again so much sooner than they had expected. When the kirtan came to an end, Bhajahari came forward with an offering of fruit. He was feeling self-conscious because he was wearing white, having just married Ramya. His *brahmachari* friends had been teasing him about his new status. He and Ramya had made a fruit salad for Prabhupada, and now he placed it in front of his teacher. As he did so he heard Malati's voice.

'Bhajahari's taken a wife since you were here last time Prabhupada.' His face turned red.

'That's alright,' Prabhupada reassured him. 'One wife is *brahmachari* life.' His kindness in saying these words, which silenced the *brahmachari* critics, was appreciated by Bhajahari.

Sharadiya had finished her painting of Sri Chaitanya and his associates and now had a one-month-old daughter, Brajarani. She sat with her baby among the devotees. Prabhupada had known Sharadiya since she had been a schoolgirl visiting the San Francisco temple in 1967. He was pleased to see she had a child.

'You have a beautiful baby,' he said, looking at her kindly. She felt she and her daughter were blessed.

His long journey from India had left Prabhupada exhausted. Bombay to Nairobi took him nine hours, followed by a six-hour wait in Nairobi airport and a further nine-hour flight to London. The whole experience had been a great strain, and he needed to rest.[4] Nothing, however, would stand in the way of his translating work, and while he was at the Manor he continued as usual, working at night.

Outside his room in the darkness Advaita Acharya stood guard. He had joined the devotees in Cardiff nearly two years previously, along with Bhajahari and Vichitravirya. Now his main service was to cook, but he had volunteered for this nighttime duty as a way to get closer to his spiritual master.

Prabhupada had been up since just after midnight, translating *Chaitanya-charitamrita.* Advaita, hand in bead bag, sat on the broad windowsill opposite Prabhupada's door. In the silence of the night he occasionally heard the low murmur of Prabhupada speaking into his Dictaphone. An hour slipped by as Advaita drifted in and out of sleep. At about two in the morning he was awakened by a gentle voice.

'*Haribol,* Prabhu?' Advaita opened his eyes with a start and saw Prabhupada standing in front of him, silhouetted against the light from his open door.

'I need some help. Can you help me?' Advaita jumped up.

'Yes, Srila Prabhupada!' he gasped, and followed him into his room.

Prabhupada explained that his coal fire was burning low and that he was getting cold. Advaita earnestly assured him that he would fix his fire, then added more coal and stoked it up. As he did so Prabhupada stood observing his disciple, to whom he had never spoken.

'What is your name?'

'Advaita Acharya, Prabhupada.' He was named after one of Sri Chaitanya's chief associates. At that time Prabhupada was writing about the original Advaita Acharya, who had made it his mission to preach to the ordinary people, the ones neglected by the high-caste brahmins. Before Prabhupada had left India he had prayed to Advaita Acharya for his blessings to teach in the West.

'This is a very nice name.'

'If you need anything, Srila Prabhupada, please let me know!'

'If I need anything I will come to see you.'

Advaita went back to his windowsill feeling fortunate beyond his dreams.

A group of devotees assembled in Prabhupada's room, preparing to receive second initiation. 'Is everyone chanting their sixteen rounds?' he asked.

Two girls giggled and admitted they weren't. Prabhupada was concerned and considered calling off the initiations, but in the end they went ahead as planned. Rebatinandan presided over a fire sacrifice in the temple, and next morning the initiates were called to Prabhupada's room one by one.

Raghubhir was first. He knelt near Prabhupada, who saw he was already wearing a sacred thread.

'Why are you wearing your thread? Who put it there?'

'Rebatinandan Swami,' he replied.

'Why did he do that? I want to put it on.' He called Mukunda.

'Why has this boy got his thread on? *I* must put on his thread. You are the temple president. You are responsible for this.'

Mukunda couldn't say much and Prabhupada told him to go. Then he read the mantras, speaking quickly, and asked Raghubhir to repeat them. Anxiously he did so, expecting to be corrected, but he finished without a mistake. This was the only time Raghubhir was alone with Prabhupada, and he was glad to leave without further incident.

In his room one afternoon, a dozen devotees sat in Prabhupada's company. Rebatinandan described how as a teenager he had taken a holiday job in a canning factory in California and how the monotonous work had almost driven him crazy. Bhajahari joined in, saying that when he was sixteen he had worked in a plant in South Wales manufacturing steel bathtubs. He described the process. 'It was all noise and steam, and after a couple of weeks they put me on night shifts. I felt I was going to have a nervous breakdown.'

Prabhupada listened attentively. 'You could not tolerate these conditions because in your past lives you were all brahmins. Otherwise, how could you so quickly come to the platform of Krishna consciousness?' He smiled as he looked around the room at each of them. 'My spiritual master ordered you all to take birth and help me spread this movement. Now we are all together again.'

Raghubhir was there and asked what they should say when distributing his books on the street. Prabhupada picked up a book and stood to demonstrate.

'You approach a person and give him the book. Then you say, "My dear sir, I can see you are such an intelligent man. In fact, I have not met a man intelligent like you. But I have one request of you, sir. Please give up all your nonsense and take this book." ' He laughed as he showed them.

Julia Burroughs visited the Manor and stayed the night as a guest. She found the atmosphere the next morning electric. Prabhupada came down to lecture. As he walked in, the 'Govindam' music played, the curtains opened, and everyone bowed down with him in front of Radha-Gokulananda. She could not help crying as the devotees danced and chanted. She went up and offered Prabhupada a flower. Then, while he spoke, she sat near him. He didn't smile, but it seemed right to her that he appeared so grave and holy. She took in every word he said. He had chosen a verse from the *Bhagavatam:* 'The clouds showered all the water that people needed, and the earth produced all the necessities of man in profusion.' He then discussed simple living.

> Here we see there are so many open fields where the cows are grazing. But they cannot be happy because they are being raised to be killed. Instead of cutting the throat of the cows, you can grow your food: why you are cutting the throat of the cows? Why don't you get your eatables from the land – grains, fruits, flowers? And if you keep the cows happy you will get so much milk. All economic problems will be solved.
>
> Why go to London to the factories? There is no need – and then you require petrol, which is scarce. Simply keep to the land and produce your food. The cows will give you milk. Why go anywhere else? Remain where you are and God will help you, if you have land and the rain is regular. And how do you get regular rainfall? By executing your prescribed duties.[5]

Later that morning he gave initiation to several devotees, and there was a fire ceremony in the temple room. In the afternoon Jaya Lakshmana followed him as he walked round the garden talking with his disciples. Prabhupada was still disturbed about Kenya: how could they have refused him entry with no explanation and disappointed so many devotees who were waiting for him?

Jaya Lakshmana thought to himself that he would like to know from Prabhupada how he could be more Krishna conscious, but he was afraid to ask. Prabhupada turned to him. '*Harer nama, harer nama,*' he murmured in a deep voice. These words meant, 'Chant the holy names, chant the holy names,' and answered Jaya Lakshmana's unspoken question.

The next morning he again gave class. Julia had volunteered to polish the brass arati paraphernalia. Sitting at the far end of the temple room while Prabhupada lectured, trying not to make a sound, she let a plate slip from her lap with a resounding crash. She froze as frowning faces turned to look at her. Prabhupada paused, then carried on as if nothing had happened. She was grateful for his patience.

Prabhupada didn't stay long. After three nights at the Manor, from 23rd to 26th November, he left in the morning for New York. At the airport Julia sat on the floor with forty other devotees gathered round his feet and chanted quietly for half an hour. She was proud to be with him but sad he was leaving. Again his reserved and sombre expression made him seem to her all the more awesome.

CHAPTER 20

Love and Trust

With the acquisition of Bhaktivedanta Manor, the demands upon the devotees in England increased. Overheads doubled as the community expanded and comings and goings multiplied. Mukunda, helped by Bhajahari, managed affairs at the Manor, and Prabhavishnu, in charge at Bury Place, spent most of his time on the road leading book distribution while Janananda ran the temple. Sarvamangala assisted Malati in the deity department at the Manor and looked after Prabhupada's rooms in his absence. In London the deities continued to be served by Lilashakti, who made do with whatever resources she could find.

Prabhupada saw the potential for gaining financial support from the Indian community in England, and wrote to Mukunda asking him to do all he could to cultivate them. 'There is great opportunity for spreading Krishna consciousness among the Indians and expanding all our programmes there in England.'[1]

To help Mukunda, Prabhupada sent Madhavananda, who had done well in India recruiting Life Members. Now Prabhupada encouraged him to do the same in England so as to 'construct very big temples.'[2] Madhavananda arrived at the Manor with his wife Kaushalya and worked hard to bring in support.

The main source of income, however, remained street sales of *Back to Godhead* magazines and the new *Krishna* book trilogy of paperbacks, attractively packaged as a boxed set. The books were stockpiled at the Manor in the dining room, where the oak floor sagged beneath their weight. Devotees wondered how they would ever be able to sell so many books. Several teams travelling round the country in converted vans were dedicated to this work, which they saw as the best service they could possibly offer their spiritual master.

Now that Shyamsundar was absent, the devotees lacked a clear leader. Mukunda's mild and reserved nature was not suited to the task of raising money to pay off debts. In contrast, Madhavananda was enthusiastic to take up the fund-raising challenge and to demonstrate his leadership abilities. Prabhupada wrote to him encouraging cooperation. 'You have to work with Mukunda, the local president,' he said.[3] Hearing that disagreements were arising, he also wrote to Malati, urging her to use her influence to promote harmony among her godbrothers.

> Do not cause a crack there with any fighting spirit or competition. Whenever I hear complaints or disturbances in our centres my mind becomes too much disturbed and I cannot properly translate my books. Please spare me such disturbance by cooperating all together, godbrothers and godsisters.[4]

Despite Prabhupada's plea, rivalry at the Manor grew between supporters of Mukunda and Madhavananda. Three months later Prabhupada wrote, appealing for calm.

> Stop the bickering and conflicting camps. You must work hard to absolve the debts you have massed so we will not lose our standing there. If everyone is chanting at least 16 rounds daily and reading the books

> and observing the regulative principles then the management will be at our finger's end, and there will be no difficulty in maintaining Krishna consciousness.[5]

He requested Hamsadutta, dynamic leader of the German devotees, to help restore financial stability in England. Hamsadutta and his wife Himavati had been among Prabhupada's first disciples in New York in 1967, and were at the forefront of the early expansion in America. They had come to Europe in 1970 to take charge of the mission in Germany, where they had worked hard to build up the devotee community and publish books. Hamsadutta was a man of charisma, an accomplished musician, and an energetic preacher and leader of devotees.

Amid reports of the temple's impending financial collapse, Hamsadutta arrived at Bhaktivedanta Manor in April 1974 and took charge. Prabhupada had developed a clear policy, based on experiences all over ISKCON, of uniting preaching and fund-raising under the single banner of book distribution. It was a way to achieve many things at once: to broadcast Krishna consciousness, bring in money, and engage his disciples in devotional service. Hamsadutta, with Prabhupada's backing, brought all his energies and talent to achieving success with book distribution in England.

Hamsadutta's new fund-raising strategy had been pioneered in Germany. He wanted to sell records of Krishna music to the public on the streets, and pass out books along with the records. At the Manor he organised workshops to train the English devotees in street sales, using phrases like 'by hook or by crook' or 'the money is the honey'. Not all the book distributors were happy with his hard-sell approach, but many of them had owned record collections before joining and could relate to the concept of selling records as a vehicle for increasing book distribution. Hamsadutta appointed Prabhavishnu as coordinator of the growing squad of travelling record and book distributors based out of the Manor, and asked Vichitravirya to manage the day-to-day affairs at Bury Place. Sales of records and books quickly picked up.

Young men who had joined over the previous two years travelled the country in vans laden with records, which they sold on the streets and in shopping centres. Alongside the records they gave out Prabhupada's books. It was the book distribution that they regarded as their true purpose: the records were a means to that end. For some purchasers, though, the Krishna music was exciting, mystical, and original – and a way to experience Krishna consciousness. As a result of this new approach the financial problems began to subside and large quantities of *Krishna* trilogies were distributed.

Prabhupada encouraged Madhavananda in his Life Membership work and told him to aim toward building a temple in the Manor grounds.

> I am very glad to learn you had a successful Janmashtami celebration. This is Krishna's special mercy upon you. I think our next big upcoming project will be in London. I am looking forward to ever-growing success there. You are a fortunate boy, both you and your wife.[6]

He told Madhavananda he wanted a replica of the temple that his Dutch architect-disciple, Saurabha, had designed for Vrindavan.[7]

Meanwhile, Shyamsundar, still hoping for success in his business ventures, wrote to Prabhupada from New York, resigning his post on ISKCON's Governing Body and agreeing to hand over charge of England to Hamsadutta. Prabhupada wrote back advising him to carry on his business, settle his debts, and 'always chant and follow the regulative principles.' He added that he hoped to meet Shyamsundar soon to discuss all that had happened.[8]

With the leadership crisis in England seemingly resolved, in May 1974 Prabhupada embarked from India on a two-month tour of twelve cities on three continents, intended to bring him back to India in time for the scheduled opening of the Vrindavan temple in July. In Europe he visited Rome, Geneva, Paris, and Frankfurt, before flying to Australia, then crossing the Pacific to San Francisco and Chicago. In the last week of July 1974 he embarked from New York on his way back to India, and decided at the last minute to make a stopover in London.

Late in the afternoon Yaduvendu was on the stairs at Bury Place when the front door opened and in walked Prabhupada. With a single leap, Yaduvendu cleared half a flight of stairs to throw himself on the floor at Prabhupada's feet. When he looked up he saw a big smile on his master's face: Prabhupada was always cheered by surrendered devotees. That day, 24th July 1974, was a high point in Yaduvendu's life.

Prabhupada went into the temple room to see Radha and Krishna just as Lilashakti was opening the curtains. A smile and a nod showed her that he liked the way the deities were being dressed and worshipped. 'Krishna is happy,' he said.

Prabhupada stayed in London for an hour, then drove out to the Manor, arriving there mid-afternoon. In his brief arrival talk given in the temple, he spoke about having met with leaders of the Catholic faith in Australia. He reported with satisfaction that they had recognised devotees of Krishna to be members of an authentic religious sect. In particular he had preached there to the staff and students of a Franciscan seminary in Melbourne, who had joined with the devotees to chant Hare Krishna.

'The young Franciscan monks listened very respectfully,' he had written after the Melbourne meeting. 'When speaking to Christians we never say our religious system is better than theirs, but we speak on the principles of love of God.'[9]

After his initiation in 1972 at the hall in Wembley, Yaduvendu had married and returned to Cardiff to reopen the preaching centre there. He had heard of Prabhupada's impending visit, and travelled all night to see him. He had a dilemma he needed to place before his guru. That afternoon at the Manor he entered Prabhupada's room.

Prabhupada listened as Yaduvendu described how one of his friends was learning to be Krishna conscious and this was causing tension in his marriage. His wife had dismantled his altar and would not let him offer his food to Krishna. This friend had asked Yaduvendu to seek Prabhupada's guidance. Should he tolerate her opposition to Krishna, or should he leave her? Prabhupada heard Yaduvendu gravely, then shook his head.

'No, no, even though Krishna consciousness may be very nice, he cannot leave his wife. You can never please Krishna by neglecting your wife and children.' Then his expression lightened. 'Tell him to keep chanting and Krishna will deliver him.'

The following morning Prabhupada flew on to Bombay. The *pujaris* at Bury Place sent him a package of sweets from Radha-Londonishvara with handwritten notes. From Bombay, dated 26th July 1974, came an unexpected reply.

> My Dear Daughters,
>
> I beg to acknowledge receipt of your notes, and I thank you very much for your dakshine. It was very nice to visit the Bury Place temple. It is from there that we started our London activities, and I am so glad to see that the deities are being decorated there the best. You are all working very hard, and this will not go in vain. Whatever we do for Krishna, that is to our eternal credit. Thank you very much.[10]

Every time Prabhupada came to see Radha-Londonishvara he showed his appreciation for how well the worship was going. Once he said Krishna had told him, 'We are happy here.' When Lilashakti heard such things she never took the credit for herself; the credit belonged to the whole *pujari* team. Knowing that Prabhupada was pleased made their hard work seem worthwhile.

As soon as Prabhupada returned to Vrindavan he was dismayed to find that contrary to the reports he had received, the Krishna-Balaram temple was nowhere near complete. This added to the pressure he was already under: in America his leaders were quarrelling with one another; Karandhar, one of his most trusted managers, had resigned; his two-month world tour had left his strength depleted; the temples in England were in debt; and now the Vrindavan temple was not ready. All these factors combined with an exceptionally hot and humid post-monsoon season in Vrindavan and he contracted malaria. He lapsed into a sustained 104-degree fever.

Word went out across the society that Prabhupada's health was in danger, and for the second time in his life his disciples united to pray for his recovery. 'Our dear Lord Krishna,' they prayed, 'please cure Srila Prabhupada.' They accompanied their prayers with twenty-four-hour kirtan in all the temples. Their prayers reached Vrindavan.

'Krishna is very kind,' Prabhupada wrote. 'By all your prayers He will surely take care of me.'[11] But he also said that his sickness was caused by his leading disciples failing to keep their vows. He had accepted too many disciples, he said, but if he was to spread Krishna consciousness all over the world he had no alternative.

After two weeks, his fever lifted.

'I was lying almost unconscious,' he wrote to a disciple. 'Now by the grace of Krishna I am walking in the morning. I am still very weak and I do not feel any proper appetite, but I feel I am progressing a little each day.'[12]

As his health returned he prepared to go Mayapur, where he planned to rest for a full month. On his way he wrote a letter to all his disciples.

> My Dear Devotees,
>
> I thank you very much for your prayers for my health. By your prayers and by your chanting Hare Krishna, and by the grace of Lord Nrisinghadeva I am much recovered from serious illness. So let us go on with the spreading of this sublime cult of Sri Chaitanya Mahaprabhu all over the world. My only request is that you all remain enthusiastic and pure by strictly following all the rules and regulations and the devotional practices of chanting 16 rounds.[13]

In Mayapur he resumed his regular translation work, which had been interrupted by his illness. He began hearing more reports of unrest among the devotees at Bhaktivedanta Manor. For several months, disputes had been going on over who should be the president, some favouring Madhavananda and some Mukunda. The community had polarised into two camps. In September Mukunda resigned as president and Hamsadutta appointed Prabhavishnu in his place. Madhavananda's supporters were not happy. Rebatinandan Swami, whose vigorous preaching had inspired young *brahmacharis* in England for the last three years, went back to California. Several groups of householders left to join the Paris temple.

Meanwhile, the devotees in Scotland were maintaining the large old building in Greyfriars Market. Wanting to consolidate his workforce, Hamsadutta decided to close the Edinburgh temple and bring all the devotees to the Manor. When news of this closure reached Prabhupada in India he was pained to hear of it. The Edinburgh temple had carried symbolic importance in one of the world's great capital cities. At Prabhupada's insistence the temple was reopened, staffed by several householder couples. He wrote to Hamsadutta, disapproving of his management style. 'I made the GBC to give me relief, but if you do like this, then where is the relief? It is anxiety for me.'[14]

Sarvamangala was one of the devotees who left. She had worked tirelessly in London, Edinburgh, and at the Manor since 1971. Now, along with five other women, she decided to join Prabhupada, who was wintering in Bombay. There she and her friends accepted the hardships of living on an undeveloped plot of land amid the steamy heat and the mosquitoes, but they were rewarded with daily contact with Prabhupada. He heard from them first-hand about the troubles at the Manor. He wrote to Malati: 'Why the devotees in London are unhappy? What is the situation?'[15]

An atmosphere of unease hung over the Manor.

Finally, by the end of the year, rivalries died down and Madhavananda was persuaded to leave England. However, a serious new crisis erupted in Germany. Under Hamsadutta's leadership the German devotees had been selling records using ISKCON's Indian food relief work as a charitable cause to increase sales. But they had been keeping the money instead of sending it to India. In December 1974, the German police, after secretly investigating their finances for months, raided their temple and froze their bank accounts. The resulting publicity disgraced the good name of Hare Krishna in Germany. Prabhupada took this as a great blow for ISKCON and appealed to Bhagavan in France for help:

I am very much depressed by the recent incidences in Germany. It is now evident that some of our top men are very much ambitious and there have been so many falldowns. Under the circumstances I have asked Hamsadutta to come to Hawaii and remain with me. Try to manage Germany, London, and Paris.[16]

After the German scandal, at Prabhupada's insistence record sales in England and elsewhere were discontinued. He had always expressed doubts as to the value of records, and now he unambiguously returned the emphasis to selling books. Prabhavishnu, president at the Manor, set about providing stable leadership after the prolonged unrest of the past year.

One young woman who witnessed the upheavals at the Manor was Krishnavesha, a newly initiated disciple. Upset by the atmosphere of discord around her, and uncertain where to turn for help, she wrote to Prabhupada and asked his advice. He replied, asking her to follow her temple authorities.

'Our movement is based on love and trust,' he wrote, 'so if we do not cooperate, how is that love and trust?'[17]

Krishnavesha had come to the temple through a long and testing journey. She was born Christine Dawn Fraser in South London in 1958. Her father was an Air Force pilot, which meant her family was always on the move. She was a shy girl who found it difficult to make friends, and whenever she did find a friend, she had to leave her behind whenever her father moved to a new posting and she to a new school. Her parents also had a tempestuous marriage, so her home was not peaceful. As a consequence of all this, Christine grew up lonely and insecure, praying to God for protection.

She kept a picture of George Harrison on her wall, and listened to 'My Sweet Lord' and the *Radha Krishna Temple* records. When she put 'Govindam' on her turntable the devotees' voices cleared her mind and her troubles faded. At fourteen she took her younger sister to the

British Museum. They got lost and were in Bury Place, just round the corner from the museum, when a kindly-looking woman dressed in a sari helped them. Her name was Gangamayi.

'Do you know where you are? You're standing outside the Radha Krishna Temple. Why don't you come inside?'

Christine dragged her sister in, bowed before Krishna, tasted prasadam, and heard things she couldn't understand. So began her love affair with Krishna. By the time they got home she had decided that as soon as she could leave school she would join the temple.

It was 1973, the year Prabhupada stayed at the Manor all summer. At the end of term Christine met a devotee on Oxford Street and bought the Rathayatra souvenir magazine from him. In it was a poster of Krishna smiling and playing the flute, with the caption: 'My dear friend, if you still have any inclination to enjoy material life, with its society, friendship, and love, then please do not see the boy named Krishna standing in a three-curved way, smiling and playing his flute, with his lips brightened by the full moonshine.'

Christine went back to the temple with the devotee. This time when she bowed down to Krishna, tears welled up in her eyes and she felt a burden lifted from her shoulders. She continued to attend the Bury Place temple each Sunday that summer. Once she visited the Manor and spent the night sleeping on the floor with blankets lent her by one of the women. In the morning, when Prabhupada came down to lecture, she listened to him with awe.

She wrote to Prabhupada telling him she wanted to run away from home, and a few weeks later, having received no answer, she packed her things in a cardboard box, crept downstairs before dawn, and fled to the temple. When she got there she learned the police were looking for her. She wrote to her parents telling them she was safe, and for nine months she was on the run, staying with devotees around Europe.

Prabhupada had replied to her letter, and his answer eventually reached her in Amsterdam. He counselled her not to run away but to stay at home and chant on her beads; when she finished school and gained some skills, he said, she could move into the temple.

With that she returned to England, was taken into custody at the border, and put into state care. At a court hearing she told the magistrate that away from the temple she felt like a fish out of water. Advised by her social worker, the court ruled that the temple should be appointed her legal guardian. Her story appeared in a Gujarati newspaper, headlined 'Modern-day Mirabhai' in memory of the sixteenth-century Rajasthani princess who fled her husband for a life of devotion to Krishna. Christine, just sixteen years old, settled into life at Bury Place, where she was initiated as Krishnavesha and learned to help Lilashakti serve the deities.

Ray McLennan was born in New Zealand in 1950. After training as a schoolteacher, he hitchhiked round Europe, North Africa, and the Middle East to educate himself about life. He arrived in London in 1972 and found work tunnelling the new Jubilee underground line beneath the city centre. His inquisitive nature led him to read voraciously, especially about the meaning of life. He believed in reincarnation and practised meditation daily. When his fellow workers, tough Irish navvies, learned he was vegetarian, they scoffed at him. But he prayed to God to help him realise the purpose of life, and to that end he read the philosophers and mystics of East and West. He always had a book in his hand.

Ray shared a flat with friends from New Zealand, all of whom were intrigued by the Hare Krishna devotees they saw chanting on Oxford Street. One day Richard Naismith, one of Ray's friends, arrived from Australia. Within a few days of his arrival Richard joined the temple, where he was later initiated as Raghubhir. Influenced by his friend, Ray started reading the *Bhagavad Gita As It Is* and visiting Richard at the temple. In the summer of 1973 Ray heard Prabhupada speak at Bhaktivedanta Manor. When Prabhupada looked at him he felt humbled, exposed by his penetrating gaze. Ray slept in the ashram a few times, but resisted invitations to stay: he had travelling to do.

He set off hitchhiking through Eastern Europe, where he discussed politics, the Rolling Stones, and the meaning of life with students in Warsaw, Prague, and Budapest. Eventually he reached Lebanon, where he worked all summer on a farm in the mountains. There, despite misgivings, he got involved in a dangerous escapade to smuggle hashish into Europe. He narrowly escaped being picked up by the police at an Italian port, and on the spot promised Krishna to give up drugs for good and surrender to Prabhupada.

Back in London Ray moved into the Bury Place temple, where he made himself indispensable cleaning, serving meals, shopping, and organising. He became expert at selling books and magazines, and earned the respect of all the devotees, who liked his friendly ways.

One day someone came to the door with a package for him. It contained his share of the profits from his Lebanese adventure. Not certain what to do with it he put it before Prabhavishnu, who advised him that the only way to absolve himself of the karma of his past was to give the money to Krishna. He was besieged with requests from devotees wanting fares to India or support for pet projects. Partha urged him to become a Life Member. In the end he decided to give the money to buy two vans, one for preaching programmes and the other for travelling book distribution – and he enrolled as a Life Member.

While in the temple he contemplated all that he had learned over the past four years. He had read Marx and Engels and lived under communism; studied the Koran and Sufi literature and lived under Islam; read the Christian mystics and fasted for forty day and nights in the same Syrian desert where Jesus was said to have fasted; now he was living as a disciple of a Vaishnava guru. One day after class, when he had asked a difficult question and not got a satisfactory answer, his friend Narahari put his arm round him.

'You know what's for breakfast today? Have you tried *halava*? Come with me.' With a broad smile Narahari led the way to the dining room, where the sweet buttery semolina was served for breakfast. That was the moment Ray let go. There were always going to be competing philosophies and new adventures, but friendship was what mattered most. He decided he was home, and he wanted to serve the man who had changed his life. Over the following months he received many revelations about his eternal self and his relationship with the all-pervading presence of Krishna. He decided he would dedicate himself to the welfare of the world by serving Prabhupada. That was something tangible, he thought – the service of a pure devotee.

When he was nine, Michael Harrison told his mum he wanted to be a Buddhist monk with a shaven head and orange robes. It was hardly surprising, then, that when he first saw devotees at a pop festival in Derbyshire, he stood mesmerised in the rain-soaked field until his friends dragged him away.

Michael grew up in Cornwall, where his father was a policeman. When he was thirteen his parents separated, and he and his father moved to Nottingham. He began to hear about Krishna, first through the 'Hare Krishna Mantra' record, then by seeing devotees on the streets. He was reading Eastern philosophy and had a translation of the *Bhagavad-gita,* when he met a devotee and bought a *Back to Godhead.* He read about Krishna and Arjuna on the battlefield of life, and for the first time the *Bhagavad-gita* made sense to him. The pictures fascinated him, showing people who had changed everything about their lives because of their commitment to a spiritual path.

Then came his encounter with devotees in the rain at Buxton Festival. There he saw them chanting in the mud, rain dripping from their shaven heads. They seemed oblivious to their surroundings and to the incredulous stares of the crowd. Beside them, from a bright yellow van with Radha and Krishna framed in a pink lotus painted on its side, someone was passing out cups of hot *kichari.*

That summer Michael saw the devotees at several festivals, and finally, in late August 1974, he spoke with them at the Windsor Free Festival. Their confident and joyful rejection of the lures of sex, drugs, and rock 'n' roll astonished the wide-eyed seventeen-year-old.

'Do you believe everyone else is wrong and you're the only ones who have it right?' he asked, sitting round their campfire.

'Oh, no. Everyone's on Krishna's path.'

Michael was reassured, but he had so much yet to discover of the world. A girl wrapped her arms round him and pulled him away to her tent. From nowhere a devotee appeared.

'Michael, don't do this – it's *maya*.' It was Tribhuvanatha. He took Michael to the same yellow van and sat there chanting his rounds, watching over Michael late into the night.

In the morning Michael and the devotees drove to Bhaktivedanta

Manor. Michael loved the place – its simplicity, the singing, the sense of mission, and the chanting on beads which filled him with inner peace. He later began to travel with the devotees in one of their vans, selling books for weeks at a time. Although it was a tough life he loved every bracing minute of it.

At the end of the summer his father came to bring him back to school, where he was halfway through his A-levels. After a long conversation with Prabhavishnu, however, Michael's father was persuaded that his son had made a free choice and had chosen the right thing, so he sadly departed.

Six months later Michael received a letter from Prabhupada with his new name: Kripamoya, 'merciful one.'

David Webb was born in the East End in 1943 during an air raid. Although his parents were atheists they sent him to Sunday school and Bible class, where he discovered Jesus and grew up praying secretly to him under his bedclothes. He was a gifted student, and gained a place at Oxford University, where he called himself a reverent agnostic. He learned to play guitar, violin, banjo, and harmonium. After he got his master's degree in Chemistry he went to Ghana to teach science. Africa took him on a mystical journey that eventually led him to Zen Buddhism.

Returning to England, he set off on a new journey. He travelled by rail across Russia to Japan, where he spent two years practicing Zen meditation in a monastery near Kyoto. He learned about Pure Land Buddhism, which included devotional chanting. Then he read the *Upanishads* and realised he needed to find his way to serving a personal God. Back in London, still dressed as a Buddhist monk, he prayed, 'God, if you exist, please help me. Otherwise I'm finished.'

The next day he met a Krishna devotee. The two of them, one wearing a kimono, the other in saffron robes, stood and talked in a street in Kensington. David said he had been living in Japan studying Buddhism.

'That must have been dry.'

'Yes, it was, actually.'

‘What are you doing now?’

‘I’m looking for a spiritual way of life, and I want to chant a holy name, but I don’t know what name.’

‘Then you should come with me, because we chant all the time.’

David arrived at the temple in time for the Sunday feast just before Christmas in 1973. Within days of accepting the chanting, the abstraction of his two years of Zen practise was replaced by a concrete sense of his own identity and a feeling of reality. To him it was like night and day. Before long he too was travelling in the back of a van with Prabhavishnu and Janananda selling books and records all over England. A few months later he received his initiated name: Jñana, ‘wisdom’.

CHAPTER 21

London Cold and Damp

Prabhupada's health recovered, and at the end of January 1975 he set off from India on his ninth world tour. He was following events in London by letter, and before leaving he delegated one of his most trusted leaders, Brahmananda Swami, to visit Bhaktivedanta Manor and see how things were going. 'See what is the actual situation there in London. Study it carefully and let me know,' he told him.[1]

Prabhupada flew by the Pacific route to Los Angeles and other temples in America, planning to return to India for the annual festival in Mayapur. So it was that on his return leg he arrived at the Manor on 7th March 1975 and stayed for six days.

Kripamoya – who had been listening to tapes of Prabhupada's lectures every morning during breakfast, distributing his books, singing his name, and worshipping his picture – was cleaning the temple room at the Manor. With a crunch of tyres Prabhupada's car pulled up outside the front door, and Prabhupada entered the temple room followed by a crowd of devotees. Kripamoya threw himself to the floor and burst into tears. Prabhupada walked past him and sat on the *vyasasana* to give a short address. While he spoke, Kripamoya sat right in front, bolt upright, straining to hear every word.

Jñana was also present. He too was seeing Prabhupada for the first time. During his years of austerity in search of truth he had hardly felt any emotion; it had not been admitted as a valid part of the Zen path. Even when he practised Krishna consciousness he did so with the same detached spirit he had learned as a Zen monk. Now, at the sight of his spiritual master, he was surprised to experience a sudden rush of emotion, and found himself choking back tears.

When Prabhupada went up to his room, Kripamoya ran ahead of everyone else, eager to be the first to follow him in. The room filled up. Prabhupada recognised Devadatta, whose son Dhruvananda was now in America at the recently established ISKCON school.

'I have just seen your son in Dallas. He is a very happy boy.'

Devadatta had sent his six-year-old son to be educated at the society's recently established school in Dallas. The boy's mother, Draupadi, had hated to send her son away, but she had agreed because Prabhupada had wanted it. Now Devadatta was relieved that Prabhupada remembered the little boy whom he had named during those first weeks at Tittenhurst, and to hear that his son was doing well in America. To Kripamoya it was a revelation to learn that Prabhupada was friends with his disciples and knew their children.

During Prabhupada's stay a log fire was kept burning in the grate in his room. Shrutakirti, still Prabhupada's servant, came in search of the recently appointed temple president, Bhajahari, to investigate why the building was so cold. Bhajahari explained that since they had stopped selling records they were always short of money. The antiquated central heating system needed constant repair, and they couldn't afford to keep the boilers fired. When Prabhupada heard this he considered what to do.

'Tell him that if they can't make any money without selling records, then they can sell them, but they must give a book with every record.'

So for the time being the record sales were resumed and money started to come in again.

Prabhupada's sensitivity to the English cold became a topic of conversation following an exchange that took place one morning after his lecture, when Krishnavesha asked a question. She had read in the *Bhagavad-gita* that Krishna had taught Arjuna in other times and places. She wondered where those places could have been. Her question didn't come out quite as planned.

'Does Krishna speak *Bhagavad-gita* on the hellish planets?' she asked. Her words mystified the devotees, but not Prabhupada.

'Yes, this London is a hellish planet – always cold and damp,' he answered, 'and Krishna is speaking *Bhagavad-gita* here!'

Everyone laughed except Krishnavesha, who felt confused and embarrassed. Had Prabhupada misunderstood her question? But then she realised that his answer was just for her. She had always been attached to London – it was where she had been born. Prabhupada wanted her to give up this attachment and see herself as an eternal soul who now had the chance to hear Krishna speak the *Bhagavad-gita* right here in twentieth-century London. For the rest of the devotees his answer confirmed what they already knew: Prabhupada didn't like the cold English weather.

There were other things that were troubling Prabhupada. Crises were forever bubbling up in different parts of his movement as his leading disciples vied for position. He was grave and the atmosphere around him sombre.

Despite the cold, damp weather, next morning Prabhupada went on his usual walk. His discomfort with the British climate was now a talking point, and as he paced the country lane with a large following, occasionally stepping aside to allow cars to pass, he repeated his opinion.

'There is no sunshine. It is wet always. The trees have moss. A place where there is no sunshine is condemned.'[2]

'You write that the sun purifies a dirty place,' put in Brahmananda Swami, 'but we don't rely on the sun.'

‘We have the Krishna sun,’ agreed Prabhupada.

He had been lecturing on the *Bhagavad-gita,* seventh chapter, where Krishna said that only one among thousands would take up Krishna consciousness.

‘Will the Krishna consciousness movement take over the world eventually?’ asked a devotee.

‘No, that is not possible. Only the fortunate persons will take it. You will have to become very expert at preaching.’

Several Indian families had visited Prabhupada since he had arrived, bringing with them their children. This prompted another question.

‘Do you think the young Indians will grow up to be pious like their parents?’

‘Why just Indians?’ responded Prabhupada. ‘We are talking of the whole world.’

He was still pondering the lack of sunlight. It reminded him of the 1906 visit to India of the young Prince of Wales, who later became George V.

‘We were schoolchildren,’ he recalled, ‘and we were given flags to wave. Twice I saw him – once when he entered Calcutta, and again at a military parade. When he saw the bright sunshine he was surprised.’

‘The British built a big memorial there in Calcutta?’ asked Brahmananda.

‘Yes, the Victoria Memorial. It took twenty years to build. While it was under construction I went to the top by climbing the scaffolding.’

‘You must have been very brave, Prabhupada,’ said Brahmananda, recalling the conversation of the previous year.

‘Yes, I am still brave. Otherwise, how could I have come alone to preach Krishna consciousness? When I was a boy an astrologer predicted that for executing my purpose I would enter fire.’

For three consecutive mornings Prabhupada lectured in the temple to his assembled disciples. One morning he said,

> The process is very easy. Wherever you live, at home or outside home, just keep a picture of Sri Chaitanya Mahaprabhu and chant Hare Krishna mantra before him. Then your life will be successful.[3]

As he traveled round the world he saw the growing contradictions of modern society, and the problems it was storing up for the future. He advised his disciples to keep their lives simple:

> Modern civilization says increase your necessities: have a machine for shaving your cheek. Formerly you could go to a blacksmith and he would prepare a razor that would last for your life and shave your cheek very nicely daily. But modern civilization means that for everything there must be a machine. If you create some convenience by this machine you create so many other inconveniences. Just like we have got the motorcar. Of course it is convenient, but there are many inconveniences. People used to find everything within the village. Now we have to go thirty miles for a doctor, and we have to flatter the Iranians to give us petrol. In this way we are forgetting our real business: self-realisation.[4]

The devotees were working selflessly to distribute Prabhupada's books in all kinds of conditions, and he knew that in the process they had to face many difficulties. People insulted them, the police chased them away, and they had to meet with both success and failure and still be enthusiastic.

> People are working so hard day and night to fill the belly. They do not know there is something other. Modern civilization keeps them in darkness and lets them work hard like hog and dog, and then die like hog and dog. This is not human life. They will say, Why do you bother us? But why we are bothering? Because we are servants of Krishna. Krishna wants them to be informed, to be raised from this state of ignorance. That is our mission. Therefore we are pleading that you kindly purchase one book and read it. We are flattering you, falling down on your feet: Please hear. Whatever nonsense you have learned, forget. This is our only solicitation. Try to hear Chaitanya Mahaprabhu and be perfect. Thank you very much.[5]

A young journalist came to interview Prabhupada. He was polite and respectful, and had taken the trouble to read some of Prabhupada's writings beforehand. His interest was in how Krishna consciousness differed from Christianity. As he always did with representatives of the press, Prabhupada preached to him as if he were just another guest, being more interested in the individual than in what he represented. The young man asked if it was difficult for Prabhupada to bring his teachings from India to the West.

'It is not a question of East and West,' Prabhupada replied, 'it is a question of human life. Western people and Eastern people – both have this living force. It is the concern of the whole human society.'

'What do you say about the Christian teaching?'

'Christian teaching is good. It is giving the idea of God. The teaching is the same – what Jesus Christ taught and what we are teaching. But no one is following. Christ said, "Thou shalt not kill," and the Christian people are very expert in killing. Do you admit?'

'Yes, I admit.'

'The difficulty is, I am claiming to be Hindu but I am not following the Vedic rules. You are claiming to be Christian but you are not following the Christian rules. We don't say the Bible is bad and the *Vedas* are good. Real spiritual understanding is that every living entity is a servant of God. We are all dependent on God's mercy. God is one, and we are all servants of God. So let us serve God.'

They talked for twenty minutes, and when the reporter ran out of questions Prabhupada continued to preach energetically.

Initiations were held for a dozen new devotees, bringing the total of devotees initiated in England to 230, a third of them women. Ray was on the list for initiation, but he decided he wasn't ready. It was something he knew he must eventually do, yet for a free spirit like him it was a big step. He kept his long hair and beard and avoided the ceremony, preferring to stay in the kitchen washing pots. It was where he thought he belonged.

Partha was also in the kitchen. He had been initiated three years earlier in Trafalgar Square, and since then had become an expert cook, specialising in preparing feasts for the whole community. His other service was fund-raising, a task he was so good at that he now led the Life Membership department at the Manor. It was an important service at a time when money was scarce, and it provided the community with a steady income. Whenever he could find time he was fond of studying

He sat on a seat of red velvet cushions and addressed a crowd of Hindu guests. He delivered a powerful oration, aimed at an audience far beyond those walls.

He sat among his disciples, motionless and silent. Not a word passed his lips, but his eyes were bright, though shaded behind sunglasses.

At 7 Bury Place awaited Radha-Londonishvara and their loyal devotees. (Left to right: Savitri, Yashasvini, Ramadevi, Lilashakti, Padma, unknown, Bhavani, Shila, Biti, Kulangana; back row: Andy, Yashoda Dulala, unknown, Triveni, unknown, unknown, unknown, Subhaga, Vichitravirya, Krishnadas)

Each day Prabhupada had an event-free ride down the stairs to the temple room, with his seat freshly decked with flowers, and accompanied by loving devotees. (Amita is the front bearer, Upendra, Bhajahari and Krishnadas look on; Tamal Krishna Goswami walks alongside.)

Prabhupada sat gazing fixedly at Krishna, his eyes streaming tears. Around him were the temple devotees and members of the German *yatra;* at his side his servants wiped away his tears.

Prabhupada's books, and he often taught classes at the temple and in the homes of Life Members.

In the midst of all this work Partha had never taken the opportunity to personally meet or converse with Prabhupada. Like many disciples he regarded the work itself as his reward, thinking that his duty was to hear Prabhupada's teachings, study his books, serve him, and to not expect personal contact.

One morning during the daily *guru-puja* ceremony Partha came before the *vyasasana* to offer a flower. Usually this would be to a picture of Prabhupada, but for these few days while Prabhupada was staying with them, he could offer his flower personally at Prabhupada's feet. As he did so he looked up and their eyes met. It was only for a fleeting moment, but Prabhupada looked at him, smiled, and nodded. In that moment Partha knew that he was acknowledged as Prabhupada's disciple.

Until then he had felt himself an outsider during his entire life; he never felt connected with the centre of things. But in that instant his relationship with Prabhupada changed. From then on he felt secure, close to his guru even without the physical contact. He continued to read Prabhupada's books repeatedly, finding in his written words ever more inspiration.

Govardhan was living at the Manor with her husband and her new baby. She arranged for her mother and three of her five sisters to come and see Prabhupada. It was all planned in advance: during the morning *guru-puja* she gave each of her sisters a rose and her mother a bouquet. She then led them to Prabhupada's *vyasasana,* where they offered their flowers and received his blessings. This made them very happy.

Some maintenance work was needed in Prabhupada's room. He wanted to lock up his valuables, but the key to his cupboard had been lost. Mohan was called to fit a new lock. He entered cautiously to find Prabhupada walking up and down, his hand in his bead bag, chanting his rounds. He indicated to Mohan that he should go ahead and fix the lock. While Mohan was chiselling at the wood, trying to be as quiet as possible, Prabhupada continued chanting in a low voice. Then he paused and came over to look with interest at his disciple.

'Oh? You are a carpenter?'

Prabhupada wanted to talk with him, but Mohan was shy and unable to answer. 'No, Prabhupada,' he mumbled. In fact he could turn his hand to almost any practical task, but in front of Prabhupada he felt tongue-tied.

'Oh,' was all Prabhupada said, and went back to his chanting.

Mohan never forgot Prabhupada's fatherly interest in him, or the way he had acknowledged his service.

Ever since his encounter with Prabhupada at Conway Hall in 1969 as a young law student, Vishnu Sharma had remembered him. He was now a barrister practicing law at the Inns of Court in London, and a married man. In 1975 Vichitravirya and Mukunda came to see him to ask his help. The temple in London was threatened with closure for breach of planning regulations, and Camden Council, in response to complaints from neighbours, had given them three months' notice to shut the temple down. Vishnu was brought to meet Prabhupada, and found him sitting at his desk, quietly chanting on his beads.

'I understand you are a lawyer,' Prabhupada said. 'Please sit down.'

Vishnu felt as if he was in the presence of his father. Prabhupada asked him about himself and his background, learning that he was from a brahmin family and had been brought up as a Vaishnava devotee of Krishna.

'We have no money,' Prabhupada told him. Vishnu knew what was meant by this: he was being asked to volunteer his help. This was as it should be. His father had taught him that there was no question of taking money from a temple. He gave Prabhupada his word.

'We will do the work and I will keep in touch with Mukunda and Vichitravirya. My friend and legal junior, David Mole, will help.'

From then on a legal battle went back and forth through repeated court appearances, for the right to worship Krishna at Bury Place. Vishnu Sharma succeeded in keeping the temple open for another four years. This was his service to Prabhupada, and it gave him the opportunity to see him several times. During their conversations Prabhupada never blamed his disciples for the problems the temple was facing, although he might have had cause to. He said they were doing their best and that it was the duty of an Indian to help them. 'When you retire,' he told Vishnu at their last meeting, 'you should go live in Vrindavan.'

Ashtasakhi had moved to Amsterdam, where she was married to the temple president, Harikrishnadas. They heard that Prabhupada was coming to London. They had been having leadership disputes in their temple community, affected by the same unrest as the London devotees. Relieved that Prabhupada was coming and hoping that he would sort everything out, they travelled to London to see him.

Ashtasakhi listened attentively to Prabhupada's lectures, but she felt her unhappiness unresolved. This had never happened when she had listened to Prabhupada before. As everyone was getting up and he too was beginning to rise from his seat, she felt troubled. He looked directly at her and sat back down on the *vyasasana*.

'Happiness and distress,' he quoted the *Bhagavad-gita*. 'Sometimes in life it may be your destiny to be in happiness, and sometimes it may be your destiny to be in unhappiness.' As he spoke he brought his hands down on the arms of the *vyasasana* with a thud. 'But it is our business to become equipoised in both.' While he said this he looked right at Ashtasakhi, and she accepted his words.

A few months earlier Lilashakti had written to Prabhupada and sent him a photograph of Radha-Londonishvara, whom she had described as 'my Krishna'. He had replied, thanking her for the photograph of 'your Krishna' and assuring her, 'Krishna is so kind that although he is *ajit,* unconquerable, he can be possessed by the devotee. From love he allows this. I am glad to see that you are advancing in Krishna consciousness by this worship of the deity. I also follow this process. Every morning I go to the temple and see the deity and offer obeisances.'[6]

Now, on his last morning in England, he was driven into London to see Radha-Londonishvara and their loyal servants. His visit was anticipated with more than usual eagerness by the devotees at Bury Place. This was because there was a controversy between those who were selling books, mainly young men, and those who served the deities, mainly young women. The men had the upper hand because they were the ones bringing in the money and administering the temple. Their leader, Sarvasagara, told his friends that when Prabhupada came he was going to put a question to him with the expectation that the men's view would be confirmed.

As usual when Prabhupada arrived he went straight in front of Radha and Krishna and appreciated how nicely they were dressed. Then he gave a short lecture to a packed audience. He chose to talk about devotional service, explaining that there were many ways to serve Krishna, beginning with hearing and chanting, and that all of these were of equal spiritual value.

> Somebody is cooking, somebody is decorating the deity, somebody is cleansing the floor, somebody is going to sell books. All these activities are in relationship with Krishna. Therefore they are complete. Here in the material world somebody is sitting in the office chair and somebody is cleaning the office – the cleaner is supposed to be lower than the officer. In the spiritual world there is no such distinction.
>
> In Vrindavan the cowherd boys are playing with Krishna on equal terms. They do not know Krishna is God. They simply know how to love Krishna, that's all. Simply the centre is Krishna. All the inhabitants of Vrindavan love Krishna: one knows Krishna is my son, one knows Krishna is my master, one is thinking Krishna is my lover. Everyone's centre is Krishna, and how Krishna will be happy. This is Vrindavan life. If we try to follow the footsteps of the residents of Vrindavan, then our life is successful. That is the recommendation of Sri Chaitanya Mahaprabhu. This is the goal of life.[7]

When Prabhupada finished speaking there was a stunned silence. It was as if he had known exactly what was on their minds and had addressed the very issue that divided them. But Sarvasagara was still determined to ask his question. He raised his hand.

'Srila Prabhupada, what is the service that will please you the most?'

'Rendering service to Radha and Krishna, even the most insignificant service, is the best thing anyone can do,' said Prabhupada. 'Take for example a small insect – say an ant – who happens to climb onto a flower in Krishna's garland. He accidentally falls on Krishna's feet. Krishna will say this ant is kindly massaging my feet. He will see that ant in the position of a devotee rendering service. What to speak of someone who consciously decides to serve? Krishna will take your service as pure devotional service. What an opportunity you have!'[8]

Afterwards, Lilashakti, in charge of the *pujari* department, spoke to some of her devotee brothers. 'Well, does anyone want to make garlands for Krishna, polish some brass, or offer an arati? There's plenty of service for everyone.' And so for a while some of the young men of the temple volunteered to make garlands and polish brass for their Krishna.

During Prabhupada's talk Yashasvini had been downstairs preparing a plate of fruit for his afternoon snack. She spent her days selling books on the street – she was the only woman in the London temple who was doing that. She loved talking to the people she met, but she was under pressure to sell more books and she had been hoping to hear Prabhupada's talk so as to gain some much-needed encouragement. Instead she had been asked to cut up his fruit. Realising she had missed his talk she sat in the basement cloakroom, chanting on her beads and crying quietly. That was where Shrutakirti found her.

'What's the matter?' he asked, and she explained her disappointment.

'You are just like a *gopi* crying for Krishna. Do you want to see him? I'll see what I can do.' He went upstairs and soon returned.

'Prabhupada will see you. Go up now.'

Yashasvini sat timidly in front of Prabhupada. He asked her name, but when she replied he was unable to understand her Lancashire accent. In silence he laid himself down to rest on the temporary bed Ramadevi had made up for him on the floor. Propping his head on one hand, he spoke again.

‘Pardon?’ she replied, confused. He repeated his words, but she still couldn’t understand. For a few moments he looked at her, seeming to peer deep into her soul.

‘Thank you very much,’ he said at last.

‘Oh, no, Prabhupada, please don’t thank me!’ she burst out. ‘Thank *you* for everything.’

Prabhupada smiled. Gently Shrutakirti informed her that Prabhupada needed to rest now. Once outside, he asked if she had understood what Prabhupada had said to her in his room. She shook her head.

‘She is a great sage and Krishna will bless her,’ Shrutakirti repeated. Stunned, she supposed Prabhupada must have known she was selling his books all day long, though she had not told him. She thanked Shrutakirti for allowing her a glimpse of her master.

From Bury Place Prabhupada went directly to the airport and flew via Tehran to India. There he joined his assembled disciples in Mayapur to celebrate Sri Chaitanya’s birthday. Then he went to Vrindavan, where on the Appearance Day of Lord Rama, 16th April 1975, in a weeklong festival, he opened the Krishna-Balaram temple. For Prabhupada, in the midst of so many competing pressures, it was a triumph.

In England, as increasing numbers of books went out, young people continued to come to the temples.

Martin Fleming grew up in a Presbyterian family in Belfast. His school and social life were structured so that he and his friends never had to meet a Catholic, but his mother was from the south, so he did occasionally get to see the other side on family visits across the border. When the troubles erupted in Belfast in the summer of 1969, he was fourteen. Soldiers arrived, barricades went up, and the city polarised. At first he and his friends were excited; during lessons they would hear a bomb go off and their teacher would send them out to investigate. They felt no fear. Then, when he was in town one day, a bomb exploded a few shops away. He was lucky – neither he nor his friends got hurt – but he no longer found the bombs exciting.

In Bible class he was never satisfied. 'You've told us about life after death,' he asked, 'but what about life before birth?' He got no answers. The idea of reincarnation and karma appealed to him, and he developed a fascination with Indian philosophy.

On Easter Sunday 1973, when he was alone at home revising for exams, he answered a knock at the door. On the doorstep stood a man dressed in saffron robes offering him a book on Eastern philosophy. The man's name was Varaha Murti, and he was a member of Prabhavishnu's book distribution team. To Martin he appeared like a shining being, and his answers to Martin's questions made perfect sense. By the time he left, Martin was holding a copy of the *Ishopanishad*, with a painting of Vishnu on its bright pink cover. He treasured the book, giving it pride of place in his room, and dedicated himself to following its teachings. He accepted its author, whose picture was on the back, as his spiritual teacher.

As soon as he turned eighteen Martin left Belfast for good, as did most of his friends. He started student life at the University of Bristol, where before long he met devotees when they held a festival in the middle of the campus. He saw at once that they were living the philosophy that until then he had only read about. Two years later, in the summer of 1975, he handed in his notice at university, wrote to his parents, and moved to the Manor. Bhajahari and Rohininandan welcomed him with lunch on the lawn. He spent a month looking after the cows, then went out selling books on the streets of London.

The first time Lyn Halley saw devotees was in California. She was studying art when in 1968, as a twenty-first birthday present, her father paid for her and her best friend to tour North America. They reached Los Angeles and met a group of devotees chanting on Hollywood Boulevard. She thought they were wonderful.

A few years later in Kenya, a friend taught her to chant Hare Krishna. She returned to Europe and was living in France when she received a parcel from her friend in Kenya. It contained japa beads and copies of

Bhagavad-gita As It Is and *The Nectar of Devotion*. She had already tried Buddhism, Guru Maharaj Ji, and a Sufi master, but none of these paths were for her. She started chanting on the beads, studying Prabhupada's books, and painting pictures of Krishna. One day she heard that Prabhupada was visiting Geneva, just across the Swiss border, so she went to see him on what was to be his only visit to Switzerland.

It was a beautiful summer's day in 1974. She was ushered into a garden where she watched a sacred fire burning surrounded by a handful of devotees, while Prabhupada sat on a *vyasasana* in the shade of a silk umbrella. The occasion was an initiation ceremony. Suddenly he looked straight at her and she felt her soul bared. She became aware of how impure she was – she had never thought of that before. She wanted the ground to open up and swallow her. At the same time, just from that look, she knew he was her spiritual master. She was ready to drop everything there and then and stay with the devotees, but no one came up to speak with her. Another year passed before she found herself in Prabhupada's presence again.

After opening the Vrindavan temple, despite his weakening health, Prabhupada embarked on yet another tour of the world. He spent two weeks in Australia, four weeks resting and translating in Hawaii, and then visited twelve temples across North America. Seven weeks into his tour, when he was in Toronto, a telegram arrived from Delhi saying that Indira Gandhi, Prime Minister of India, had agreed to see him. For a long time he had been requesting her government to give visas to his European and American disciples. He decided to cut short his stay in America and hasten back to India.

On the way to India Prabhupada stopped in England, on 12th August 1975, for twenty-four hours. In the early morning sunshine, Prabhupada walked along the lane toward Round Bush, and Lyn Halley followed behind him. She had returned to England, married a Krishna devotee, and was now staying near the Manor, pregnant with her first child.

Prabhupada crossed the broad expanse of ripened wheat, chanting on his beads and surrounded by the murmur of twenty-five voices. Lyn's troubled mind felt soothed in his presence, floating in his wake, borne upon the sound of the holy names of Krishna.

Also on the walk was Martin Fleming. He had been worried that Prabhupada might not live up to his expectations, but when he had seen him the previous day at the airport he felt a wave of energy such as he had never felt before and knew that Prabhupada must be his true spiritual master.

Back at the temple Prabhupada lectured from the *Bhagavatam*, using simple examples to communicate Vedic knowledge. He began by describing the sunshine:

> The sunshine which we daily see is made of very small shining particles. We are like that – very small part and parcel of Krishna, like fire and small sparks of fire. As there are material atoms nobody can count, similarly we are atomic sparks of God....
>
> We have come to this world, like the Europeans who go to other countries to colonise and use the resources for their gratification. America was discovered and the Europeans went there, now they are trying to go to the moon. This is the tendency of the conditioned soul: Krishna is the enjoyer and we are imitating Krishna. Everyone is trying to become Krishna....
>
> The hand is part and parcel of the body. What is the duty of this hand? The duty is to fulfil the desire of the person. Similarly we are part and parcel of God, of Krishna, and our only business is to fulfil the desire of Krishna....
>
> One is sure to suffer the material pangs of life. To our eyes the so-called poor man and rich man, they are all suffering. Not that simply the poor man is suffering and the rich man is not suffering. Everyone is poor. One who has no knowledge of Krishna is poor. Therefore we give them prasadam and they get the opportunity to associate with Krishna.[9]

Then he was gone, first to Bombay for a week, then on to Delhi where he had his meeting with Indira Gandhi. She had just declared her state of emergency – it was to last for two years in defiance of international opposition – and she was in no mood to discuss Krishna consciousness. She did, however, agree to help with the visas.

After Prabhupada left England, Lyn Halley moved to the Edinburgh temple, now led by Mahavishnu. There she gave birth to her daughter, who she named Rasalila. On the day her daughter was born she received her initiation letter from Prabhupada, giving her the name Srikama.

Martin Fleming was initiated at the same time. He was called Akhandadhi, a name for Krishna's father. He joined Partha at the Manor, where he helped to recruit Life Members.

Ray McLennan shaved off his beard, and eventually his hair, and took up the daily mission to sell as many of Prabhupada's books and magazines as he could.

The final volumes of the *Chaitanya-charitamrita* had just been published, and all over ISKCON an ever greater emphasis was being placed upon book distribution. In Britain a core of dedicated book distributors had emerged, and Ray became one of the most active. He had read in the *Chaitanya-charitamrita* the five-hundred-year-old prophesy that the name of Sri Chaitanya would be heard in every town and village of the world.[10] Inspired by this he channelled the same sense of adventure that had spurred him to explore the planet into spreading Krishna consciousness for the benefit of people everywhere.

As Christmas approached and London filled with shoppers, Ray descended into the underground system every morning carrying great piles of magazines. He would work through a train, making announcements, and sometimes he would leave fifty people in a single carriage reading *Back to Godhead* magazine. At the end of each twelve-hour day he emerged from beneath the city, his nostrils blackened with soot but his heart filled with satisfaction. At the temple he compared results with other devotees, ate supper, danced, sang with them, then tried to sleep, impatient to get up and do it all again the next day. Now he felt ready to accept initiation. He prayed for a short name. He was a popular devotee, and was awarded the name Amita, which means, simply, 'friend'.

The growing street sales meant that at last devotees could eat properly and pay the bills. The Bury Place temple was still under threat of closure, but Vichitravirya continued working through the law courts with Vishnu Sharma to keep it open for as long as possible.

At the Manor, key members had gone – some of the householders to France, Sarvamangala and her friends, followed by Tribhuvanatha and Subhaga, to India. In the autumn Prabhavishnu handed the presidency to Vichitravirya and also left for India. The Edinburgh temple was finally closed, and Mahavishnu went to join Prabhavishnu in India, where together they began a new adventure selling Prabhupada's books. Despite all that had gone wrong, Hamsadutta remained overall in charge in England, but by the spring of 1976 he was exhausted and dispirited. It was time for a change of leadership.

BOOK FIVE

Farewell to the West 1976–77

CHAPTER 22

So Many Centres, So Little Time

By the time Prabhupada reached New York in July 1976 at the end of a demanding three-month tour of Australia, the Pacific, and North America, he was showing the strain. He was now eighty years old, with diabetes and persistent insomnia. His disciples begged him to slow down.

'I want the benediction to die fighting on the battlefield like Arjuna,' he insisted, even though he could hardly walk. In this mood he crossed the Atlantic on 21st July.

At the Manor, change was in the air. Prabhupada had appointed Jayatirtha, one of his best leaders, to replace Hamsadutta as Governing Body Commissioner for the UK. Jayatirtha was born James Immel in 1948 on a U.S. Air Force base in the Pacific. His father was a pilot and a tough man, and the sensitive young boy had never felt comfortable with him. Instead, he learned to distinguish himself from a young age as a creative and intelligent rebel.

He graduated from high school two years ahead of his age group and attended law school at the University of California. Soon, however, thirsting for spiritual adventure, he dropped out to join a commune where he took part in Timothy Leary's psychedelic research into the nature of consciousness. In 1969, at the age of twenty, and after some life-changing experiences, he moved into the Hare Krishna temple in Laguna Beach. He was initiated as Jayatirtha and appointed to head the movement's Spiritual Sky incense business in Los Angeles. Within three years he built it into a $4,000,000 business that supported temples across North America. Prabhupada made him GBC secretary for the West Coast and a trustee of the Bhaktivedanta Book Trust. Jayatirtha's projects flourished. Then at the Mayapur festival in March 1976, Prabhupada asked him to give up his West Coast responsibilities and come to England.

Jayatirtha brought with him his wife, Manjuali, and their six-week-old son. Mary Leona had grown up in California. She studied Art and English at the University of Chicago. She too had dropped out to search for a spiritually-based community where she could feel at home. At the 1969 Woodstock festival in upstate New York she met members of a hippie commune in the Catskill Mountains and moved in with them. There she learned yoga and meditation. While visiting her mother in Chicago she met devotees, and over the next two years, moving from commune to commune in California and Oregon, she kept in touch with them.

Mary loved chanting Hare Krishna, and she felt safe with the devotees. In 1971 she saw Prabhupada at the Los Angeles temple. When she bowed down at his feet she saw them glowing with spiritual light. She thought an extraordinary human being had appeared on the planet and that it was her good fortune to be in his presence. From that day on she never left the temple. Three months later she was initiated as Manjuali, and in early 1972 she married Jayatirtha. The Los Angeles Krishna community became her family, and along with her young husband she dedicated herself to serving and caring for the young men and women who came there for spiritual shelter.

These two arrived in England bringing with them hope and optimism. Soon the insecurity of the past two years' leadership was swept away, and the Manor became a hive of activity in preparation for Prabhupada's expected visit.

That summer the lake evaporated in a heat wave and the lawns were parched and yellow. Jayatirtha decided to spend money to redecorate the Manor. For weeks a hose slowly refilled the lake; devotees planted roses and tidied the grounds; the driveways were spread with new gravel; Manjuali, her baby strapped in front of her, sewed curtains; the temple room got a new floor, gold wallpaper, a new *vyasasana,* and its beams gold-leafed; in the reception room a long bookcase was built to house the full set of Prabhupada's books, displays were made for the walls, and a new painting of Prabhupada was hung; and his rooms were redecorated in blue with peach curtains.

Jayatirtha and Manjuali were everywhere encouraging and befriending the devotees and urging on the work. Vichitravirya was now president at the Manor. He combined a clear sense of purpose with a mild and friendly nature, which gained him the trust and cooperation of the community. Everyone felt a fresh start was being made.

Jaya Lakshmana, now the treasurer, was less enthusiastic about the changes. He worried about the money being spent, much of it on credit, and feared a repeat of the past when they had run up unmanageable debts. But Jayatirtha was an astute manager and kept control of the finances. He set up a UK branch of the BBT, putting Raghubhir in charge of producing a range of publications designed to appeal to British tastes and rejuvenating the book distributors. To increase the cash flow he created a dedicated group of young women fund-raisers, who went every day into the West End of London to sell flowers and books on the streets.

One of these fund-raisers was Janaki. Born Janet Leithead in Leicester, she had trained as a psychiatric nurse, then gone with her husband to India on pilgrimage to find a guru. The couple were disappointed and close to abandoning their search, when on their travels they met devotees and bought some of Prabhupada's books. By the time they got home to Leicester they were convinced of the truth of Krishna consciousness, and in 1975 they joined the Manor community, accepting the names Janaki and Ramasharana.

Janaki drove each day into London with armfuls of flowers. She told people she met that their donations were supporting charity work to save the world, and whenever she could she sold them a book. She found it difficult to hustle people on the streets, but she wanted to serve her spiritual master, so she and her devotee sisters worked hard and waited for Prabhupada's arrival.

Another new member was Greg Clarke, from near Uxbridge on the western edge of London. From the age of ten, on visits to Central London, he had seen devotees chanting in the street and felt a powerful attraction to them.

In 1974 he bought one of the Krishna records from a devotee on the street. It featured Hamsadutta leading kirtan, and had a dazzling picture of a golden Radharani on the sleeve. The sound captivated him and he began to chant. He kept meeting devotees, and finally visited the Manor in early 1976. He phoned his mother and told her he had decided to live with the Hare Krishnas. She came to see what it was all about, met Mukunda, and by the end of the day gave approval for her eighteen-year-old son to join. But two days later, when she delivered some of his belongings, she found him dressed in saffron robes with his long, fair hair shaven off, and she burst into tears.

'You have to come home now, Greg. I've spoken to people, and they say you've been brainwashed.' When he refused to go with her she was inconsolable and ran away down the corridor. Greg loved his mother, and he was anxious.

'Don't worry,' reassured Narahari. 'Call her tonight and everything will be fine.'

When Greg called she apologised for the scene.

'I was testing you to see if you're really serious about this. You are, and it's okay with me,' she assured him. The following weekend she brought the whole family – his grandmother, aunt and uncle. They ate the feast, chanted and watched a play staged by the devotees, and thought the Manor a wonderful place.

Greg stayed, working in the kitchen, studying the books, gardening, and going out to chant on the streets. In the van on the way home each day he talked excitedly about when Prabhupada would come to visit.

Crossing the Atlantic in the first-class cabin of a jumbo jet, Prabhupada passed a sleepless night and arrived at Heathrow exhausted and ill. Aided by his new servant, Hari Sauri, he struggled through immigration and customs and was greeted by a large crowd of chanting devotees. They knew nothing of his poor health, and he appeared to them as effulgent as ever. His attendants cleared a path to the waiting Rolls Royce, which belonged to Charles Patel, a Hindu businessman who had become a good friend of the temple.

By the time Prabhupada reached the Manor, word had gone ahead that he was ill, and he was greeted by a subdued kirtan. As his car entered the gravel drive, a conch shell sounded from the rooftop, and inside the building, Greg, assigned at the last minute to sweep the stairs, hurried to finish. Suddenly he came face-to-face with his spiritual master, who was being assisted through the garden door.

Greg stood, trembling in awe, hands folded, as Prabhupada paused to survey the reception room. Along the length of one wall was the hand-built book display, a painted portrait of himself hung above the fireplace, and beside it in painted relief the new crest of the Manor. The crest was the work of Sakshi Gopala and showed the four symbols of Vishnu flanked by two swans and surmounted by the leaves of the sacred *tulasi,* beneath which an open book held the Sanskrit characters *ve-da*, knowledge, above the motto *Krishnas tu bhagavan swayam,* 'Krishna is the Supreme Personality of Godhead'.

When he saw all this Prabhupada's face lit up with a golden smile of approval. He came before Radha-Gokulananda and, with the whole community clustered around him, lowered himself full length to the floor. He rose painfully and stood there for a long time, hands folded in silent prayer ('I was praying that I will not fall down,' he said afterwards), then moved toward the stairs, leaning heavily on his cane. He was in no condition to climb them, and he paused while devotees ran to find a chair on which to carry him up. Amid the sparse furnishings of the Manor a chair was difficult to find. Soon, growing impatient, he ascended slowly, step by step, aided by his servant. A hush descended as a hundred anxious disciples watched helplessly, seeing how weak he had become. When he reached the top a cry went up, '*Jaya* Prabhupada!' Then he disappeared into his room.

Manjuali had bought a new bed for him, deep and soft with eiderdowns and many pillows. It was perhaps the first such bed he would ever sleep in. Beside it she had placed a large creamy magnolia blossom cut from the tree outside his window. There he rested for twenty-four hours and ate nothing.

Only one man was brought in to see him. From his window Prabhupada had caught sight of an Indian devotee sitting on the lawn chanting on his beads. It was Kshirodakshayi, who had come to see him but had been turned away from his door. Prabhupada asked for him, and he entered to find his master sitting up in bed, coughing painfully.

'I have been sick for three days. Please call Dr Trivedi.'

Dr Trivedi was an ayurvedic physician who lived in Luton. Since he could not be located, Kshirodakshayi telephoned home and told his son Chaturbhuja to bring an ayurvedic remedy called *chayvana-prasha*. Then he prepared ginger tea and sat with Prabhupada.

Next morning Prabhupada went down briefly to see the deities but had real difficulty climbing back up the long flight of stairs. He spent most of the day in bed. He spoke for a while with Jayatirtha and Vichitravirya. He was concerned to know how the devotees were. They gave him all their good news and avoided burdening him with any management problems.

Kshirodakshayi returned and cooked *kichari* with lemon pickle, which Prabhupada ate sparingly, watched by Jayatirtha and Vichitravirya. Again he took *chayvana-prasha* and ginger tea. Slowly he was recovering.

On the third day he was up and walking around his room. Again he ate Kshirodakshayi's *kichari*, this time with chapatis. Seeing Prabhupada gaining strength, Kshirodakshayi invited him to visit his home to see his deities.

'If by Krishna's grace I am feeling better,' he promised, 'on Sunday I will go to see Radha-Londonishvara, and afterwards I will come to your house to see Radha-Govinda.'

Sakshi Gopala and Harernamananda had made an opulent new *vyasasana* for his visit. It was richly upholstered and had gilded lion's feet, crafted by Sakshi. After working on it for four weeks they were disappointed to be told that Prabhupada would be too ill to come to the temple room to sit on it. But on the third day of his visit he did come down, and they were delighted, as everyone was, when he sat on the new *vyasasana* and gave a talk.

Behind the curtains *pujaris* rushed to get the altar ready. Every morning they bathed and dressed the deities in time for the seven o'clock arati. Their two hours' labour would culminate when the curtains opened to reveal to the assembled devotees Radha and Krishna newly adorned for the day, with fresh garlands and flowers amid clouds of incense.

During these few days in July the *pujaris*' efforts acquired a new intensity. Dressing the deities knowing that Prabhupada was going to see them brought on a kind of ecstasy. In the final rush before opening the curtains, as they hurried back and forth, a flow developed between them all: the last adjustment to Krishna's flute, the posy of flowers in Radha's hand, the polish applied to the marble steps, the incense and candles lit, the sounding of the conch, the curtains opening, the *Govindam* prayers resounding, then running out into the temple room to throw themselves down like sticks with the others. And there was Prabhupada, glowing in freshly-pressed saffron silk, hands joined to see his Radha and Krishna. All eyes were upon him: instead of looking at Radha-Gokulananda the devotees gazed at Prabhupada as he saw Radha-Gokulananda and they saw Krishna through his eyes.

He sat on the *vyasasana* and accepted their homage. As soon as he began to speak, a child's voice called out. It was the two-year-old daughter of Govatsa and Jaya Lakshmana, sitting on her mother's lap.

She had suddenly recognised the man on the big seat in front of her and had stood up amid a sea of adults to point excitedly.

'Oh! Prabhupada!' her little voice interrupted his lecture and caused heads to turn.

'Yes,' he responded gravely, pausing the lecture to confirm that indeed it was he. Then he went on to speak.

> The ultimate knowledge is Krishna. If you understand Krishna you understand everything, because Krishna is the source of everything. Believe in the words of Krishna, then you have studied thoroughly. It does not require much education – simply you believe. In human life we can understand what is God, but if we do not take advantage of this chance then we are lowest of mankind. Take seriously the conclusion of the scripture, and your life will be successful.[1]

Mukunda brought Colin Cross, religious correspondent for *The Observer*, to interview Prabhupada. The young man sat hunched on the floor with his notebook, while his photographer moved about the room to capture his subject from different angles. Prabhupada was surprised to hear that Cross knew little of the Krishna movement.

'Your paper is *Observer*,' Prabhupada teased. 'Why you did not observe us for the last seven years?'

Mr Cross was keen to learn, though, and engaged Prabhupada with a series of practical and revealing questions. 'In England, the Christian Church in recent years has been losing support. Could your teaching provide a substitute for traditional Christian teaching?'

'Yes, this is science. Religion without scientific idea is sentiment. It has no value.'

'What impelled you, at a late stage in your life, to come to the West to teach?'

'I must be prepared to teach – teaching is not so easy thing. I was ordered to teach at the age of twenty-five years, but I was finding out the opportunity how to take up the work. It took me so many years. At seventy I came out for teaching.'

'Why particularly in the West?'

'Because my Guru Maharaj ordered that, "You go and teach this gospel in the Western world." '

'And are you surprised at the great success you've had?'

'That is my Guru Maharaj's blessing. He ordered me and I tried my best. When I see so many boys under such shelter, living peacefully in a nice house, getting good prasadam, having good knowledge in the books, reforming their character, getting good home, that is my success. Otherwise they were loitering – no hope, no character, no peace of mind. I have given so many boys a life – that is my success.'

Before long the interview came to an end.

'Well, I am very honoured to have met you. I have read some of your work and I intend to read more. Thank you very much.'

With these words Colin Cross 'backed from his presence', as he put it in that Sunday's edition of *The Observer*, which included an intimate portrait of Prabhupada across four columns at the top of page three. He summed up his impressions:

> It was an unnerving experience to interview His Divine Grace A.C. Bhaktivedanta Swami Prabhupada, founder ten years ago of the rapidly growing Hare Krishna movement. 'It is a great honour you are being paid,' I was told. 'There are many of His Divine Grace's own devotees who have never met him in person.' We – a group of about a dozen monks and laymen – ascended the stairs barefoot. Swami Prabhupada sat cross-legged on a low cushioned throne. He gestured us to sit down and asked if I would like a chair. We listened intently – every word spoken by the Swami is revered – and a tape recorder whirred. He declared himself thirty-third in an unbroken succession of teachers stemming back to Krishna himself. 'I was ordered to teach this gospel,' he said. 'I have tried my best and my success is that I have given so many boys a life.' Then we backed from his presence.[2]

One of those who was in the room that afternoon was Alun Thomas, deputy headmaster of a large rural school in Leicestershire. He had come to visit his daughter Jane, whom he had not seen since she left home to go to India a year ago.

Jane Thomas discovered mysticism while studying English at

university in Colchester. She had once seen devotees singing in London and been struck by the contrast between their carefree appearance and the anxious faces of those around. She decided to become a vegetarian and delve into Eastern philosophy.

In 1973 she met a young Krishna monk in Colchester who sold her a record. The title was simply *India*. On the cover was a picture of Hare Krishna devotees singing and dancing in Bengal. She listened to it whenever she was alone, and felt in touch with something mystical and profound. The following year she bought a *Krishna* book from another monk in Nottingham city centre and was fascinated by its stories of an enchanting blue cowherd boy.

As soon as she got her degree in 1975 she began her spiritual quest. Inspired by the many books she had read, she wanted to travel overland to India in search of a teacher. On her way south she met devotees again, singing their way through the early morning mist among sleeping revellers at Knebworth open-air festival. They gave her prasadam and a ride back to the Manor, where she danced with them and stayed the night. From there she crossed by ferry to France, where she spent the rest of the summer fasting, reading, and chanting. When she reached Rome she went to the temple and again stayed with devotees. There she decided to give her life to Krishna. Eventually she made it to India where, at the newly-opened Krishna-Balaram temple in Vrindavana, she met Prabhupada and he named her Jagannatheshvari.

She had just returned to England as one of a small group of fund-raisers who sold books and collected donations to support the Vrindavan temple. Her father had come to see her. While waiting for her to return from her day on the street, he was invited up to Prabhupada's room along with the two men from *The Observer*. There he found a man of masterful demeanour, sitting behind a low table giving instructions to his assistant. He was introduced, and listened respectfully as the interview proceeded, occasionally responding to a query from Prabhupada.

After the interview was over and the reporters had left, Prabhupada spoke to Mr Thomas. 'Your daughter is very fortunate,' he said, and gave him his blessings and some prasadam.

The following day the book distributors were called into Prabhupada's room – about twenty men and women. Jagannatheshvari was there, as was Kripamoya. Given the opportunity to sit in the company of their spiritual master, they drank it in. They asked what should they say to people on the street, and he repeated the same formula he had given before: 'My dear sir, you are so intelligent, so fortunate and wealthy. Now please take this book.' He allowed his glance to rest on each of them as he looked round the room, letting them feel personally his appreciation for what they were doing for him.

In the evening many devotees came in to see him, filling up the room. Jagat Bandhu was there, visiting the temple, for he no longer lived in the ashram. He had worked hard since 1972 selling Prabhupada's books, travelling in vans all over the country, but he had found it difficult being the only black devotee, in spartan conditions, and had retreated home to his mother for a while. Now he saw Prabhupada looking so strong and determined, like a spiritual warrior. When he got home he wrote him a letter, telling him of his unhappiness. He didn't intend to send it, but his mother found it and put it in the post. A few months later he got a reply. 'You are a very intelligent boy,' Prabhupada wrote, and invited him to come and meet him in India – an invitation Jagat Bandhu never managed to fulfil.

Prabhupada wanted to encourage the devotees from Germany, who had gone through considerable turmoil since the government had seized their funds. Word was sent that they should come to London, and as soon as they arrived they came up to his room. He examined them.

'What is the most important thing?'

Hands went up. 'Book distribution, preaching.'

Then someone quoted a line of Bengali from the *Chaitanya-charitamrita*: *yare dekha tare kaha krishna upadesha* – which translated as, 'Tell whomever you meet about the teachings of Krishna.'[3]

'Yes, this is right. What does it mean, *krishna upadesha*? It means the instruction of Krishna. And what is that?' He waited, looking round the room. 'Surrender to Krishna. That is what you should preach.' He paused.

'I know you distribute a lot of books, but you should also read my books. That is very important, because otherwise you cannot maintain your Krishna consciousness.'[4]

Manjuali was deputed by her husband to take charge of the housekeeping for Prabhupada. It kept her busy eighteen or more hours a day, since even when he was unwell he was active for more than twenty hours a day. She loved every moment of it, seeing how relaxed and at home Prabhupada appeared to be at the Manor.

She organised the daily cleaning of his quarters, which was more difficult than usual because he was not going out and the cleaners had to work around him. She had a team of women helping her, including Srikama, whose daughter Rasalila was now nine months old, and some other young mothers. They took turns looking after each other's children.

One day Manjuali had just finished cleaning and came flying into Prabhupada's room with two fresh vases, ready to place them on his low, glass-topped desk. She was surprised to find him sitting bare-chested, chanting the *gayatri-mantra*. Embarrassed, she bowed to the floor, holding the vases up in the air. He looked straight at her, motionless in the midst of his meditation, and dropped his eyes to where the vases were supposed to be, allowing her to enter his space, deposit the vases, and leave.

The next day was Sunday 25th July, the day Prabhupada had promised to visit London. Charles Patel had found a four-storey building in Soho. It was a shabby public house with a restaurant upstairs, typical of the rundown premises that abounded in Soho in the seventies. The building was in poor repair and not officially on the market, but the freehold was available through a friend of Charles for the discount price of £108,000. Jayatirtha wanted to open a restaurant there with a reading room upstairs, and at the Mayapur festival that year Prabhupada had offered a loan to help buy the building. Charles Patel drove Prabhupada and his party into London in his Rolls Royce. They stopped outside the property in Soho Street.

'Where is Oxford Street?' asked Prabhupada.

'Just behind us.'

'Then buy it.'

Their finances had been improving since Jayatirtha's arrival, and they didn't even need the loan.

Nearby at 7 Bury Place were Radha-Londonishvara and their loyal devotees. When Prabhupada arrived he sat in the temple room, close to Radharani, and gave a short talk.

> I am very glad to see that you are taking care of the deities so nicely. Whenever I come I see, and it is very encouraging.
>
> The more beautifully you decorate Krishna, the more your heart will be beautifully decorated. And when your heart is beautifully decorated very soon you will see Krishna.
>
> God consciousness means you have to face difficulty and not be discouraged. Go on with your business and success is sure. Those who humbly, tolerantly, go on with Krishna consciousness with determination – for them, going back home back to Godhead is guaranteed.
>
> Now we have so many centres I am sorry that I cannot spend more than fifteen minutes in any one place. Therefore I am simply praying that in my absence Lord Krishna will give you the intelligence how to serve him nicely.'[5]

After breakfast and a rest in his room upstairs he continued on his way. By midmorning he reached Kshirodakshayi's house at 108 Ellesmere Road, Willesden. Guests showered him with petals as he entered the small front hall. Radha-Govinda's altar was on the main ground-floor room at the back of the house, facing the garden. He sat beside them on a low seat of red velvet cushions while his feet were being bathed, then addressed a crowd of Hindu guests. As they were settling themselves he reminded them of the nonsectarian nature of Krishna consciousness.

> Sri Chaitanya Mahaprabhu's mission makes no distinction of caste, creed,

> nation or religion. Anyone, even from low-grade family, can be elevated to the transcendental platform.

Once the hubbub had died down he delivered a powerful oration, aimed at an audience far beyond those walls – an urgent call to take up spiritual life:

> The modern world has taken the vow of sense gratification: to somehow or other satisfy the senses. They are going toward hell, because this unrestricted sense gratification creates a mentality that will be prominent at the time of death, and according to that mentality you will get your next birth....
>
> We should be very careful. In this life I may be born an Englishman or American, but if I do not take advantage of this human form of life and remain dull, as the trees or the animals, then in my next life I will have to accept a similar body to theirs. This is the law of nature. You can say you do not believe in the next life, but nature's law will drag you. You will have to accept another body according to your mentality at the time of death....
>
> We have to make our choice: whether we are going to hell or going back to Godhead. If you miss this opportunity you are committing suicide – knowingly drinking poison. As Narottama das Thakur has sung, "My Lord, Krishna, I have wasted my time without any good result. I got this human form of life. It was an opportunity to worship Radha-Krishna but I did not do it. I simply wasted my time in sense gratification. This means knowingly I have drunk poison." Anyone can drink poison if he likes – nobody can check. But it is a fact that if one does not become Krishna consciousness in this human form of life, he is drinking poison....
>
> Take advantage of this Krishna consciousness movement. Don't think these people are sentimentally chanting and dancing. This is the process for this age. But if you think yourself a scientist or philosopher, then we have eighty-four books of four hundred pages, for you to study and become convinced....
>
> Either you are Indian or Englishman or American or Hindu or Muslim, it doesn't matter. Krishna Consciousness means God consciousness – I may say Krishna or you may say some other name. Human life is meant for this purpose, to understand Krishna, or God. How you can know God? Krishna explains himself: 'I am like this. You can see me, know me.' Please take to Krishna consciousness and be happy.[6]

Upstairs he bathed and ate prasadam, cooked by his disciple Kirtima. Meanwhile, more than a hundred guests assembled downstairs, waiting to hear him speak. After talking privately with a few special guests he gave a second lecture, this time in Hindi, for the benefit of the many older Indians with little knowledge of English.

On his return to the Manor a crowd of guests awaited him, including many Hindus gathered from far and wide to witness the leader of the Hare Krishna movement on this Sunday afternoon. At the end of a tiring day, Prabhupada agreed to Jayatirtha's proposal that he address them on the lawn. His *vyasasana* was positioned on the terrace, and a crowd of several hundred guests sat patiently on the sloping lawns – including Lyn, and Greg's mother, grandmother, aunt, and uncle. While Jaya Lakshmana fanned him, Prabhupada spoke over a background of children's laughter, chattering birds, and the occasional drone of light aircraft passing overhead.

> Freedom can be achieved when we surrender to Krishna. We are not presenting something manufactured. There is no need. Perfection is already there in the *Bhagavad-gita*. Simply we have to accept it and apply it in life. Then our life will be successful.'
>
> … My request is, to all the Indians here in this foreign country, keep your culture – don't be bewildered. *Bhagavad-gita* is easy to understand. If you want to understand Krishna through science and philosophy, read this book. Otherwise, very easy method, come here, chant Hare Krishna, that's all. There is no difficulty.'[7]

Another day of preaching ended, with evening bringing a chill to the air, as Prabhupada slowly mounted the long stairway to his rooms. Such busy days had once been routine for him, even in times of ill health. But this was different: his ageing body was close to exhaustion. The next day he was unable to get up. From his bed he dictated a letter to Jayapataka in India: 'Because you are helping me, all this has become possible. How can I do anything alone? Sri Chaitanya Mahaprabhu says, "Alone I am helpless." So what to speak of me?'[8]

That afternoon, 26th July, Gurudas and Mukunda brought George Harrison to see Prabhupada. After Gurudas and Yamuna had gone to India in 1970 they had spent five years helping to build the Krishna-Balaram temple in Vrindavan. When the temple finally opened in 1975 Gurudas fell ill and was nursed back to health by Yamuna. Since then they had returned to America and gone their separate ways, she living with devotee friends in a rural community in Oregon and he, at Prabhupada's request, becoming a reluctant *sannyasi*.

Gurudas had travelled in America for a year teaching Krishna consciousness and then followed Prabhupada to England. While Gurudas stayed at the Manor, each morning he sat in the orchard under the shade of a tree and recounted stories of Prabhupada. His audience, young devotees who would never get the chance to meet Prabhupada themselves, crowded round to hear Gurudas's tales, which he told with humour and affection.

Mukunda and Gurudas had been to visit their old friend George, and now they brought him to see Prabhupada. After the previous day's exertions, Prabhupada was resting in bed. Propped up by pillows, he received George, who asked about his health.

'I have old man's disease – cough and cold. But still work is going on. I shall complete eighty years this month. So now, due to old age, it is becoming little difficult.'[9]

Prabhupada asked George about himself. 'Chanting is going on?'

'Yes.'

'Thank you. That is our life and soul.'

'I suppose some day the whole of the world will just be chanting in the countryside,' said George wistfully.

'That is not possible. But if some of the leading men take it seriously, then others will follow and people will be happy.'

'Will you ever stop travelling?'

'It is Krishna's desire. I don't want, personally, but if Krishna wants, that is everything. We have got 102 centres in different parts of the world.'

'Still six more to go.'

Prabhupada laughed. He had always said he would open 108 centres.

A richly prepared meal was brought in, served on silver dishes. Though Prabhupada apologised and ate nothing, he insisted that George have seconds and thirds. When George could eat no more he and Jayatirtha both wanted Prabhupada to rest.

'I am taking rest now these twenty-four hours. I have no other business than to take rest.' Everyone laughed, knowing that nothing could be further from the truth.

'Always resting at the lotus feet of Sri Krishna,' said Jayatirtha.

'That is real rest,' Prabhupada observed, and chanted in Sanskrit the prayer of King Kulashekhara. 'O Krishna,' he translated, 'let the swan of my mind be entangled with the stem of your lotus feet. That is the swan's sport – to be entangled deep with the lotus stem. For at the time of death, when the body will be in disorder, I shall not be able to chant Hare Krishna. Now, while I am in good health, let me finish this business.

'At the time of death, if one remembers Krishna, then his life is successful. This practice means that whatever we do all through life, this remembrance will come at the time of death. The mother of one of my students was attached to her boy and heard several times from him "Krishna". At the time of her death she asked her son, "Is your Krishna here?" and died. Very fortunate. On account of her son she got salvation.'

'When my mother died in 1970,' George told Prabhupada, 'I just chanted Hare Krishna.'

'Oh, very nice. Could she hear?'

'I don't know, I don't know. She was in a coma and it was the only thing I could think of that may be of value, you know.'

'If she has heard Hare Krishna, she will get the benefit. Either she chants or she hears somebody chanting – both the same thing,' assured Prabhupada. 'Let us practice in such a way that at the time of death we may remember. That is success.'

Prabhupada called for Manjuali and asked her to prepare a package of *samosas* for George to take home with him. Seeing George reminded him of their efforts to publish the *Krishna* book and how George had paid for the printing.

‘Are you reading the *Krishna* book?’ he enquired. ‘Are you reading it repeatedly?’

‘Well, you know, I read it every so often. I always take the *Gita* with me wherever I go. I mean, that’s the one I just keep all the time. But you know, I’ll just sometimes read a little of something, a little bit of something else. I’ve never been a great reader.’

‘But on account of your chanting Krishna’s name so many people are chanting.’

‘I don’t think it’s on my account.’

‘No, they say, “George chants Hare Krishna,” do they not?’ He turned to Mukunda, who assured them both that this was what people often said.

‘And you have got many thousands of followers.’

In front of Prabhupada, George felt bashful to acknowledge the influence he had in the world.

‘Anyway, you go on chanting. That will influence. There is a verse, I think in the *Chaitanya-charitamrita,* written by Rupa Goswami. He is wondering, “I do not know what sweetness there is in these two syllables, *krish-na.*” Find this verse.’ The final volumes of Prabhupada’s translation, including this verse, had just been published.

‘These books are so much work,’ commented George. ‘I don’t know how you did it all.’

‘While everyone else sleeps,’ said Gurudas. ‘Isn’t that right, Prabhupada?’

‘Yes, at night I don’t sleep. At most two hours, that’s all. I take little rest during the daytime. But actually I do not like to sleep. I think, when I go to sleep, now I am going to waste my time.’

George recalled how he had been inspired, following his recent visit to Vrindavan, to write a song based on a mantra – *Jaya Krishna, Jaya Sri Krishna, Jaya Radhe, Jaya Sri Radhe*. He recited some of the words.

‘He whose eyes have seen what our lives have been and who we really are, it is he, *Jaya* Sri Krishna. He whose sweetness flows to any one of those that cares to look his way, see his smile, *Jaya* Sri Radhe.’

‘So in your next record you can give this mantra,’ said Prabhupada.

While they talked a call had gone out to find a devotee who knew the *Chaitanya-charitamrita*. He had been found outside on the lawn. He looked up the verse Prabhupada wanted and hurried upstairs bringing with him the relevant volume. When he entered he saw Prabhupada in bed, with George sitting beside him on a low chair, surrounded by Mukunda, Gurudas, Pradyumna, Jayatirtha, and Vichitravirya. Pradyumna chanted the verse in its original melodious Sanskrit, full of rhythm, rhyme, and alliteration. Jayatirtha read out the translation.

> I do not know how much nectar the two syllables *krish-na* have produced. When the holy name of Krishna is chanted, it appears to dance within the mouth. We then desire many, many mouths. When that name enters the holes of the ears, we desire many millions of ears. And when the holy name dances in the courtyard of the heart, it conquers the mind and all the senses become inert.[10]

'Chant this mantra,' Prabhupada said to George, 'and your admirers will take it very nicely. That will be a great benefit to the mass of people. This word, *krishna,* if they hear, will be sufficient.'

Manjuali arrived with the *samosas* packed with chutney and sweets from the deities. George left with the prasadam and with Prabhupada's blessings ringing in his ears, '*Jaya*! Long live.'

Prabhupada decided to cut short his planned European itinerary and go straight to the welcoming heat of India, where he hoped to regain his strength. That evening, however, Bhagavan arrived from France with samples of the new French editions of the *Srimad-Bhagavatam* and photos of the recently acquired chateau in the heart of France. There, deities of Krishna and Balaram were ready to be installed, and nearly two hundred devotees were hoping to see their guru. It didn't take long for Prabhupada to change his mind and agree to leave for France as soon as it could be arranged.

One more task remained. Mukunda had arranged for Prabhupada to be interviewed by Mike Robinson of the London Broadcasting Company.

On the last afternoon of Prabhupada's stay Mukunda showed in the radio presenter, who was eager to introduce his listeners to a genuine holy man with something challenging to say. The conversation that followed ranged wide and long.

'Can you tell me what you believe?' began Robinson.

'It is not a question of belief. It is a science. What is the difference between a man who is living and who is dead? The difference is that the spirit soul, the living force, is out of the body. Our movement begins when one understands that he is soul, or something other than this body.'

'Why did you leave it so late in life before you founded this movement?'

'I must be prepared – I must be bone fide to preach. Not that all of a sudden one becomes M.A. He must be qualified.'

'So what are you doing now? You've come to England for a brief stay?'

'Just to guide my disciples and to see how they are doing things.'

'I gather you travel a lot?'

'Yes. But now I am getting old. So it is little difficult for me. Still, I have to come and see.'

'And that is your mission in life?'

'Yes. I have established it and I want to see that it is not spoiled.'

'How does the philosophy of Hare Krishna affect the way people live?'

'They are suffering for want of this knowledge. Supposing you misunderstand that you are coat and shirt, and you sew and wash the coat and shirt. Will you be happy?'

'No, I won't.'

'So similarly, they are simply washing the coat and shirt. They have no information. They will say, "I am Englishman, I am this coat." You have this body, but what are you? Nobody is thinking over this. The whole civilisation is going on misunderstanding.'

'Apart from giving spiritual enlightenment, are you concerned for people's physical well-being? Would you help the sick?'

'If you have a car to drive, naturally you take care of the car also. But not that you identify yourself, "I am this car." They are doing that. They are taking too much care of the car, forgetting that they are different from the car. They cannot eat the petrol and be satisfied.'

'What do you believe to be the meaning of life? Why do we exist in the first place?'

'The meaning of life is to enjoy. Everyone is struggling for existence. What is the aim? Enjoyment of life. But at the present moment our life is not enjoyment. It is suffering. Do you admit or not?'

'Yes, I would agree with that.'

'Then the question should be, "I want to enjoy – why am I suffering?" That is spiritual knowledge.'

They went on for over an hour before the interview was brought to a close.

'Finally, could I ask, do you ever have any doubts?' The question surprised Prabhupada.

'If I have doubts, how am I preaching? That means I am cheating. Do you think a man with doubt can produce, in doubtful condition, so many books?'

'So you never doubt any of this, anything at all?'

'We are sure.'

'You are sure this is the truth?'

'Yes.'

'Thank you for talking to me. It's been a great pleasure.'

'Hare Krishna. Give him prasadam.'

When the interview was over, Prabhupada was deeply satisfied. He asked for a transcript of the discussion to be reproduced in *Back to Godhead* magazine, and for weeks afterwards devotees were talking about the things he had said.

The following morning, Wednesday 28th July 1976, it was time to go. After seeing Radha-Gokulananda, Prabhupada turned in the hallway to Jayatirtha. All he had seen during his stay persuaded him that his movement in Britain was now in good hands. He gave his disciple a magnanimous hug and, amid a tearful kirtan, left for the airport.

CHAPTER 23

Saying Goodbye

More than a year had passed when, in late August 1977, Vichitravirya took a call from India. The line crackled, then cut out. All he managed to hear was 'Prabhupada's coming.'

So Raghubhir booked a line to Vrindavan. He told the operator it was an emergency: someone was dying. She called back a few minutes later with a connection straight through, and he gathered a little more information before the line went dead again. He got through a second time, then a third, and gradually he and the others pieced together the message: Prabhupada was flying to the West and would be arriving at Heathrow the very next day, 28th August 1977.

Ever since he had returned to India the previous year Prabhupada's health had been in steady decline. He gave his last public talk at the Mayapur festival in March – the *Bhagavatam* class on the third morning of the festival before four hundred disciples. Since then he no longer had the strength to speak for any length of time. He had not left India but had moved to different places in the hope of recovering: to Orissa where he encouraged the founding of a temple in Bhubaneswar; to Allahabad to bathe one last time at the confluence during the Kumbha Mela, where three million Hindus bathed in the Ganges on the same day; to Bombay to occupy his rooms, even though they were still under construction; to Rishikesh, where he lodged in a house overlooking the Ganga stream; then finally, when all else failed, he retreated to Vrindavan and prepared to leave this world.

'Now I have come back to my home,' he wrote. 'If anything should go wrong, at least I will be here in Vrindavan.'[1]

There he was cared for by a team of half a dozen devotees headed by Tamal Krishna Goswami. Prabhupada called for Abhirama[2] to be his general secretary, assisted by his wife Shrutirupa.

By the end of July he had lost the energy to work on his books. He felt that without his translating he was simply dying slowly. His disciples all over the world were praying for him. Then, amazingly, he began to talk of going to the West.

'What is the use of living like this? My disciples will be very enlivened if I come, even at the risk of my life,' he told Abhirama.

After much discussion it was decided to bring Prabhupada to London. From there he could go on to America. The party would include Tamal Krishna, Abhirama and Shrutirupa, the barefoot Pradyumna laden with his books, his wife Arundhati with their small son Aniruddha, and Upendra, Prabhupada's original servant from San Francisco. A bed was prepared in the back seat of the car, and Prabhupada was driven to the airport. Once in the air he spent most of the journey lying across his disciples' seats. In Rome the Air India flight was held on the tarmac for three hours, but he waited patiently.

'I am just thinking of that innocent smiling boy in London,' he murmured, meaning his Krishna, Londonishvara, who had come to him so miraculously.

The devotees at the airport in England were shocked when he emerged in a wheelchair. There seemed nothing left of him. He still glowed, but his frail state appeared beyond recovery. They had brought basketfuls of garlands, which they distributed to every member of his retinue. His cheeks were sunken, his hands swollen, his eyes shaded by dark glasses. They wondered that he would travel to see them in such a condition.

Prabhupada's car navigated the busy roads from the airport with Janananda at the wheel. He drove with meticulous care, trying his best not to betray his distress at seeing how ill his guru was. Prabhupada asked him how many cows they now had at the Manor. Though Janananda knew all about how many books were going out and how many new devotees coming in, he had no idea about the cows. Yet Prabhupada wanted to know not only how many there were but how much milk they gave and who was looking after them. This was a theme he would return to in his closing days: the need to be self-sufficient and to live off the land.

At the Manor he was carried through the crowded reception room full of chanting devotees from Britain, Ireland, France, Holland, and Germany, and brought before Radha-Gokulananda. He was surrounded by a sea of love and at once felt at home.

The palanquin on which he was carried was itself a work of love. The chair was from Akhandadhi's desk – the only one that had arms – to which Mohan had fixed two long wooden poles with handles carved at either end and a padded foot-rest to prevent Prabhupada sliding forward. Sarvamangala, Janaki, and Srikama covered it with cloth, and decorated it each day with flowers. While he was carried up the stairs, precariously manoeuvred by four strong men, he recognised one of them.

'Kulashekara?'

His whisper was heard by those beside him and echoed forwards. Kulashekara turned and smiled in response to Prabhupada's happiness to see his first English disciple.

Settled in his room behind his low table, Prabhupada was engulfed by a wave of adoring men, women, and children. A soft kirtan went on as he was offered a plate of fruit. He took a small portion, and the rest was distributed round the room. The kirtan came to an end. When he spoke, his voice was barely audible.

'Is everyone alright? Are there any complaints?'

Yes, Prabhupada, came the answer from all sides. We are all very happy. No, we have no complaints. Everything is going very well.

And it was true, for since Jayatirtha's arrival the previous year, the *yatra* had flourished in every way.

Then he tried to cough – a sort of choking sound racked his frail form and sent a shiver round the room as they all saw how very ill he was. Yet he had come all this way for them.

Here in England, he told Tamal Krishna, things had improved in all respects. In India he had encountered so much resistance from the government. Instead of helping him they had blocked visas for his disciples, and in Bengal they were hindering the development of Mayapur.

'I have given my best energy there, but they do not appreciate. I was so much suppressed that sometimes I would cry.' As he remembered, he wept. 'I have no desire to return. I have sufficient preaching field here. When I sit in the temple, Radha-Gokulananda are so beautiful and there are such nice devotees chanting. They have beautiful features, nicely dressed. It is Vaikuntha. Here I have no anxiety. You are all taking so much nice care of me.'

The weather was warm, and his appetite was returning. He talked of becoming a UK citizen and basing himself at the Manor. 'Either they make me a Commonwealth citizen here or I get my permanent residency in the United States. I shall be glad to die among the devotees, seeing Gokulananda.'

A hush descended on the building: doors were fitted with foam pads so they closed silently; metal dinner plates were replaced with paper ones; cars were restricted from coming near the main building; kirtans were kept to a low volume; and during the day the building emptied out as most devotees went to sell books. They offered their efforts as a continual prayer for Prabhupada's recovery: 'My dear Lord Krishna, if you so desire, please cure Srila Prabhupada.' A sign with this prayer hung above his seat in the temple room and was their constant meditation.

Going down to see the deities and be surrounded by his devotees was the focal point of Prabhupada's day. Amita was appointed as bearer, along with Adikarta. They practised for hours, using a sack of flour to simulate Prabhupada's weight. Up and down they went, rehearsing until they could navigate safely and without jolting, keeping the seat level. What made it tricky was that Amita, who went first, refused to turn his back on Prabhupada; he walked backwards. They mastered it, and each day Prabhupada had an event-free ride down and back up the stairs, his seat freshly decked with flowers, accompanied by his loving devotees.

Mothers with children waited outside his room as he came out. Nabhasvati, over from Amsterdam, was there with her two-year-old son. Prabhupada recognised her straight away and greeted her with joined hands, then patted her son's head. It was hard for her to see him so ill: she thought surely he must get better because she still had so much more to learn from him. At the top of the stairs he had his bearers wait while Ashtasakhi's small son Baladeva came and grasped his two fingers, then holding hands they went down the stairs together. Later, he told her she must never change his name – it was a good name.

He was carried up to the altar, where he looked for a long time at Radha-Gokulananda, hands joined in prayer. While he looked at them all the devotees had their eyes only on him, feeling his prayers and sensing his connection with Krishna. Then he was taken to the dais at the back, his seat positioned in front of the *vysasasana,* and there he listened to their kirtan.

In the beginning of his visit they had offered *guru-puja* – two hundred devotees leaping, arms extended, in unrestrained adoration of their spiritual master. Suddenly tears had started from his eyes, streaming down and dripping from his chin. He had gripped the arms of his chair and tried to stand. After that they abandoned *guru-puja* – the emotions were too strong for him to take – and opted for a mellow Hare Krishna kirtan while they sat on the floor.

On the first day he had tried to speak to them, telling them how merciful his guru had been to him, but his voice choked. He remained still, eyes closed, while everyone waited in breathless silence. A minute passed, then Tamal Krishna told them to chant. They put their hands in their bead bags and softly murmured the *maha-mantra*. Finally he opened his eyes and said one word, 'Kirtan.' The tears were rolling down his face as fast as his servant could wipe them away.

After that they just went straight to chanting, sitting down and taking it in turns leading. Bhagavan arrived from France. He picked up the drum and led a powerful kirtan. The exchange of love intensified. At one point Prabhupada slightly raised the palm of one hand. That was all the encouragement they needed. Suddenly they were off the floor, crying and jumping, dancing in a circle in front of him, running backwards and forwards toward him: they felt as if they would leap through the ceiling. What added to the intensity, if they were honest with themselves, was the knowledge that they probably wouldn't see him again.

He sat among his disciples, motionless and silent. Not a word passed his lips. Only his eyes were bright, though shaded behind sunglasses. The glasses, a gift from Shrutirupa, responded to light, so that indoors their tint faded and allowed his eyes to see and be seen.

The spirit that had propelled his voice for so long now revealed itself through those eyes, which glistened with tears. It was as if he no longer had the strength to check his feelings, and the merest mention of a fondly remembered name or the sight of a dear disciple was enough to bring forth his tears.

His lack of speech made his gaze all the more expressive. He looked at his disciples' faces and they looked at him. They couldn't take their eyes off him, like the *gopis* who regretted having eyelids that blinked when they looked at Krishna. Nikunjavasini, visiting from Amsterdam, sat with her little daughter. Her vision of Prabhupada was hindered when her child got up to dance, so she forced her back down into her lap, only to see Prabhupada looking directly at her, his glance telling her, 'Don't do that. Let the child dance.' She took that as a direction for life.

Anyone whose eyes met his felt touched to the core, convinced he was seeing their hearts and responding to their unspoken desires. Jaya Radhe, who had sewn Krishna's outfit, pleaded, 'Tell me if you like it.' He looked straight at her and she got her answer. Another devotee, seeing Prabhupada for the first time, heard his voice when their eyes met, asking, 'Are you a devotee?' 'Yes, I am a devotee, and I offer you my life.' Immediately Prabhupada smiled at him, bringing such emotion that he had to look down and wipe the sudden tears from his eyes. He missed receiving formal initiation from Prabhupada, but was later given the name Jayatirthacaran.

Krishnavesha, normally so unsentimental, travelled in from the London temple whenever she could. She brought offerings – one day a garland made from flowers collected in the park, still wet with dew, another day *burfi* she had made, prematurely turned to toffee. She was inexpert, but she wanted to show the sudden attachment she felt for him – just when he was leaving her.

Even Vishnu Sharma, normally so reserved, couldn't help crying when he saw Prabhupada, as if he were losing his own father.

Afterwards they waited at the bottom of the stairs as he was carried up by Amita and Adikarta – so carefully. When the bearers reached the half-landing they turned the palanquin so he could face the devotees and acknowledge them, taking their leave with folded hands. Again their chanting reached a crescendo. They felt closer to him than ever because he was so completely in their hands.

They had never known him like this, without the sound of his voice constantly calling them to ever more faith in Krishna and ever more service. He had always been the one who was pushing his disciples. Now all that was changed.

Manjuali, who as the presiding mother of the community was old for her years, found it heartbreaking to see his fragile state. When she brought him grape juice, blended and strained, he was childlike. The lion who had inspired awe had become a lamb, and she wanted to cuddle him.

Most of the time when he was in his room he sat absolutely still with his eyes closed in meditation. But the day Bhagavan arrived and presented him with new translations of his books in Italian, French, and Dutch, Prabhupada took Bhagavan's head in both hands and cried, 'This is my life.'

Another favoured devotee came – Ghanashyama – who was placing Prabhupada's books in academic libraries all over Europe, including behind the Iron Curtain. He had been sacrificing everything for Prabhupada, who drew him close and stroked his head and shoulders for a long time.

'My Guru Maharaj pushed me. Now I am pushing you and you are pushing others. Just like a train.'

News came that his entry to America had been cleared and that the immigration officials had been open and welcoming.

'America has been so good to me,' he whispered tearfully. 'They gave me men, money, everything. I cannot forget them, I want to make them happy, and through them the whole world.'

A large group of devotees came over from Germany. Their commitment to distributing his books was unrivalled, and he called for them to be shown into his bedroom so he could thank them personally. They entered, falling flat on the floor one by one.

'First understand that you are eternal spirit, and then surrender to Krishna,' he told them. They left his room thrilled by his words and the attention he had shown them.

Jayatirtha, who had been carrying out responsibilities in South Africa, arrived and came straight in to see him.

'Your name is Jayatirtha,' said Prabhupada. '*Tirtha* means shelter, and I have come to take shelter of you.' A few days later Jayatirtha had to return to South Africa, and there was an emotional parting.

'Since last time I was here there is so much improvement,' he murmured and rubbed his disciple's head. They were both crying. 'Anyway, be happy.'

Prabhupada was so weak now that he couldn't move without assistance. If he wanted to get up he wrapped his arms round a disciple's neck and was carried like a child. Despite his frailty he said he felt no pain. There were only feelings of ecstasy accompanied by copious tears. The slightest thing – hearing Krishna's name, seeing a picture of Krishna, meeting a devotee – could prompt streams of tears.

Out on the streets his disciples were performing heroic deeds to sell his books. When Tamal Krishna read out their results in his room each day he could not contain his emotions. One day he told Pradyumna he had had a dream in which he saw the Vishnudutas, agents of Vishnu, coming to take him to the spiritual world – and they were fair-skinned and blue-eyed, like his Western disciples.

On Janmashtami, 6th September, Prabhupada visited the Bury Place temple in Bloomsbury for the last time. The German devotees went with him, his white Rolls Royce followed by a string of white Volkswagen buses jumping the lights to keep up with him all the way down Finchley Road.

The London devotees had stayed at their posts serving Radha-Londonishvara and receiving a daily stream of guests. Prabhupada had sent out an important letter at the beginning of the year:

> *To all ISKCON temple presidents*
>
> Now you must arrange in every temple sufficient stock of prasadam for distribution. Whenever a guest comes he must get prasadam – puris and *subji, halava* and *pakoras*. The temple is managed by Radharani, so why should there be any want? If we believe that Krishna is providing and maintaining everyone, then why should we be misers? Let the whole world come, we can feed them.[3]

Inspired by this letter Rohininandan had established a lunch programme at Bury Place. Guests were invited by the devotees they met on the street, and every day at lunchtime the temple was packed. Sakshi Gopala had created a window display of Prabhupada's books, the deities were well looked after, and a full schedule of classes was offered. The temple was flourishing.

Prabhupada was carried into the temple room to the sound of conches and kirtan as the curtains were pulled back to reveal Radha-Londonishvara. The *pujaris* had spent hours preparing a special display for Prabhupada. Radha and Krishna were dressed in a multi-coloured gypsy outfit, Krishna in a turban, sewn by Lilashakti, Jalasthita, and Krishnavesha, wreathed with greenery and flowers that transformed the altar into a forest bower.

The devotee performing arati turned to offer incense to Prabhupada and was astonished by the scene. Prabhupada sat right at the foot of the altar, gazing fixedly at Krishna, his eyes streaming tears. As Prabhupada accepted the incense he looked up at the devotee, whose heart melted when he saw Prabhupada's soft smile. Around him, tier upon tier, were the temple devotees and the massed members of the German *yatra;* at his side stood his faithful servants wiping away his tears. It seemed that the whole spiritual world was assembled for Prabhupada to say farewell to his beloved Radha and Krishna, whom he had brought here by his devotion eight years earlier. Now he was back one last time, the tide of his love carrying him to the Manor and finally as far as the feet of Radha-Londonishvara.

On the way out his glance lingered on Sakshi Gopala's book display. Then he was in the car. As it pulled away, Jñana, once a wintry Buddhist, ran after him unable to stifle his tears.

One more visit remained. Girigovardhan drove the Rolls a few blocks west to Soho Street, where the previous year Prabhupada had approved the purchase of a small building, now temporarily being used for devotee accommodations and book storage. In Bloomsbury, time was finally running out for the temple, under notice from Camden Council, and there was a proposal to move Radha-Londonishvara to this new building. Cradled in the back of the car, Prabhupada looked up at the façade. On the first floor a row of windows marked a decent-sized room – intended as the deities' new home. He nodded his approval.

Throughout the trip he had remained silent. Now, from the back of the car, as it sped home to the Manor, Girigovardhan heard him say only one word: 'Bloomsbury.'

The next day was his birthday. Instead of the customary chanting during his morning visit to the temple, they all listened to an address by Tamal Krishna Goswami, who told at length the story of Prabhupada's mission to the West. While he spoke, Prabhupada occasionally interjected a word or two, allowing his voice to be heard in public for the first time since his arrival.

'1922,' Prabhupada recalled, when Tamal Krishna described his first meeting with his guru, Srila Bhaktsiddhanta, when he surrendered himself as his disciple.

Tamal Krishna referred to the instructions Prabhupada had received.

'If you ever get money, print books,' Prabhupada added, referring to the advice his guru gave him in 1935.

Tamal told how in New York in 1966 he had preached, even when no one came to hear.

'I preached to the walls,' he said.

In Los Angeles in 1968 the devotees had no temple, so they met with Prabhupada wherever they could.

'Even in a garage,' he commented.

His head tilted as he listened, and tears rolled down his cheeks. Sometimes he smiled. As Tamal Krishna's account neared the present day, Prabhupada began to have a look of determination, and that old energy gleamed in his eyes. He sat tall, holding the sides of his chair – at any moment he might start to preach.

A cake was brought in with eighty-one candles. On it was inscribed a prayer to Lord Krishna to cure Srila Prabhupada. He counted the candles and called for an extra one, because according to Indian calculation his age was eighty-two.

Afterwards, initiations were presided over by Harikesh Swami, and the last of Prabhupada's disciples in England took their vows, bringing their number to 299 in all.

For the past ten days Prabhupada had appeared stable, giving grounds for a slight optimism. But his health remained precarious. 'No matter what happens,' he had told Abhirama during one massage, 'my death must be glorious – no tubes or pipes.'

The day after his birthday he suffered a crisis when he was unable to pass water. He was rapidly fading and talking of heading straight back to India when he had a seizure and briefly lost consciousness. His disciples feared he would not survive the plane journey, so they rushed him to hospital for a minor operation to relieve the blockage. An ambulance came to take him to Watford Peace Memorial Hospital, where he was treated by Dr McIrving. Vichitravirya, Abhirama, and Upendra waited in fearful suspense while Tamal Krishna accompanied him into the operating theatre. Pradyumna and Akhandadhi arrived an hour later full of apprehension and bringing Prabhupada's japa beads. But they found everyone filled with momentary euphoria: the operation had been a success and Prabhupada was comfortable.

After that America seemed an impossibility. Prabhupada called for kirtan in his room and again spoke of returning to India, first to see the opening of the Bombay temple and then to go home to Vrindavan. The next night around eleven, while Tamal sat up with him, he expressed his wish.

'I want to go back.'

'But Prabhupada, you should go on to New York, where you began this.' Prabhupada looked at him, crying.

'If you do one thing for me, please take me back.' When Tamal heard that he knew there could be no more doubts. Vichitravirya stayed up all night, phoning round their Hindu friends, and by morning he had booked four first-class seats to Bombay on British Airways.

'There is nothing to lament,' Prabhupada told them. 'If I expire, my age is ripe. Everything is going on. You all maintain.'

On the last morning, 13th September, before he left his room Ashtasakhi was there with a few others.

'When I leave I want everything kept exactly as it is.' He pointed around the room, even at the pictures on his table. 'Don't move a thing.'

In front of Radha-Gokulananda he prayed for a long time with his head bowed and his hands clasped together. Amid general distress he was carried through the temple side door to the white Rolls, parked in the circle. Harry Edwards, the village policeman known to Prabhupada since 1973, came through the crowd to say goodbye.

'Thank you very much,' managed Prabhupada, and smiled at him weakly.

Mohan blinked through his thick spectacles. A magnolia tree grew beside the garden door. He saw a single large blossom extending from a lower branch. Carefully he plucked it and ran forward. Prabhupada opened his hand and took it as he went. Mohan felt this was the perfect moment of his life.

At Heathrow his car was parked outside the terminal as delays were announced. In the back he sat majestically, illuminated by a ray of sunlight, relaxing with one leg up. He might have been behind his desk, his head tilted, his hand rubbing his knee. As devotees crowded round heedless of decorum, he appeared relaxed and at peace, ready to accept whatever Krishna wanted.

Finally the call came and he was wheeled toward the departure gate. He passed a devotee lying full length on the ground. It was Sakshi Gopala. 'Please don't go, please don't go,' Sakshi was praying. He didn't see Prabhupada's wheelchair halt and turn, and the look of care Prabhupada gave him.

Srikama ran up behind him, thinking she would never see him again. She gave her daughter Rasalila a yellow rose, Prabhupada's favourite.

'Give this to Srila Prabhupada,' she said, and the little girl ran up and held the flower out to him.

His eyes lit up like the sunshine, and he beamed at her. Then they wheeled him through the gates and he was gone.

Epilogue

LONDON, 10TH SEPTEMBER 1977

After returning from the Manor, where I saw Srila Prabhupada for the last time, I sat in my office staring through the back window at the dull brick walls of the adjoining Bloomsbury houses. I wondered what the future would hold now. How long would Prabhupada remain with us? Perhaps he would regain his strength, go to America, and live another ten years to teach us how to organise self-sufficient communities, as he had said he would.

Whatever came to pass, I did not want to ever forget the last few days. While they were fresh in my mind I decided to write to the devotees in Nairobi, where I had just been to paint the deities. In the temple there lived Tribhangananda and Shuchi, friends from England – they would want to know what they were missing. I got out some paper and a sheet of carbon, and wrote them a letter.

Prabhupada has been at the Manor a few weeks now. His presence is the most unexpected blessing. We thought he would never again travel out of India, and maybe not even live this long, but he has improved his health dramatically. When he arrived at Heathrow he appeared desperately weak and unbelievably thin. Daily at the Manor he has been regaining his strength.

Each morning he is carried down on a palanquin and sits out in front of Radha-Gokulananda for three or four minutes. He told Upendra that he prays to them for the advancement of all the devotees.

Then he is carried back and his chair is placed on a dais in front of the *vyasasana*. The devotees sit down around him and begin kirtan. He prefers us to chant Hare Krishna, so we don't sing *guru-puja* at this time. Sometimes he closes his eyes, and appears to forget or lose interest in his whereabouts. Sometimes he gazes at Radha-Gokulananda, sometimes he moves his beautiful head slowly from side to side, absorbed in some secret ecstasy, and sometimes tears flow from his eyes – when that happens Upendra wipes them away for him (he is very weak and even to move his arms is strenuous).

Then he may become more alert and look at the devotees, watching them with satisfaction and approval, filled with grave pleasure. Sometimes he smiles gently, and we all stand and dance in ecstasy, and he may even raise an arm with great effort. Then the kirtan becomes uncontrollable. After about half an hour he is returned upstairs, leaving everyone breathless and often emotionally overcome.

On his appearance day he sat for one hour while Tamal Krishna spoke his biography and glorified him. It was a memorable occasion which will surely remain in the minds of all those who were present. We have the entire German and Swiss *yatras* as well as numerous other devotees from Europe here. As Tamal went through the different periods of his life, Prabhupada became absorbed in the recitation, and frequently, large tears fell down his soft cheeks. Sometimes he made a brief comment – a date or a place – and benedicted us with the nectarean vibration of his honeylike voice for the first time since arriving in England. As Tamal Krishna neared the present day and began talking of his successes in India, Prabhupada appeared to be gaining strength. He began stirring in his chair and looked almost as if he was going to stand up.

Prabhupada's pattern of behaviour is different from previously. He has become almost continuously absorbed in thoughts of Krishna (visibly, I mean, whereas previously he was externally engaged in so many affairs) and manifests ecstasies. His personal attendants are often in anxiety in case he becomes overpowered by these ecstatic moods – Upendra spoke of torrents of tears. Prabhupada embraced Jayatirtha, and later Ghanashyama, with tears of affection.

I pray that I may be able to serve him forever and ever, and never cease serving him for a moment. He has shown us the way. Now we must simply follow and be his menial servants.

I signed the letter and addressed an airmail envelope. I took the carbon copy, folded it in half, and placed it for safekeeping inside the pages of my *Bhagavad-gita*.

Two months later, in Vrindavan, on 14th November 1977, His Divine Grace A C Bhaktivedanta Swami Prabhupada, surrounded by his disciples, passed from this world.

GOVARDHAN HILL, 5TH FEBRUARY 2008

That carbon copy is still in my *Gita* along with treasured photographs from the seventies. Those days seem far away now, but while writing this book I have felt back among them, anticipating Prabhupada's arrival, walking beside him in Russell Square or sitting with him in his room at Bury Place or the Manor.

I think that although all in this world must pass, and these events live now only as memories, still, they possess a reality beyond time and space. No one in history ever spoke and acted as Srila Prabhupada did to bring devotion for Krishna from the East to the West. His influence echoes across the years of my life, and I firmly believe his words will echo around the world for centuries to come, for those with the ears and hearts to hear, like ripples from a touchstone dropped into a still pond.

PRABHUPADA DISCIPLES INITIATED IN BRITAIN

NAME	INITIATION DATE	NAME	INITIATION DATE
Digvijaya das	69/07	Bhushakti devi dasi	70/08
Kulashekhara das	69/07	Purnananda das	70/10
Tirthapada das	69/07	Svati dd	70/10
Vishakha dd	69/07	Bala Gopala dd	71/01
Devadatta das	69/09	Pratejas das	71/03
Dhananjaya das	69/09	Ranchor das	71/03
Draupadi dd	69/09	Jayajagadisha das	71/04
Pritha dd	69/09	Sananda Kumara das	71/04
Radharamana das	69/09	Birasingha das	71/08
Chaturbhuja das	69/12	Charanaravinda das	71/08
Jaihari das	69/12	Damayanti dd	71/08
Karanodakshayi das	69/12	Devamaya devi dasi	71/08
Kirtima dd	69/12	Gunarnava das	71/08
Kshirodakshayi das	69/12	Jagaddeva das	71/08
Sandipani Muni das	69/12	Jijñasi dd	71/08
Ilavati devi dasi (Hamburg)	70/01	Kishor das	71/08
Jyotirmayi dd	70/01	Kunjamandana dd	71/08
Mondakini dd	70/01	Mahavishnu das	71/08
Aditi dd	70/06	Narendra das	71/08
Lilashakti dd	70/06	Shambhunatha das	71/08
Tribhuvanatha das	70/06	Subhaga das	71/08
Trilokanatha das	70/06	Sudurjaya das	71/08

Sukarma das	71/08
Svayambhur das	71/08
Vidyabhadu dd	71/08
Ksama dd (Amsterdam)	71/11
Ananta Shesa Naga das	71/?
Bhoumadeva das (Amsterdam)	71/?
Bhajahari das	72/02
Narahari das	72/02
Prabhavishnu das (Paris)	72/02
Sarvamangala dd	72/02
Smarahari das	72/02
Achintyarupa das	72/04
Ekanatha das	72/06
Bhaktipramoda das	72/07
Vrajendra Kumar das	72/07
Devadharma das	72/07
Dhirashanta das	72/07
Gangamayi dd	72/07
Harernamananda das (Paris)	72/07
Haribolananda das	72/07
Janakaraja das	72/07
Janananda das	72/07
Nabhasvati dd	72/07
Nisha dd	72/07
Nishkala das	72/07
Partha das	72/07
Shastra Chakshus das	72/07
Shyamasundari dd	72/07
Tirthanga das	72/07
Tirthasadhaka das	72/07
Tribhangananda das	72/07
Vichitravirya das	72/07
Vimuktasanga das	72/07
Vrindavana Viharini dd	72/07
Yashodamayi dd	72/07
Abhimanyu das	72/08
Ashtasakhi dd	72/08
Divyashakti dd	72/08
Girivaradhari das	72/08
Jagat Bandhu das	72/08
Kamalakanti dd	72/08
Manu das	72/08
Padmalochana das	72/08
Ratimanjari dd	72/08
Sakshi Gopala das	72/08
Sanatana das	72/08
Shatadruti dd	72/08
Sitanatha das	72/08
Srivatsa das	72/08
Yaduvendu das	72/08
Dayamayi dd	72/11
Ramadevi dd	72/11
Shuchi dd	72/11
Govindananda das	73/01
Kamadhuk dd	73/02
Mohan das	73/02
Rohininandan das	73/02
Haripriya dd	73/03
Ishvara das	73/03
Premarupa das	73/04
Archanananda das	73/05
Brahmajanani dd	73/05
Govardhan dd	73/05
Kapardini dd	73/05
Krishnapremanandi dd	73/05
Niraga Deva das	73/05
Parthasarathi das	73/05
Radhagiridhari das	73/05
Rajashekhara das	73/05
Sambhavi dd	73/05
Shramana das	73/05
Sukhaprada das	73/05
Tanumadhya das	73/05
Vishvadharini dd	73/05
Yashasvini dd	73/05
Rukmini Priya dd	73/07
Bhadrakrishna das	73/08
Bhaktilata dd	73/08
Nitya dd	73/08
Abhinanda das	73/09

Adishakti dd	73/09	Amekhala dd	74/06
Anakhadundubhi	73/09	Dharmagub das	74/06
Anandi dd	73/09	Jalasthita dd	74/06
Bhadracharu das	73/09	Mahakratu das	74/06
Bhajananandi das	73/09	Manihara das	74/06
Bhavani dd	73/09	Parardhi das	74/06
Chitraketu das	73/09	Rasamandala das	74/06
Hladini Shakti dd	73/09	Ratnanabha das	74/06
Ishvari dd	73/09	Ravilochana das	74/06
Jaya Lakshmana das	73/09	Aliptavani dd	74/07
Kamalangi dd	73/09	Balabhadra das	74/07
Komala-kara das	73/09	Dhenuvati dd	74/07
Kshamarupa das	73/09	Jñaneshvara das	74/07
Mahadeva das	73/09	Krishnanga dd	74/07
Mahajana das	73/09	Kulangana dd	74/07
Mahavidya das	73/09	Mahabhuja das	74/07
Pankajanghri das	73/09	Mahamana das	74/07
Parameshvara das	73/09	Pratapavana das	74/07
Raghubhir das	73/09	Radhasakhi das	74/07
Shailendriya dd	73/09	Ragashakta das	74/07
Siddheshvari dd	73/09	Raghudvaha das	74/07
Tejovati dd	73/09	Rajavidya dd	74/07
Vrishabha das	73/09	Rauhineya das	74/07
Trivarga	73/10	Svargavasini dd	74/07
Archa dd (Sweden)	73/?	Svetavarna das	74/07
Asita das	73/?	Triveni das	74/07
Barhishati das	73/?	Vrindavani dd	74/07
Gaurachand das	73/?	Aksunnashakti dd	74/12
Gunaraja dd	73/?	Janardana Prita dd	74/12
Harikrishnadas (Amsterdam)	73/?	Sarvasagara das	74/12
Janardradhi das	73/?	Advaita Acharya das	74/?
Muktananda das	73/?	Dhiranga das	74/?
Prabharupa das	73/?	Jagadbandhu das	74/?
Puridas das	73/?	Jñana das	74/?
Purnachandra dd	73/?	Krishnavesha dd	74/?
Ramya dd	73/?	Premananda das	74/?
Shaktimati dd	73/?	Raghava das	74/?
Varaha Murti das	73/?	Ratnaranjini dd	74/?
Sharadi dd	74/04	Sucharudeva das	74/?
Trinavarta-ghatana das	74/04	Chitta Vinodana das	75/01

Gokulananda das 75/01
Gopipriya dd 75/01
Kripamoya das 75/01
Lalita devi dd 75/01
Premaniketana das 75/01
Radhapriya dd 75/01
Rasa-rasika das 75/01
Rupamanohara das 75/01
Vamshivadana das 75/01
Yamuna Jivana das 75/01
Yashoda Dulala das 75/01
Brajendranandana das 75/02
Adikarta das 75/03
Anandamoya das 75/03
Anjana dd 75/03
Dhanvantari das 75/03
Gokularani dd 75/03
Halayudha das 75/03
Jagaddhatri dd 75/03
Karabhajana das 75/03
Mahashanta das 75/03
Radhakrishna das 75/03
Ruchira dd 75/03
Savitri dd 75/03
Tyagishvara das 75/03
Krodhaha das 75/04
Mahaksha das 75/04
Medhavi das 75/04
Amita das 75/08
Ilapati das 75/08
Kaliyaphani das 75/08
Nandapriya dd 75/08
Niralamba das 75/08
Paradhyeya das 75/08
Parajñana das 75/08
Paramapurusha das 75/08
Punyashloka das 75/08
Satyavak das 75/08
Ravi das 75/09
Adikurma das 75/11
Akhandadhi das 75/11
Dharanidhara das 75/11
Prithvipati das 75/11
Srikama dd 75/11
Yajñanga das 75/11
Lalita-priya dd 75/?
Naimisharanya das 76/03
Raseshvari dd 76/03
Atindra das 76/04
Atmatattva das 76/09
Atmatma das 76/09
Bhagavatabhakta das 76/09
Bhajanananda das 76/09
Gauranitai das 76/09
Girigovardhan das 76/09
Janaki dd 76/09
Lalagopala dd 76/09
Ramasharana das 76/09
Tulasipriya das 76/09
Gopala-sakhi dd 76/?
Punyatma das 76/?
Andhaka das 77/03
Ankottha das 77/03
Bhuvaneshvara das 77/03
Dama das 77/03
Indranuja das 77/03
Jaya dd 77/03
Keshidamana das 77/03
Lilamohini dd 77/03
Toshapita das 77/03
Vinoda das 77/03
Brajajana das 77/04
Govatsa Rakhala dd 77/04
Nabanita-chora das 77/04
Yashomati-stanya-payi dd 77/04
Gaurapurusha das 77/10
Rukmini Ramana das 77/10
Sanatani dd 77/10
Gopimata dd 77/?
Haridas Thakur das 77/?

Jami dd	77/?
Karnamrita das	77/?
Adiguru das	?
Dhiranayaka das	?
Ganga das	?
Gopati das	?
Krishnaparayani dd	?
Lokaguru das	?
Mahabala das	?
Nandapatni dd	?
Nityachanda das	?
Pundarika das	?
Shachinandana das	?
Shardhunya dd	?
Yaduratna das	?

(299 records; 99 women, 200 men)

NUMBERS INITIATED EACH YEAR

	TOTAL	CUMULATIVE
1969	15	15
1970	10	25
1971	25	50
1972	47	97
1973	65	162
1974	41	203
1975	47	250
1976	15	265
1977	21	286
date unknown	13	299

PRABHUPADA IN ENGLAND TIMELINE

1965

13th August	A C Bhaktivedanta Swami embarks on *Jaladuta,* Calcutta
17th September	Arrives at Boston Harbour
19th September	Disembarks at Brooklyn Pier, New York Harbour
20th September	Stays with the Agarwal family in Butler, Pennsylvania
18th October	Guest of Dr Mishra, 33 Riverside Drive, Manhattan
November	Moves to Dr Mishra's yoga studio at 501, 100 West 72nd Street, Manhattan

1966

15th February	Swami rents his own room at 307, 100 West 72nd Street, Manhattan
April	Moves to a loft at 94 Bowery, Lower East Side
May	Meets Mike and Jan
end of June	Establishes his first temple 26 Second Avenue
September	Initiates Janaki and Mukunda, who are married next day (25 devotees initiated during this period in New York)
November	Mukunda rents 518 Frederick Street in San Francisco

1967

16th January	Swamiji arrives in San Francisco
29th January	Appears at Mantra-Rock Dance, San Francisco
January	Initiates Malati and Shyamsundar
7th April	Initiates Yamuna and Gurudas (17 devotees initiated during this period in San Francisco)

9th April	Flies to New York
28th May	Admitted to Beth Israel Hospital in New York
8th June–5th July	Recuperates in Long Branch, New Jersey
6–20th July	Rests in beach house at Stinson Beach
24th July	First sets foot in England, en route to India
14th December	Arrives in San Francisco, back from India

1968

3rd June–30th Aug.	Stays in Montreal
10th–19th August	The London party stay in Montreal for rehearsals
25th–30th August	London party flies from New York to Amsterdam
3rd–5th September	Shyamsundar and Malati arrive in London and move to 80 Herne Hill
10th September	The first street kirtan (Trafalgar Square) and kirtan at the Hindu Centre, Grafton Terrace – all three families are now in London
1st November	They move to 22 Betterton Street, Covent Garden
16th December	Syamasundara has met George Harrison (who offers to buy '5-storey' building)
18th December	The Alchemical Wedding at Albert Hall

1969

4th January	First annual convocation, held at Betterton Street, is addressed by Prabhupada via a tape recording
16th January	Syamasundara visits Beatles on set of Let It Be at Twickenham Film Studios
29th January	First English devotees join: Colin Jury (Kulashekhara) and Richard Withey (Digvijaya)
17th February	First authorised street sankirtan, Hanover Square
20th March	John marries Yoko
14th April	Syamasundara & Malati have moved to 11 Balham Park Road – the others are elsewhere in South London
20th April	George gives guarantee to Camden Council for buying a mortuary
29th April	'New hope for getting a nice temple'
4th May	John Lennon purchases Tittenhurst
15th May	John is refused a US visa
1st June	During John and Yoko's Montreal Bed-In they speak with Hare Krishna devotees
5th June	They find 7 Bury Place
25th June	Lease signed for 7 Bury Place, guaranteed by Apple

27th June	Kirtan held at Oxford University
1st July	John and Yoko's car accident
7th July	'Hare Krishna Mantra' recorded at Abbey Road Studios
24th July	George plugs 'Hare Krishna Mantra' and Rathayatra on the Kenny Everett show
27th July	Rathayatra
28th July	Record 'Govindam' at Abbey Road
31st July	Prabhupada initiates by letter Kulashekhara, Digvijaya and Tirthapada, the first English initiates
11th August	John and Yoko move to Tittenhurst
24th August	'Cold Turkey'
27th August	Beatles last photo session
28th August	'Hare Krishna Mantra' launched by George at press conference in Sydenham
11th September	2.30 pm Prabhupada arrives at Heathrow Airport
16th September	International Society for Krishna Consciousness incorporated as a registered charity
16 September	Prabhupada appears on Late Night Line-Up
28th September	Radha Krishna Temple perform at the Marquee
6th, 15th, 20th Oct.	Conway Hall lectures (7.30 pm)
30th October	Lecture at Oxford Town Hall
3rd November	Move to Baker Street
3rd December	Radha-Krishna Temple perform at Queens College
14th December	Opening of London Temple
21st December	Prabhupada leaves

1970

14th January	George Harrison buys Friar Park, Henley-on-Thames
6th March	'Govindam' record released

1971

28th May	*Radha Krishna Temple* album released
2nd August	Prabhupada arrives from Los Angeles
12th August	Hampstead Town Hall programme
15th August	Initiation ceremony
17th August	St Pancras Town Hall programme
10th September	Prabhupada leaves for Mombasa

1972

6th July	Prabhupada arrives in London from Los Angeles via New York
13th July	Visited George Harrison at Henley
16th July	Rathayatra
20th–28th July	Paris and Amsterdam
29th–30th July	Edinburgh
1st August	London
3rd August	With George to Runneymede Farm
15th August	Prabhupada leaves for Los Angeles

1973

24th–31st May	Prabhupada visits Bhaktivedanta Manor
7th July	Prabhupada arrives at Bhaktivedanta Manor
8th July	Rathayatra
8th–14th August	Paris (installation 10 August)
21st August	Janmastami – Radha-Gokulananda installation
22nd August	Vyasa Puja
5th–10th Sept.	Stockholm
14th September	Prabhupada departs
23rd–25th Nov.	Prabhupada was refused entry to Nairobi and instead stays at Bhaktivedanta Manor

1974

24th–25th July	Prabhupada visits London

1975

7th–12th March	Prabhupada visits Bhaktivedanta Manor
16th April	Opening of Krishna-Balaram Mandir, Vrindavan
13th–14th August	Prabhupada overnight stopover at Bhaktivedanta Manor

1976

21st July	Prabhupada arrives at Bhaktivedanta Manor
25th July	Visit to Bury Place and Kshirodakshayi's house
28th July	Prabhupada departs for Paris on mid-morning flight

1977

28th Aug.–13th Sept.	Prabhupada's last visit to Bhaktivedanta Manor

BIBLIOGRAPHY

Goswami, Satsvarupa dasa. *Srila Prabhupada-lilamrita,* 2nd edition. Grödinge, Sweden: Bhaktivedanta Book Trust, 2002.

Goswami, Tamal Krishna. *Servant of the Servant.* Los Angeles, CA: Bhaktivedanta Book Trust, 1984.

———. *TKG's Diary.* Dallas, TX: Pundits Press, 1998.

Greene, Joshua M. *Here Comes the Sun: The Spiritual and Musical Journey of George Harrison.* Bantam Books, 2006.

Gurudas. *By His Example: The Wit and Wisdom of A C Bhaktivedanta Swami Prabhupada.* Badger, CA: Torchlight Publishing, 2004.

Hari Sauri Dasa. *A Transcendental Diary: Travels with His Divine Grace A C Bhaktivedanta Swami Prabhupada,* vol. 5. Alachua, FL: HS Books, Lotus Imprints, 1995.

Harrison, George. *I, Me, Mine.* London: W H Allen, 1982.

Hayagriva Dasa. *The Hare Krishna Explosion: The Birth of Krishna Consciousness in America, 1966–1969.* USA: Palace Press, 1985.

Maharaj, Ksirodak Shayee Vishnu. *Sweet Memories of Srila Prabhupada.* Mathura, India: Bhaktivedanta Swami Ashram Trust, 1997.

Mulaprakrti Devi Dasi. *Our Srila Prabhupada: A Friend to All.* Brij Books, 2004.

Siddhanta Das. *Memories: Anecdotes of a Modern-day Saint,* vols. 1 and 2. Culver City, CA: Monsoon Media, 2002–2003.

Srutakirti Dasa. *What is the Difficulty? Intimate Moments in the Personal Service of His Divine Grace A C Bhaktivedanta Swami Prabhupada.* Radlett, Herts: Dharma Publications, 2006.

Shukavak N. Dasa. *Hindu Encounter with Modernity: Kedarnath Datta Bhaktivinoda, Vaisnava Theologian.* Pioneertown, CA: Sri, 1999.

Vedavyasa Dasa. *Srila Prabhupada and His Disciples in Germany.* Alicante, Spain: Mandir Media Group, 1996.

NOTES

INTRODUCTION

1 Scottish Churches College was founded in 1830 as India's first missionary college. Since the 1930s it has been known as Scottish Church College.

2 The most widely read book of Sri Chaitanya's teachings is the poetic biography written by Krishnadas Kaviraj – to this day a classic of Bengali literature – *Sri Chaitanya-charitamrita.*

3 See *Hindu Encounter with Modernity,* chapter one, "19th Century Bengal".

4 *A Literary History of India* by R W Frazer, published by T Fisher Unwin, London 1898.

5 *My First Year in England,* by Tridandi Swami B H Bon, London 1934.

6 Recalled by Nayanananda dasa Babaji, as recorded in *Our Srila Prabhupada: A Friend To All.*

7 Devi Prasad Maskara remembrance, *ibid.*

8 Narayana Maharaj remembrance, *ibid.*

9 Remembrance of a *pujari* from Sri Advaita Acharya's house in Shantipura, West Bengal, *ibid.*

10 A complete list of disciples Prabhupada initiated in England can be found in the appendix.

CHAPTER 1: CHILDREN OF THE FIFTIES

1 The story of Prabhupada's first year in America is told in vivid detail by Satsvarupa dasa Goswami in the *Srila Prabhupada-lilamrita.*

2 Prabhupada wrote of his plan to go to California in a letter to Sally Agarwal, 19th November 1965.

CHAPTER 2: THE TEACHER LIVES AMONG THEM

1 *The Hare Krishna Explosion,* Hayagriva Dasa, p. 131.

2 In San Francisco Prabhupada spent time daily guiding Hayagriva in editing his *Bhagavad-gita* manuscript. He told him to 'edit for force and clarity.' I have followed this maxim when editing excerpts of Prabhupada's lectures and conversations for this book. See *The Hare Krishna Explosion,* Hayagriva Dasa, p. 178.

3 Letter to Satsvarupa Dasa, 15th February 1967.

4 *By His Example,* Gurudas, p. 11.

5 *The Hare Krishna Explosion,* Hayagriva Dasa, p. 136.

6 *By His Example,* by Gurudas, p. 22.

7 Prabhupada approved a translation of the *Chaitanya-charitamrita* by Nogen Roy in his letter to Rayarama and Satsvarupa, 30th March 1967.

8 *Srila Prabhupada-lilamrita,* Satsvarupa dasa Goswami, p. 96.

9 Prabhupada wrote instructions to Brahmananda in New York on how to observe Sri Chaitanya's birthday, 14th March 1967.

CHAPTER 3: THE IDEA OF LONDON

1 Letter to Rayarama and Satsvarupa, 30th March 1967.

2 Letter to Mukunda, 6th June 1967.

3 Letter to devotees in New York, 5th June 1967.

4 Letter to Mukunda, 10th June 1967.

5 Letter to New York devotees, 26th July 1967.

6 *ibid.*

7 Prabhupada entrusted the editing of his *Bhagavad-gita* to Rayarama in his letter of 15th November 1967. It is clear from this and other letters written around that time that Prabhupada put a great deal of time and effort into finishing his *Bhagavad-gita As It Is,* though he ultimately left finalising the text in the hands of his disciples.

8 Letter to Brahmananda, 27th August 1967.

9 Yamuna memorised Prabhupada's seminal words at the time he spoke them.

10 Released in 1967, on the Beatles' *Sergeant Pepper* album.

11 *Here Comes the Sun,* Joshua Greene (Yogeshvara), p. 124.

12 Letter to Mukunda, 6th May 1968.

13 Letter to Shyamsundar, 7th June 1968.

14 Letter to Gurudas, 23rd May 1968.

15 As defined by Prabhupada in his lecture on *Srimad-Bhagavatam* 1.2.2, London, 10th August 1972.

CHAPTER 4: SEARCHING FOR GEORGE

1 To enter the country they shared the sum of £1000, which allowed each couple to gain six-month entry visas by showing the cash. They then wired it back to Amsterdam for the next couple to use.
2 Letter to Janaki, 17th September 1968.
3 Letter to Malati, 23rd November 1968.
4 The clay *tilaka* mark, composed of two vertical lines on the forehead above a leaf shape drawn on the bridge of the nose, denotes a worshipper of Vishnu, or Krishna.
5 Summarised from original recording.
6 Told to the author by Kulashekara.
7 *The International Times,* 28th February 1969.
8 Letter to Mukunda, 20th February 1969.
9 Letter to Yamuna, Malati, and Janaki, 20th February 1969.
10 Letter to Mukunda and Colin Jury, 9th February 1969.
11 Letter to Shyamsundar, 12th June 1969.
12 Letter to Shyamsundar, 12th June 1969.
13 George first recorded the song 'All Things Must Pass' in January 1969. It was considered for inclusion on the final Beatles album, *Let It Be,* before eventually becoming the title track of his triple album released in 1970.
14 Letter to Gurudas, 31st July 1969.
15 Letter to Shyamsundar, 13th August 1969.
16 Letter to Shyamsundar, 13th August 1969.

CHAPTER 5: UNDERNEATH THE CEDARS

1 For the full story of Srila Prabhupada and his disciples in Germany, see Vedavyasa Dasa's book of that title, The Bhaktivedanta Book Trust, 1996.
2 For the full text of this conversation, see *Conversations With Srila Prabhupada,* vol. 2.
3 Paraphrased from *Srimad-Bhagavatam* 7. 5.30–32, spoken by Prahlada to his father.
4 Letter to Sethji, 22nd September 1969.
5 Letter to Prahladananda, 5th October 1969.
6 Letter to Tamal Krishna, 18th October 1969.
7 Letter to Gargamuni, 22th September 1969.
8 Laurence Dundas, Marquess of Zetland, Governor of Bengal from 1917–1922, and Secretary of State for India from 1935–1937, was noted for his opinion that Indians should be allowed to govern their own country. He introduced Swami Bon, a disciple of Bhaktisiddhanta Saraswati, to King George V at Buckingham Palace in 1933.

CHAPTER 6: SPREADING THE WORD

1 From Shakespeare's *Hamlet:* 'This above all: to thine own self be true, and it must follow, as the night the day, thou canst not then be false to any man.'

2 This summary is based on Prabhupada's lecture given in London on 15th September 1969.

3 Letter to Mukunda, 28th July 1969.

4 Years later in an interview, George said that seeing the Radha-Krishna Temple perform on Top of the Pops was one of the greatest thrills of his life. Making the single had been 'more fun, really, than trying to make a pop hit record. It was a feeling of utilising your skills to do some spiritual service for Krishna' (quoted in a *Rolling Stone* commemorative issue published in 2002, after George's passing).

5 Letter to Tamal Krishna, 25th October 1969.

CHAPTER 7: RADHA AND KRISHNA IN BLOOMSBURY

1 Letter to Pradyumna and Arundhati, 14th November 1969.

2 Letter to Satsvarupa, 14th November 1969.

3 Letter to Gaursundara, 20th November 1969.

4 Letter to Sridhar Maharaj, 7th December 1969.

5 Prabhupada's plans for the deities donated a year earlier by Dalmia Trust and Birla Trust are detailed in his letter to Hit Sharanji, 5th December 1969.

6 Letter to Himavati, 20th December 1969.

CHAPTER 8: CALL TO INDIA

1 Letters to Mondakini and Ilavati, 8th February 1970.

2 During Prabhupada's seven-month stay in Los Angeles, which began 1st January 1970, he wrote 427 letters (now published by the Bhaktivedanta Archives) – around a quarter of a million words.

3 Letter to Shyamsundar, 16th February 1970.

4 Letter to Gurudas, 29th June 1970.

5 Letter to Yamuna, 2nd March 1970.

6 Letter to Shyamsundar, 8th March 1970.

7 Letter to Gurudas, 27th January 1970.

8 Letter to Gurudas, 15th March 1970.

9 Letter to Mukunda, 8th February 1970.

10 Letter to Umapati, 18th February 1970.

11 Letter to Tamal Krishna, 17th March 1970.

12 Letter to Shyamsundar, 19th July 1970.

CHAPTER 9: YOUTHFUL TEMPLE

1 Words from 'The Inner Light', George Harrison, released by the Beatles in 1968 on the 'B' side of their single 'Lady Madonna'.
2 Letter to Mukunda, 31st December 1970.
3 Letter to Mukunda, 17th March 1971.
4 Letter to Mukunda, 23rd May 1971.
5 Letter to London devotees, 12th June 1971.
6 Letter to Tribhuvanatha, 4th July 1971.

CHAPTER 10: THE MASTER RETURNS

1 These words were noted by Kshirodakshayi in the journal he kept at the time.
2 Letter to Kirtanananda, 22nd August 1971.
3 See 'Room conversation with member of Mensa Society,' 4th September 1971, *Conversations with Srila Prabhupada,* vol. 3.
4 Letter to Sarvamangala, in her possession, 7th October 1971.

CHAPTER 11: EXPANDING MISSION

1 Letter to Dayananda and Nandarani, 13th October 1971.
2 Letter to Sridama, 22nd December 1971.
3 Letter to Dayananda, 5th December 1971.
4 See letter to Vaikunthanath, 21st February 1972.
5 Shyamsundar's letter is reproduced in full in the *Srila Prabhupada-lilamrita,* vol. 2, p. 85.
6 Letter to Hamsadutta, 14th February 1972.
7 Letter to Upendra, 19th February 1972.
8 Letter to Bhargava, 13th June 1972.
9 Letter to Mukunda, 28th December 1971.
10 Letter to Dayananda, 20th May 1972.
11 Letter to Rebatinandan, 2nd April 1972.
12 Letter to Hamsadutta, 22nd June 1972.

CHAPTER 12: THE BEST RATHAYATRA EVER

1 Lecture on *Srimad-Bhagavatam* 1.1.5, London, 22nd August 1972.
2 Lecture on *Srimad-Bhagavatam* 1.1.1, London, 8th August 1972.
3 Lecture on *Srimad-Bhagavatam* 1.1.2, London, 18th August 1972.
4 Lecture on *Srimad-Bhagavatam* 1.1.2, London, 18th August 1972.
5 Lecture on *Srimad-Bhagavatam* 1.1.6, London, 22nd August 1972.
6 Many of these 1972 lectures have not been released but are held in the reserve collection of the Bhaktivedanta Archives because of the poor quality of the original recordings.

7 See 'Room conversation, London, 14th August, 1972, *Conversations with Srila Prabhupada:* vol. 2 [the conversation is mistakenly dated 1971].

8 The Old Kensington Town Hall, a grand Italianate building, was demolished in 1982 to make way for an office block.

9 Summarized from Prabhupada's address, London, 10th August 1972.

10 Summarized from Prabhupada's lecture, London, 13th July 1972.

11 Letter to Karandhara, 19th July 1972.

12 Letter to Jayapataka, 22nd July 1972.

13 Letter to Hridayananda, 29th July 1972.

CHAPTER 13: AUSTERITIES IN EDINBURGH

1 Letter to Kishor, 25th December 1972.

2 Letter to Gurudas, 14th July 1972.

3 George Harrison recalls this meeting and how it inspired his song, in his autobiography *I Me Mine*, page 254.

4 Letter to Gurudas, 1st August 1972.

5 Nanda Kumar remembrance, as recorded in *Memories*, volume 2, p. 207.

6 *I Me Mine*, page 254.

7 Letter to Gurudas and Yamuna, 3rd August 1972.

8 Letter to Jagadish, 11th August 1972.

CHAPTER 14: SEARCH FOR A TEMPLE

1 Letter to Prabhavishnu, 3rd January 1973.

2 Letter to Rebatinandan, 31st December 1972.

3 Letter to Sri Govinda, 31st January 1973.

4 Letter to Kshirodakshayi, 29th January 1973.

5 Letter to Dhananjaya, 31st December 1972.

6 Letter to George Harrison, 4th January 1973.

7 In 1980 George arranged for the Manor to pass permanently into the ownership of ISKCON. The Material World Foundation sold the freehold to ISKCON for £190,000, out of which George paid £145,000 from his own pocket, leaving the temple to find the remaining £45,000.

8 Summarised from Prabhupada's lecture titled 'Arrival at the Manor, 1973'.

9 Letter to Jaihari, 28th June 1973.

CHAPTER 16: KRISHNA'S MANOR HOUSE

1 Letter to Tamal Krishna Maharaj and Giriraja, 14th July 1973.

2 Shrutakirti remembrance.

3 Vyasa-puja lecture, 22nd August 1973.

4 Letter to Kirtanananda, 8th August 1973.

5 Summarised from Prabhupada's lecture on *Bhagavad-gita* 1.24–25, London, 20th July 1973.

6 Summarised from Prabhupada's lecture on *Bhagavad-gita* 1.26–27, London, 21st July 1973.

7 *ibid.*

8 *ibid.*

9 Summarised from Prabhupada's lecture on *Bhagavad-gita* 1.30, London, 23rd July 1973.

10 Reported by Bhagavan, as retold by Satsvarupa dasa Goswami in *Srila Prabhupada-lilamrita*, vol. 2, p. 171.

11 Summarised from Prabhupada's Vyasa-puja lecture, 22nd August 1973.

12 Plans for the temple were made and sent to Prabhupada in India, where he said he would consider their use.

13 Summarised from Prabhupada's Vyasa-puja lecture, London, 22nd August 1973.

CHAPTER 17: MANY MEETINGS

1 Letter to Karandhara, 10th July 1973.

2 Letter to Sir Alister Hardy, FRS, 28th July 1973.

3 The following conversation abridged from 'Room conversation with Lord Brockway, London, 23rd July 1973', *Conversations with Srila Prabhupada,* vol. 5.

4 The following conversation abridged from 'Garden conversation with Mahadeva's mother and Jesuit priest, London, 25th July 1973', *Conversations with Srila Prabhupada,* vol. 5.

5 The following conversation abridged from 'Room conversation with E F Schumacher, London, 20th July 1973', *Conversations with Srila Prabhupada,* vol. 5.

6 The following conversation abridged from 'Room conversation with Indian guest, London, 11th July 1973', *Conversations with Srila Prabhupada,* vol. 4.

7 The following conversation abridged from 'Room conversation with David Wynne, sculptor, London, 9th July 1973', *Conversations with Srila Prabhupada,* vol. 4.

8 The following conversation abridged from 'Room conversation with Harry Edwards, London, 30th August 1973', *Conversations with Srila Prabhupada,* vol. 4.

9 The following conversation abridged from 'Room conversation with David Lawrence, London, 12th July 1973', *Conversations with Srila Prabhupada,* vol. 4.

CHAPTER 18: LIVING WITH PRABHUPADA

1 Letter to Rameshvara, 3rd August 1973.

2 Summarised from Prabhupada's Radhashtami lecture, London, 5th September 1973.

3 Ashtasakhi remembrance.

4 Summarised from Prabhupada's lecture on *Srimad-Bhagavatam* 1.5.11, London, 12th September 1973.

5 Letter to Dhananjaya, 23rd December 1973.

CHAPTER 19: AN UNEXPECTED VISIT

1 Letter to Kirtanananda, 18th October 1973.

2 Letter to Mukunda, 6th October 1973.

3 Letter to Kirtanananda, 24th November 1973.

4 Letter to Tamal Krishna Goswami, 5th December 1973.

5 Summarized from Prabhupada's lecture on *Srimad-Bhagavatam* 1.10.4, London, 25th November 1973.

CHAPTER 20: LOVE AND TRUST

1 Letter to Mukunda, 1st January 1974.

2 Letter to Madhavananda, 1st January 1974.

3 *ibid.*

4 Letter to Malati, 7th January 1974.

5 Letter to Puranjana, 7th April 1974.

6 Letter to Madhavananda, 16th August 1974.

7 Letter to Madhavananda, 6th August 1974.

8 Letter to Shyamsundar, 8th June 1974.

9 I heard Prabhupada's talk on this occasion, but since I cannot find a recording of it I have inserted this passage from an earlier letter to Pancha Dravida Swami, 28th June 1974, to illustrate the spirit of what he said.

10 Letter to daughters in London, 26th July 1974.

11 Letter to Rameshvara, 3rd September 1974.

12 Letter to Tamal Krishna Goswami, 8th September 1974.

13 Letter to devotees, 24th September 1974.

14 Letter to Hamsadutta, 12th September 1974

15 Letter to Malati, 8th December 1974

16 Letter to Bhagavan, 27th January 1975

17 Letter to Krishnavesha, 16th January 1975

CHAPTER 21: LONDON COLD AND DAMP

1 Letter to Brahmananda Swami, 7th January 1975.

2 Summarised from 'Morning Walk, London, 11th March 1975.

3 Excerpt from Prabhupada's lecture on *Bhagavad-gita* 7.2, London, 10th March 1975.

4 Lecture on *Bhagavad-gita* 7.3, London, 11th March 1975.

5 *ibid.*

6 Letter to Lilashakti, 3rd November 1974.

7 Summarised from Prabhupada's lecture, London, 12th March 1975.

8 Amita remembrance.

9 Abridged from Prabhupada's lecture on *Srimad-Bhagavatam* 6.1.55, London, 13th August 1975.

10 See Prabhupada's commentary to *Chaitanya-charitamrita, Adi-lila* 17.203.

CHAPTER 22: SO MANY CENTRES, SO LITTLE TIME

1 Summarised from Prabhupada's lecture on *Chaitanya-charitamrita, Madhya-lila,* 20–113, London, 23rd July 1976.

2 'Meeting His Divine Grace,' Colin Cross, *The Observer,* 25th July 1976.

3 *Chaitanya-charitamrita, Madhya-lila* 7.128.

4 Prithu remembrance.

5 This talk is reconstructed from notes by Hari Sauri, and the memories of Lilashakti and myself.

6 Summarised from Prabhupada's 'Lecture to Indian Community, London, 27th July 1976' (although the lecture was actually given on 25th July 1976).

7 Summarised from Prabhupada's lecture on *Bhagavad-gita* 13.3, London, 25th July 1976.

8 Letter to Jayapataka Swami, 26th July 1976.

9 The following is abridged from 'Conversation with George Harrison, London, 26th July 1976'.

10 *Chaitanya-charitamrita, Antya-lila* 1.99.

CHAPTER 23: SAYING GOODBYE

1 Letter to Guru Kripa Swami, 18th May 1977.

2 Much of this chapter is based upon the journals of Tamal Krishna Goswami and Abhirama Das.

3 Letter to all ISKCON temple presidents, 18th January 1977.

INDEX

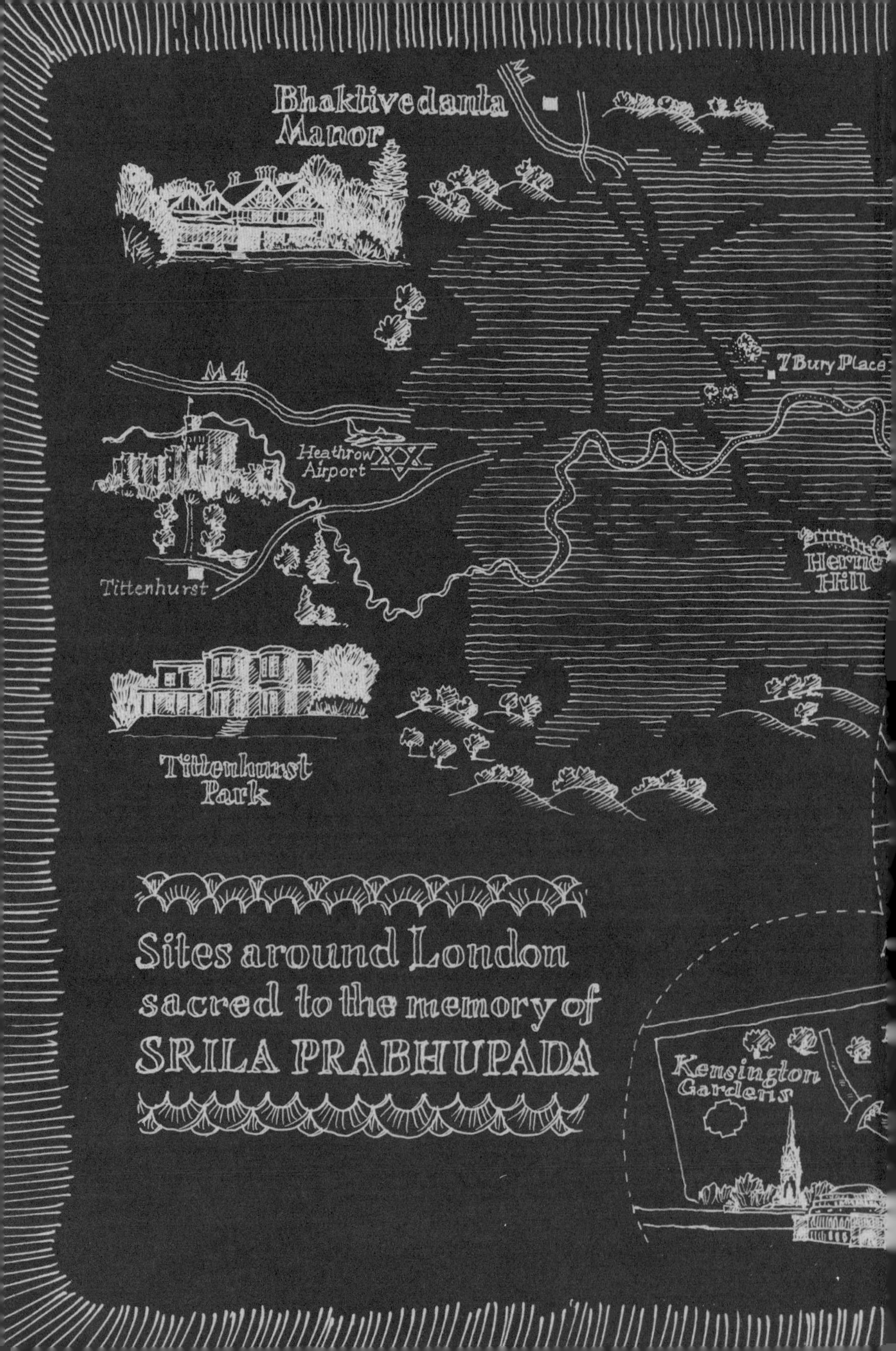
Bhaktivedanta
Manor
M1
7 Bury Place
M 4
Heathrow
Airport
Tittenhurst
Herne
Hill
Tittenhurst
Park
Sites around London
sacred to the memory of
SRILA PRABHUPADA
Kensington
Gardens